THE CAMBRIDGE
COMPANION TO
# LIBERATION
# THEOLOGY

Liberation theology is widely referred to in discussions of politics and religion but not always adequately understood. The new edition of this *Companion* brings the story of the movement's continuing importance and impact up to date. Additional essays, which complement those in the original edition, expand upon the issues by dealing with gender and sexuality and the important matter of epistemology. In the light of a more conservative ethos in Roman Catholicism, and in theology generally, liberation theology is often said to have been an intellectual movement tied to a particular period of ecumenical and political theology. These essays indicate its continuing importance in different contexts and enable readers to locate its distinctive intellectual ethos within the evolving contextual and cultural concerns of theology and religious studies. This book will be of interest to students of theology as well as to sociologists, political theorists and historians.

CHRISTOPHER ROWLAND is Dean Ireland's Professor of the Exegesis of Holy Scripture, University of Oxford. His most recent publications include *Radical Christian Writings: A Reader* (2002) with Andrew Bradstock.

# CAMBRIDGE COMPANIONS TO RELIGION

A series of companions to major topics and key figures in theology and religious studies. Each volume contains specially commissioned chapters by international scholars which provide an accessible and stimulating introduction to the subject for new readers and non-specialists.

*The Cambridge Companion to Reformation Theology*
edited by David Bagchi and David Steinmetz (2004)
ISBN 0 521 77224 9 hardback ISBN 0 521 77662 7 paperback

*The Cambridge Companion to American Judaism*
edited by Dana Evan Kaplan (2005)
ISBN 0 521 82204 1 hardback ISBN 0 521 52951 4 paperback

*The Cambridge Companion to Karl Rahner*
edited by Declan Marmion and Mary E. Hines (2005)
ISBN 0 521 83288 8 hardback ISBN 0 521 54045 3 paperback

*The Cambridge Companion to Friedrich Schleiermacher*
edited by Jacqueline Mariña (2005)
ISBN 0 521 81448 0 hardback ISBN 0 521 89137 x paperback

*The Cambridge Companion to the Gospels*
edited by Stephen C. Barton (2006)
ISBN 0 521 80766 2 hardback ISBN 0 521 00261 3 paperback

*The Cambridge Companion to the Qur'an*
edited by Jane Dammen McAuliffe (2006)
ISBN 0 521 83160 1 hardback ISBN 0 521 53934 x paperback

*The Cambridge Companion to Jonathan Edwards*
edited by Stephen J. Stein (2007)
ISBN 0 521 85290 0 hardback ISBN 0 521 61805 3 paperback

*The Cambridge Companion to Evangelical Theology*
edited by Timothy Larsen and Daniel J. Trier (2007)
ISBN 0 521 84698 6 hardback ISBN 0 521 60974 7 paperback

*The Cambridge Companion to Modern Jewish Philosophy*
edited by Michael L. Morgan and Peter Eli Gordon
ISBN 0 521 81312 3 hardback ISBN 0 521 01255 4 paperback

*The Cambridge Companion to the Talmud and Rabbinic Literature*
edited by Charlotte E. Fonrobert and Martin S. Jaffee
ISBN 0 521 84390 1 hardback ISBN 0 521 60508 3 paperback

Forthcoming
*The Cambridge Companion to Islamic Theology*
edited by Tim Winter

*The Cambridge Companion to the Virgin Mary*
edited by Sarah Boss

*The Cambridge Companion to Ancient Christianity*
edited by Rebecca Lyman

# THE CAMBRIDGE
# COMPANION TO
# LIBERATION
# THEOLOGY

Second Edition

EDITED BY

CHRISTOPHER ROWLAND

*Dean Ireland's Professor of the Exegesis of Holy Scripture,*
*University of Oxford*

CAMBRIDGE
UNIVERSITY PRESS

CAMBRIDGE UNIVERSITY PRESS
Cambridge, New York, Melbourne, Madrid, Cape Town,
Singapore, São Paulo, Delhi, Tokyo, Mexico City

Cambridge University Press
The Edinburgh Building, Cambridge CB2 8RU, UK

Published in the United States of America by Cambridge University Press, New York

www.cambridge.org
Information on this title: www.cambridge.org/9780521688932

© Cambridge University Press 2007

This publication is in copyright. Subject to statutory exception
and to the provisions of relevant collective licensing agreements,
no reproduction of any part may take place without the written
permission of Cambridge University Press.

First edition published 1999
Second edition published 2007

*A catalogue record for this publication is available from the British Library*

ISBN 978-0-521-86883-9 Hardback
ISBN 978-0-521-68893-2 Paperback

Cambridge University Press has no responsibility for the persistence or
accuracy of URLs for external or third-party internet websites referred to in
this publication, and does not guarantee that any content on such websites is,
or will remain, accurate or appropriate. Information regarding prices, travel
timetables, and other factual information given in this work is correct at
the time of first printing but Cambridge University Press does not guarantee
the accuracy of such information thereafter.

# CONTENTS

# NOTES ON CONTRIBUTORS

MARCELLA MARIA ALTHAUS-REID is an Argentinian theologian and holds a Chair in Contextual Theology in the School of Divinity, University of Edinburgh. She has published extensively in the area of Liberation Theology and Sexuality, and her books include *Indecent Theology* (London, Routledge, 2000); *The Queer God* (London, Routledge, 2003); *From Feminist Theology to Indecent Theology* (London, SCM, 2004) and the edited *Liberation Theology and Sexuality* (London, Ashgate, 2006).

EDWARD ANTONIO is Associate Professor of Theology and Social Theory at Iliff School of Theology, Denver, Colorado. Originally from Zimbabwe where he grew up on the streets and taught himself how to read and write, he holds the M.Litt. degree of the University of Aberdeen and a Ph.D. from Cambridge. He taught Political Theology at the University of Zimbabwe from 1989 to 1996. Before taking up his present position at Iliff, he was a lecturer at the University of Witwatersrand in Johannesburg, South Africa. He has written a number of articles in the areas of Black and African theologies, ecology and African traditional religions as well as on sexuality in African culture.

ZOË BENNETT is the Director of Postgraduate Studies in Pastoral Theology, Anglia Ruskin University and Cambridge Theological Federation. She is the Director of a Masters programme and a Professional Doctorate programme in Pastoral and Practical Theology. Her current research interests are in theological education in an ecumenical context, the Bible and practical theology, and the work of John Ruskin in dialogue with practical theology. Recent publications include 'Ecumenical Theological Education as a Practice of Peace' in *Religious Education*, 101, 3 (Summer 2006), pp. 331–46; and, with Christopher Rowland, 'Action is the Life of All: New Testament Theology and Practical Theology' in C. Rowland and C. Tuckett eds., *The Nature of New Testament Theology* (Oxford, Blackwell, 2006).

ANDREW DAWSON lectures in Religious Studies at Lancaster University. He researches and publishes on religion and society in South America, particularly Brazil. His publications include *New Era – New Religions: Religious*

*Transformation in Contemporary Brazil* (Aldershot, Ashgate, 2007) and *The Emergence and Impact of the Base Ecclesial Community and Liberative Theological Discourse in Brazil* (Lanham, International Scholars Publications, 1998).

VALPY FITZGERALD is Professor of International Development at Oxford University and Fellow of St Antony's College. He teaches and researches on international finance and development economics, and has extensive experience of working with Christian groups in Latin America on economic change and social justice issues. He is an advisor to CAFOD, UNICEF, UNRISD and UNCTAD on economic and social policy. He has recently edited *The Transmission of Economic Ideas in Latin America* (Palgrave, Macmillan, 2005) and completed *Economic Growth and Welfare in 20th Century Latin America* (Oxford University Press, forthcoming 2008).

MARY GREY is Emeritus Professor of Theology at the University of Wales, Lampeter. She was formerly Professor of Feminism and Christianity at the Catholic University of Nijmegen, The Netherlands. Her publications include *Redeeming the Dream: Christianity, Feminism and Redemption* (London, SPCK, 1989); *The Wisdom of Fools? Seeking Revelation for Today* (London, SPCK, 1993); *Prophecy and Mysticism: The Heart of the Post-Modern Church* (Edinburgh, T&T Clark, 1997); and *Beyond the Dark Night: A Way Forward for the Church?* (London, Cassell, 1997). She is editor, with Elizabeth Green, of *'Ecofeminism and Theology', Yearbook of the European Society of Women in Theological Research* (1994). She is also co-founder and Trustee of the charity 'Wells for India'.

GUSTAVO GUTIERREZ is John Cardinal O'Hara Professor of Theology at the University of Notre Dame. He has been a principal professor at the Pontifical University of Peru, and Visiting Professor at many major universities in North America and Europe. He is author of *A Theology of Liberation* (Maryknoll, NY, Orbis, 1971); *The Power of the Poor in History* (Maryknoll, NY, Orbis, 1979); *We Drink from Our Own Wells* (Maryknoll, NY, Orbis, 1983); *God-talk and the Suffering of the Innocent* (Maryknoll, NY, Orbis, 1986); *The Truth Shall Make You Free* (Maryknoll, NY, Orbis, 1986); *The God Life* (Maryknoll, NY, Orbis, 1989); *In Search of the Poor of Jesus* (Maryknoll, NY, Orbis, 1992); and *Sharing the Word through the Liturgical Year* (Maryknoll, NY, Orbis, 1997).

PETER HEBBLETHWAITE, who died in December 1994, was the Vatican affairs writer for the *National Catholic Reporter* of the USA. Trained as a Jesuit theologian, his reporting of current church affairs went back to the final session of Vatican II. His books include *Theology and the Church* (London, Collins, 1975); *The Christian–Marxist Dialogue* (New York, Paulist Press, 1977); *The Year of the Three Popes* (London, Collins, 1978); *Introducing John Paul II* (London, Collins, 1982); *John XXIII: Pope of the Council* (London, Geoffrey

Chapman, 1984); *In the Vatican* (London, Sidgwick and Jackson, 1986); and *Paul VI: The First Modern Pope* (London, HarperCollins, 1993).

OLIVER O'DONOVAN has been Professor of Christian Ethics and Practical Theology at the University of Edinburgh since 2006, before which he was Regius Professor of Moral and Pastoral Theology and Canon of Christ Church, Oxford, from 1982. Born in England and educated at Oxford and Princeton Universities, he has also taught in Toronto, Canada, and is an Anglican priest. He is a past President of the Society for the Study of Christian Ethics and a Fellow of the British Academy. His publications include *The Problem of Self-Love in St Augustine* (New Haven, Yale University Press, 1980; Eugene, Wipf & Stock, 2006); *Begotten or Made?* (Oxford University Press, 1984); *Resurrection and Moral Order* (Grand Rapids, Eerdmans, and Leicester, Apollos, 1986); *Peace and Certainty* (Oxford University Press and Grand Rapids, Eerdmans, 1989); *The Desire of the Nations* (Cambridge University Press, 1996); (with Joan Lockwood O'Donovan), *From Irenaeus to Grotius* (Grand Rapids, Eerdmans, 1999); *Common Objects of Love* (Grand Rapids, Eerdmans, 2002); *The Just War Revisited* (Cambridge University Press, 2003); (with Joan Lockwood O'Donovan), *Bonds of Imperfection* (Grand Rapids, Eerdmans, 2004); *The Ways of Judgment* (Grand Rapids, Eerdmans, 2005).

IVAN PETRELLA is an assistant professor of Religious Studies at the University of Miami. A citizen of Argentina, he spends almost half the year in Buenos Aires, where he participates in political and social debates about the country's future. He is the author of *Beyond Liberation Theology: A Polemic* and *The Future of Liberation Theology: An Argument and Manifesto*, editor of *Latin American Liberation Theology: The Next Generation Reclaiming Liberation Theology* and executive editor, with Marcella Althaus-Reid, of the series for SCM Press. In his spare time he roams Buenos Aires and Miami Beach in search of pickup soccer games.

CHRISTOPHER ROWLAND is Dean Ireland's Professor of the Exegesis of Holy Scripture in the University of Oxford. He has written on Jewish and Christian apocalypticism, including *The Open Heaven* (London, SPCK, 1982) and 'Revelation' in the *New Interpreters' Bible* (1998). He was for ten years a member of the board of Christian Aid, London, and chair of its Latin American and Caribbean Committee. He has written on liberation theology in *Radical Christianity* (Cambridge, Polity Press, 1988) and *Liberating Exegesis* (London, SPCK, 1990). Together with John Vincent he edits *British Liberation Theology* published by the Urban Theology Unit in Sheffield.

DENYS TURNER is Horace Tracy Pitkin Professor of Historical Theology at Yale University. He is author of *Marxism and Christianity* (Oxford, Blackwell, 1983) and of many articles and papers on Marxism, social theory and Christian Theology. His more recent publications include *The Darkness of*

*God* (Cambridge University Press, 1995) and *Faith, Reason and the Existence of God* (Cambridge University Press, 2004).

CHARLES VILLA-VICENCIO is Executive Director of the Institute for Justice and Reconciliation in South Africa. His publications include *A Theology of Reconciliation: Nation Building and Human Rights* (Cambridge University Press, 1992) and *The Spirit of Freedom: Conversations with South African Leaders on Religion and Politics* (Berkeley, University of California Press, 1995).

GERALD WEST is Professor in the School of Theology at the University of Natal, South Africa. He is also Director of the Institute for the Study of the Bible, a project that brings together socially engaged biblical scholars and ordinary readers of the Bible from poor and marginalised communities. He is author of *Biblical Hermeneutics of Liberation: Modes of Reading the Bible in the South African Context* (Maryknoll, NY, Orbis, 2nd edn, 1995).

BASTIAAN WIELENGA has been teaching Biblical Theology as well as Social Analysis at the Tamilnadu Theological Seminary in Madurai, South India, since 1975. Earlier, he was a research scholar in the Christian Institute for the Study of Religion and Society in Bangalore, and co-worker in the Ecumenical Centre, Hendrik Kraemer House, Berlin. He has published in the fields of Christian–Marxist dialogue, politics and theology. His *It's a Long Road to Freedom* (Mandurai, Tamil Nadu Theological Seminary, 1998) discusses perspectives of biblical theology; *Introduction to Marxism* (Bangalore, Centre for Social Action, 1991) presents a pluralist approach to Marxist theory; and *Towards Understanding Indian Society, 3rd Edition* (Mandurai, Centre for Social Analysis, 2002), co-authored with Gabrielle Dietrich, relates social analysis to social movements and alternative development perspectives.

# FOREWORD TO THE SECOND EDITION

I recall a reviewer of an earlier book I wrote on liberation theology commenting that the book was now redundant, given the collapse of communism. That assessment reflects a widespread assumption that liberation theology is simply Marxism with a Christian gloss and that, with the dramatically changed situation since the fall of the Eastern bloc, the theology which was inspired by it was likewise to be consigned to the dustbin of history. There is a problem with this view. First of all, it assumes that, without Marxism, liberation theology would not have any rationale. This view is widespread (as also is the assumption that liberation theology is linked with the use of violence for political ends). What such views fail to recognise, however, is that liberation theology has never been greatly indebted to Marxism, even if in certain important respects (such as its epistemology and commitment to human history as the arena for the fulfilment of the divine purposes), it has some parallels to it. But those parallels are less indicative of indebtedness than of the recovery in liberation theology of components of the Christian way of life which more mainstream theology has lost sight of. Nevertheless, there is one sense in which the reviewer might have had a point. If liberation theology had stayed as it was in the period before 1990, such criticism would be justified. It has not, and a new generation of liberation theologians has continued with the essential features of the liberation theology method, albeit in changed circumstances. Those changed circumstances also include a more hostile environment in the Roman Catholic Church. One can get a flavour of this when one recalls that the present pope, then Cardinal Josef Ratzinger, not only was an important part of the investigation and critique of liberation theology in the 1990s but also wrote some rather harsh things about it, comparing it to the illusory fanaticism reflected in the violent preparations for the Kingdom of God in the War Scroll from Qumran.[1]

The bulk of the book remains the same as the first edition. What we have in the new chapters by Marcella Althaus-Reid, Zoë Bennett and Ivan Petrella is evidence of the continuing history of liberation theology and examples of the contours of that new generation. Liberation theology has pervaded much contextual theology. Thus, action/reflection models of engagement are commonplace. Zoë Bennett, writing from a background in contemporary practical theology, demonstrates the extent of this influence and contrasts what is central to liberation theology with this kind of 'pastoral cycle' method. At the same time, she fills a gap in the earlier edition by exploring what is perhaps the most important component of liberation theology: the basis of its epistemology in practice. She does this by reference to one of the most important texts of the earlier generation of liberation theology – Clodovis Boff's *Theology and Praxis*[2] – indicates its strengths and weaknesses and points to the indispensability of the discussions raised by this question for the wider theological debate. Ivan Petrella and Marcella Althaus-Reid are representative of a new wave of liberation theologians. Their respective contributions demonstrate the extent of the continuity with the original inspiration, though both indicate the ways in which some recent liberationist discussion has lost touch with that original vision. They also point out the ways in which the original advocates of liberation theology ignored central issues in human experience, linked with sexuality and gender, which continue to be key areas of human need and oppression. Ivan Petrella indicates what is central to liberation theology: commitment to projects for social change within history. When liberation theology loses its commitment to engagement in historical projects, to bringing life where there is death, it has lost its soul.

All three writers demonstrate the ways in which, despite all the attempts by ecclesiastical officialdom to disinfect Christian culture of what they deem to be the virus of the politicised theology of liberation theology, at the grassroots level this way of understanding God is alive and well. Those who have been drawn to liberation theology practise this approach not so much because of its intellectual sophistication, as if it were one option in the academic market, but because liberation theology enables one to put one's finger on the pulse of a world of suffering and death, personal tragedy and injustice. As a result the discernment of Christ in the persons of the needy and vulnerable, and service to them, is then the motor of theological insight. So, theological understanding comes through commitment and action. It is a form of contextual theology, therefore, in which experience and circumstances have a prime importance as the first step in seeking to be a disciple of Jesus.

CHRISTOPHER ROWLAND

## NOTES

1. J. Ratzinger, 'Eschatology and Utopia', in *Church, Ecumenism and Politics* (Slough, St Paul, 1988), pp. 237ff.
2. Clodovis Boff, *Theology and Praxis: Epistemological Foundations*, tr. Robert R. Barr (Maryknoll, NY, Orbis, 1987).

Liberation theology has been one of the most significant movements in Christian theology in the last thirty years. For a decade or more liberation theology dominated the intellectual horizon of theologians in universities and seminaries throughout the world. Recent evidence of a declining profile cannot mask the enormous influence this approach to theology has had on the contemporary Church. It emerged in Latin America, though there have been parallel developments in other parts of the world, in which experiences of oppression, vulnerability or marginalisation have led to a sustained reflection on the Christian tradition. The Third World setting in situations of abject poverty and human need has given the theology a particular urgency and distinctive outline. The concern with human well-being and an understanding of the Church's mission which includes practical measures for human betterment have embraced theologians as co-workers in practical expressions of Christian commitment. The agenda is distinctive in its emphasis on the dialogue between Christian tradition, social theory and the insight of the poor and marginalised into their situation, leading to action for change. Liberation theology is not only of interest to theologians but also to all those studying the role of religion in contemporary society. The emphasis on the political dimensions of the Church's mission within situations of extreme poverty has made it the most compelling example of political theology in the late twentieth century. Liberation theology has a certain novelty value in the popular imagination. Many of its practitioners, however, have been quick to point out how deep are its roots in Christianity's emphasis on the life of prayer and commitment to neighbour as the necessary contexts for understanding God.

The initial dynamism may have been in Latin America, but there have emerged parallel movements in Africa, Asia and also Europe and North America. Not all of these are called liberation theology. Contextual theology is a term now widely used to designate theological reflection which explicitly explores the dialogue between social context and Scripture and tradition.[1] It is not an ideal term, however, as it suggests that there exists a form of theology in which context plays no determining role, a notion that many, including liberation theologians themselves, would want to challenge. The greatest examples of Christian theology down the centuries (Augustine's *City of God* is a case in point) have all arisen from, and been directed to, specific historical and social contexts. There are enough common threads linking theologians in Asia, Latin America and South Africa to justify a common perspective, not least organisations like the Ecumenical Alliance of Third World Theologians which have enabled dialogue and common interests to emerge as the result of a series of influential conferences with a common sense of direction and purpose.

The chapters of this *Companion* offer a survey of examples of theology in different parts of the world which may be labelled liberation theology. The chapters have been written by contributors, some of whom live and work in the countries whose theology they write about. The first part enables readers to have some understanding of the main features of contemporary liberation theology in Latin America, Asia and Africa and the related feminist theology. In Part II specific issues which arise in the emergence of liberation theology are explored in chapters on the emergence of the base ecclesial communities, so important for the growth of liberation theology in Latin America, and the distinctive ways in which Scripture is studied. One new issue to have arisen since Gustavo Gutiérrez's pioneering *A Theology of Liberation* was published thirty years ago has been the emergence of a situation in which theologians of protest have found themselves engaged in reconstruction and reconciliation. That new situation is reflected in a chapter which examines the case of South Africa. In Part III writers turn to analysis of aspects of liberation theology and specific criticisms made of it. This starts with a posthumously published essay by Peter Hebblethwaite on the emerging critique of liberation theology from the Vatican. I am particularly grateful to Peter's widow, Margaret Hebblethwaite, for all her help in providing me with material which Peter left in a fragmentary state at his death. The extent of the indebtedness to Marxism has also been a subject of controversy from liberation theology's very earliest days, as also has the extent of the influence of a particular economic theory. Finally, its distinctive standpoint on political theology is contrasted with other traditions of political theology.

This volume should enable the student beginning a course in liberation theology to have some idea of the contours of the varied aspects of this

---

[1] In the Pontifical Biblical Commission's recent document (ed. J. L. Houlden, *The Interpretation of the Bible in the Church*, London, 1995) liberationist and feminist interpretations are both given the label 'contextual approaches'.

significant movement and will permit someone who wants a panoramic view of the various forms of liberation theology to get some sense of the overall situation. As editor I am aware of the many other matters which could legitimately have been included in a volume of this kind: the relationship of liberation theology and evangelisation, Catholic and Protestant; the evidence of an indigenous liberationist tradition in Europe and North America; the story of Christianity in post-revolutionary Nicaragua, and an analysis of the way in which liberation theology has revolutionised much Christian pedagogy in the Northern Hemisphere even when it seems to remain peripheral to the life of most of the Christian churches.

I am grateful to colleagues at the Centro Missionário de Evangelização e Educação Popular in Valença, Bahia, Brazil for giving me permission to take photographs of their popular education material during my visit to them in 1990, an example of which forms the illustration on the front of this book. My daughter, Rebekah, has helped with proof-reading and the preparation of an index. I am grateful to her for her help and her continuing interest in, and support for, the subject of this book.

**apophatic theology:** that which is beyond expression in language. It involves a denial that human language can ever properly be affirmed of God. It contrasts with **cataphatic theology/cataphaticism.**

**caste:** a hereditary group which maintained social distance from members of other castes.

**catechesis/catechetical:** teaching or instruction, a way of describing the preparatory teaching given to a candidate for baptism in the Christian Church.

**chiliasm:** the expectation of a 1000-year reign of God on earth based on Revelation 20, but which has come to be linked with any this-worldly expectation of God's eschatological reign.

**christology:** teaching about the person of Jesus Christ.

**Dalit:** the name chosen for itself by the outcaste group in India; it means 'crushed' or 'oppressed'.

**dialectical:** concerning the understanding of or reconciliation of contradictions, e.g., in theology between God and humanity and different social and economic phenomena. It is a word used both in political philosophy influenced by Hegel and Marx, where it is used of the progressive resolution of contradictions in history, and also in the theology of Karl Barth, which contrasted human ways of knowing and the revelation of God.

**encyclical:** in modern Roman Catholicism refers to a circular document sent to the church by the Pope.

**epistemology:** concerned with the theory of knowledge and how humans know anything about themselves, the external world, and God.

**eschatology:** the hope for the future, both for the individual and the world. There has been a divide in Christian theology between a this-worldly hope and an other-worldly hope.

**exegesis:** the practice of interpretation and exposition, specifically of the Bible.

**fetishism:** according to Marx, the bestowal in a capitalist society on material objects of certain characteristics, such that they appear to possess these naturally.

**Feuerbachian:** referring to Ludwig Feuerbach (1804–72), who demanded that theology be understood as a projection on to the transcendent of ideas concerning humanity and society.

**fideism:** a doctrine which places emphasis on the need for faith and rejects the ability of the human mind to understand God, with the consequent denial of the possibility of the need for rational justification.

**hermeneutics:** the task of reflecting on how we go about doing our interpretation of texts, life and culture.

**hermeneutics of suspicion:** interpretation linked with what Paul Ricoeur has called the masters of suspicion, Marx, Freud and Nietzsche. Its major characteristic is suspicion of the validity of received narratives and explanations with a demand to probe to get at the underlying truth behind appearances.

**immanentism:** in contrast with **transcendence** in theology this doctrine stresses God's nearness and involvement in history, including ordinary events and situations.

**neo-liberal:** a way of characterising the free-market economic theory which has been influential in global economics in the last decades of the twentieth century.

**orthopraxy:** right way of behaving, contrasted with **orthodoxy**, right belief, which is held to be less interested in the practical demands of faith.

**praxis** or **practice:** action, a term often used in liberation theology to describe the actions and commitments which provide the context for theological reflection.

**proletariat:** the working class which in Marxist theory would be the agent of the defeat of capitalism.

**Promethean:** referring to Prometheus, the figure in Greek mythology who stole fire from the gods and taught humankind divine wisdom, for which he was imprisoned for having aspired to divinity.

**soteriology:** the doctrine of God's saving work, especially through the life, death and resurrection of Jesus Christ.

**typology:** the relation of different persons and narratives (usually in the Old and New Testaments), so that the character of one is informed by the character of the other (so the sacrifice of Isaac informs the understanding of the death of Jesus).

# ABBREVIATIONS

| | |
|---|---|
| CCA | Christian Conference of Asia |
| CDF | Congregation for the Doctrine of the Faith. The major institution of the Roman Catholic Church responsible for the church's faith and morals |
| CEB/BCC | Basic Ecclesial Community or Basic Christian Community |
| CELAM | The Latin American (Roman Catholic) Bishops' Conference |
| CIIR | The Catholic Institute for International Relations |
| CISRS | Christian Institute for the Study of Religion and Society |
| CLAR | The Latin American Conference of Religious |
| CSR | Centre for Social Research |
| EATWOT | Ecumenical Association of Third World Theologians |
| ECLA | Economic Commission for Latin America |
| EFECW | European Ecumenical Forum of Christian Women |
| ESWTR | European Society for Women in Theological Research |
| GATT | The General Agreement on Tariffs and Trade |
| GS | *Gaudium et Spes*. The major document of the Second Vatican Council dealing with relations between the Church and the World |
| IMF | The International Monetary Fund |
| ISB | Institute for the Study of the Bible |
| MNC | Multi-National Corporation. Also called Trans-National Corporation |
| NGO | Non-Governmental Organisation. A term used to describe organisations like charities or intermediate groups engaged in development work in the Third World |
| OECD | The Organisation for Economic Co-operation and Development |
| ST | *Summa Theologiae* of Thomas Aquinas |
| URM | Urban-Rural Mission |
| WCC | The World Council of Churches |
| WSCF | World Student Christian Fellowship |

CHRISTOPHER ROWLAND

# Introduction: the theology of liberation

May Day in 1983 will always remain indelibly etched on my memory. It was my first Saturday in Brazil, in the middle of a period of military dictatorship in that country, and I was taken to visit some theologians working with base ecclesial communities in São Paulo. I recall entering a large building which served as a community centre for one of the shanty towns on the periphery of this enormous city. Inside there were about forty men and women listening to a woman expound the first chapter of the book of Revelation. She was standing at a table at which were sitting two men. Her lecture was constantly interrupted by her audience sharing their experience of situations parallel with that of John on Patmos: witness, endurance, and tribulation. One man who had been active in trade unions spoke with me after the meeting describing the way in which the book of Revelation spoke to his situation: he had been imprisoned without trial, and a Church which had seemed so irrelevant and remote had become a shelter and inspiration for his life. There was an atmosphere of utter comprehension of, and accord with, John's situation, as trade union activists, catechists and human rights workers shared their experiences of persecution and harassment as a result of their work with the poor and marginalised. They found in John a kindred spirit as they sought to understand and build up their communities in the face of the contemporary beast of poverty and oppression. It was readily apparent as I listened to their eager attempts to relate Revelation to their situation that they had discovered a text which spoke to them because they had not been desensitised by an ordered and respectable life of accommodation and assimilation. The woman and one of the men at the front of the meeting were teachers at the local seminary and the other man the local Roman Catholic bishop. They had been conducting a regular training day for representatives from the hundreds of base ecclesial communities who had gathered for training in Scripture and its interpretation.

That occasion embodies so many of the features which have distinguished liberation theology. First of all, it is rooted in ordinary people's everyday experience of poverty. Second, it involves a use of Scripture the interpretation of which is closely related to that experience. Third, it is a theology which in many parts of the world has deep roots within the life of the Church (this is nowhere more true than in Brazil where a liberation theology perspective has permeated, and in turn been influenced by, the pastoral practice of many Roman Catholic dioceses). Fourth, it has flourished in the meetings of groups within urban or rural settings, worshipping and reflecting on Scripture and joining in common projects for human welfare in health and education. Fifth, there is a theology which is explored not just in the tutorial or seminar but engages the whole person in the midst of a life of struggle and deprivation. It is theology which, above all, often starts from the insights of those men and women who have found themselves caught up in the midst of that struggle, rather than being evolved and handed down to them by ecclesiastical or theological experts. Finally, books of the Bible (like the book of Revelation) and parts of the theological tradition, often ignored or despised, become a vehicle of hope and insight in these situations of oppression and deprivation as new hope in God's purposes are discovered.

## Theology and experience: a way of doing theology from the perspective of the poor and marginalised

Theology as it has developed over the centuries can seem abstract from ordinary life as is evident in the way in which 'theological' has come to be used to describe irrelevant discussion of a topic. In contrast, liberation theology has its origins in the reality of the 'premature and unjust death of many people' as Gustavo Gutiérrez has put it. However sophisticated the books and articles from the liberation theologians may seem to be, it is their experience and that of those with whom they work that is the motor which drives their theology. The struggle for survival of millions linked with Christian social teaching prompted priests and religious to think again about their vocation. In so doing, they have learnt afresh from the poor as they have lived and worked with them. In a situation where hundreds of thousands of peasants were driven off the land their families have farmed for generations, because of international demand for economic growth to service foreign debt, and where many have drifted to the shanty towns which have sprung up on the periphery of large cities, liberation theology has flourished. So the starting place is not detached reflection on Scripture and tradition but the present life of the shanty towns and land struggles, the lack of basic amenities, the carelessness about the welfare of human persons, the death squads and the shattered lives of refugees. It is here in particular that its distinctiveness as compared with the theology of North American and European academies is most marked. In the words of Gustavo Gutiérrez:

> ...the question in Latin America will not be how to speak of God in a world come of age, but rather how to proclaim God as Father in a world that is inhumane. What can it mean to tell a non-person that he or she is God's child?[1]

It was a similar question which was posed in the very earliest years of Christianity's presence in South America for priests like Bartolomé de las Casas who took up the cause of the oppressed indigenous people of the sub-continent. As a young priest he prepared a homily on Ecclesiasticus 34.21–7: the words 'Like one who kills before his father's eyes is a person who offers a sacrifice from the property of the poor' crystallised a sense of the injustice of the economic system of which he was a part and which exploited indigenous peoples. The rest of his life was devoted to obtaining rights for indigenous peoples from the Spanish crown.[2]

Liberation theology is being worked out in shanty towns, land struggles, oppressed and humiliated groups, as well as areas of urban deprivation in the Northern hemisphere, wherever the rebuilding of shattered lives takes place. The point is well made by Jon Sobrino who has for years worked in war-torn Central America. He suggests that the agenda of European theology has been more interested in thinking about and explaining the truth of faith, whereas for liberation theologians faith runs parallel to real life and is in dialectical relationship with it. Thereby the meaning of faith and doctrine is illuminated at the same time as the world's wretched condition is confronted and alleviated. Commitment to the poor becomes the context of reflection, and so practical discipleship becomes the dynamic within which theological understanding takes place. Understanding of God and the world is a gift of grace and means an altered perspective in a life of service to those who are the least of Christ's brothers and sisters.[3]

## Liberation theology: a means of ethical and intellectual orientation

When Carlos Mesters, a liberation theologian from Brazil, writes of 'interpreting life by means of the Bible', he encapsulates this way of doing theology. Liberation theology is not the accumulation of, or learning about, a distinctive body of distinctive information, though the perspective may well produce an approach to parts of the spectrum of the Christian tradition which are either ignored or denied. Liberation theology is above all a new way of *doing* theology rather than being itself a new theology. It is new in the sense that it contrasts with much of the theology that has emerged in the last two centuries, centred, as it so often is, in university or seminary, with the priority placed on intellectual discourse detached from life and, increasingly, the practice of prayer and charity. In many respects, liberation theology harks back to the theological method of an earlier age, when worship, service to humanity and theological reflection were more closely integrated and when the conduct of the Christian life was an indispensable context for theological reflection. What has been rediscovered, in particular, is the commitment to the poor and marginalised as a determining moment for theology rather than the agenda of detachment and reflection within the academy. Such a discovery may involve a disorientation of life, a conversion indeed. The commitment to, and solidarity with, the poor and vulnerable are the necessary environment for stimulating the intellectual activity which enables liberation theology to begin. The key thing is that one first of all *does* liberation theology rather than learns about it. Or, to put it another way, one can only learn about it by embarking on it. To ask the question, 'What is liberation theology?' and think that one can answer without commitment and the understanding which emerges from it is to miss out on the central ingredient of liberation theology. This experience cannot adequately be communicated except by committing oneself and taking the first step along the road of solidarity and action. Therein lies the root of understanding.

Liberation theology is a way, a discipline, an exercise which has to be lived rather than acquired as a body of information. It has its parallels in the classic texts of Western Christian spirituality. The Spiritual Exercises of Ignatius Loyola, the founder of the Jesuits, for example, seems at first sight to be a rag-bag of Christian platitudes. To read them without putting the advice into practice for oneself, however, fails to do justice to the fact that it is only when one actually *uses* them that the significance and function of the Exercises becomes apparent.[4] What one is offered in them is a means of intellectual and ethical re-orientation. Similarly, engagement with the texts of liberation theology offers an understanding of God from within a commitment to the poor and marginalised and a means of thinking afresh about reality or the ways in which we articulate it to one another. Therein lies their peculiar power. It is not so much their fascinating ideas (many may be paralleled in other areas of contemporary intellectual enquiry) or the originality of the information they convey (there are many text books about the Third World which give a fuller picture of life in the various countries in which the liberation theologians are writing). Rather, it is the process of wrestling with texts like these which explicitly start from a situation of oppression and vulnerability and in that situation discovering

God that makes liberation theology peculiarly powerful. Because of the deep-rooted connection of this theology with particular contexts and experiences, liberation theology presents peculiar problems for those who seek to write *about* it. A proper understanding of it demands something more than an intellectual appreciation alone. Understanding involves more than the exercise of the mind and includes the move from a previous position of detachment, to be open to that transformation of perspective which comes, either at the margins, or in social estrangement. Thereby one may be enabled to 'see the Kingdom of God'.[5]

## Liberation theology and the Church

Liberation theology has emerged within the wider context of Catholic social teaching and, in particular, the significant development of Roman Catholic theology based on the Second Vatican Council, and the encyclicals associated with it. The decisions taken by the Latin American bishops at their epoch-making meeting at Medellín, affirmed at Puebla, with the explicit commitment to take a 'preferential option for the poor'[6] and reaffirmed at the most recent conference of Latin American bishops at Santo Domingo,[7] have offered a foundation for those Christians committed to the betterment of the poor enabling them to see their task as an integral part of the Church's vocation to evangelisation. Working within the parameters of international and national episcopal decisions, exponents of the theology of liberation respond to the 'reality' which confronts millions: poverty, appalling living conditions, malnutrition, inadequate health care, contrasting with the affluence not only of the 'North', but, even more glaring still, the wealth and affluence of the wealthy elites of Latin American cities.

In the Roman Catholic Church the power of diocesan bishops is such that those attempting to get the grassroots movement off the ground where there is no episcopal support have found the going very tough indeed, even though the social conditions of large numbers of people may be every bit as bad as in other dioceses where the theology has taken root. Equally, in those dioceses where the diocesan bishop is supportive, that power can be used to push a diocese in a progressive direction far more quickly than would be possible in the Protestant churches.[8] The particular circumstances of the Church in Brazil have offered a context for the development of liberation theology which has been unique in Latin America (though there has been a trend to less progressive positions by the Brazilian Bishops' Conference in recent years and the mushrooming of Protestant churches[9]). While it may be possible to detect an apparent similarity of concern and expression in theology which has a liberationist perspective, we need to take care that we avoid assuming that community of interest necessarily means that we can easily distil the different perspectives and emphases, whether of Latin American theologians[10] linked with liberation theology, or, of theologians in Asia, Africa and those representing minority groups in the 'North'. While it is usual to speak of Latin America as the starting-place of liberation theology, in fact there have been different emphases in the different countries, as related movements have emerged in other parts of the world.

## The base ecclesial communities

Liberation theology as it has developed has become rooted in the Basic Christian Communities or base ecclesial communities (the CEBs). The base communities are a significant component of the contemporary political as well as ecclesiastical scene, particularly in Brazil, where it is difficult to drive a wedge between the so-called 'popular church' with more tenuous links to bishops and priests and mainstream Catholicism. Certainly there are tensions, particularly in those dioceses where there is less sympathy towards the CEBs. But Brazilian Catholicism, for example, is characterised by a widespread acceptance of the CEBs and their central role in being the church in contemporary Brazil, a fact which is evident from the episcopal support of the regular CEBs' assembly. An ecclesial agenda is being set for the interpretative enterprise which is firmly based in the struggles of millions for recognition and justice.

A constant refrain of all the different approaches which are grouped together under liberation theology is that the perspective of the poor and the marginalised offers another story, an alternative to that told by the wielders of economic power whose story becomes the 'normal' account. Its encouragement of the study of popular religion, whether Christian, Indian or Afro-American, is part of its project to enable the story of the 'little people' to be heard. In addition, it has championed the recovery of the religion of those within the Christian tradition who resisted the practice of conquest and despoliation, like Bartolomé de las Casas and Antonio Valdivieso, whose ministry takes its part alongside those whom the conquerors would prefer to forget. It is part of the task suggested in Walter Benjamin's words: 'In every era the attempt must be made anew to wrest tradition away from a conformism that is about to overpower it.'[11]

Oppressed persons have become the particular means whereby the divine perspective on human existence is offered. They are the 'little ones' who are vouchsafed a peculiar insight into the identity of the divine wisdom: 'I thank thee, Father, Lord of heaven and earth, that you have kept these things from the wise and intelligent and revealed them to babes' (Matt. 11.25). The oppressed call into question assumptions about the character of human relationships, both local and international, in a suffering and unjust world.[12] What some liberation theologians are claiming is that the vantage point of the poor is particularly, and especially, the vantage point of the crucified God and can act as a criterion for theological reflection, biblical exegesis, and the life of the Church. The poor are the means whereby the Church can learn to discern the truth, direction and content of its mission, and they can assure the Church of being the place where the Lord is to be found.[13]

## The Bible and liberation theology

Among grassroots groups the Bible has become a catalyst for the exploration of pressing contemporary issues relevant to the community and offers a language so that the voice of the voiceless may be heard. The biblical tradition becomes a catalyst for new thought and action related to the circumstances of everyday commitments. In the CEBs there is an immediacy in the way in which the text is used because resonances are found with the experience set out in the stories of biblical characters which seems remote from the world of most people in the more affluent Europe and North America. The Bible offers a means by which the present difficulties can be shown to be surmountable in the life of faith and community commitment. To enable the poor to read the Bible has involved a programme of education about the contents of the biblical material, so that it can be a resource for thousands who are illiterate. In such programmes full recognition is taken of the value of the experience of life.[14] It can be a form of Bible study which goes straight to the text with no concern to ask questions about its original historical context.[15] Such a reading of the text can serve to encourage faith and confidence in the individual's relationship with his/ her Lord. The community setting means an avoidance of a narrowly individualist 'religious' reading. The approach to Bible reading in the CEBs has many similarities with Protestant forms of Bible study which are increasingly prevalent in Latin America. Indeed, one should not ignore the enormous inroads into Latin American Catholicism of evangelical Christianity with its similar 'direct' way of reading the Bible, though with less overt political content to the interpretation.

As we have seen, the experience of poverty and oppression (often termed 'life' or 'reality') is as important a text as the text of Scripture itself. It represents another text to be studied alongside that contained between the covers of the Bible. God's word is to be found in the dialectic between the literary memory of the people of God and the continuing story to be discerned in the contemporary world, particularly among those people with whom God has chosen to be identified. This twofold aspect is well brought out by Carlos Mesters:

> ... the emphasis is not placed on the text's meaning in itself but rather on the meaning the text has for the people reading it. At the start the people tend to draw any and every sort of meaning, however well or ill founded, from the text ... the common people are also eliminating the alleged 'neutrality' of scholarly exegesis ... the common people are putting the Bible in its proper place, the place where God intended it to be. They are putting it in second place. Life takes first place! In so doing, the people are showing us the enormous importance of the Bible, and at the same time, its relative value – relative to life.[16]

This biblical study may seem to be an example of the dangerous reading into the text of the readers' own prejudices. But Karl Barth reminds us of the inevitability that some kind of reading into the text is always at work in any biblical interpretation as we seek to make sense of the meaning of the words, when he writes 'Why should parallels drawn from the ancient world be of more value for our understanding of the epistle than the situation in which we ourselves actually are and to which we can therefore bear witness?'[17] This neatly encapsulates the way of reading Scripture in the CEBs and represents the difference between so much mainstream contemporary biblical exegesis and a liberationist approach.

## Responses to liberation theology

In the course of the development of Latin American theology which has followed in the footsteps of Gutiérrez's pioneering study of the early 1970s, there has been a development and response to criticisms that have been made. There has been a greater appreciation of gender and race alongside poverty as factors which need to be taken into account in any liberation theology. Also the Roman Catholic representatives of the liberationist perspective have been in dialogue with wider catholic theology and consider their work as in continuity, and in dialogue, with the Magisterium (teaching office) of the Church (often to the frustration of some of their Protestant colleagues). Of course, the Congregation for the Doctrine of the Faith has had significant differences of opinion over the years with certain Latin American theologians (not to mention also with some Brazilian cardinals and the Brazilian Bishops' Conference). Nevertheless many of the theological expositions, particularly as liberation theology has developed, have been consciously moulded within the Magisterium and its application within the successive conferences of the Latin American bishops and their regional conferences' decisions (in Latin America at Medellín and Puebla, reaffirmed substantially at Santo Domingo). It is this which, along with the experience of pastoral work and the peculiar insight and contribution of the poor, forms their response to questions about poverty.

The contributions of liberation theologians form a small part of a long debate within Christianity, both modern and ancient, about appropriate attitudes and responses to the poor and vulnerable and the Church's relations with the political powers. Liberation theology has emerged, in Roman Catholic circles at least, as applications of the Magisterium's emphasis on the preferential option for the poor, the insight vouchsafed to the poor 'to highlight aspects of the Word of God, the richness of which had not yet been fully grasped' (Congregation of the Doctrine of the Faith's Instruction 70), and the important contribution of the CEBs. Liberation theologians see themselves engaged in mediation between the poor and the Magisterium together with the appropriate 'secular' wisdom which contributes to theological reflection (*Gaudium et Spes* 62), though with a clear commitment to the poor rather than being neutral theological brokers.[18]

Assessment of liberation theology in the Roman Catholic Church has not been entirely negative. In contrast with the tone of the Congregation for the Doctrine of the Faith's *Libertatis Nuntius*, in a recent survey of biblical hermeneutics members of the Pontifical Biblical Commission[19] include a more positive assessment of liberation theology. Among the criticisms of the Commission are the concentration on narrative and prophetic texts in liberation theology, which highlight situations of oppression and which inspire a praxis leading to social change. While admitting that exegesis cannot be neutral, they discern a danger that those engaged in liberation theology might be too one-sided, and find themselves engaged in social and political action which is not the main task of the exegete. The use of Marxist analysis of social reality as a frame of reference for reading the Bible is questioned, as is its emphasis on a hope for God's reign on earth 'to the detriment', as they put it, 'of the more transcendent dimensions of scriptural eschatology'.[20] Liberationist and feminist interpretations are both given the label 'contextual approaches' (as if interpretative approaches like the historical-critical method are not contextual, though, clearly, members of the Commission regard the historical method as having a privileged position in biblical hermeneutics).

The response to liberation theology in the academies of Europe has been mixed. On the one hand there is evidence of the considerable influence of the importance of experience and context in theological reflection in seminary training, but mainstream biblical exegesis and dogmatics have been largely unaffected by a liberationist perspective. Although there is an admiration of 'Southern' theologians on the part of 'Northern' colleagues, there has been a certain wariness about liberation theology in the 'North'. Liberation theology's overt commitment and practical involvement can make it an obvious target for criticism from those who favour a more detached and dispassionate form of theological reflection. Liberation theologians seem to some to bypass the careful questioning and necessary provisionality of much of our interpretation. Liberation theologians insist that all theology is inevitably contextual and conditioned by the environment and activity in which the theologians are themselves engaged, even if they would want to assert the existence of a universal demand to opt for the poor. 'Northern' theologians have been somewhat coy about their own interpretative interests, social and economic as well as ideological, however. The overtly committed reading from liberation theologians at least has the merit of being more clear about where they are approaching the text from and posing a challenge to those of us who are more ideologically complacent. The apparent absence of partiality in 'Northern' academic readings should not lead us to suppose that there may be no interest at stake. All of us involved in mainstream academic theology need to examine our consciences and ask ourselves how far our theology breathes a spirit of detachment and objectivity. There will often be struggles in the academy but they will often be individualised and detached from the growing gap between rich and poor throughout the world. We in the 'North' need to learn to be part of a community of interpretation and action in a Church committed to the poor where the concerns of the academy contribute to the challenge to the priorities of an increasingly individualistic age lacking global concern. There is nothing new in what is expected of both the Church and theology. Frequently despite itself, the Christian Church has for two thousand years managed to keep alive an antidote to that unfettered individualism which seeks to fragment and destroy.

Critics often find the liberationist agenda inapplicable to the complex democracies of the 'the North', or, while accepting the challenge that liberation theologians pose, indicate that there are other issues which 'Northern' theologians find pressing in their context.[21] Others find the theological approach too simplistic or too much infected with a philosophy alien to Christianity. The emphasis on the experience of the everyday world and its injustices as an essential part of the knowledge of God is a recurrent theme in a small but growing grassroots theology in Europe as well as being the cornerstone of the theology of liberation. The primary text of oppression, poverty and dehumanising attitudes and circumstances as a result makes theologians out of all God's people. The experts do not have a privileged position in the understanding of God as there is emphasis on the insight of the poor as interpreters of the word of God. There is evidence of a wide-spread practice of a way of doing theology in which experience of life in inner cities or on the margins of life resonates with Scripture either as a direct result of the influence of liberation theology or, sometimes, as a parallel development. Often such examples in the 'North' are related to one another only loosely at most and lack the institutional networks of the liberation theology of Latin America or the Ecumenical Association of Third World Theologians (EATWOT).[22] Theology which may be termed liberationist has grown up in a variety of situations in Europe and America over the last two decades, much of it not yet adequately catalogued.[23] Among its theological ancestors one might include the radical Barthian William Stringfellow[24] and Jacques Ellul[25] in North America and Europe respectively. Neither has been influenced by liberation theology; indeed, in some respects each has been opposed to it.

## Historical antecedents to liberation theology

Liberationist perspectives have a long pedigree in Christian theology. They are already evident in, for example, the words of the mid-sixteenth-century English writer, Gerrard Winstanley, that 'tradesmen will speak by experience the things they have seen in God, and the learned clergy will be slighted'.[26] Here priority is given to that inner prompting of God peculiarly derived from the experience of poverty and vulnerability which offers a glimpse of the mind of God. Scripture then acts as confirmation of that intuitive knowledge of God. As in many radical movements in Christianity there is a stress on the immanence of God in the persons of the poor as a catalyst for theology in history (though in liberation theology it is the presence of God in the poor whereas in the writings of the Radical Reformation understanding of the ways of God tends to be viewed in a more individualist manner).[27] From Paul's letter to the Galatians where the meaning of Scripture and the tradition is subordinated to experience of the Spirit to the use of the Bible in the CEBs in contemporary Latin America the emphasis is on experience as a prior 'text' which must condition the way in which Scripture and tradition are read and the 'signs of the times' interpreted. William Blake is another of a long line of radical exponents of Scripture whose myth-making and creative use of Scripture is filtered through personal experience and social upheaval. Blake explored ways in which to liberate the Bible from the dominant patterns of interpretation of his day. He was no exegete or theologian in any conventional sense. He offered a different perspective to tell the story in language which might subvert a Bible in support of a system which oppressed the poor. William Blake used words and designs to open eyes to other dimensions to life and an awareness of the epistemological shift which was required of dulled human intellects.[28] What is apparent in the writings of all these ancestors of liberation theology is the enormity of the task confronting those who would persuade supporters of great institutions of their need for a change of heart and practice. Theirs is no utopian optimism for there is a recognition that the task of persuasion requires a variety of stratagems to jolt complacent mind-sets into seeing things differently.

The positions of liberation theologians, varied as they are, do seem to exhibit certain tendencies and influences (the presence of God in the persons of the poor, the emphasis on action rather than belief, the hope for the reign of God on earth, and a reliance on an action-reflection model). What runs like a thread through all liberation theology is a commitment based on contemplation of God in the suffering Christ whose presence is hidden in the poor.[29] One could compare that moment of commitment about which Gutiérrez writes to the insight of Job when he contrasts past knowledge with present experience which enlivens that knowledge: 'I had heard of thee by the hearing of the ear, but now my eye sees thee' (Job 42.5f).

In recent years several commentators have sounded the death-knell of liberation theology. Yet, there is the disturbing fact that even if liberation theologians have made some mistakes, they have put their finger on something fundamental to the theological task: speaking of God in a world that is inhumane. Such a standpoint is a central component of catholic Christianity, and it is necessary for a Church seeking conformity with the way of Jesus[30] to discern the standpoint of those who may be particularly well able to perceive Christ. Perhaps this is the most disturbing thing about the theological tradition which liberation theology represents: that there exists a hermeneutical privilege for the poor and marginalised and a consequent loss of privilege and status in academy or church. As one English ancestor of liberation theology put it:

> Nay let me tell you, that the poorest man, that sees his Maker, and lives in the light, though he could never read a letter in a book, dares throw the glove to all the humane learning in the world, and declare the deceit of it.[31]

Words which echo those of Jesus, 'I thank you, Father, Lord of heaven and earth, that you have hidden these things from the wise and intelligent and revealed them to infants' (Matt. 11.25). A salutary warning for all theologians.

## NOTES

1 Gustavo Gutiérrez, *The Power of the Poor in History* (London, SCM, 1983), p. 57.

2 Bartolomé de las Casas, *A Short Account of the Destruction of the Indians*, 1552 (London, Penguin, 1992); and G. Gutiérrez, *Las Casas. In Search of the Poor of Jesus Christ* (Maryknoll, NY, Orbis, 1994).

3 C. and L. Boff, *Introducing Liberation Theology* (London, Burns and Oates, 1987); G. Gutiérrez, *A Theology of Liberation*, rev. edn. (London, SCM, 1988); T. Witvliet, *A Place in the Sun* (London, SCM, 1985). There is an important discussion of the epistemology of the theology of liberation in Clodovis Boff, *Theology and Praxis* (Maryknoll, NY, Orbis, 1987); and see further the discussion in J. Milbank, *Theology and Social Theory* (Oxford, Blackwell, 1990), p. 234.

4 Similarly Theodor Adorno's *Minima Moralia* (London, Verso, 1974) and Ludwig Wittgenstein's *Philosophical Investigations* (Oxford, Blackwell, 1953), aphoristic in character as they are, are examples of texts to be used rather than interpreted as one is puzzled and perplexed when asked to reflect on language and the contradictions of life.

5 D. Rensberger, *Overcoming the World* (London, SPCK, 1988), p. 52.

6 For the final documents see *Medellín Conclusions* (New York, US Catholic Conference, 1973) and *Puebla Conclusions* (London, CIIR, 1973); also in A. T. Hennelly (ed.), *Liberation Theology. A Documentary History* (Maryknoll, NY, Orbis, 1990). The basic texts relevant for understanding evangelisation are to be found in the collection *Proclaiming Justice and Peace*, eds. M. Walsh and B. Davies (London, CIIR/CAFOD, 1984).

7 *Santo Domingo Conclusions*, tr. P. Berryman (London, Fourth General Conference of Latin American Bishops, 1993) and the *Puebla Conclusions* 1134ff.; and G. Gutiérrez, *Santo Domingo and After: the Challenge for the Latin American Church* (London, CIIR, 1993).

8 On Brazilian Catholicism see T. C. Bruneau, *The Political Transformation of the Brazilian Catholic Church* (Cambridge, Cambridge University Press, 1974), and *The Catholic Church in Brazil. The Politics of Religion* (Austin, University of Texas, 1982); E. de Kadt, *Catholic Radicals in Brazil* (Oxford, Oxford University Press, 1970); M. Burdick, *Looking for God in Brazil: the Progressive Catholic Church in Urban Brazil's Religious Arena* (Berkeley, University of California, 1993); and for an introduction to the CEBs see M. Hebblethwaite, *Basic Communities. An Introduction* (London, Chapman, 1993).

9 See e.g., David Martin, *Tongues of Fire: the Explosion of Protestantism in Latin America* (Oxford, Blackwell, 1990), and D. Lehmann, *Struggle for the Spirit: Religious Transformation and Popular Culture in Latin America* (Oxford, Polity Press, 1996).

10 One of the problems of the discussion of liberation theology in the first *Instruction* by the Congregation for the Doctrine of the Faith (*Libertatis Nuntius*) is the lack of sophistication in the approach taken to what is a very complex phenomenon. The first document has been subjected to critical scrutiny by J. L. Segundo

in his *Theology and the Church* (London, Chapman, 1985). For reactions to liberation theology see also A. McGovern, *Liberation Theology and its Critics* (Maryknoll, NY, Orbis, 1989) and M. Novak, *The Spirit of Democratic Capitalism* (London, Institute of Economic Affairs, 1991).

11 From his 'Theses on the Philosophy of History' in *Illuminations* (New York, Schocken, 1978).

12 J. Sobrino, *The True Church and the Church of the Poor* (London, SCM, 1985), p. 222.

13 Ibid., p. 95.

14 Examples of material produced by the Archdiocese of São Paulo may be found in C. Rowland and M. Corner, *Liberating Exegesis* (London, SPCK, 1990), pp. 7ff.

15 C. Boff, *Theology and Praxis*, discussed in Rowland and Corner, *Liberating Exegesis*, p. 55; and R. Sugirtharajah (ed.), *Voices from the Margins* (London, SPCK, 1992). Boff speaks of a difference between the immediate paralleling of ancient text and modern situation (what he calls an exegesis of 'the correspondence of terms') and a more nuanced approach in which the contemporary social and political struggles of modern communities are used as an interpretative lens through which to view the text's witness to the social and political struggles of ancient biblical communities (an exegesis he describes as 'correspondence of relationships'). See also Tim Gorringe's essay 'Political Readings of Scripture' in J. Barton (ed.), *The Cambridge Companion to Biblical Interpretation* (Cambridge, Cambridge University Press, 1998, pp. 67–80).

16 C. Mesters, 'The use of the Bible in Christian Communities of the Common People' in Norman Gottwald (ed.), *The Bible and Liberation* (Maryknoll, NY, Orbis, 1983), and C. Mesters, *Defenseless Flower* (London, CIIR/CAFOD, 1989); G. West, *Biblical Hermeneutics of Liberation: Modes of Reading the Bible in the South African Context* (Maryknoll, NY, Orbis, 1995); J. Siker, 'Uses of the Bible in the Theology of Gustavo Gutiérrez: Liberating the Scriptures of the Poor', *Biblical Interpretation*, 4 (1996), pp. 40–72.

17 K. Barth, *The Epistle to the Romans* (Oxford, Oxford University Press, 1933), p. 11.

18 Rowland and Corner, *Liberating Exegesis*, p. 44; cf. the description of John Wesley as a 'cultural broker' in J. Walsh, in 'John Wesley and the Urban Poor', *Revue Française de Civilisation Britannique*, vol. 6, pp. 18–30.

19 Reprinted with commentary in J. L. Houlden (ed.), *The Interpretation of the Bible in the Church* (London, SPCK, 1995), pp. 38ff.

20 See also J. Ratzinger, *Church Ecumenism and Politics* (Slough, St Paul, 1988); and see the critique in Rowland and Corner, *Liberating Exegesis*, pp. 114ff.

21 O. O'Donovan, *The Desire of Nations* (Cambridge, Cambridge University Press, 1996).

22 The EATWOT Proceedings (see Select Bibliography) offer a good guide to many of the issues which have dominated Third World theology over the last twenty years. EATWOT publishes a regular bulletin entitled *Voices*, available from EATWOT, 63 Millers Road, POB 4635, Bangalore 560046, India.

23 For an outline of the emergence of a British liberation theology see John Vincent, 'Liberation Theology in Britain, 1970–1995' in C. Rowland and J. Vincent, *Liberation Theology UK* (*British Liberation Theology 1*, Sheffield,

The Urban Theology Unit, 1995) and Mike Simpson and Joan Sharples' account of the emergence of a British liberation theology network, 'British Liberation Theology Consultation and Celebration Weekends, 1989–1995' in *British Liberation Theology* 3 (forthcoming). On European basic communities see M. and I. Fraser, *Wind and Fire: the Spirit Reshapes the Church in Basic Christian Communities* (Dunblane, Scottish Churches House, 1986). See also K. Leech, *True God: an exploration in Spiritual Theology* (London, Sheldon, 1985; Bob Holman, *Towards Equality: A Christian Manifesto* (London, SPCK, 1997); J. Reader, *Local Theology* (London, SPCK, 1994); and P. Ballard and J. Pritchard, *Practical Theology in Action: Christian Theology in the Service of Society* (London, SPCK, 1996), esp. pp. 73–86. There are echoes of a liberationist perspective in Anglican theology: e.g., D. Sheppard, *Bias to the Poor* (London, Hodder and Stoughton, 1983) and the Archbishop of Canterbury's report on the churches in the inner cities, *Faith in the City* (London, CIO, 1985). See also *The Cities*, a Methodist report (London, The Methodist Church and NCH Action for Children, 1997).

24 W. Stringfellow has influenced Jim Wallis and groups like the Sojourners in the USA. His concern to propound a theology of the principalities and powers anticipates the writing of Walter Wink, the final volume of whose trilogy on the biblical doctrine of the heavenly powers has an avowedly contemporary concern (*Engaging the Powers*, Philadelphia, Fortress, 1992). Stringfellow's *An Ethic for Christians and Other Aliens in a Strange Land* (Waco, Word, 1975) is an example of a contextual theology dominated by protests against the Vietnam War and what he perceives to be the complacency of American Christianity. He later supported the Berrigan brothers in their campaign against weapons of mass destruction.

25 E.g., J. Ellul, *The Presence of the Kingdom* (London, 1951) and *Jesus and Marx. From Gospel to Ideology* (Grand Rapids, Eerdmans, 1988).

26 Quoted in C. Rowland, *Radical Christianity* (Oxford, Polity Press, 1988), p. 110. On the biblical interpretation of radical theology in early-modern England see C. Hill, *The English Bible and the Seventeenth Century Revolution* (London, Penguin, 1993). Winstanley's theology is compared with that of the German reformation radical Thomas Muentzer in A. Bradstock, *Faith in the Revolution* (London, SPCK, 1997).

27 See Rowland, *Radical Christianity*; and on the emphasis on immanentist theology in the writings and illustrations of William Blake as a protest at the hegemonic theology of his day, see J. Mee, *Dangerous Enthusiasm: William Blake and the Culture of Radicalism in the 1790s* (Oxford, Oxford University Press, 1992).

28 See *William Blake's Illuminated Books*, General Editor David Bindman, 6 vols. (London, Tate Gallery Publications/William Blake Trust, 1991–5); D. V. Erdman, *Blake Prophet against Empire* (Princeton, Princeton University Press, 1977); N. Frye, *Fearful Symmetry: A Study of William Blake* (Princeton, Princeton University Press, 1947).

29 G. Gutiérrez, *The Truth Shall Make You Free* (Maryknoll, NY, Orbis, 1990), p. 3.

30 Many liberation theologians, influenced as they are by the modern concern for the historical Jesus, lay greater emphasis on the Jesus of history and on the

synoptic Gospels, in which understanding and insight seem peculiarly available to the insignificant and marginal. See, e.g., J. Sobrino, *Christology at the Crossroads* (London, SCM, 1978).

31 Gerrard Winstanley (fl. 1650), New Law of Righteousness, quoted in Rowland, *Radical Christianity*, p. 110.

# PART I

# Contemporary Liberation Theology

# I

G. GUTIERREZ translated by JUDITH CONDOR

# The task and content of liberation theology

The urgency and the richness of the commitment that many Christians in Latin America and the Caribbean began to feel in the 1960s as part of the struggle for justice and solidarity with the poor raised new questions, as well as pointing to fertile new pathways in the discourse about faith. These circumstances helped convert such reflection into a theology of liberation; that is, a way to understand the grace and salvation of Jesus in the context of the present and from the situation of the poor.

From the start, therefore, this theological perspective is bound up with the life of grassroots Christian communities and their commitment, as well as with the evangelising mission of the Church. This is the reason for its great impact, also from the outset, in the magisterium of the Church. Medellín and other Latin American Bishops' conferences, as well as many other texts, bear witness to this fact.

The theology of liberation, like any theology is about God. God and God's love are, ultimately, its only theme. But since for Christian revelation (the starting point for any theology) the love of God is a mystery, the immediate question is how to talk of a mystery? The humble and respectful advice of Thomas Aquinas remains valid: 'we cannot know what God is, only what he is not' (*ST* I.9.3 introd.). It is in this context that, nearly thirty years ago, we asked ourselves what path the theological task ought to take in the context of Latin America.

In order to try to answer this question it is useful to remind ourselves about the challenges that are posed for such a reflection; how this reflection understands its present and future tasks; and its orientation towards the proclamation of the God of life in a reality characterised by the premature and unjust death of many people.

## Challenged by poverty

There is one clear and determining fact about the last few decades in the life of the Latin American Church: the way of understanding the task of announcing the gospel changed from the moment that the Church took new consciousness of the 'inhuman misery' (Medellín, *Pobreza* n. 1) in which the majority of the population lives. Poverty continues to be the great challenge to Christian witness in our continent. The attempts of some, on the eve of the Bishops' conference at Puebla – and at Santo Domingo – to tone down the concern about this situation of poverty and to shift the focus of attention to other matters were in vain. Our reality and the demands of the gospel combined to head off any possibility of evading these issues.

Thus, theological reflection cannot be the same either. It sets out on new pathways which lead – not without difficulties or misunderstandings – to rich possibilities for the proclamation of the Kingdom of God as these last years have proved.

### *The presence of the absent*

The participation of Christians in the process of liberation in Latin America that some time ago we used to call the 'most important fact' (*hecho mayor*) in the life of the Church is nothing other than an expression of the immense historical process that we know as the 'irruption' of the poor. This has helped us see with unusual force and clarity the longstanding, cruel poverty in which the great majority of Latin Americans live. These people have burst upon the social scene with 'their poverty on their shoulders' – as Las Casas commented referring to the Indian nations of his time. But this situation of poverty has led to a better appreciation of the energies and values of these people.

These times, therefore, bear the imprint of a new presence of the poor, the marginalised and the oppressed. Those who were for so long 'absent' in our society and in the Church have made themselves – and are continuing to make themselves – present. It is not a matter of physical absence: we are talking of those who have had scant or no significance, and who therefore have not felt (and in many cases still do not feel) in a position to make plain their suffering, their aspirations and their hopes. But this is what has started to change.

It is always difficult to date the beginning of any historical process; in these examples, dates are often approximate and conventional. Nevertheless, we can affirm that the process we have described has been going on for thirty or forty years in Latin America and the Caribbean. Initially, it was evident in developments such as the growth of the popular movements, in an intensification of the struggle for justice, in an increase in expectations, in the emergence of new social and political organisations, in a greater awareness of personal dignity and in the rights of the old indigenous peoples, in attempts by those in power to undertake meaningful social reforms, and even – in some cases – in unfruitful outbreaks of guerrilla violence. All of which brought in response new types of authoritarian and repressive governments, in a world still characterised by the cold war.

The facts are complex, and not free of ambivalence. However, we are on the threshold of something challenging and hopeful, which has meant that the poor begin to see themselves as subjects of their own history, as being able to take their destiny in their own hands. This is clearly a crucial discovery and a profound conviction, replete with social and pastoral implications. It is a case of what today is known as 'self image' and of the appearance of new social and pastoral actors. It has left a decisive mark both on the nature of the political task in Latin American society, as well as on the activity of the Church.

The challenge becomes even more dramatic for the task of evangelisation if we bear in mind that the people who erupted on to the historical scene are at the same time both poor and Christian. Their Christian faith affects in many different ways their experience of poverty and oppression, and this experience of poverty and oppression makes its mark on their experience of the gospel.

## A new social awareness

For a long time we Latin Americans have lived in great ignorance about the reality of our countries. Occasional voices – some of which were certainly very authoritative – alerted us in the past to the problems created by enormous social divides. But often they were rendered ineffectual by indifference and the lack of sensitivity to the marginalisation of the poor. During the 1950s various international factors led to a concern for what came to be called development, both social and economic. In the wake of the Bandung Conference (1955), such terminology came to express the aspirations of backward countries which sought to achieve more humane living conditions. Developmentalist policies came to be applied at this time in Latin America and the Caribbean with a view to rescuing these countries from their backwardness. But the initial optimism in such policies soon gave way to disillusion.

Confronting developmentalism – not development itself which is a technical concept and a necessity for all countries – there emerged dependency theory. This received its initial elaboration in the neo-structuralist domain of the Economic Commission for Latin America (ECLA), a UN body. This perspective gradually gained substance through contributions from various aspects of the social sciences, both with and without the influence of Marxist analysis. Unlike developmentalism, dependency theory involves acute and sustained study of the causes of poverty in Latin America and places it in an international context. It also seeks – a key point – to concentrate on the process which has led up to this state of affairs, stressing the view that nations form part of a history which is increasingly universal. A fundamental requirement for this perspective, therefore, is to look for ways to break the dependency on the main centres of power.

This last point, coupled with the analysis of the causes of poverty, linked this approach with the path opened up by the increased awareness of the poverty in which the majority of Latin Americans lived, and also with the new pastoral and spiritual paths that stemmed from it. In this way, dependency theory – which was at its peak in the 1960s and 1970s – became a crucial tool for understanding the socio-economic reality of Latin America. It made possible a structural analysis of the evils present in this reality, and suggested courses for remedying them.

Without any doubt this theory represented a qualitative step forward in efforts to understand the Latin American situation. Its presence in the framework for liberation theology (and in the Medellín documents) derives precisely from its contribution to social analysis. In this way dependency theory fulfils a role as a tool of understanding those aspects of the socio-economic reality for which it was designed. Its contribution was significant during the first few years of the development of the theology of liberation in Latin America. This is clear and a well-known fact. However, as always in the history of theology, the understanding of faith is not necessarily identified with the intellectual path taken to understand a specific aspect of existence, in this case the socio-economic dimension. This should not be taken to mean that the use of social analysis, by giving a better picture of the challenges that the social and economic dimensions of society pose to faith, does not help to establish priorities which leave a mark on theological reflection oriented to transforming society, so long as this coincides with the task of evangelisation. It is important to be clear about connections and distinctions to be drawn on such matters.

Like any theory, dependency theory necessarily advances and adapts in the light of changes in the situation it seeks to understand. Indeed, the tools of social analysis vary with time, according to their ability to explain the phenomena to which they relate, and in accordance with the efficacy of the solutions they propose. What characterises science is its capacity to be critical about its own presuppositions and its own results; scientific knowledge advances permanently by means of new interpretative hypotheses.

A variety of learned studies in more recent years have aimed to critique dependency theory. For many today it represents – without denying its contribution at a specific moment – an instrument that fails to explain the complexity of the present situation. Indeed, in retrospect, the limitations it always had have become clearer (for example, its excessive emphasis on external factors in explaining underdevelopment). This is normal. It is always the case with attempts to understand terrain such as ours where the surface soil is sandy and shifting. The same happens in human sciences (social and psychological). Time is implacably relentless in such attempts at understanding.

While it would be a serious error not to acknowledge the contribution of this theory, it would be worse to remain tied to a tool which clearly no longer responds adequately to the diversity of the present situation, and which pays no heed to new aspects. Many such changes are the product of important changes on the international scene. They also arise from different perceptions of elements which, while they may have long formed part of the social framework in Latin America, now help provide a better picture of its contours.

### The current situation

First we need to remind ourselves that poverty has increased dramatically. The gap between the rich and poor nations is today wider than two decades ago. The same is the case within each Latin American country. This has led to the virtual disappearance of sectors of the middle class which have been plunged into poverty. It has given rise to what has been called 'neo-dualism': the population is ever increasingly polarised at the two extremes of the social and economic spectrum. In this context, the 1980s is often referred to as a 'lost decade', although for some countries the period has in fact been much longer. Nevertheless, it is important to note that in this period those countries have managed to improve their strategies to alleviate or even solve their problems.

Many things have also changed in the international arena. Following the collapse of the authoritarian socialism of the Eastern European countries – which neither respected the basic rights nor took into account the diversity of aspirations of their citizens – we have moved from a bipolar world to one in which in political and military terms there is but one pole, although in the economic sphere the situation is more complex. This collapse has also led to a reaffirmation of market economics, even though these cannot work properly except within parameters which reflect concern for social and human inequality. The technological revolution in the sphere of knowledge has radically transformed the process of accumulation and reduced the role played by the raw materials that poor countries produce. This has rendered redundant a number of the analytical concepts which were used previously. The burden of debt has distorted the economies of the poor countries, while the rigidity of international organisations on this issue has acted as a straitjacket limiting the possibilities for responding to the needs of the poorest.

All this has brought new forms of interchange between North and South. In many cases, the inequalities have become more marked, these deep chasms at times posing a threat to world peace, even if we believe that economic and military might can control the situation at the moment.

Neo-liberal ideology (one of its main texts proclaims, not without unconscious humour, 'the end of history') rereads in its own fashion the historical evolution of humanity. In this way it deprives the poor nations of their history and disguises those economic and social processes which have increased the asymmetries mentioned above. All this leads to a concentration of power in certain sectors of society that reduces the ways out available to poor nations, and to the poor living in them. The signs of exhaustion implicit in neo-liberalism are already beginning to appear and they may change the picture in the future, although the present trends are clear enough.

On the other hand, the passage of time has helped us to understand better the concrete situation facing the poor and oppressed in Latin America. From the beginning, from the perspective of the theology of liberation, we spoke of subjugated peoples, exploited classes, despised races, and marginalised cultures. Then, there was expressed a concern for the discrimination against women, an attitude frequently hidden that becomes a daily habit, a cultural tradition, even though for that no less persistent and unhealthy. But what is clear is that these different aspects did not take on their most strident and demanding form until solidarity with the world of the poor became deeper in the last few years. Factors of race, culture and gender have become increasingly important in helping to draw a more accurate picture of the condition of the poor in Latin America. Thanks to such commitment we became more aware that ultimately – without omitting of course its social and economic dimensions – poverty means death, unjust and premature death.

From this arises the reaffirmation of life as the prime human right, and, from the Christian viewpoint, as a gift of God that we must defend. This became the hallmark of our experience and reflection at the end of the 1970s (for example, in Peru and Central America), and has become the catalyst for our endeavour and commitment. It helped us recover an evangelical perspective (so present in men like Las Casas in the sixteenth century) on the idolatrous character of profit propagated by a 'savage capitalism' that crushes the dignity of human beings under foot, turning them into the victims of a cruel and sacrilegious cult.

At the same time it is important to understand that poverty is not only about deficiencies. The poor person is someone brimming over with capacities and possibilities, whose culture has its own values, derived from racial background, history and language. Such energies have been revealed throughout Latin America by women's organisations fighting for life, in their creativity and originality which challenges, in spite of everything, the so-called 'crisis of paradigms' which we hear so much of today. We are talking about poor people who, despite the way they have been affected by circumstances (often seriously), resist all attempts to mutilate or manipulate their hopes for the future.

### Poverty and theological reflection

At around the middle of the twentieth century, a number of developments helped to revive and to relaunch the theme of poverty within the universal Church. There was a demand for a radical and authentic witness of poverty arising from new religious communities. This came from among those concerned with the growing estrangement from faith evident among the labour movement, in the development of the social teaching of the Church and in some spiritual and pastoral tendencies, especially in Europe. This concern was categorically and prophetically expressed by Pope John XXIII at the Vatican Council: in the call for the Church to become the Church of all, and in particular the Church of the poor (11 September 1962).

Vatican II, for reasons that are well known and easy to understand, did not fully take up John XXIII's proposal, even though this concern was at the fore during much of the work of the Council. However, it was heard, in large measure because of the developments we have already touched upon (albeit not without some reservations and vacillation), where the great majority is both poor and Christian: in Latin America. Alongside the fact of the new presence of the poor, the idea of a Church of the poor stimulated considerable theological reflection.

That is why in around July 1967, a distinction was made between three concepts of poverty:

(1)　Real poverty (frequently called material poverty), defined as the lack of those goods required to satisfy the most basic needs of human beings. This poverty is an outrage in terms of the message of the Bible. It is a situation wholly contrary to the will of God.

(2)  Spiritual poverty. This is not primarily the putting aside of worldly goods; it is rather an attitude of openness and acceptance towards the will of God. The gospel also calls this spiritual childhood, of which the renunciation of worldly goods is a consequence.

(3)  Poverty as a commitment to be assumed by all Christians, which expresses itself in solidarity with the poor and in protest against poverty. Jesus assumes the sins of humanity in this way, both out of love for the sinner and in rejection of sin.[1]

Such an approach presupposes a particular analysis of poverty and its causes. It also implies a biblical foundation both in relation to a rejection of this inhuman situation as well as towards an understanding of spiritual poverty. Finally it sets out the reasons – leaving aside all idealism – for Christian commitment in this field. This contribution was taken up a year later at Medellín in August and September 1968, and helped clarify the commitment which many Christians had begun to assume.[2]

Closely linked to the theme of poverty emanating from a situation of injustice, a little before Medellín there emerged the theme of liberation, which embodies a number of perspectives. Although the term liberation exists also in the social and political spheres, it comes from a very ancient biblical and theological tradition. It was within this tradition that we sought to locate the term from the beginning. In using the word 'liberation' we distinguished between:

(1)  Political and social liberation, which points towards the elimination of the immediate causes of poverty and injustice, especially with regard to socio-economic structures. On this basis, an attempt can be made to construct a society based on respect for the other, and especially for the weakest and the insignificant;

(2)  human liberation, meaning that, although aware that changing social structures is important, we need to go deeper. It means liberating human beings of all those things – not just in the social sphere – that limit their capacity to develop themselves freely and in dignity. Here we are speaking of what Vatican II called a 'new humanism' (cf. GS 55);

(3)  and, crucially, liberation from selfishness and sin. In the analysis of faith, this is the last root of injustice that has to be eliminated. Overcoming this leads to re-establishing friendship with God and with other people (cf. Lumen Gentium n. 1). It is clear that only the grace of God, the redeeming work of Christ, can overcome sin.

Divergent, but at the same time linked, these three dimensions of liberation portray a radical and integral reality, a broad process whose meaning is ultimately to be found in the salvation of Christ. This provides the concept of liberation with its permanent relevance and the demanding appeal, as well as the context for dealing with the issue of poverty.

From the distinctions noted above between notions of poverty, the expression 'preferential option for the poor' emerged from within Christian communities, between the time of the conferences of Medellín and Puebla (1979). Here, the three notions of poverty are bound together with one another, and are made dynamic. *Poor*, here refers to victims of material poverty; *preferential* is inspired by the notion of spiritual childhood or the capacity to accept the will of God in our lives; and *option* relates to the idea of commitment that – as we have suggested – means solidarity with the poor and rejection of poverty as something contrary to the will of God. This option, adopted at the Bishops' conference at Puebla,[3] represents today a point of orientation for the pastoral activities of the Church and an important guideline for being a Christian – in other words, what we call spirituality, one of the fundamental concerns of liberation theology. As is well known, this is a perspective which is widely accepted in the teaching of the universal Church.

All this provides the approach which has become the central plank in the evangelising mission of the contemporary Church in Latin America. It combines a profound sense of the gratuitous love of God with the urgency of solidarity with the 'little ones' of history. These are the two elements, the two pillars of what we call liberation theology. The theme of encounter with our Lord in the suffering faces of the dispossessed and despised of our continent beautifully and concisely expresses a process which has been under way for some years now. It is evident even from the very dawn of Latin American theological reflection inspired by the gospel. We refer to the reflections of the Peruvian Indian Felipe Huamán Poma de Ayala at the beginning of the seventeenth century; to the ideas we find a little earlier in the writing of Bartolomé de Las Casas. Both illustrated their Christian understanding of the cruel predicament facing the Indians through reference to chapter 25 of Matthew's Gospel. This is a text which occupies a central place in the theology of liberation as well, being taken up both in Puebla (1979) and Santo Domingo (1992).

## Theology as critical reflection

The theology of liberation is reflection on practice in the light of faith. In order to understand the scope of such an affirmation, it is helpful to examine the question posed at the outset of this discourse on faith, to see how in this perspective theological method and spirituality interrelate closely; and finally we can set out the present challenges.

## A point of departure

A good part of contemporary theology, since the Age of Enlightenment, appears to take as a point of departure the challenge raised by the (often unbelieving) modern spirit. The modern mentality questions the religious world and demands of it a purification and renewal. Bonhoeffer takes up this challenge and incisively formulates the question that lies at the roots of much contemporary theology: 'how to announce God in a world that has come of age (*mündig*)?'

But in a continent like Latin America and the Caribbean, the challenge comes not in the first instance from the non-believer, but from the 'non-persons', those who are not recognised as people by the existing social order: the poor, the exploited, those systematically and legally deprived of their status as human beings, those who barely realise what it is to be a human being. The 'non-person' questions not so much our religious universe but above all our economic, social, political and cultural order, calling for a transformation of the very foundations of a dehumanising society.

The question we face, therefore, is not so much how to talk of God in a world come of age, but how to proclaim God as Father in an inhuman world? How do we tell the 'non-persons' that they are the sons and daughters of God? These are the key questions for a theology that emerges from Latin America, and doubtless for other parts of the world in similar situations. These were the questions which, in a way, Bartolomé de Las Casas and many others posed in the sixteenth century following their encounter with the indigenous population of America.

This does not mean that the questions posed by modernity are irrelevant for us. It is a question of emphasis, and in this light, poverty without doubt is the most important challenge.

## Reflection on praxis

How to find a way to talk about a God who reveals Himself to us as love in a reality characterised by poverty and oppression? From the perspective of the theology of liberation, it is argued that the first step is to contemplate God and put God's will into practice; and only in a second moment can we think about God. What we mean to say by this is that the veneration of God and the doing of God's will are the necessary conditions for reflection on Him. In fact, only as a consequence of prayer and commitment is it possible to work out an authentic and respectful discourse about God. Through commitment, concretely commitment towards the poor, do we find the Lord (cf. Matt. 25.31–46); but at the same time this discovery deepens and renders more genuine our solidarity with the poor. Contemplation and commitment in human history are fundamental dimensions of Christian existence; in consequence, they cannot be avoided in the understanding of faith. The mystery is revealed through contemplation and solidarity with the poor; it is what we call the *first act*, Christian life, practice. Only thereafter can this life inspire reasoning: that is the *second act*.

Theology, as a critical reflection in the light of the Word adopted through faith on the presence of Christians in a tumultuous world, should help us to understand the relationship between the life of faith and the urgent need to build a society that is humane and just. It is called upon to make explicit the values of faith, hope and charity that that commitment involves. But it also helps to correct possible deviations, as well as to recall some aspects of the Christian life which risk being forgotten in view of immediate political priorities, however charitable those may be. This is the function of critical reflection which, by definition, should not be a Christian justification *a posteriori*. In essence, theology helps the commitment to liberation to be more evangelical, more concrete, more effective. Theology is at the service of the Church's task of evangelisation; it arises out of it as an ecclesial function.[4]

The starting point for all theology is to be found in the act of faith. However, rather than being an intellectual adherence to the message, it should be a vital embracing of the gift of the Word as heard in the ecclesial community, as an encounter with God, and as love of one's brother and sister. It is about existence in its totality. To receive the Word, to give it life, to make it a concrete gesture; this is where understanding of faith begins. This is the meaning of Saint Anselm's *credo ut intelligam*. The primacy of the love of God and the grace of faith give theology its *raison d'être*. Authentic theology is always spiritual, as was understood by the Fathers of the Church. All this means that the life of faith is not only a starting point, it is also the goal of theological reflection. To believe (life) and to understand (reflection) are therefore always part of a circular relationship.

## A way of living and thinking

The distinction between the two moments (first and second acts) is a crucial point in the method of liberation theology; in other words, the process (method, *hodos*, the way) that should be followed for reflection in the light of the faith. This is indeed more traditional than many think, but what we need to underline here is that it is not only a question of theological methodology, rather it implies a lifestyle, a way of being, and of becoming a disciple of Jesus.

In the book which tells of the Acts of the first Christian communities, this is given a particular and original name: 'the way'. The term is used frequently in an absolute way without qualification. To follow the Way implies a pattern of conduct; the Hebrew word *derek*, which translates into Greek as *hodos*, in fact means both things at the same time: the way and conduct. Christians were characterised by their conduct and by their lifestyle. This is what distinguished the Christian communities in their early years in the Jewish and pagan world in which they lived and bore witness. Such conduct is a way of thinking and behaving, 'of walking according to the Holy Spirit' (Rom. 8.4).

Following Jesus defines the Christian. It is a journey which, according to biblical sources, is a communitarian experience, because it is indeed a people that is on the move. The poor in Latin America have started to move in the struggle to affirm their human dignity and their status as sons and daughters of God. This movement embodies a spiritual experience. In other words, this is the place and the moment of an encounter with the Lord; it represents a way of following Jesus Christ.

This is a fundamental point of reference for the theological reflection taking place in Latin America. It is aware that it is preceded by the spiritual experience of Christians committed to the process of liberation. This encounter with God and the discipleship of the Lord – sometimes extending to surrendering one's life, to martyrdom – has been made more urgent and fruitful by the events of recent years. In the context of the struggle for liberation motivated by love and justice for all, there has possibly opened up a new way of following Jesus in Latin America. There is a new spirituality which, for this very reason, resists clear definition and any attempt to imprison it in description, but which nevertheless is no less real or full of potential.

Following Jesus Christ is the basis of the direction that is adopted for doing theology. For this reason, it could be said that our methodology is our spirituality (in other words, a way of being Christian). Reflection on the mystery of God can only be undertaken if we follow in the steps of Jesus. Only if we walk in the way of the Spirit is it possible to understand and announce the gratuitous love of the Father for all people. Perhaps it is because of this relationship between Christian life and theological method that the Base Ecclesial Communities in Latin America are becoming ever more the agents of such theological reflection.

## A *continent* of all bloods

From the outset, Latin American theological reflection raised the question of the 'other' in our society. The inadequacy, and indeed the errors, in the concentration on the reality of poverty adopted at that time made it necessary to analyse first the social and economic reasons for the marginalisation suffered by different categories of the poor (social class, culture, ethnicity and gender). Indeed, although a description of poverty is important, so long as its causes are not identified we are unable to do anything about it, or we are limited to trying to heal social rifts that require much deeper and broader solutions. Many of those causes – although not all – are social and economic. These are most unsettling for the power groups within Latin America and beyond, because they remind them of their responsibility for the conditions in which the majorities live. For this reason, they continually try to ascribe the differences to factors that mask the degree of social injustice. We should not forget this when with the best will in the world – and to some extent correctly – we are sensitive to certain aspects such as the race, culture and gender of the heterogeneous population of Latin America. We need to be clear about the different facets of the problem.

To adopt this perspective, to embark on a structural analysis, was one of the novelties of Medellín. Many of the positions taken in recent years reveal the extent to which this approach has been engraved on the Latin American mind, and has been constantly reworked. At the same time, these positions show with great clarity the need to immerse ourselves in the multifaceted world of the poor, remaining attentive to its cultural and racial dimensions.

Although a longstanding concern, the last few decades have allowed us to become more deeply involved in this complexity. The year 1992 stimulated the need to undertake a critical evaluation of the last 500 years of the continent's history, and helped give more attention to the predicament of the various indigenous nations and to the black population which have been violently incorporated into our world. In many ways we have been witnesses over this period to the force given by the voices of these peoples; they remind us that the expression used by the Peruvian writer José María Arguedas to describe Peru as a country 'of all bloods' can be applied to the whole continent.

All this affects the way of living and announcing the gospel, and certainly the theological reflection that accompanies it. The emphasis that these types of theology adopt, depending on which angle of poverty is the starting point, should not make us lose sight of the global dimension of the issue, nor to forget the horizon of understanding of our languages about

God: the language of the marginalised and oppressed, the language of their liberation and the language of the gospel of Jesus.

It is necessary to avoid the possibility that the deepening of reflection on the suffering of the poor in Latin America transforms itself into fruitless searches for theological spaces, anguishing priorities and misunderstandings – with undisguised (in spite of appearances) intellectualist features – that in the long run only undermine the effort of the 'little ones' of history in their struggle for life, justice and the right to be different. We also observe the existence of indigenous groups that are particularly forgotten and excluded. We refer to the aborigines of the Amazon, a region where – as pointed out in one of the texts of the bishops and missionaries – governments are more interested in natural resources than in the inhabitants.[5] This is also the case of the Kunas of Panama and the Mapuche in Chile, amongst others. The distance we need to cover in order to understand these peoples and to express solidarity with them is still long. Nevertheless, these peoples are beginning to make it clear that they live in lands that have always been theirs. This fact is partly a result of the liberating dimension of the gospel. However, it also constitutes a challenge to Christian faith.

What we have just mentioned continues to provide colour and flavour to the new role of the poor we referred to earlier. It too forms part of the – prolonged and stormy – search for identity in a continent of many colours which still finds difficulty in knowing what it is. For this very reason, the state and values of the poor in general, and of indigenous and black people in particular (and among them the women), constitute a challenge for evangelisation in our countries and a stimulus for different types of theological reflection. We face a real upsurge in fruitful understanding of faith, coming from cultural and human backgrounds of great importance. The initial perception of the other thus turns into a much more precise image, providing invaluable enrichment for the theology of liberation. However, much still needs to be done in this area.

## Announcing the gospel of liberation

To know that the Lord loves us, to accept the gratuitous gift of his love, is the profound source of happiness of those who live according to the Word. To communicate this happiness is to evangelise. Such communication is the purpose of the reflection we call liberation theology. It concerns itself with a proclamation which is, in a way, gratuitous, just as the love which motivates it is gratuitous. What is received free, should be given freely, as the Gospel says. In the starting point for evangelisation there is always the experience of the Lord, a living out of the love of the Father that makes us

His sons and daughters, transforming us, making us ever more fully brothers and sisters.

For us, all of this comes together – as we have pointed out – in the question: how to proclaim a God who is revealed as love in a world of poverty and exclusion? How to proclaim the God of life to people who suffer premature and unjust death? How to proclaim the 'Gospel of liberation'?[6]

## A *universal call*

To proclaim the gospel is to announce the mystery of 'sonship' and 'brotherhood', a mystery hidden – as Paul says – from the beginning of time and revealed now in Christ dead and resurrected. For this reason, to evangelise is to come together in *ecclesia*, to assemble together. Only in community can faith be lived, celebrated, and deepened, lived out through one act as fidelity to the Lord and solidarity towards all people. To accept the Word is to turn ourselves to 'the Other' in others. It is with them that we live the Word. Faith is not to be found in private or in intimacy; faith is the denial of the retreat into ourselves.

'Make disciples of all the nations' (Matt. 28.19) is the mission entrusted to his disciples by the resurrected Jesus in Galilee, the very scene of his preaching. The universality of the message bears the mark of that land of Galilee, forgotten and despised. The God announced by Jesus Christ is the God whose call is universal, aimed at all people. However, at the same time it is a God whose preferential love is for the poor and dispossessed. The universality of God's call not only does not contradict that preference (which is not exclusivity) but demands it to give meaning to this universality. The preference lies in the call of God to every human being.

This double requisite of universality and preference is a challenge to the community of the Lord's disciples. This is explicitly and authentically the place that John XXIII calls the 'Church of the poor', the vocation of the whole Church, afterwards insisted upon by Medellín, Puebla and John Paul II. This is also the framework for the preferential option for the poor, the central point of liberation theology, the axis for the task of evangelisation of the Church in Latin America and beyond.

This leads us to the very heart of the gospel message, the proclamation of the Kingdom of God. This was the purpose of Jesus, according to the Gospels. The Kingdom expresses the Father's will for life and love. This will of God comes to us through the saving and liberating actions of Jesus.

The growth of the Kingdom is a process that takes place historically through liberation, in as much as this is taken to mean the fulfilment of the human being in a new and fraternal society. But we cannot identify the Kingdom with the forms of its presence in human history. The Kingdom manifests itself in historical deeds that lead towards liberation. It decries their limitations and ambiguities, announces its fulfilment and pushes these events towards complete communion. Without historical moments of liberation, the Kingdom does not grow, but the process of liberation will not destroy the roots of oppression, of exploitation amongst human beings, unless the advent of the Kingdom is above all a grace, a gift.

Moreover, we could even say that the historical moment of liberation is itself an expression of the growth of the Kingdom, to some extent a moment of salvation, although not the advent of the Kingdom itself or of complete salvation. It is a realisation of the Kingdom in history, and as such an announcement of the fullness of the Kingdom which is beyond history.

### Proclamation and martyrdom

The path of the solidarity with the oppressed and dispossessed, the announcement of the gospel in the here and now in Latin America, is plagued with difficulties. Since the end of the 1960s there have been cases of Christians killed because of their evangelical witness.[7] Such painful events became more frequent and threatening in the following years. The murder of Mons. Oscar Romero (Archbishop of San Salvador who was brutally assassinated in 1980) tolled like a bell, loud enough to awaken the most indifferent to such events. Surrender to death – unsought but serenely accepted – has been a sign of many from within the Christian community in Latin America.

Spirituality, the way of being Christian that has emerged in Latin America, carries with it now the mark of martyrdom. It is not an attitude of complacency towards that which causes it, something which we have no alternative but to reject, but – painful as it is – it is also an enrichment of the life of the Christian community. Indeed, the same route followed by many Christians (catechists, peasants, religious, urban dwellers, priests and bishops) to martyrdom is still followed by many others still alive. Not because they search or hope for death, but because of their fidelity to the God of life and to solidarity with the poor. There may have been moments of rest on the way, occasional deviations to avoid stumbling blocks, slowness in the way forward, but it is not possible to turn back from the road which defines us as the followers of Jesus.

The type of news that the media tend to prefer when it comes to the Church are specific conflicts, authoritarian and abrupt changes of direction, the intellectual brilliance of some which leaves others in the shadows. These tend to downgrade what is most valuable about the Church in Latin America and the Caribbean. Humbly, without seeking to feature on the covers of the newspapers, situated in different corners of the continent, there are people who every day give up their lives, their energy, their time, their affection for those who are oppressed or marginalised for the love of the gospel. To speak of a spirituality of martyrdom goes beyond the reality of bloody and violent loss of life. Everyday commitment, generous, disinterested, undertaken at very high personal cost but in a spirit of joy and peace, in the midst of profound threats and rewards, of suspicions (even within the Church itself) and fraternal support, all are part of the 'martyred' following of Jesus along the highways and byways of Latin America.

According to a traditional affirmation, which derives from historical experience, the Church is born from the blood of martyrs. Something similar is happening to us today, the Church is renewing its presence in this continent in the radical witness (martyrdom) of many of its members. These lives, taken by those who refuse to recognise the rights of all people to a just and human existence, are profound expressions of the solidarity and sad reminders that Christians ought to be, like the God in whom we believe, 'friends of life'. In this way is formed an ecclesial community, capable of stubbornly sustaining the hope of the dispossessed.

### The horizon of creation

The Latin American experience of these years has enlarged the perspectives for social solidarity. This has to take into account also a respectful bond with nature. The question of ecology is not posed solely to those countries that most destroy the natural human habitat. It is something which affects the whole of humanity. As is frequently said when these issues arise, the planet earth is a great ship on which all of us find ourselves. This is very true. However, the same image can help to remind us that on this ship not all of us travel in the same class. There are those who travel first class, with wonderful food, ballrooms and swimming pools; and there are those who make the crossing in third class, if not in the hold. No one can escape the task of avoiding the destruction of our environment, but we in this continent should be particularly attentive to the situation facing the weakest in humanity. We must avoid, for example, becoming the rubbish tip of the industrialised countries.

On the other hand, this is an area in which much can be learnt from the ancient peoples of our continent. Throughout their long period of survival, they knew how to make these lands their home, they tamed its high altitudes, its excesses, its rainfall and its deserts. They did so with deep respect for the land that gave them life. Without falling into the facile romanticism which is common among members of the urban and industrialised countries when they consider simple people attuned to their natural environment, it is true that there are important lessons to be learned from ancestral wisdom. Consequently, in defending their rights and in proclaiming respect for life, indigenous peoples make an important contribution for the rest of us.

The ecological perspective can draw strength from the corrections that the Bible itself makes to an abusive interpretation of the phrase 'dominate the earth' which we find in the book of Genesis. For instance, those ideas found in the book of Job, whose author seeks to convince us that it is not the human being, rather the gratuitous love of God, which is the heart and meaning of all creation. This emphasis can be used to provide oxygen in the struggle for justice, and to widen our horizons. It reminds us as well of the aesthetic dimensions of a process of liberation which seeks to take into account all aspects of what it is to be human; the right to beauty is an expression (more pressing than some suppose) of the right to life.

### At the crossroads of two languages

From the perspective of theological reflection, within the framework of liberation, the challenge in Latin America is to find a language about God which arises out of the situation created by the injustice and poverty in which the great majority live, whether they be disparaged races, exploited classes, excluded cultures or women who suffer discrimination. At the same time, it has to be a discourse nourished by the hopes of a people who seek liberation. In that context of suffering and joy, uncertainty and conviction, generous commitment and ambiguity, our understanding of the faith should continually shine through.

Indeed, we believe that a prophetic and mystical language about God is being born in these lands of exploitation and hope. It is a question of talking of God – just as in the book of Job – from the suffering of the innocent. The language of contemplation recognises that all stems from the gratuitous love of the Father. The language of prophecy denounces the situation (and its structural causes) of injustice and exploitation, as lived by the poor of Latin America. In this respect, Puebla speaks of knowing how to discover 'the suffering features of Christ the Lord in the faces' furrowed by the pain of an oppressed people (nn. 31–9; a text taken up and developed at Santo Domingo).

Without prophecy, the language of contemplation risks not involving itself in the history in which God acts and where we find him. Without the mystical dimension, the language of prophecy can narrow the vision, and weaken the understanding, of Him who makes all things new. 'Sing to Yahweh, praise Yahweh, for he has liberated the poor from the hands of evil men' (Jer. 20.13). Sing and liberate, the act of thanksgiving and the demand for justice.

Between thanksgiving and demand runs Christian existence. In the beginning, and enveloping all is the free and gratuitous love of God. But this gift requires behaviour which translates into acts of love towards our neighbour, and especially the weakest among them. This is the challenge of Christian life, which seeks (beyond all possible spiritual evasion and political reductionism) to be faithful to the God of Jesus Christ.

These two languages try to communicate the gift of the Kingdom of God revealed in the life, death and resurrection of Jesus. This is the heart of the message that we go on rediscovering from our own reality. It is this that brings us together as a community, as a Church, within which we try to think through our faith. Theology is done in a Church which must provide in human history the testimony to a life victorious over death. To be a witness to the resurrection means choosing life, life in all its forms, since nothing escapes the universality of the Kingdom of God. This testimony of life (material and spiritual life, personal and social life, life present and future) assumes particular importance in a continent characterised by premature and unjust death, and also by the struggle for freedom from oppression. This reality of death and sin is a negation of the resurrection. For this reason, the witness of the resurrection is he who can always ask ironically (according to Scripture) 'Death, where is your victory?'

This life we celebrate in the Eucharist, the first duty of the ecclesial community. In sharing bread, we remember the love and trust of Jesus who was taken to His death, and the confirmation of His mission towards the poor through the resurrection. The breaking of bread is both the point of departure and the destination of the Christian community. This act represents the profound communion with human suffering caused in many cases by the lack of bread, and it is the recognition, in joy, of the Resurrected Jesus who gives life and lifts the hopes of the people brought together by his acts and his word.

The theology of liberation tries – in ecclesial communion – to be a language about God. It is an attempt to make present in this world of oppression, injustice and death, the Word of life.

## NOTES

1 I highlighted this distinction in a course in Lima, a little later, on 'Church and Poverty'. The course was also given at the University of Montreal University on the date mentioned.

2 Cf. the document *Pobreza de la Iglesia*, in the conclusions of Medellín.

3 Cf. the document *Opción Preferencial por los Pobres*. This option was endorsed at the Bishops' conference at Santo Domingo (1992).

4 G. Gutiérrez, 'La teología: una funcíon eclesial', in *Páginas* (Lima, 1994), pp. 10–17 n. 130.

5 A meeting in Melgar (April 1968), which drew attention to the values of these peoples, provided one of the most vivid memories in the preparations for Medellín. This was also an element in a similar meeting in Iquitos, Peru (1971).

6 John Paul II, *Letter to the bishops of Brazil* (April 1986).

7 One of the first was Henrique Antonio Pereira Neto, a black priest from Recife (Brazil), cruelly murdered in May 1969. My first book *Teología de la Liberación* was dedicated to him and to the Peruvian writer on indigenous culture, José María Arguedas.

# 2

ZOË BENNETT

# 'Action is the life of all': the praxis-based epistemology of liberation theology

If you continue in my word then you are truly my disciples; and you will know the truth and the truth will make you free.

(John 8.31, 32)

That practice, truth and freedom are inseparable is axiomatic for liberation theology.

The defining characteristic of liberation theology is that it is a lived praxis in solidarity with the poor and oppressed. It is defined as theology, and not simply as an ethical or pragmatic stance, in that the key question concerns the living of a specifically *Christian* life, and the story of the Bible is brought into dialogue with the story of life, the story of the world. Freedom is the goal towards which practice is oriented. In this committed and value-laden practice, truth will be made manifest; the true character of the ideologically distorted structures of this world will be unmasked; and, for the truth of God's fullness of life for all humanity, men and women will live and die.

The commitment and practice of liberation theology requires three moments: the moment of praxis, the moment of reflection on praxis, and the moment of return to a renewed praxis. It begins and ends in praxis.[1] Given this primacy, and the claim to a new way of doing theology founded in it, the question arises whether praxis is in itself epistemologically significant. Can we know through praxis? And if so, what can we know?

This question is significant not only for liberation theology, but for a wide variety of theologies of practice.[2] The epistemological significance of practice is a question raised by the extensive contemporary use of the Pastoral Cycle, a model of doing theology which begins in concrete experience and practice.

In this chapter, I will do some ground-clearing, by examining what claims are made for the epistemological status of praxis. I will consider and critique the argument of Clodovis Boff's *Theology and Praxis*. This work sets out the 'classic' liberation theology position on its own epistemological foundations. I will then consider the grounds of the possibility of giving praxis a more substantial epistemological role than Boff does, and further consider what practices might enable such knowing.

## What might we know through praxis?

The notion that practice is a key locus of disclosure is embedded in much contemporary theology, not only in that which is written under the umbrella of 'liberation' or 'practical' theology. Manuel Mejido[3] writes that 'progressive theologies of Western Europe and North America' have 'posited praxis as the very condition of possibility for interpreting the meaning of transcendence'. Praxis is at the root of their hermeneutical, critical and constructive projects. For example, Elaine Graham, Heather Walton and Frances Ward, referring to Graham's earlier work *Transforming Practice*, which 'inscribe[s] a turn to *practice* in contemporary theology',[4] argue that 'the method of theology-in-action represents a paradigm shift in the epistemology of theology. It insists on a unity of action and reflection, emerging from concrete experiential knowledge':[5] 'In turn, an emphasis on the performative and enacted realm of human practice – in Christian terms, the value-directed activities of pastoral action – offers pastoral theology a new role as the *primary expression and generator of theological disclosure* [my italics].'[6]

Having identified this characteristic of progressive Western theology, Mejido goes on to note characteristics of contemporary liberation theology which demonstrate the same rootedness in praxis but with some radical differences in focus of interest. He, and with him Petrella and the other authors writing in 2005 in *Latin American Liberation Theology: the Next Generation*, is interested in going beyond the role of theology as it appeared in classic liberation theology. They want to take liberation theology in the direction of historical projects, not in the direction of a hermeneutic of transcendence. So Mejido contrasts the progressive theologies of Western Europe and North America with 'theologies of liberation [which], rather, establish a theological knowledge that is interested in the *making* of transcendence', not its interpretation, which he interprets as the making of liberation and of '"better" history' through praxis.

An important question has not yet been answered with regard to a praxis-based epistemology. When the hermeneutical, the critical and the constructive tasks of theology are thus founded in praxis, what kind of theological truth does praxis disclose? Is praxis able to disclose what is right, good and truthful practice – orthopraxy? Or is praxis able to disclose what is right, good and truthful belief – orthodoxy? To use an image loosely borrowed from Hans Urs von Balthasar, does the fact that my mother loves me mean that I know something about how to treat my own children, or that I know something about the fundamental graced structure of 'how things are'?

These are questions which are not yet answered within liberation theology or theologies of practice. Graham poses the question 'whether one can speak of the infinite, undetermined world in the language of the contingent, finite world of practice' and implies that her answer is in the negative.[7] Just what praxis will deliver epistemologically needs to be developed further.

A second fundamental question is: what exactly is meant by praxis? Practical theology, as it has taken root in professional education for ministry and in adult Christian education in Western Europe and North America, uses models for theological reflection which have one historical root in liberation theology, but which should be clearly distinguished from liberation theology in other respects. Failure to see this difference is widespread. The basic model of liberation theology arises from a Marxist dialectical context and involves the movement from praxis to theory to changed praxis. The basic model of practical theology is the pastoral cycle, whose model appears in myriad forms, but whose root form is a cycle, or spiral, running from concrete experience through sociological analysis, through reflection in the light of the Christian tradition, to renewed action/praxis. While this is also sometimes referred to the process of 'See, Judge, Act' in liberation theology, as well as to the dialectical method, it is important to note that it has another quite different contextual root. This is the movement of professional reflective practice, rooted in the work of Donald Schön.[8] While there are significant resemblances in method and epistemological suppositions between this and a liberationist practice, there are also crucial differences. Of these, the most important relates to context, commitment and intentionality. In the reflective practice movement, and the experiential educational tradition which is often associated with it, there is no necessary solidarity with the poor and oppressed, and no necessary intention for radical social change. Indeed, in some contexts, professional reflective practice becomes an instrument of conservative political and religious ends – serving the conservative ends of personal advancement such as meeting targets, getting value for money and enhancing professional effectiveness, and the organisational ends of efficiency and enhancement of the existing social, political and economic status quo. Unless this difference is recognised there is inappropriate elision of liberation theology and practical theology, which is part of the annexing of liberation theology to the establishment and the diluting of its potency in a Western/ Northern educational context. Praxis in liberation theology is in solidarity with the poor and oppressed and has an intention of bringing liberation and humanisation through radical, transformative social and political change.

Corresponding to this important differentiation in the understanding of praxis is a necessary differentiation in the understanding of the person doing the theological reflection. Clodovis Boff makes the person of the liberation theologian a key plank in his development of epistemology, stressing the theologian's social location, choices of subject matter for theological reflection, and commitments.[9] The use of the word 'practitioner' may obscure the fact that a practitioner is not necessarily a person with radical social/political commitments. Such a committed person might be better described as an 'activist'.

I will illustrate the difference through a personal story.[10] On a visit to my daughter who is a political activist in Nazareth we went to stay with some of her friends in Sakhnin, an Arab village in the Galilee. Our host was a Palestinian man who had spent several years in prison and was at the time under house arrest. I was there for Land Day, an annual day of protest against the confiscation of Arab land, and a Dutch journalist, a woman with a senior job on a Dutch radio foreign news desk, visited for the weekend to cover the protests. Her husband is Irish and she was at the time researching a book on women's involvement in the IRA hunger strikes. After a while I noticed an interesting difference between our host's treatment of the journalist and his treatment of me. 'Why' I asked my daughter, 'am I being treated to pleasant and superficial conversation whereas she is engaged in high-powered intellectual debate?' Her answer was one of those conversion moments, when you see yourself as others see you: 'She's an activist and you're not.' In that moment I understood the difference between being a practitioner and being an activist. My protest that I was no ivory-tower academic but involved as a practitioner in theological education died on my lips as I saw that difference. It made sense of my nagging worries that a certain sort of reflection on practice can become totally divorced from that commitment to radical change that is integral to the Marxist roots of the theory/practice dialectic. I saw the reality of a context in which theory is so deeply intertwined with action that only the activists are able to enter the intellectual arena.

These crucial differences between practical theology in Western/Northern contexts and liberation theology correspond to the distinction which Manuel Mejido makes[11] between a practical cognitive interest and an emancipatory cognitive interest.

## Clodovis Boff's *Theology and Praxis*

Clodovis Boff's *Theology and Praxis: Epistemological Foundations*, published in Portuguese in 1978 and in English in 1987, is the classic text expressing the epistemological foundations of liberation theology. Boff's work is divided into three parts. In the first, 'Socio-analytic Mediation', he seeks to establish the claim that the 'sciences of the social' are the appropriate instrument in liberation theology for the analysis of life situations. This socio-analytic exercise is seen as independent of theology, but as furnishing the essential data on which theology is to work. Among the sciences of the social, Marxist tools of analysis are privileged as yielding clarity, particularly in relation to possible ideological distortion.

Boff's whole work arises from practice – the practice of Christians who have acted in the political situation in which they have found themselves. His entire project in the book must be seen in the context of the problematic created by action, which introduces a *new* situation for theology. In the first part he establishes a distinction between 'second theology', such as the theology of the political, and 'first theology', which asks questions such as 'Can God be known?' It is the *object* of theological reflection which makes the difference. In the case of political theology this object is social realities – and it is the work of second theology to explicate them. Furthermore, social realities must be given contours which make them a real object about which to theologise. This is the work of the 'sciences of the social'. They, by their own autonomous scientific method, delineate the object which one may then theologise about. It should be noted that he does not allow the 'first theology' questions to be in any way determined by action or socio-analytic mediation.

Boff is concerned to establish a role for the social sciences over against Catholic theologies, which speak in generalities because they have not delineated any concrete objects on which to theologise in the political realm. This is because they have regarded the social sciences as illegitimate in the theological enterprise. He stresses the need not to confuse the social scientific task and the theological task, nor to confuse the languages they use (chapter 2). Boff regards himself as undertaking the same enterprise in respect of the social sciences as Christians in the past have done in respect of philosophy. Aquinas (Aristotelianism) is his key analogue here, though he also refers to the Fathers (Hellenistic philosophy) and to Bultmann (Existentialism).

No science, he says, has the right to absolutise itself. That includes all social sciences. It also includes theology itself, as its object is 'Mystery as incomprehensible Reality, comprehended only as incomprehensible'. By virtue of its engagement with mystery and incomprehensibility, theology is able to contribute to the de-absolutisation of 'scientificist' thought (pp. 54–5). In this, Boff emphasises theology's mystical/apophatic nature.

The point is strongly made that faith/religion is not the same thing as theology. Boff speaks of both the horizontal (sex, aesthetics, political action) and the vertical (religious) dimensions of faith and says they must always be anchored as concretions in history; for example, in the Good Samaritan story, 'love' is anchored in a specific concretion, as 'species of concrete universal' (p. 39). As for theology, he says this also is inevitably 'a regional discourse' (p. 61). Theology must not ignore its historicity nor claim that it 'coincides with the voice of revelation itself, otherwise it becomes an ideology' (p. 40).

In Part 2, 'Hermeneutic Mediation', Boff deals with the role of theology. It is doubtful whether the role he assigns to theology enables us to construct an epistemology of praxis/action. He is quite clear about the priority of practice for Christians, but he says that this is an attitude and an orientation:

> The priority of practice is a practical, not a theoretical, priority. Therefore, it is not and cannot be a principle of theory, governing the theological process. Indeed, when theologians undertake to theologize the consciousness and practice of the community, they obey only the norms of theological practice – norms that, after all, exist in virtue of a 'breach' with those of the spontaneous language of this same community.                                         (p. 151)

This is an absolutely key passage. It contains much of the argument of Part 2. First there is his definition of theology which he works out according to Althusser's model of theoretical practice, involving 'three generalities'. Within these, theology (classic theology, which is in itself the third generality of first theology, and the Christian writings including scripture) acts as the second generality, operating on the first generality (the situation, as mediated by the socio-analytic mediation which is in itself the third generality of another discipline, social theory) to yield a third generality which is political theology (p. 83).

Second there is the breach, including an epistemological breach (p. 109) between faith and theology. He posits three orders: (1) the word of revelation, or faith (he sees these as two sides of a coin); (2) religious discourse, including such things as sermons; (3) theology, which involves critical distance and systematisation. He sees the crucial breach as being between (2) and (3). It is the modus operandi not the material object which confers epistemological status (p. 68), therefore it is in the hermeneutic mediation, in which theology works on the data given in faith and in the socio-analytic mediation, that the epistemological work is done.

His is a narrow definition of 'theology' which restricts it to the critical, systematising function. It is also a highly rational definition of 'doing theology' and raises questions for the engagement of other faculties – intuitive, imaginative, body-centred – in the production of theological knowledge and understanding: 'Theology is the language of theory, not the discourse of passion or action' (p. 111). Boff is aware that his definition is contrary to an Orthodox approach of a more contemplative and existential style (p. 114, see note 21). It also raises questions for a contemporary 'ordinary theology'[12] based on a democratisation of the theological process.

The place which Boff gives to classic theology, and indeed to the scriptures and tradition (the 'Christian writings'), as the means of reading life and situation beg the question: is theological knowledge generated through practice? That is to say: is practice theologically disclosive in Boff's understanding? His model of 'correspondence of relationships' (p. 147) seems to imply a 'yes'. The process is apparently two-way and cannot be restricted to reading life through the scriptures as it also implies inevitably that we can read the scriptures through life. But I am not sure Boff would concur: witness his reference to Augustine (p. 151 and note 84) – while political theology gives priority to the present context, the world is read through scripture. Augustine said God gave two books, the book of the world and the book of the Bible. It was because the former became unreadable through sin that God gave us the latter, so we could read the former through it. Witness also his comment (p. 69 notes 8 and 9) on Belo – that it would be more epistemologically sound to talk of reading Marx through Mark not vice versa: 'To think Christianity, to reflect upon Christianity, with Marxism as a tool, in socioanalytic mediation, is possible and even desirable. But to reduce the reflection to this, and to pass off its product as theology, is "selling cat for rabbit".' It would therefore seem that for Boff practice cannot shape first theology but can shape second (in this case, political) theology. In terms of my original question: the situation, socio-analytically mediated, can shape orthopraxis, but not orthodoxy.

In talking about first theology Boff talks about something 'even deeper', 'at zero degrees on the theological scale' which is natural theology. This is the discourse of transcendental reflection and is a precondition of the possibility of revelation. It depends on the fact that 'the *nous* that is in the human being is of divine nature' (p. 80 note 64, referring to Aristotle). Faith apprehends revelation; the scriptures and the ecclesial community are the nexus of revelation. This opens up possibilities for understanding the epistemology of praxis, as I shall discuss below.

In Part 3, 'Dialectic of Theory and Praxis', Boff reiterates the primacy of praxis over theory. He sees the work of theology as a theoretical work, which he describes as being the minor key of the dialectic, in which theory takes the dominant role. This is embedded in the larger dialectic of the historical process, the major key, in which praxis takes the dominant role. We are constrained to admit the priority of praxis, of life, of world, of history, over their representation in the field of awareness (p. 176). This, he says, is classical critical realism. The movement runs from praxis (interested) to theory (disinterested) to praxis. Praxis is the beginning and end of the dialectic, the driver and the goal. Dialectic is a style rather than a fossilised method, a perpetual movement, 'transgression of limits, journey through the desert endlessly' (p. 206), thrusting, ricocheting, dislocating (p. 216). Dialectic as a method of relating theological theory and praxis is not 'smooth and pacific' nor is it something systematisable. It seems to me that there is within this vision the possibility of moving beyond the strictly compartmentalised epistemological roles which he sets out for praxis and for theological theory.

Boff, however, retains the designation 'epistemological' for the theoretical practice of theology, opening up the question of whether it may be used of praxis (p. 156), which he describes as pistic or agapic practice. There is an epistemological breach, leap, rupture (p. 193) between praxis and theory as they operate in quite different ways – theory and praxis represent irreducible orders. Theological criteriology and pistic criteriology are different – the former is epistemological, the latter existential. This distinction is vital to Boff and he is critical of 'strident manifestos in behalf of praxis. [Political theology] exalts the "epistemological density"[13] of praxis to the point of threatening the autonomy of theoretical practice – to the detriment of praxis itself' (p. 198).

He is absolutely insistent on the need for critically distant theoretical reflection for the project of ethics and political effectiveness, and on the importance of 'cool rational calculation', as well as indignation and hope and 'doing something' (p. 203 note 5). If the dialectical moment is derailed, praxis becomes pragmatism, and theory idealism. But there is also a continuity, a rooting and an immersion (p. 213). The one is embedded in and connected with the other. There is formal breach but material continuity (p. 209).

In answer to the question whether praxis can be the criterion of truth, Boff says that it cannot, as praxis itself is ambiguous. Which praxis would be the criterion of truth? It is empiricism to take reality unmediated into theory. It is ideological, at least in the sense of ideology as uncriticised common sense, and possibly also in the sense of ideology as reality distorted by power. However, theology cannot know God outside of praxis, as any kind of absolute knowing is eschatological: 'After all, God can only be known within the purview of historical possibilities, especially our cultural possibilities' (p. 167).

## Critique of Boff

Boff does not purport to furnish us with an epistemology of action/praxis, but with the beginnings of a 'second theology' or a "second moment" in a *single* theological process'.[14] His work, however, has important implications for the epistemological status of praxis. Explicitly his model gives to theology – a first theology which has been derived from sources other than praxis – the evaluative and epistemological significance within the dialectic of theory and praxis. This will become clear in the two important critiques of Boff's position which I shall examine. Implicitly, however, there are pointers in Boff's work towards a more positive assessment of the epistemological significance of praxis – namely the dialectical method, the mysterious and apophatic, the christological and pneumatological, the human appropriation of revelation, and his hermeneutic of scripture, particularly the 'correspondence of relationships'.

Critique of Boff has focused on the place he gives to theology in his system, and I now turn to two of these critiques, which come from quite different quarters.

Ivan Petrella[15] has claimed that sociological analysis is not properly theological in Boff's scheme and that therefore the theological is not allowed to be incorporated into the practical mediation.[16] Theology and practice are kept apart. His own claim is that the clarification of theological concepts and the constructive role of the social sciences are co-inherent: 'Thus for liberation theology the construction of historical projects should not be a secondary moment in the historical task, coming after the clarification of our theological concepts, but rather must become a central means by which those concepts are clarified, given analytical rigor and understood.'[17]

The necessity for the construction of historical projects as part of the work of liberation theology is the issue to which Petrella is committed. He identifies Boff's epistemological scheme as a key factor in the wrong tack which classic liberation theology has taken, away from the construction of historical projects. In particular he names the way in which Boff gives theology a role isolated from the socio-analytical, and thus condemns the socio-analytical to a non-theological role. By contrast Petrella wishes to assert that 'the social sciences do not just read reality, they are the realm where God's promise of life fails or succeeds'.[18] This view insists that the socio-analytic mediation is properly theological, and also by implication has epistemological significance within liberation theology. Petrella's explanation of the possibility of this is based on an analogy of Segundo's. The tenets of liberation theology – that God has a preferential option for the poor and that God is a God of life and body – are related to the actual working out of these tenets in historical practice and projects in the same way that faith is related to the realisation of faith in practice in a particular historical context.[19]

If Petrella's critique indicts Boff for *undervaluing* the socio-analytical mediation by not allowing it to be properly theological, the earlier critique of John Milbank[20] indicts him for the opposite – overvaluing the socio-analytical by allowing it weight independent of the theological: 'For there to be salvation with a specifiable Christian content, there must be a directly theological discourse about the socio-historical; without this, theology occupies the pre-theologically-determined site of transcendentalist metaphysics.'[21]

Without direct theological discourse about the socio-historical, theological theory and praxis – God and action – are not truly integrated. Milbank himself explicates this integration of theology and action through the work of Maurice Blondel.[22] Language, knowledge, act, text and common tradition are bound together in this account in reference to the infinite, divine reality. So, for Milbank, the practice of the ecclesial community is the means of reading all reality. Liberation theologians would want to ask here about the necessity to criticise the historical practices of this community, and indeed to assert that there is not a single monolithic community. It is significant that Nelson Maldonado-Torres[23] accuses Milbank of only having Western secular reason on his horizon and not seeing that there is more than one history of the Church and history of sociology – in short, of ignoring the 'colonial difference': 'In part then the difference between Milbank and liberation theologians is that that they are reflecting from a different history of the church. What appears in their work is thus not only the *theological* difference but also the *colonial* difference, which remains hidden for Milbank and for the project of radical orthodoxy.'[24]

It is interesting to note, however, that Milbank explicitly suggests that, although liberation theology has neglected the relevance of the Church, 'Of course this may be to say that liberation theology has not properly theorized the significance of the "base communities" in Latin America itself.'[25] He offers here an important alternative way of understanding the epistemology of praxis in liberation theology.

These critiques of Boff point to the need to overcome the split between theology and praxis, the 'epistemological breach', which exists in his work. From the perspective of practical theology, which has much in common with liberation theology in its epistemological base in practice, there is a similar concern that, in many theorists and practitioners, the move from theology to practice is one of shaping, having an impact, and forming, whereas the move from practice to theology is weaker, described as informing and asking questions. Robert Mager characterises this as an emphasis on the theme of Incarnation – whereby theology reaches into practice – but the neglect of its opposite term, Theosis or Divinisation: 'To put it in a blunt way; human practice is hardly understood as a *locus theologicus* in the full sense of the phrase, that is, as a God-revealing process. Rather it is there to be questioned by God's revelation, as if revelation were somehow given beforehand.'[26]

## The grounds of the possibility of an epistemology of praxis

The project of establishing 'human practice as a *locus theologicus* in the full sense of the phrase' is a much larger project than can be undertaken in this chapter. What I would like to offer, by way of a contribution to that project, are some preliminary suggestions as to the underlying grounds of possibility, and some key contours of what a Christian epistemology of praxis might look like, and what practices might enable such knowing through action.

Fundamental to the possibility of an epistemology of praxis is the understanding that knowledge is participatory. The knowing subject is determinative of the knowledge, and is implicated in it.

> It is to be noted that there is a type of theology that wants to adopt *only a
> historical attitude* towards religion; it even has an abundance of cognition,
> though only of a historical kind. This cognition is no concern of ours, for if the
> cognition of religion were merely historical, we would have to compare such
> theologians with counting-house clerks, who keep the ledgers and accounts of
> other people's wealth, a wealth that passes through their hands without their
> retaining any of it, clerks who act only for others without acquiring any assets of
> their own. They do of course receive a salary, but their merit lies only in keeping
> records of the assets of other people. In philosophy and religion, however, the
> essential thing is that one's own spirit itself should recognise a possession and
> content, deem itself worthy of cognition, and not keep itself humbly outside.[27]

To know something from the outside, claims Hegel, is an impoverished form
of knowledge. True knowledge of God, of the world, and of ourselves, is
participative knowledge; is not available to the detached observer. Human
practice and involvement therefore is a fundamental constituent of epistemology. The dialectical method of relating theory and practice, as set out
classically for liberation theology by Clodovis Boff, potentially enables the
integration of human practice into theoretical understanding.

Second, a certain provisionality inevitably attends an epistemology of
praxis. This has two intimately related aspects. The first is attention to the
mysterious and the apophatic dimension of any talk about God. The second
is the fact that praxis itself is never given in advance of the event – the logic of
reality, including our actions within that reality, is never identical with the
logic of prior thinking and awareness. We do not know in advance what we
will do, what will happen, and how what happens and is done will be
interpreted by ourselves or by others. Our understanding of God and of
human reality is eschatological. This provisionality may take the form of
what Boff calls classical critical realism, or of the more agnostic approach
to transcendence expressed by Graham.[28]

These factors hold for any epistemology of practice. Specifically in relation
to a Christian epistemology, there are further theological categories which
pertain. An epistemology of praxis must be based in: Christology, the Spirit,
Creation, and the Church.

A Christian theological epistemology of praxis must be Christological
because Jesus Christ, the centre of Christianity, is a historical human being
acting in the midst of human history. His life of service to humanity, his acts
of witness to the work of God, and his death on the cross are pivotal to our
understanding of what it is to be fully human and what it is to be God. Here

we can find the possibility of an epistemology which, to use Mager's terms, not only employs the category of *incarnation* but also that of *theosis*. Human action is taken up into the divine action. Christology alone, however, does not take us far enough; we also need a doctrine of the Spirit to understand the presence of God in ongoing human praxis:

> For Mercy has human heart
> Pity, a human face;
> And Love, the human form divine,
> And Peace, the human dress . . .

> And all must love the human form.
> In heathen, turk, or jew,
> Where Mercy, Love and Pity dwell,
> There God is dwelling too.[29]

Consideration of God's Spirit dwelling in humanity is one way to enable an understanding which connects the human and the divine in human practice. God's Spirit, the same Spirit as was in Jesus, animates both human practice and human understanding of that practice.

When Clodovis Boff explicates the grounds of the possibility of the epistemological connection between the human and the divine he speaks of faith apprehending revelation. His analogy between the human and the divine which makes this a possibility is the Aristotelian *nous* – the mind of the human being which shares the divine nature.[30] If we trace this idea through pneumatology and Christology, or indeed through Genesis and the doctrine of creation, rather than through Aristotle and the mind, we can transcend the rational, critical systematising functions of the role Boff assigns to the epistemology and include intuition, imagination, love, action and bodily apprehension. A theological epistemology of praxis must be founded on this holistic appreciation of the human being and of the analogy between the human and the divine.

Finally, a Christian epistemology of praxis is rooted in the actions of the Christian community, the Church. I have already noted Milbank's suggestion that the liberation theologians might explicate the significance of base communities, as part of an epistemology of praxis. The actions of discipleship form part of a complex nexus which includes the inherited story, the scriptures and the historical communities which bear testimony to that story, and the contingent realities of the contemporary world and life. The gospels themselves indicate the 'contingent basis of theological understanding in action rather than in contemplation and detachment . . . The understanding of the Christian scriptures in particular is an activity and a discipline inseparable from that action which is epistemologically fundamental.'[31]

Here we pick up the theme of provisionality again, as all attempts to construct praxis which truly enacts and reveals the divine are just that, provisional – contributions to the dialectic of praxis and theology which is the path of understanding. As Nicholas Lash says, there are no 'exceptions to the rule that it is only in risking the construction of a story that human beings have given content, shape and specificity to their hopes and fears'.[32]

## Witness and risk: practices which underlie an epistemology of praxis

As a practical theologian whose context of practice is ecumenical theological education, I find the twin concepts and practices of witness and risk illuminating and fruitful, both for understanding and for story- and community-building. Among the different ecclesial traditions represented in my educational context there are some which put a high premium on commitment and on trust. The Orthodox and the Evangelicals, and some Roman Catholics, work primarily and self-consciously from a trustful inhabiting of text and of tradition, whether these be liturgical, biblical or magisterial. Others, mainly from the liberal Protestant traditions, are more oriented to critique and suspicion of texts and traditions. We have wrestled with the poles of commitment and critique, of trust and suspicion together, seeking to create and interpret stories which give 'specificity to ... hopes and fears', and in particular stories which speak, and lives which act, faithfully in a Christian context:

> In an attempt to move beyond the suspicion/trust polarity, there are two concepts I find particularly helpful: witness and risk. Witness and risk both arise from and imply immersion in action as well as reflection, the actions of the believing community and also the action of engagement with others who are 'strangers' to us. Risk allows us to trust with due suspicion. It involves the kind of commitment and moving forward in faith which trust implies: an acknowledgement that all trust is fraught with the danger that we may have trusted inappropriately; that things may be more complicated than we at first believed. Witness allows us to say what we have found to be the truth, to say it with personal conviction and commitment, but to say it without claiming that it is universal, full or incorrigible truth. We can trust but we do not thereby close down the possibility of the questions and suspicion either coming from others or indeed coming out of our own self-reflection. We can explore, but explore with engagement rather than detachment. The word witness also points us to the relational nature of our exploration; we witness to others and we attend to their witness.[33]

These practices are significant for liberation theology and for an epistemology of praxis. Witness points to the Christological roots of the epistemology of praxis, to the human history of Jesus Christ and of those who would be his disciples. It indicates the 'martyrdom' (witness) which has been the lot of many committed to liberation. Furthermore, it suggests the co-inherence of speech and act, of practice and interpretation, of what is testified to with the lips and what is testified to in the life.

A specific contribution which witness can have to the epistemology of praxis is that, through witness, we are enabled to articulate and suggest those truths which are only partially or ambiguously grasped. I alluded earlier to the necessary element of mystery and apophasis in speech about God. This does not only apply to classic apophatic theology, but to a wide variety of genres of religious speech or interpretation of praxis, for example, the mystical, the visionary, the apocalyptic, the prophetic, the parabolic. These things reveal and conceal at the same time.[34] Witness points but does not contain or fully circumscribe.

Witness also invites imaginative engagement and action. In this it is close, and indeed is a counterpart, to my other category – risk. Action is risky, ambiguous, and invites imaginative engagement and new theological language and interpretation.

The epistemology of praxis is predicated upon commitment, as is clear in all liberation theology. Committed action is risky. Specifically the risk revolves around two factors – relationships and transgression. The epistemology of praxis is a holistic epistemology based on subjectivity and context. Human contexts are webs of relationships, and praxis involves reconfiguring those relationships through our actions. Theological reflection on that action seeks to discern what is learned for new praxis and for belief (for orthopraxy and for orthodoxy). Often that praxis is transgressive of the status quo. This was clear in classic liberation theology which transgressed the status quo of the economic order and of the Church's blessing of that economic order, and it is clear in relation to the transgression of the patriarchal, heterosexual order in Marcella Althaus-Reid's chapter in this volume. Dissent and transgression is the risky, disclosive praxis of liberation theology. While the epistemology of liberation theology shares with Milbank's epistemology of practice a rootedness in the life of the Christian community, it differs from his in that it is not predicated on the faithful repetition within a tradition of ever new instantiations, but looks for disclosure of faithfulness and of the ways of God in risky practices of dissent and transgression.

## Conclusion

In Clodovis Boff's work, liberation theology has had the classic statement of its epistemology. But this statement is inadequate from the perspective of anyone, liberation theologian or otherwise, who wishes to locate human experience and action itself as the locus of theological disclosure. The questions 'Can we know through praxis? And if so, what can we know?' remain.

I have attempted to sketch in a preliminary way some pointers towards the shape of an epistemology of praxis. Such a theological epistemology would be participatory, eschatological, Christological, pneumatological, and would take account of the nature of the human being created in the divine image and of the contingent realities of Christian discipleship in Christian communities. Witness and risk are practices which enable the understanding of truth in action.

All this points to a necessary constructive theological project to understand further the epistemology of praxis. If this project is to be of service to liberation theology it must have its base in emancipatory, not merely practical, intention and cognitive interest, and must be a 'theological knowledge that is interested in the *making* of transcendence' not just in its interpretation.

## NOTES

1. As is made clear in Clodovis Boff, *Theology and Praxis: Epistemological Foundations*, tr. Robert R. Barr (Maryknoll, NY, Orbis, 1987), despite Boff's aversion to assigning a theologically epistemological function to praxis.
2. The title of this chapter is in part borrowed from an essay which explores the relationship between New Testament theology and practical theology: Christopher Rowland and Zoë Bennett, '"Action is the Life of All": New Testament Theology and Practical Theology' in Christopher Rowland and Christopher Tuckett (eds.), *The Nature of New Testament Theology* (Oxford, Blackwell, 2006), 186–206.
3. 'Beyond the Postmodern Condition, or the Turn toward Psychoanalysis', in Ivan Petrella (ed.), *Latin American Liberation Theology: the Next Generation* (Maryknoll, NY, Orbis, 2005), pp. 119–20.
4. Elaine L. Graham, *Transforming Practice: Pastoral Theology in an Age of Uncertainty*, 2nd edn (Eugene, OR, Wipf & Stock, 2002 [1996]).
5. Elaine Graham, Heather Walton and Frances Ward, *Theological Reflection: Methods* (London, SCM Press, 2005), p. 196.
6. Graham, *Transforming Practice*, p. 10.
7. Graham et al., *Theological Reflection*, p. 195.
8. Donald A. Schön, *The Reflective Practitioner: How Professionals Think in Action* (London, Temple Smith, 1983).
9. Boff, *Theology and Praxis*, ch. 9.
10. See Zoë Bennett, *Incorrigible Plurality: Teaching Pastoral Theology in an Ecumenical Context*, Contact Pastoral Monograph No. 14 (Edinburgh, Contact Pastoral Trust, 2004), p. 22.
11. 'Beyond the Postmodern', pp. 119–20.
12. Jeff Astley, 'In Defence of "Ordinary Theology"', *British Journal of Theological Education* 13(1) (August 2002), pp. 21–35.

13. The English text has 'destiny' here but as (a) the Portuguese has 'densidade', and (b) the note has 'density' in the English, 'destiny' is presumably a misprint.
14. Clodovis Boff, 'Epistemology and Method of the Theology of Liberation', in Ignacio Ellacurìa and Jon Sobrino (eds.), *Mysterium Liberations: Fundamental Concepts of Liberation Theology* (Maryknoll: Orbis, 1993), pp. 57–84.
15. In two important new works setting out an agenda for liberation theology – Ivan Petrella, *The Future of Liberation Theology: An Argument and a Manifesto* (Aldershot, Ashgate, 2004), and Petrella (ed.), *Latin American Liberation Theology*.
16. Petrella, *The Future of Liberation Theology*, p. 29.
17. Ibid., p. 37.
18. Ibid., p. 33.
19. Ibid., pp. 35ff.
20. John Milbank, *Theology and Social Theory: Beyond Secular Reason* (Oxford, Blackwell, 1990).
21. Ibid., p. 249.
22. Ibid., pp. 210ff.
23. 'Liberation Theology and the Search for the Lost Paradigm: From Radical Orthodoxy to Radical Diversality', in Petrella (ed.), *Latin American Liberation Theology*, pp. 39–61.
24. Ibid., pp. 45–6.
25. Milbank, *Theology and Social Theory*, p. 244.
26. Robert Mager, 'Do We Learn To Know God from What We Do?' in Elaine Graham and Anna Rowlands (eds.), *Pathways to the Public Square: Practical Theology in an Age of Pluralism, International Academy of Practical Theology, Manchester 2003* (Munster, LIT Verlag, 2005), p. 193.
27. G. W. F. Hegel, *Introduction To Lectures on the Philosophy of Religion of 1824*, ed. P. Hodgson, tr. R. F. Brown *et al.*, vol. I: *Introduction and Concept* (Berkeley, University of California Press, 1984–7), p. 128.
28. Graham *et al.*, *Theological Reflection*, p. 195.
29. William Blake 'The Divine Image', in *Blake's Illuminated Books*, vol. II: *Songs of Innocence and Experience*, edited with an Introduction and Notes by Andrew Lincoln (London, The William Blake Trust/The Tate Gallery, 1991), p. 18.
30. Boff, *Theology and Praxis*, p. 80 n. 64.
31. Christopher Rowland, 'Liberation Theology', in Kathryn Tanner, Ian Torrance and John Webster (eds.), *The Oxford Handbook to Systematic Theology* (forthcoming) 634–52, where he illustrates this through Matthew 18 – the practice of forgiveness – and Matthew 25 – the service to the 'least'.
32. Nicholas Lash, *Theology on the Way to Emmaus* (London, SCM, 1986), p. 97.
33. Bennett, *Incorrigible Plurality*, pp. 31–2.
34. For a discussion of this in relation to the language of the Bible, see Christopher Rowland, 'The Evidence from the Reception History of the Book of Revelation', in Abbas Amanat and John Collins (eds.), *Apocalypse and Violence* (Yale Center for International and Area Studies, Council on Middle Eastern Studies, May 2002), pp. 1–18. This simultaneous revealing and concealing puts me in mind of a multiple-choice examination question in which a false choice for the definition of a 'Freudian slip' was 'a garment which draws attention to that which it conceals'.

# 3

BASTIAAN WIELENGA

# Liberation theology in Asia

## The Asian context

Liberation theology differs from other theologies in that it starts with an analysis of the context, as it wants to respond to the cries of the people arising from it. As contextual theology we can distinguish it by regions – Latin American, African, Asian, European – and by social groups such as the poor, women, blacks, Dalits, indigenous peoples. However, none of these social or geographical identities can be understood in isolation. Contexts and identities are multiple and overlapping. The realities of class, caste, patriarchy and ethnicity, and of local, regional and global economy are intertwined. A Dalit girl working in a factory in an export-processing zone in India is exploited as an underpaid worker – like other workers around the globe – and suffers from a lack of protection by trade-union rights, while as a woman she suffers from male domination and violence – as other women do – whereas she shares her plight as an 'untouchable' suffering from caste oppression with other outcastes, male and female, in India.

What is specific about Asia, especially in contrast with Latin America, is the religio-cultural context. The overwhelming majority of the poor and oppressed in Asia are non-Christians, many of whom adhere to a wide variety of popular religious traditions which are more or less connected with the traditions of the great religions which have shaped dominant Asian cultures. Yet within Asia there are again tremendous differences. Latin America is, compared to Asia, a relatively homogeneous continent in terms of history, language, economic and political developments. Asia has to be subdivided into various regions with different cultural, religious, political and economic histories. In this chapter only a few areas come into view, primarily India, Sri Lanka, South Korea, Taiwan and the Philippines as places where liberation theological perspectives are being articulated. From the various attempts to analyse the common Asian context, as tried in study centres and ecumenical gatherings, the following basic points may be highlighted: the persistence of mass poverty, the threat to democratic rights, the double role of religion and the ecological problem.

## The persistence of mass poverty

Poverty in Asia has many faces: the landless peasant in search of work, the child labourer longing for rest, the coolie collapsing under the luggage of wealthy tourists, the traditional fisherman who fishes in vain because high-tech fishing vessels have emptied the sea, the village girl in what nowadays is called the sex industry, the destitute who is discarded by the economic system and the state.

The causes of their poverty cannot be discussed in detail. In the first decades after shaking off the yoke of colonialism the tendency was to see mass poverty as the combined product of an economically stagnating tra-ditional type of Asian society and the deprivation caused by imperialist plunder, exploitation, and withholding of Western science and technology. The devastating impact of colonialism is beyond doubt, but the percep-tion and evaluation of traditional Asian society was misled by a dominant 'development' ideology which measured poverty in terms of per capita income in US dollars and Western living standards. As a result subsistence producers with a satisfactory and sustainable livelihood were classified and treated as 'poor' because of a low monetary income, lack of electricity, toilets, mechanisation and the like. They lived an austere life, but became poor only as a result of development policies which deprived them of their livelihood through the process of monetisation and modernisation. Thus subsistence producers turned into landless labourers, migrants and slum dwellers, joining the ranks of the poor and deprived. This process becomes aggravated in recent years through the world-wide triumph of trade policies favouring the freedom of global capital and MNCs to move in and out of national economies in pursuit of profit. The policies of IMF, World Bank and WTO – whatever their claims – are contributing to a further pauperisation and marginalisation of millions of people for whom there is no role and no use in a global market economy dominated by the logic of capital. Theology in Asia – as elsewhere – is facing the destructive power of Mammon as never before.

## The threat to democratic rights

Asia has been the scene of great anti-colonial and anti-imperialist struggles. But in many of the countries which gained independence the leadership failed to foster democratic participation and space. Dictatorial set-ups developed rather soon, as alienation of the disappointed masses and state repression grew side by side. Dictatorship took different forms, from military regimes in Indonesia, Pakistan and Burma, to martial law regimes in the Philippines (under Marcos) and South Korea or one-party dictatorship as in Taiwan. The countries where the anti-imperialist struggle had been led by communist parties came under the dictatorial rule of the vanguard party which in the case of Kampuchea established a most murderous regime. India and to some extent Sri Lanka seem to have been exceptions as they kept up more or less functioning parliamentary democracies. However, even there the record of violation of human and democratic rights is depressing, the redeeming feature being, especially in India, that there is some democratic space for movements within the country to raise their voices in protest.

As a result of the repressive role of the state the struggle for democratic rights has been a top priority in popular movements all over Asia. In those struggles protest against traditional forms of oppression – such as caste, patriarchy, discrimination of minorities – converges with protest against new forms of victimisation, caused by modern development promoted by the state and hitting the same vulnerable groups first of all. Workers and peasants struggling for survival are fighting for their rights to organise. Women's movements fighting patriarchy and violence in the family and in daily life expose the militarisation of state and society as a culmination of the same. Eco-movements protesting against ecologically destructive dams or large-scale logging of tropical forests are defending the livelihood of tribals and forest-dwellers, who have been the victims of marginalisation by traditional society long before. Ethnic and religious minorities are protesting that they are denied jobs and other benefits of modern development and deprived of their rights to protest. Sometimes students are in the forefront of these movements. What emerges, as is being pointed out by some of the new social movements, is that the post-colonial state which pursues the modernisation of the economy unavoidably tends to become repressive and dictatorial as it turns out to benefit only some at the cost of others.

In this respect there is little difference between countries with a dictatorial regime and those with a parliamentary set-up. The fall of dictators and the change of governments through elections do not solve the basic problems of the modernisation project. Victims of modern development, masses of uprooted and marginalised people, are asking what sort of development it is which makes them redundant. The state responds with repression and the curbing of democratic rights. Increasingly it does so in the context of implementing 'structural adjustment' programmes in accordance with IMF and World Bank conditions. People's movements experience their state more and more as the police force of global capital, that most undemocratic, uncontrolled concentration of power. Theology in Asia is facing the despotism of uncontrolled Pharaonic power.

## The double role of religion

The struggle for justice and freedom in Asia is complicated through the multi-ethnic and multi-religious character of Asian societies. Religion plays a powerful role both in justifying oppression and in inspiring and sustaining thirst, and struggles, for justice. The oppressive role of religion is notorious in the legitimation of patriarchy and of caste. It further appears where dominant religions justify discrimination against religious minorities. On the other hand, protest movements may also appeal to religious motives.

Mahatma Gandhi in India and Khomeini in Iran are well-known examples of the power of religious motivation in anti-imperialist struggles. But they also show the problems involved. Gandhi was able to mobilise the masses, he tried to overcome oppressive practices of Hinduism like child-marriage and untouchability, and chauvinist attitudes towards other religions. Yet his commitment to Hinduism, including a reformed caste system, alienated the Dalits – the untouchable outcast groups – who are still enraged today about his treatment of their leader Dr Ambedkar, and it contributed to the India–Pakistan break-up along religious lines.

The oppressive role of religion is conspicuous in the legitimation of patriarchy, affecting women all over Asia. No religious tradition is free from it. Women rising up to free themselves and society from this oldest form of oppression find it often hard to identify liberating undercurrents in their religious traditions. This led some of them to opt for a secularist course of struggle for emancipation. However, others insist on the reform of religion rather than its abolition as a more liberative perspective.

Religion plays a divisive and oppressive role in many social and political conflicts. Dalits are oppressed by Brahminical Hinduism in India. Many of them have rejected Hinduism and have become Neo-Buddhists in their search for equality and human dignity. The ethnic conflict in Sri Lanka has a religious aspect as dominant Buddhism is based on the Sinhala majority. Tamils are Hindu or Muslim, while Christians are on both sides. Buddhists are driven out of Bangla Desh which is dominated by a Muslim majority. Muslims in the southern Philippines are fighting against a state dominated by a Christian majority. Christians in north-east India are fighting against the Indian state. Many of these armed ethnic struggles aiming at a separate state turn exclusive, create new minorities and evolve into internecine conflicts. Similarly the Dalits find it difficult to unite. One of the factors which divides them is religion, as some have converted to Buddhism, others to Christianity or Islam, whereas again others remain within the setting of Hindu traditions.

It is not surprising in view of all this that secular nationalist reformers, leftist revolutionaries, and many feminists rather opted for radical modernisation and a secular state as the way to a more free and just society. In the communist-ruled countries of Asia – China, North Korea, Vietnam, Kampuchea, and Laos – this took the form of repression or severe restriction of religious practices and traditions. In China this found its brutal, iconoclastic expression in Mao's Cultural Revolution. In a country like India it took the soft form of a modernising state which left all religious traditions free while its Prime Minister Jawaharlal Nehru spoke of nuclear reactors as the new temples of India. Both approaches have lost their momentum. The whole of Asia is now exposed to the devastating impact of the global media on cultural traditions. The integration into global capitalism and its nivellating, homogenising effects provokes various responses. Not all religious fundamentalist movements can be taken to be genuine responses of protest. Political manipulation and calculation may play a significant role. Careful studies are needed in each case. Certain movements, like the Hindu chauvinistic movement in India, are committed to modernisation and integration into global capitalism, but see a chance to come to power by projecting a sort of religious nationalism at the cost of Muslims. But others turn to their religious traditions in order to oppose consumerist-mammonist secularism. For liberation theology this poses the question on which basis it might be possible to develop a common opposition to the powers that be.

### The ecological problem

Ecological concerns are more and more penetrating the agendas in Asia also, though the 'tiger' economies are still rushing forward blind to the disasters they are preparing. Indigenous peoples, women in subsistence peasant economies, fish workers and other marginalised groups are the first to register the threat to life, as they are most directly in touch with nature and dependent on it. Workers in factories will take more time to notice. In their case it is catastrophes like that in Bhopal which alert them. Bank directors will be the last to notice and to be affected. Earlier, Asia has seen peasant struggles against exploitation and repression by landlordism and the state. Such struggles often got linked up with a Maoist-revolutionary perspective in our century. In the process the cultural and religious values of peasant communities were ignored or suppressed. On the other hand a leader like Gandhi tended to romanticise the peasantry without addressing its class and caste problems. This time indigenous peoples, hill farmers and other subsistence producers, often with women in the forefront, are raising issues of economic survival and social justice as well as of ecological sustainability. In the process traditional values regarding the relationship to nature, the down-to-earth cosmic spirituality of village religion and folk assumptions have come across to other sections of people in eco-movements as precious elements of people's and humankind's heritage. What used to be dismissed as superstition now attracts much more serious attention. People's myths are rediscovered. A Christian painter in India, Jyoti Sahi, explores tribal myths in his paintings and brings out their ecological significance and their challenge to Christians.

These developments – which cannot be spelled out in detail – are bringing a new openness to appreciate popular religion, as distinct from the highly abstract religious thought systems and world-views, the religion of the elite which used to be called the 'high tradition'. Of course, for many modern revolutionaries it is quite a long and difficult process of reorientation, as they had expected all these myths and rituals to have been long forgotten. Among liberation theologians the process has started.

## Christian responses with a liberative perspective

Liberation theology does not have a broad popular base in the churches of Asia comparable to the Basic Communities in Latin America. Mostly being tiny marginalised minorities Christians and churches in Asia tend to avoid confrontation with the powers that be. Usually an individualistic-pietistic outlook prevails. Exceptions can be found in the Philippines – which with its Christian majority and experience of Spanish colonialism is more comparable with a Latin American situation – and in South Korea and Taiwan.

Liberative theological responses to the social and political situation on the local and continental level have been primarily stimulated through ecumenical gatherings and networks, through study centres, individual theological teachers and some theological seminaries. The Ecumenical Association of Third World Theologians (EATWOT), the Conference of Churches in Asia (CCA), the World Student Christian Federation Asia/Pacific, centres like the Christian Institute for the Study of Religion and Society (CISRS) and the Indian Social Institute in Bangalore/India, the Centre for Society and Religion (CSR) in Colombo, and others, have through conferences and publications made major contributions to the formation of a liberative theological response in the Asian context. Their role and impact in the churches may appear rather marginal, but they have stimulated and supported groups which got directly involved in social and political action, relating to trade unions, peasant organisations, fish workers' movements, women, students and human rights organisations. The Urban Industrial Mission in South Korea, the Christian Workers' Fellowship and the Devasanara Collective Farm in Sri Lanka may be mentioned as examples.

Another significant form of involvement has been and is that of individual Christians joining secular mass organisations and popular movements. They may rarely articulate their motivation in theological terms, they may seldom appear in church gatherings, but they are – often anonymously – present as salt, working together with non-Christians in practical solidarity. They have overcome the marginalisation of Christians, they are there where the basic conflicts of society are being fought out. There they face the problem how to relate to their Christian faith tradition, as a living spiritual source without causing divisions along religious lines.

Here appears a major difference with the situation in Latin America. Christianity has played a highly problematic role in colonial times. There has been an embarrassing number of Christians among Asia's dictators in post-colonial times – such as Chiang Kai-Shek in China and Taiwan, Ngo Diem in South Vietnam, Park in South Korea, and Marcos in the Philippines – but there has not been a Christian state ideology. State repression of popular movements has been and is being justified by national security, anti-communism, development etc. but not in the name of Christ. Of course, obliging statements of status-quo minded church leaders are always welcome and the charity of Mother Teresa may be prominently projected as the proper response to the problems of poverty. But the God of the Bible does not figure in the ideological defence of the state and its policies. If religion is used for ideological purposes, then the gods, the traditions and the godmen of the majority community are more useful.

Liberation theology in Asia, therefore, does not have the function of criticising a pseudo-Christian legitimation of the prevailing system. But its critique of other forms of religious ideological idolatry is easily misunderstood in the social context of conflicting and competing religions. Traditionally Christians have calumniated the gods of other religions as idols, self-righteously assuming that they themselves were free of idolatry. Fundamentalist preachers do so still today. The necessary critique of Brahminical Hindu communalism or Buddhist-Sinhala chauvinism can be mistaken as a continuation of that approach in the garb of liberation theology, unless it simultaneously and effectively criticises the fetishist absolutisation of their own community among Christians and the idolatrous worship of a Christian God who is no longer associated with the affirmation of life and liberation of the poor, but rather with the forces of death hidden in the 'blessings' of prosperity and progress for some at the cost of many.

This self-critical approach implies on the other side an affirmation of the liberative thrust of biblical faith in such a way that struggles for the transformation of society can be fought in solidarity with non-Christians.

Groups like the Christian Workers' Fellowship and the Devasarana Collective Farm in Sri Lanka have developed forms of celebration and dialogue in which different religious traditions which matter to people are articulated side by side in such a way that people do not feel threatened but mutually encouraged. The ways in which non-Christian activists have been relating to such groups and to theological thinkers like M. M. Thomas, Sebastian Kappen and Samuel Rayan in India show what is possible.

This points to the crucial task of liberation theology in Asia: to speak from the core of the biblical messages in such a way that the solidarity between Christian and non-Christian Asians in their sufferings and struggles gets expressed and enhanced, without obliterating their specific identities.

One of the most striking elements of such a theological response to the Asian context is the reflection on God's suffering and its relation to the sufferings of people. The response to the suffering from colonialism and war, from poverty and disease, from discrimination and repression, from death on a mass scale is central to all liberation theology, which starts with listening to the cries of those who suffer and the attempt to understand the causes of their sufferings. But in Asia the concern with suffering and liberation from it strikes at the same time a chord with the core theme of one of its greatest religious traditions, namely that of Buddhism. The Buddha came to see life as suffering, and Asia knows of the yearning of the heart for liberation from suffering.

The Taiwanese theologian Choan-Seng Song takes up this theme by reflecting on the pain-love of God in view of human suffering and the threat of evil forces. Listening to the great Asian traditions and to the poems and stories of people, and avoiding treatises in the rationalist style of Western theology, he speaks of God as Creator and Redeemer using existential categories of the heart rather than rational categories of the mind. C. S. Song's concern in dialogue with Buddhist traditions is to take the reality of suffering seriously in such a way that in the midst of it meaning can be found and hope can be articulated which enables people to involve themselves in protest and struggle. Traditionally Buddhism may tend to seek a way out of suffering by reaching nirvana – as many pious Christians do by their longing for heaven – but the practical involvement of Buddhist monks in protest actions against the dictatorial regime of Ngo Dinh Diem in South Vietnam in the early 1970s, when some of them took to self-immolation in the streets of Saigon, suggests to Song that the Asian tradition of facing and accepting suffering can become part of people's struggles against tyranny and exploitation. Cross and Lotus symbolise different religious spiritualities, but they must meet.

> The lotus still looks as peaceful as ever. But it symbolizes peace in the midst of unrest and fear. It still appears as tranquil as ever, but its tranquility is surrounded by the fire of destruction. It still looks toward Nirvana as the destination of human striving, but its Nirvana is forced to take history seriously. Here the cross can and must meet the lotus.[1]

The involvement of Christians in protest movements in South Korea, the Philippines and Taiwan, bearing the risk of imprisonment, torture and death witnesses that a deeper understanding of the implications of Christian faith is bringing them close together with the suffering masses of Asia, and thus closer to the aching of God's heart, whose pain-love affirms life against the forces of evil and death.

The Korean Minjung theology is the strongest example in Asia of a liberative theology born in the context of people's suffering and corporate struggles.[2] It is not the theology of one theologian but indeed a people's theology worked out by a number of theologians connected with people's organisations. In it suffering people find a voice. The Korean people have gone through many sufferings: under the rule of the Yi dynasty over five centuries, under the imperialist rule of Japan (1905–45), from the traumatic post World War II division of the country and the devastating war of 1950–3, and under dictatorial rule both in North and South Korea, be it in the name of communism or for the sake of technocratic capitalism. Under all these regimes the Minjung, the common people, suffered and rose in rebellion, long ago, in the Tonghak Peasant Revolution of 1894, in the March First Independence Movement of 1919, and in the struggles for democracy in the 1970s and 1980s.

The Protestant Mission which entered Korea in the 1880s got rooted among the lower classes due to the translation of the Bible not into the Chinese language of the ruling elite but into the – neglected – Korean vernacular script of the common people, providing them with a language of liberation of oppressed people. The biblical stories, parables and symbols rather than the abstract doctrines of the missionaries appealed to the people who recognised in them their own story of enslavement and suffering, and their hopes and longing for freedom and well-being. The missionaries tried to keep the Korean Christians away from political involvement in opposition to Japanese rule. But the Christian community based among the poor at the bottom of society attracted more and more people who found in it spiritual and moral resources for the regeneration of the nation. The Christians shared the aspirations of the Korean people at large for national independence. And they suffered for it, both as Christians and as Koreans, and thus the Christian language of suffering got related to the suffering of people at large. The biblical stories of the Exodus and of the trial and passion of Jesus interpreted what happened in the present. Once again the Exodus symbol became a revolutionary paradigm.[3] The Japanese government even banned the book of Exodus. However, the *kairos* of involvement in 1919 was followed by a long period of withdrawal into a church ghetto which lasted till the end of the 1950s. The emergence of the student movement in 1960 and the military coup in 1961 followed by the brutal Park Regime (1962–79) drew Korean Christians again into social and political action, at the price of harassment and imprisonment. Continuity was provided by Kim Jai-Jun (born 1901), an Old Testament scholar who related the prophetic vision of a just society and the suffering servanthood of Christ to the mission of the Church aiming at the transformation of Korean history.[4] Students, workers, community workers and clergy were involved through such organisations as Urban Rural Mission (URM), Korea SCM, the Seoul Metropolitan Community Organisation, new institutes for mission and theological study, and new congregations and communities such as the Galilee Church for squatters, the House of Dawn, and ecumenical fellowship groups. Tremendous inspiration came from the Catholic poet Kim Chi-ha, both through his writings and through the courage with which he suffered torture and years of solitary confinement in prison. In his poems and ballad-plays the suffering Korean people, Minjung, and the suffering Christ are central.[5] He relates at the same time to the Minjung traditions of Korean history, such as the Tong Hak uprising with its messianic and shamanistic elements.

Speaking of Minjung as the subjects of history Korean theologians distinguish themselves simultaneously from a traditional and modern Christian preoccupation with the subjectivity of the individual and from a rigid sort of Marxist class analysis and revolution theory. Minjung are the exploited and oppressed people. Who belongs to them cannot be defined by socio-economic factors alone as Marxist theory does when it speaks of the proletariat. Minjung is a wider, more dynamic concept, says Kim Yong Bock:

> Woman belongs to minjung when she is politically dominated by man. An ethnic group is a minjung group when it is politically dominated by another group. A race is minjung when it is dominated by another powerful ruling race. When intellectuals are suppressed by the military power elite, they belong to minjung. Of course, the same applies to the workers and farmers.[6]

In their biblical studies the Minjung theologians have tried to identify biblical parallels to the concept of Minjung.[7] Mark's use of the term *ochlos* and his avoidance of the term *laos* distinguishes the people with whom Jesus sides both from the nation as a whole and from an organised class, according to Ahn Byung Mu. The Korean theologians obviously want to keep the concept of Minjung flexible and to avoid a rigid political-ideological fixation. Kim Chi-ha especially stresses Jesus' identification with lepers and prostitutes, with the most destitute victims of society, who would not qualify as members of the proletariat.

A significant aspect of their explorations into the history of the Korean Minjung and of cultural and religious expressions of its consciousness is the appreciation of positive elements in Shamanism and Maitreya Buddhism with its Messianic Buddha who comes to rescue the people from suffering. These are popular religious traditions among the Minjung, whereas Confucianism is the tradition of the ruling class. Here is a liberation-oriented political theology which focuses on the political but does not ignore people's piety. This may be seen as the positive outcome of the basic understanding that people who are objects of oppression are meant to become subjects of history and therefore have to be taken seriously also in what they feel and hope. Shaman priests, often women, perform rites to resolve *han*, i.e. problems caused by the grief of people who have died and cause suffering as ghosts. Usually the rites are limited to releasing the *han* of the dead. But contemporary writers have developed a political understanding of the *han* of the Minjung caused by endless injustice and of the need of exorcising it. Kim Chi-ha sees himself as a transmitter of *han*, as one who voices the bitter sense of grief and indignation of the Minjung. This can be sublimated in a dynamic way as the energy for revolution. 'People's han and rage ought to be liberated from its masochistic exercise to be a great and fervent clamor asking for God's justice. If needed, it ought to be developed into a decisive and organised explosion. This miraculous transition lies in religious commitment and in internal and spiritual transformation.'[8] It is a service of the prophetic religions of love to shake the emotions of the oppressed people, who after a long time of dehumanisation have become wretches who have lost their passion for justice. Their rage has turned into self-hatred and frustration. To awaken them is the mystery of resurrection which fashions people in God's image. Such resurrection is revolution. Kim calls it 'the unity of God and revolution'.[9]

Suffering is one basic aspect of Asian reality; the process of rapid and often revolutionary social change is another aspect which has provoked theological reflection. What God is doing in and through the 'Asian revolution' is a question which M. M. Thomas, in India, has been asking.[10] And how, accordingly, are Christians expected to participate in the process? Thomas may not be directly counted among the theologians of liberation.

But he has made a seminal contribution to a political theology and social ethics which calls for critical Christian participation in secular social and political life, thus paving the way for the concerns and perspectives of liberation theology. He has made this contribution on various levels: in India through the Christian Institute for the Study of Religion and Society of which he has been director, in Asia through the East Asia Christian Conference (later CCA), in the global ecumenical movement through the WSCF and the WCC over many years, and in his home state Kerala as a social worker in the 1930s and again in retirement writing Bible commentaries in Malayalam, inspiring new generations of students and participating himself in political life, especially in the context of human rights movements. He became nationally known through his bold critique of the emergency regime of Indira Gandhi (1975–7).

In the 1950s and 60s Thomas pleaded with church members to come out of their Christian ghettos and participate in building a secular, democratic and socialist India. This emphasis on 'Christian participation in nation-building' was the outcome of years of involvement and analysis.[11] During the time of the struggle for independence Thomas sympathised first with Gandhi, then with the communists, but he finally opted for Nehru's secular and democratic socialist nationalism. The undemocratic methods of Stalinist communist parties in India and elsewhere, and their questioning of the genuineness of Indian independence in 1947–8, caused his break with the communists. The communal bloodshed between Hindus, Muslims and Sikhs during the traumatic Partition in 1947 must have impressed on him the need for a secular state and for a common secular ethos to sustain such a state. And the problem of mass poverty convinced him with many others that modern science and technology was needed to increase productivity, while a socialist orientation should ensure that independent India would commit itself to social justice in the distribution of the fruits of economic development.

In his analysis of the process of change in Asia Thomas uses the framework of tradition and modernisation. Modern nationalism is seen as a revolutionary force which overcomes the repressive stagnation of traditional Asia of which Marx spoke long ago. In the process the people of Asia are awakened to a new sense of freedom, of selfhood and personal responsibility. Even the bearers of the great religious and cultural traditions of Asia cannot escape from the impact of humanism and modernisation and find themselves challenged to reform in response to it. Nationalism in its simultaneous search for an unique national and Asian identity could turn back to traditional culture and its authority. But Thomas pins his hope on the cultural reform movements within Asian religions, the non-totalitarian movements of secular humanism and the Christian ferment which through interaction should usher in an open, pluralistic society with a 'common framework based on common humanity' in which people of many faiths and no faith work out 'common assumptions about man and society which will inform their cooperative effort'.[12]

Theologically Thomas sees in the Asian revolution under God's creative providence 'the promise of Christ for a richer human fulfilment'. The creativeness of human freedom in the conquest of nature through science and technology, the new sense of selfhood and self-determination, and the possibility of developing communities of persons instead of traditional collectivism or modern individualism are seen as elements of progress in the conditions of humanness. Thomas does not reproduce the idea of inevitable progress, but speaks of the maturing of conditions 'which makes both hell and heaven nearer'. The same revolutionary process has inherent in it 'evil powers of both individual and collective egoism, self-righteousness and idolatry which are likely to betray its promise of fuller human life'. Through constructive participation and prophetic critique Christians should witness to the defeat of these evil powers in cross and resurrection and to the new humanity and new creation in Christ which are offered within the revolution as the fulfilment of its promises.[13]

By the end of the 1960s waves of protest were spreading through India and Asia. The independent nation-state had not brought the end of poverty. Traditional hierarchical society divided by caste and religion had not been transformed into a new, non-discriminatory national community. Christian nationalists like M. M. Thomas started to recognise that their dreams at the dawn of Independence had not come true. Interaction with social scientists and activists convinced them that a radical renewal would have to come in the course of people's awakening and organisation and struggles. From then onwards the focus shifts from 'development' and 'modernisation' to 'social liberation' and from 'nation' to 'people', meaning tribals, Dalits, women, peasants and workers getting organised in the struggle for their rights.

Theologically this leads – as in Korea – to a greater emphasis on the crucifixion of Jesus as the symbol of God's identification with the agony of oppressed humanity. It is the crucified Christ, the messianic suffering servant as distinguished from the conquering king, who with the victory of the cross provides a spiritual basis for the combat of the cruciform humanity of the oppressed.

Within the cruciform humanity of the oppressed in India the Dalits have a special significance. Their sufferings through centuries of caste-oppression under the stigma of untouchability, their 'brokenness' – as the name Dalits signifies – under the burden of exploitation at the bottom of society make their struggles a crucial test case for all other social movements in their struggle for a new society. In many respects their case is comparable with that of women suffering from and struggling against patriarchy. The fact that the oppression of Dalits unabatedly continues and that they suffered discrimination even within the churches to which they have converted in large numbers in the expectation of being treated as equal human beings is one of the reasons for the emergence of Dalit theology.[14] One of its fruits is a growing interest in Dalit traditions in the form of myths, folk stories, songs, proverbs, festivals and rituals which tell of their origins and enslavement, the degradation of their women, the alienation of their lands and their search for justice and equality. Dalit theologians demand that these traditions, along with those of Tribals, should no longer be neglected by church and theology, but should be given priority over the dominant religious traditions of India, as they are much closer to the liberative perspective of the gospel: Tribals and Dalits embraced the gospel of Christ because they experienced Him as 'liberator' not as an advaitin or Bhakta. They have more egalitarian traditions in their heritage like community sacrifice, community needs and mutual reconciliation before religious acts.[15]

Fr Sebastian Kappen (1924–93), an Indian liberation theologian who like M. M. Thomas has related to critical social activists on the margin of the Church and far beyond it and inspired them with his analysis and liberative vision, has addressed the same problem in terms of the need for 'cultural revolution'.

At a meeting of 'Third World Theologians in Dialogue' held in New York in 1979, Kappen reflected on the relevance of Jesus as the prophet of a counter-culture subverting first-century Jewish culture for counter-cultural movements in India today as well as on the relevance of Indian tradition for such movements today. Prophecy is 'the point of eruption for the repressed longings of the masses' to be freed from inherited cultural bondages and at the same time the 'point of irruption of the divine' which together result in an ultimate project of hope aiming at a 'theandric community of justice, love and freedom'. It becomes a praxis of subversion of the existing culture and creation of a counter-culture through a new dissenting community. Such counter-cultures never start from scratch. They draw upon the 'wealth of tradition', giving new meaning to old myths and symbols in a 'dialectical supersession of the past' involving the moments of abolition, preservation and sublimation.[16]

Turning to Indian history Kappen identifies the Vedic religion as a culture of the oppressors and the dissent of the Buddha as a movement towards the emancipation of the oppressed, with its morality not of exclusion – as that of caste and family – but of inclusion based on all-encompassing love and compassion. However, Buddhism was driven out of India, and what today is called Hinduism succeeded in establishing the dominance of Brahminism through a process of integrating and assimilating the deities of popular religions, while imposing simultaneously the oppressive laws of Manu. This provoked a new outbreak of dissent in the medieval Bhakti movement representing the devotion and aspirations of the oppressed masses. The Bhagavata Purana, the main scriptural authority of the movement, speaks of a God who is partial to the poor. This movement also got domesticated by Hindu orthodoxy. Again prophetic-millenarian movements erupted in the eighteenth century drawing inspiration from folk traditions and their myths and symbols. This history shows in Indian culture a mixture of two opposing strands, namely of ascetical priestly, patriarchal and elitist and of life-affirming, creative popular, matriarchal, egalitarian tendencies. Kappen concludes that a re-creation of Indian society can emerge only from the repressed culture of the lower castes, outcastes and tribals, who in the present day have to confront both orthodox Hinduism and modern capitalism.

In this process Christians should avoid claiming superiority by proclaiming the lordship of Christ and instead bring the message of the reign of God in the spirit of the Jesus of the synoptic Gospels. Then the way will be free for the Jesus tradition to give to India as well as to receive from her. Here Kappen differs from M. M. Thomas who derives much of his vision from the cosmic Christ of the letter to the Colossians and from the Syrian Orthodox bishop Mar Osthatios who bases his argument for a classless society on the orthodox doctrine of the Trinity.[17] The contribution of the Jesus tradition, as Kappen saw it, consisted in its dialogical rather than cyclic view of history, its ethical rather than cosmic religion and its communitarian approach, all aiming at the liberation of history rather than liberation from history. In its turn the Indian tradition could contribute a deeper understanding of the indwelling of the divine in nature and society, of the yogic discovering of the self within as a means towards freedom from acquisitiveness, hatred and violence, and of the motherhood of the earth. Kappen concludes:

> What I claim . . . is not the superiority of Christianity over the Indian religious tradition but the superiority of the humanizing religiosity of the Buddha, the radical Bhaktas and Jesus over the magico-ritualistic religiosity of orthodox Hinduism and the depropheticized religiosity of tradition-bound Christianity.[18]

Aloysius Pieris, a Sri Lankan Jesuit, founder and director of the Centre for Research and Dialogue at Kelaniya, has pushed the question of the relationship to the religious traditions of Asia as a crucial issue on the agenda of liberation theologians. As one who is deeply involved in dialogue with Buddhists, he has challenged EATWOT members as well as Catholic bishops to face mass poverty and (non-Christian) religion as basic characteristics of Asian reality. The tendency is to ignore one of the two; the task is to relate to both simultaneously. Churches and theologians will try in vain to overcome their isolation from Asia's non-Christian civilisations through 'indigenisation' of liturgy and theology, if they do not relate first of all to the poor of Asia. And liberation movements will remain marginal or become oppressive if they view the religion of the poor only as a bondage which has to be overcome. Religion and poverty both have an enslaving and a liberating side, and these are connected. Enslaving religion justifies the poverty which is imposed on people through exploitative structures. Liberating religion opts for voluntary poverty as the way of interior liberation from the rule of Mammon and as a political strategy of solidarity with the poor in their struggle against forced poverty, as in the case of Gandhi.

In the biblical tradition we find the distinction and connection of voluntary and enforced poverty in the call to follow Jesus who was poor then and to serve Christ who is in the poor now. Followers of Jesus opt to be poor in order to serve the poor by 'birth' who are the proxies of Christ (Matt. 25.31–46). Asian liberation theologians have pointed at the same connection by insisting that the '*God-Man* Jesus saves by being at once the *human* victim and the *divine* judge of Asia's institutionalized misery'. Pieris criticises them, however, for having counterposed this understanding of Christ against Asian religion, not discerning the prophetic-political resources in it. He identifies two versions of religious socialism in Asia's ancient traditions: that of peasants in clannic societies, and that of monks in monastic communities. The first is founded on what Pieris defines as '*cosmic religiousness*' in which 'social harmony is insured by cosmic communion with the elements of nature', the second is based on a '*metacosmic religiousness*' which does not negate cosmic reality, but points to a salvific beyond through its non-addiction to cosmic needs. The monastic tradition, however, located in a feudal context, has turned into 'the luxury of a leisure class maintained by the really poor', one of its weaknesses being the lack of respect for the dignity of labour. This happens once more in a lot of Western enthusiasm for 'oriental spirituality'. But in some rural areas of Asia a symbiosis of the religious socialism of peasants and monks can be found, in which the earth is everybody's property and 'cosmic needs are made to serve rather than to obsess the person'.[19] These two distinct traditions meet when Jesus identifies with the religious poor of the countryside asking for baptism by John the Baptist who represents the tradition of renunciation, and then after his desert experience goes to the people for his prophetic mission.

Pieris calls the Asian church and its theology to get baptised in the Jordan of Asian religion and on the cross of Asian poverty. Only then can it add to the irreconcilable antinomy between God and Mammon which is common to all religions, the irrevocable covenant between God and the poor which is unique to the biblical tradition. This raises the practice of voluntary poverty from the micro-ethical to the macro-ethical level and merges the struggle against Mammon and for God with the struggle for the poor. It implies at the same time the understanding that the struggle of the poor becomes 'God's own struggle against the principalities and powers that keep them poor'. 'It is a just war, an exercise of divine justice. A holy revolution.'[20] Pieris makes an important breakthrough as he acknowledges and integrates the Jewish-Semitic contribution to Asia's religious traditions, which often is negated as part of the Western tradition in the context of inter-religious dialogue. Pieris finds the social base for the praxis of solidarity with the poor in their struggle in basic human communities such as the Devasarana collective farm initiated by Yohan Devananda who merged his Anglican monastic tradition with that of the French worker-priests by building up a community with unemployed, largely Buddhist village youth in Sri Lanka, which later related to mass organisations of peasants struggling for survival.

Pieris' input during the Asian Theological Conference in 1979 in Sri Lanka provoked a lot of discussion.[21] The Filipino delegation expressed reservations about giving too much weight to the religious factor, suggesting that such discussions would eventually be more the concern of middle-class theologians than of the poor – the real subjects of theology – in their struggles. Carlos H. Abesamis and the group whom he represents acknowledged the need to consider native wisdom and religion, but they insisted that the 'principal characteristic of a truly Asian theology is its "Third-Worldness" which denotes the thrust towards socio-political and total human liberation of the poor, whereas "Asianness", which they defined as the question of inculturation follows on the second place'.[22] Pieris was able to show that they misunderstood his position. Their intervention represented the thrust of liberation theology as it has evolved in the Philippines which found a wider echo among activists elsewhere in Asia especially during the 1970s and early 80s. During those years a revised and reorganised communist party, with a Maoist orientation, led an armed struggle, and the building up of mass organisations brought together in the National Democratic Front, against the Marcos regime and US imperialism. This disciplined, committed and strong movement attracted a growing number of Christians who got involved in various ways. In this context grew a Filipino version of liberation theology which had close affinity with Latin American theology in its emphasis on social (class) analysis and on paradigms from biblical history. Its specificity was expressed in the title 'theology of struggle'.[23] This may be understood as the result of interaction with the Maoist outlook which dominated large sectors of the popular resistance movement. It demands and seeks clarity and commitment regarding politically organised struggle as the only means to achieve liberation. Struggle is seen as the primary context of theological reflection and the basic expression of Christian life. This approach tends to translate the theological conviction of God's partisan choice for the poor into the demand to make a concrete political choice, to take sides in the polarised political situation of the Philippines. The emphasis on struggle also implies a critique of traditional religion which focuses on Christ as the suffering servant who did not open his mouth and went as a lamb to its slaughter, a religion which would enhance passivity.[24] Instead the cross is presented as a symbol of challenge and struggle. Edicio de la Torre, one of the priests who went underground, narrates how in prison he painted a poster presenting the crucified one with one open hand and one hand closed to a fist, whilst the blood that flows down turns into a red banner.

The non-violent overthrow of the Marcos regime in 1986 in which large sections of the middle class mobilised by the Catholic church leadership were involved has created a political situation in which the Maoist-oriented left lost part of its influence and is now facing a split. This has probably reduced the appeal of the 'theology of struggle' as far as support for the armed struggle is concerned. But other aspects, such as the importance of class analysis, remain relevant, as Ed de la Torre, writing in the 1970s, shows when he asks Christians: will you be like Pharisees thanking God that you are not like others? 'We are not subject to class analysis. We are not affected by class interests. We are moved only by theology and ideas. We only need to be informed about the issues and we will immediately act in favour of the poor.'[25]

The continuation of mass poverty in the Philippines shows that the struggle for democratic rights is not enough, just as the change of governments through parliamentary elections in India or Sri Lanka is not enough. The question is not only that of the use of violent or non-violent means in the overthrow of a repressive government. The question is how and by whom the strangling grip of global capitalism and its agents can be broken and what steps are needed to initiate a liberating transformation of society. The concern of liberation theologians in other Asian countries with questions of culture and religion has not caused them to ignore the contribution of Marxist theory, as the widespread refutation of Cardinal Ratzinger's

*Instruction on Certain Aspects of the 'Theology of Liberation'* (1984) has shown. Marxism is being appreciated for its analytical focus on the reality of exploitation and alienation and for its revolutionary outlook which challenges people to take responsibility for their common life. Marx taught me, says Kappen, 'to think from below, from the heart of the fragmented, demented world around'. And this bore theological fruits in the encounter with 'the historical Jesus'.[26] However, it is commonly observed that dogmatism has affected the analytical and liberative capacity of Marxism and that class analysis has to be integrated with a thorough analysis of the social divisions caused by discrimination on the basis of race, ethnicity, caste, sex and religion. The late Lakshman Wickremesinghe, an Anglican bishop, who with the late Catholic bishop Leo was one of the inspiring promotors of liberative involvements in Sri Lanka, favoured an 'indigenous Marxian socialism', which would be 'influenced by rather than dominated by Marxism' and would relate not only to the economically poor, but also to ethnic minorities, women, unemployed youth, the disabled, the 'tourism-debased', in short to all who are deprived, made submissive or alienated. This would be in accordance with the image of Jesus as 'prophetic contestant and martyr', which should, however, be kept in dialectical tension with the images of Jesus as companion and rehabilitator of sinners and outcastes and as the 'self-sacrificing satyagrahi' who converts enemies with the soul-force of vicarious suffering love.[27]

Kim Yong Bock introduces the distinction between messianic politics and political messianism in order to distance the liberation struggles of the Minjung from Maoism and North Korean communism.[28] Political messianism is the negation of the historical subjectivity of the Minjung. The North Korean notion of *juche* refers to the autonomy not of the people but of the national totalitarian dictatorship in the name of the proletariat. 'It is a sort of "realized" subjecthood in the form of a dictatorial state.' But the Minjung, which transcends the narrow, self-contained entity of the proletariat, realises its subjectivity while suffering and struggling in the unfolding drama of history between the times of the 'not yet' and the 'already'. The politics of Jesus – and of other messianic traditions in Korea – does not make the Minjung an object of messianic claims but the subject of their own historical destiny, struggling for justice, *koinomia* and *shalom* to come. While presenting this critique of totalitarianism Kim Yong Bock avoids the trap of Western anti-communism by arguing that Japanese ultranationalism in the time of Japanese rule and modern technocracy at present are other manifestations of political messianism. It may be added that critical Marxist tendencies would find themselves in agreement with many of Kim Yong Bock's points.

In China K. H. Ting, who was WSCF Secretary together with M. M. Thomas in the late 1940s, tried as leader of the Three Self Movement, as Principal of Nanjing Theological Seminary and as an Anglican bishop to guard the independence of the Church and the sovereignty of its message over against communist ideology. At the same time he promoted its independence from a Western missionary heritage, and sought to overcome its alienation from Chinese society. One of the mottos of the Three Self Movement – meaning self-supporting, self-administering and self-propagating – was 'love the country, love the Lord'. This affirmation of national belonging corresponded with the anti-imperialist, nationalist dimension of the Chinese revolution. It was the base for welcoming all that was good for China and its people in the achievements of the communist regime. Theologically this was connected with an affirmation of God's goodness at work in creation and history, and of the scope of the redemptive lordship of the cosmic Christ of Colossians 1, 15–17. This overarching perspective creates space for a critical awareness of the sinfulness of human endeavours and efforts, which Chinese tradition from Confucius and Mencius to Mao underestimates. Ting expresses his appreciation of liberation theology and its preferential option for the poor elsewhere but he sees it as one of the tasks of church and theology in the post-liberation situation of China to avoid making the poor the bearers of salvation. The experience of the Cultural Revolution has taught where such idealisation leads. 'The poor are not the Messiahs of the world, as if it were only necessary to liberate the poor and they would then liberate the world.'[29]

In an article entitled 'Insights from Atheism' (1979) Ting expressed the hope that the revolutionary spirit of the communists would purify the institutional Church, whilst religious faith would purify the revolutionary spirit, not by dampening it, but by giving its undertakings in industry, agriculture, science and technology, art and music a 'deeper grounding' by relating its meaning 'to the ongoing creative, redemptive and sanctifying movement in the universe under what we call God'.[30]

Whatever its shadow sides the Chinese experiment has been a source of inspiration. Writing in the early 1980s Fr Tissa Balasuriya, director of the Centre for Society and Religion in Colombo, expressed the admiration of many Asians for China's achievements in overcoming the problems of hunger, unemployment, and dependency on foreign powers. 'It represents the greatest transformation for the betterment of the largest number of human beings in the shortest period of time.'[31] However, the bloody repression of the movement for democracy in June 1989, and the pursuit of economic liberalisation policies which tend to undermine some of the social achievements and to aggravate the mounting ecological problems, have increased the doubts regarding China's contribution to the solution of Asia's problems, though it may be too early to conclude, given its revolutionary past, where its present approach will lead.

A new phase in the search for a viable alternative to capitalism has started, a search which is no longer dominated by communist vanguard parties. New social movements are beginning to influence the analysis of the situation and the setting of political agendas.[32] It took time for women's movements and eco-movements to be heard, as conservatives and leftists suggested that their concerns were Western imports. However, Asian women are succeeding in making the role of patriarchal oppression in all areas of life visible and the warnings of eco-movements can no longer be ignored. In India efforts are under way to integrate the insights of social analysis based on the methodologies of the theologian and sociologist F. Houtart, of the economists S. L. Parmar and C. T. Kurien – who made crucial contributions to ecumenical social thought – and of Marxists like Ajit Roy with the insights and methods which have emerged in the context of the struggles of women and other subsistence producers, of Dalits, fish workers, trade unions with new agendas, and eco-activists. Eco-feminists have conceptualised the non-accounted-for work of subsistence-producers and women as 'production for life' which has to become central to the construction of an ecologically sustainable and socially equitable society. People's control of resources is seen as one of the crucial conditions for the realisation of this vision of a life-centred production system and society.

This process of reorientation is slowly penetrating into the realm of theological reflection. Aruna Gnanadason from India has popularised Asian feminist insights in ecumenical and theological circles. Chung Hyun Kyung has combined insights gained from personal experiences in the Korean cultural context with liberation motives found in EATWOT and CCA. She speaks of a survival-liberation centred syncretism in the struggle of poor Asian women who select those 'life-giving elements of their culture and religions' which empower them 'to claim their humanity'. Such inspiration will be found especially in the popular piety of a women-centred cosmic religion which has been repressed by the dominantly patriarchal meta-cosmic religions.[33]

Connections with eco-concerns are being spelled out by others. Sean McDonagh, working in Mindanao (Philippines) and witnessing the assault on the environment by logging companies and green revolution technologies called for a new theology which draws on sources such as Teilhard de Chardin, Buddhism and the tribal religious experience.[34] Gabriele Dietrich, a social activist and theological teacher in Tamilnadu Theological Seminary (Madurai, India) and one of the eco-feminists who coined the 'production of life' concept, has combined the economic, ecological, feminist and theological dimensions in her writings.[35]

Fears have been expressed that eco-concerns and openness to Asia's religion would lead to a withdrawal from history and politics because of a re-absorption into a cosmic/metacosmic spirituality. This happens indeed in some eco-groups and among those Christians who strive for inculturation and religious harmony in the absence of the poor. Liberation theology which is open to eco-feminist insights and non-Christian popular religion will have the task of showing that the threat of eco-catastrophes means a greater historical responsibility for humankind than ever before. It has to expose the irresponsible blindness to reality which characterises capitalist dynamics. And it cannot give up the critique of religion – Christian and non-Christian, elitist and popular – wherever and whenever it serves structures of domination and forces of death. It will, not uncritically, embrace all popular religion, but will welcome those elements which indeed affirm life and liberation. Fr Samuel Rayan, a Jesuit theologian and EATWOT member, gives voice to such an orientation when he speaks of the openness of Asian spirituality to the reality of the earth, of history and of the ultimate mystery of God, and connects contemplation and critical analysis with the ability to respond in action. Such response-ability implies conversion from capitalist development models to 'redefining development as if people mattered'.[36] A biblical basis for welcoming life and liberation affirming traditions and elements from other religions as well as secular sources and placing them in a historical-political perspective can be found in the covenantal approach to the preservation of the earth and the survival of the poor. The connection between Genesis and Exodus, between God's covenant with the earth and God's covenant with the people on the way from slavery to a society based on justice, could indeed provide crucial insights in the present search for an alternative.[37]

The question of liberation is more urgent than ever, in Asia as elsewhere. Whether Christians will be able to address the question will depend on their readiness to go against the tide of Mammon, to turn to the Galilees of those who are excluded today and enter into a common search to find how struggles for survival can become struggles for life in its fullness. Asia has its martyrs who witness to that search. Two of them, both from Sri Lanka, represent many others who have committed themselves to this search and struggle: Fr Michael Rodrigo (1927–87), a priest who identified with the poor in a predominantly Buddhist rural area, and Rajani Rajasingham (1953–89), a human rights activist and feminist in Jaffna. At Rajani's funeral people affirmed their commitment to continue the struggle for life by saying: You have not been buried, you have been sown.

## NOTES

1 C. S. Song, *Third Eye Theology: Theology in Formation in Asian Settings* (Guildford and Lowdon, Lutterworth Press, 1980), p. 122. See also: *Theology from the Womb of Asia* (Maryknoll, NY, Orbis Books, 1986).

2 See Kim Yong Bock (ed.), *Minjung Theology: People as the Subjects of History* (Singapore, Christian Conference of Asia, 1981).

3 See M. Walzer, *Exodus and Revolution* (New York, Basic Books, 1985).

4 See John C. England (ed.), *Living Theology in Asia* (London, SCM Press, 1981), p. 10.

5 See Kim Chi-ha, *The Gold-Crowned Jesus and Other Writings* (Maryknoll, NY, Orbis Books, 1978).

6 Bock, *Minjung Theology*, pp. 186f.

7 Cyris Hee Suk Moon and Ahn Byung Mu in ibid., pp. 119ff.

8 Quoted by Suh Nam Dong, 'Towards a Theology of Han', in ibid., p. 61.

9 See Kim Chi-ha, *Gold-Crowned Jesus*, pp. 23ff.

10 M. M. Thomas, *The Christian Response to the Asian Revolution* (London, SCM Press, 1966).

11 See M. M. Thomas, *Ideological Quest within Christian Commitment. 1939–1954*, Indian Christian Thought Series: No. 16 (Madras, publ. for CISRS by CLS, 1983).

12 Thomas, *Christian Response*, p. 76, n. 29; cf. M. M. Thomas, *The Acknowledged Christ of the Indian Renaissance*, Confessing the Faith in India Series No. 5 (Madras, CLS, 1970).

13 'Christ's Promise within the Revolution and the Christian Mission' (Strasbourg, WSCF, 1960) in M. M. Thomas, *Towards a Theology of Contemporary Ecumenism* (Madras, CLS, 1978), pp. 65ff.

14 A. P. Nirmal (ed.), *Towards a Common Dalit Theology* (Madras, Gurukul); X. Irudayaraj SJ, *Emerging Dalit Theology* (Madras/Madurai, Tamil Nadu Theological Seminary, 1990).

15 A. M. A. Ayrookuzhiel, 'Indian Religious Heritage and Social Transformation: Change of Perspective within the CISRS', in *Religion and Society* XXL, 1–2 (Bangalore, 1993), p. 81.

16 S. Kappen, *Jesus and Cultural Revolution. An Asian Perspective* (Bombay, Build Publications, 1983).

17 G. M. Osthatios, *Theology of a Classless Society* (Madras, CLS, 1980).

18 Kappen, *Jesus and Cultural Revolution*, pp. 70f.

19 Quotations from A. Pieris, SJ, *An Asian Theology of Liberation* (Maryknoll, NY, Orbis Books, 1988), p. 21, p. 61, p. 43f.

20 A. Pieris, *Love Meets Wisdom. A Christian Experience of Buddhism* (Maryknoll, NY, Orbis Books, 1988), p. 95.

21 See V. Fabella (ed.), *Asia's Struggle for Full Humanity: Towards a Relevant Theology* (Maryknoll, NY, Orbis Books, 1980), chs. 8, 14.

22 Ibid., pp. 123ff.

23 M. R. Battung et al. (eds.), *Religion and Society: Towards a Theology of Struggle* (1988).

24 Recent studies find a dimension of hidden protest in people's identification with the martyred Christ. See A. Ligo, 'Liberation Themes in Philippine

Popular Religiosity', in *Voices from the Third World* (EATWOT) XVI, 2 (December 1993).

25 'The Filipino Christian: Guidelines for a Response to Maoism', in England, *Living Theology*, p. 94.

26 S. Kappen, *Liberation Theology and Marxism* (Puntamba, Asha Kendra, 1986), pp. 14f. cf. S. Kappen, *Jesus and Freedom* (Maryknoll, NY, Orbis Books, 1977). See also M. M. Thomas, *The Secular Ideologies of India and the Secular Meaning of Christ* (Madras, CLS, 1976).

27 L. Wickremesinghe, 'Living in Christ with People', D. T. Niles Memorial Lecture, CCA Assembly, Bangalore 1981, in *An Asian Bishop's Quest*, Quest 81 (Colombo, CSR, 1984), pp. 101f.

28 Bock, *Minjung Theology*, pp. 185ff.

29 K. H. Ting, 'Inspirations, from Liberation Theology, Process Theology and Teilhard de Chardin', quoted in R. L. Whitehead (ed.), *No Longer Strangers, Selected Writings of K. H. Ting* (Maryknoll, NY, Orbis Books, 1989), p. 33, cf. pp. 49f.

30 Ibid., p. 127.

31 T. Balasuriya, *Planetary Theology* (Maryknoll, NY, Orbis Books, 1984), p. 142.

32 See M. Selden, 'People's Plan 21' and M. Ichiyo, 'For an Alliance of Hope', in *Bulletin of Concerned Asian Scholars* (July 1990), pp. 43–51.

33 Chung Hyun Kyung, *Struggle to be the Sun Again. Introducing Asian Women's Theology* (London, SCM Press, 1991), pp. 112f. cf. A. Pieris SJ, 'Women and Religion in Asia: Towards a Buddhist and Christian Appropriation of the Feminist Critique', in *Dialogue*, New series, vols. XIX–XX (Colombo, EISD, 1992–3), pp. 119–203.

34 Sean McDonagh, *To Care for the Earth. A Call to a New Theology* (London, Geoffrey Chapman, 1986).

35 G. Dietrich, *Reflections on the Women's Movement in India: Religion, Ecology, Development* (New Delhi, Horizon India Books, 1992); and 'Emerging Feminist and Ecological Concerns in Asia', in T. Fernando *et al.* (eds.), *Launching the Second Century. The Future of Catholic Social Thought in Asia* (Hong Kong, Asian Center for the Progress of Peoples, 1993), pp. 47–58.

36 S. Rayan, 'The Search for an Asian Spirituality of Liberation', in V. Fabella *et al.* (eds.), *Asian Christian Spirituality. Reclaiming Traditions* (Maryknoll, NY, Orbis Books, 1992), pp. 25f.

37 For Biblical reflections see R. S. Sugirtharajah, *Voices from the Margin* (London, SPCK, 1991); J. Russel Chandran (ed.), *Third World Theologies in Dialogue. Essays in Memory of J. S. Amalorpavadoss* (EATWOT, 1991); D. Carr, *Sword of the Spirit. An Activist's Understanding of the Bible*, Risk Book Series (Geneva, WCC, 1992); C. R. Hensman, *Agenda for the Poor Claiming their Inheritance. A Third World People's Reading of Luke*, Quest 109 (Colombo, CSR, 1990). Cf. B. Wielenga, 'Reorienting our Hopes', in *COELI International Intercommunications* (Brussels, 1993), also in *Voices from the Third World* XVII, 2 (December 1994).

# 4

EDWARD ANTONIO

# Black theology

## Introduction

There are several ways of approaching Black theology. One approach seeks to characterise it in terms of its history, that is, of its origins in the Civil Rights and Black Power movements of the 1960s. It maintains that the demands for racial justice embodied in these two movements provided the basis for the emergence of Black theology. I shall not follow this approach here since it is not the aim of this chapter to offer a detailed description of the relationship between movements of protest and Black theology in the 1960s. This has been done elsewhere.[1]

The second but related approach starts from an interpretation of the different ways in which African-American slaves appropriated and reworked Christian faith in the context of their experience of slavery. According to this understanding Black theology represents not just a faddish attempt to redefine Christian teaching in the light of the demands of the social and political forces of the 1960s but a critical search for a historically black Christian form of reflection on issues of racial justice and liberation. The materials for such reflection come from the twin realities of slavery in the past and the experience of racism in the present. One important difference between these two approaches is that, although they both share the same understanding of Black theology, the first is very much shaped by the politics of the recent past whereas the second locates its point of departure in the history of slavery itself, with the latter being seen as a historical expression of racism. Needless to say, these approaches are not mutually exclusive but they point to differences in methodological emphasis between the first generation of black theologians, i.e., its founders like James Cone, Gayraud Wilmore, Deotis Roberts and others and the second generation like Dwight Hopkins, Jacquelyn Grant, Josiah Young, Delores Williams and others.

The third route and one which I shall take here approaches Black theology through a critical elucidation of its main themes. This has several advantages over the other two approaches. First, it allows one to engage the actual thinking of black theologians on a variety of topics which have come to be central to Black theology's self-understanding. This has rarely been done.[2] Many works on Black theology either merely describe how it came into being, its relationship to the social movements of the 1960s or they are attempts to recover slave narratives in order to reconstitute them as appropriate modes for theological reflection. The second advantage of the approach I propose here is that it helps one to maintain a certain distance from the productions of black theologians. Such a critical distance is long overdue because, with a few exceptions, the bulk of what makes up the literature of Black theology remains largely uncritical of itself. This can perhaps be explained not only as a function of the character of that literature as a body of primary sources but also in terms of the self-understanding of Black theology as a form of social struggle rather than simply as an intellectual exercise.

What I do in this chapter, then, is to engage the writings of one of the leading black theologians of the first generation. I refer to James Cone. I choose Cone because he remains by far the most prominent and influential of all black theologians. He has, perhaps, published more works on Black theology than any living theologian and the extent of his influence can easily be seen in the fact that many of the second generation of black theologians studied under him at Union Theological Seminary where he is the Distinguished Charles Briggs Professor of Systematic Theology. Cone has thus continued to provide the framework for the articulation of Black theology whether in America or in South Africa.

By focusing on Cone I do not wish to suggest that other black theologians or other varieties of Black theology (South African or Womanist Black theologies, for example) are unimportant or that there are no real differences in approach and content between them. I wish simply to give the reader the opportunity to come to terms with the central presuppositions of Black theology as articulated in the writings of its most well-known advocate. Whatever differences may exist between black theologians, they are all agreed that the basic categories first formulated by Cone provide the most appropriate means for theological reflection on the problem of racism. The various schools of thought that have arisen within Black theology, then, fundamentally stand in continuity with Conian theology.

## Black theology defined

I have so far used the term 'Black theology' as though the meaning of that phrase is self-evident. This, however, is not so; hence we need to attend to matters of definition before proceeding further. What, then, in the perspective of its exponents, is Black theology and what connection, if any, does it have with Christian theology? According to an official statement of the National Conference of Black Churchmen issued in June of 1969 (the same year in which Cone first published his *Black Theology and Black Power*):

> Black Theology is a theology of liberation. It seeks to plumb the black condition in the light of God's revelation in Jesus Christ, so that the black community can see that the gospel is commensurate with the achievement of black humanity. Black Theology is a theology of 'blackness'. It is the affirmation of black humanity that emancipates black people from white racism, thus providing authentic freedom for both white and black people. It affirms the humanity of white people in that it says No to the encroachment of white oppression.[3]

Cone and Wilmore have defined it in the following terms.

> Black theology, therefore, is that theology which arises out of the need to articulate the religious significance of [the] Black presence in a hostile White world. It is Black people reflecting on the Black experience under the guidance of the Holy Spirit, attempting to redefine the relevance of the Christian gospel for their lives.[4]

First, both definitions make reference to 'blackness' or the 'black condition' and, second, both claim some kind of relationship between this 'black condition' and the gospel. Both definitions also link blackness to white racism. According to these definitions, the central problem which Black theology seeks to address is that of the contradiction between racism and the demands of Christian faith. In order to understand this it is important to bear in mind that the reality of white racism has been a significant and pervasive feature of the experience of modernity for both blacks and whites. It is a reality which has historically formed the context of their often vexed encounter.

The centrality of race in the modern period can be seen not only in the fact that millions of people in countries as widely different as South Africa and Brazil or France and Australia, or again, Germany and America, Britain and Italy have been the victims of racist practices; it can also be observed in the existence of a large body of knowledge both popular and academic in which the 'being' of blacks has been classified (sometimes as less than human), ordered (as inferior to whites), labelled (as primitive, barbaric etc.) and interrogated (as to its utility; slavery and the exploitation of labour in much of the Third World being perhaps the best examples of this). It has now been established by a number of scholars, both white and non-white, that the philosophers of the Enlightenment and the scientists as well as the would-be scientists of the nineteenth century showed a great interest in the question of race; an interest in which the humanity of blacks was ridiculed and sometimes denied. The gurus of western philosophical thought, Kant, Hegel, Hume, Voltaire and other less well-known scholars, all produced works in which they openly displayed their racism against blacks. It is in the works of these men that 'the grammar of racialised discourse' which underlies much of modernity's view of the self as, among other things, a racial subject, was forged. When in *Tancred or the New Crusade* Disraeli says, 'All is race. There is no other truth', he is merely repeating the sentiments of a long line of well-known figures in modernity: Renan, Taine, Le Bon, Gobineau, etc.[5]

The point is not that Black theology came into being in response to the discursive provocations of the theorists mentioned above. In fact, it has never really engaged the discourse of race in the modern period which, of course, remains one of its major theoretical weaknesses. What is important, however, is the fact that the level at which Black theology is forged as a critique of racism has been historically and sociologically determined by the pain and suffering which has resulted from the infliction of racism on blacks.

Thus when the above definitions of Black theology speak of white racism as the hostility of the world towards the black presence, it is not primarily the effects of the theoretical content of racialist discourse which form the basis of such a claim but rather the practical expression of that discourse, its lived experience, in the attitudes, institutions and modes of behaviour that constitute the oppression of blacks on the basis of their skin colour. In other words, for Black theology racism is not just a set of beliefs which say that inherited biological traits determine moral and intellectual dispositions so that some races are not only biologically but, therefore, morally and intellectually better off than others, it is also a mode of behaviour which prescribes discriminatory policies intended to work against those considered to be biologically less better off.

The basic claim of Black theology, then, is that it is in the context of the suffering caused by these discriminatory policies and modes of behaviour that black humanity has been negatively defined by whites. Its aim, therefore, is to critically reflect on what it means to be black in such a context.

According to the two definitions of Black theology quoted above this mode of reflection seeks to show that 'God's revelation in Jesus Christ . . . is commensurate with the achievement of black humanity'. Black theology is nothing short of a statement of affirmation of black humanity. The possibilities of such an affirmation, in other words, require a theology of liberation which takes race and the practices associated with belief in the idea of race seriously.

The identity of Black theology, it follows from this, is moulded by the circumstances or situation of black existence in which the gospel is appropriated, lived and reflected on such that doing Black theology becomes a dialectic between the two realities of 'context' and 'gospel', 'situation' and 'kerygma'. I shall argue in this chapter that this 'dialectic' of message and situation represents the regulative principle of the methodology of Black theology.[6]

## The twofold structure of Cone's thought

### The methodological aspect

In order to illustrate this, I shall distinguish two broad categories into which the Black theology of James Cone may be divided: the methodological and the dogmatic. One deals with his approach to Black theology and the other with the content of that theology. As far as the first is concerned, I shall address Black theology's claim regarding the contextuality of all theological discourse and of Black theology in particular. With respect to the second category, I shall elucidate Cone's thought on the nature of revelation and christology.

### The contextuality of theological discourse

Cone understands Christian theology to be 'human speech about God'. But, it is speech, like all human speech, always related to historical situations.[7] As we shall see shortly, this is an important claim for Black theology because it is committed, in all its variety, to the view that all human ideas, including theology, are marked by the identities of their productive agents: they represent the thoughts, interests and practices of those who produce them. In turn, who these are and what makes them what they are is largely a function of the social, political and economic context in which they live, move and have their existence.

For Cone this means that all theology is limited by the cultural conditions of its production and thus is not universal language. Or, to put it another way, it is precisely because it has no legitimate claims to such universality that it is interested language. Elsewhere Cone calls this the 'contextual-dialectical method'. According to this method, there are no absolute, universal truths, not even in revelation itself.[8]

What makes this method dialectical is the fact that theology arises out of a specific historical context characterised by the movement of thought and experience between the reality of racism, which spells out the content of both context and experience, and the demands of the gospel which provide the framework for the struggle for racial justice. But this movement is not exhaustive of the nature of this dialectic since the latter is, theologically, also made up of a paradox that drives our interpretation of the gospel back to the original experience of racism in order to discern whether or not that interpretation has yielded any possibilities for black liberation.

The elements of this paradox are, first, the refusal to concede the possibility of divine, universal truths and, second, the affirmation of truth as a happening from beyond history, 'a divine event that invades our history'. Both the idea that revelation is not absolute or universal and that it is a divine event which operates through a process of self-historicisation (it invades our history) are meant to express the contextuality of thought and experience. It is important to observe here that Cone's dialectic is not neutral: for the context of its verification or realisation is the event of black liberation.

In other words, the aim of Cone's emphasis on the contextuality of theology is, ultimately, to show that it makes a difference to the identity of a theology whether the theologian is a slave or a slave master; whether he/she speaks – even through elected silence – on behalf of the oppressor or the oppressed. Cone writes, '. . . thinking, or thought, can never be separated from our socio-political existence. If one is a slave, then one's thinking about God will have a different character than if one is a slave master.'[9] That is, whereas the slave's experience of God and reality is mediated through 'the attempt to define himself [in his early writings Cone consistently used sexist language] without the ordinary possibilities of self-affirmation', through the 'slave ship, the auction block and the plantation regime', that of the slave master is gained by 'extending white inhumanity to excruciating limits'.[10] Hence it follows that, even granting the similarity in their language about God, the slave and the slave master 'could not possibly be referring to the same reality'.[11] There is, therefore, a fundamental connection between thought and the social conditions of thought; between reflection and praxis, between theology and its social context, a connection illustrating the fact that black religion[12] and white religion are not 'essentially the same'.[13]

Cone puts the differences which separate these two modes of interpreting the Christian message down to the different 'mental grids' or perspectives through which they are structured. The argument here is that if we want to know why the white American apprehension of the reality of the gospel has not theologically appropriated the question of colour or racism as a central problematic in its consciousness; if we want to find out why, instead, its concern is directed at the somewhat abstract issues of the status of religious statements and the problem of faith and history posed by the challenge of the Enlightenment, we must look not to the content of white theology, that is, its assertions about God, humanity, etc., but to the social presuppositions which have determined its shape and form. We must look to its social connections; to the goals and aspirations it serves.[14]

This refusal to explain the character of a given theology simply in terms of its objective assertions or content is, as we have already seen, a consequence of Cone's belief in the contextuality of all theological language. It is, however, not contextuality in general which furnishes grounds for Cone's critique of doctrinal objectivism but contextuality in its concrete aspect. In other words, for Cone the fundamental property of the cultural context is in fact its concreteness. The constitutive attribute which most aptly describes the meaning of *Sitz im Leben* (the context or situation of life) is, so to speak, its existentiality. This being so, Cone is then enabled to search for the origins of his theological commitment not primarily in intellectual processes, nor in abstract self-elucidation, but rather in what he calls 'the existential and social formation of my faith'. In fact, he goes so far as to say that the factors of biography,[15] embedded as they are in the socio-political context, are methodologically and theologically the most decisive characteristic in the forming of a theological perspective.[16] Biography, and the existential elements mentioned here, refer, in the first instance, not to the life of the individual theologian or thinker, but to the collective self-understanding of which he is a product. This aspect of biography is linked to the use of the idea of narrative in Black theology. This can be seen in the extent to which many of the leading black theologians of the second generation are seeking to recover the memory of slavery through a rereading of slave-narratives as a framework for reworking a whole range of Christian teaching from biblical hermeneutics to eschatology and from ethics to church history in terms of blackness as a category of theological interpretation. These theologians understand blackness both as a context as well as a narrative. It is the story of how Africans were enslaved and subjected to racism by people who identified themselves and the societies they represented as Christian. That story has become the context within which the meaning of the gospel is being interrogated in the light of that narrative.

This notion of contextuality allows Black theology to formulate a hermeneutic of liberation rooted in the reality of black experience itself.

According to Cone, two aspects, one negative and the other positive, are crucial to understanding liberation as the hub of such a hermeneutic. Negatively, Black theology's *raison d'être* is the recognition that, for blacks, 'the world is not what God wills it to be'.[17] God does not will racism for the people of colour and yet that is the pervasive reality which saturates their consciousness;[18] a reality which refuses to acknowledge their humanity; which sees their blackness as a necessary condition for their negation. Positively, however, the knowledge that the world could be different leads precisely to the struggle for liberation. Thus, from the start, Black theology was, in the eyes of its exponents, nothing short of a theology of liberation. But unlike other forms of liberation theology, its perspective on oppression was not primarily elucidated through concepts such as 'class', the role of international capitalism or gender, but through the category of race, or more precisely, that of blackness.

In its early stages Black theology failed or refused to engage with questions of class and gender, because, as black theologians had it, racism was the most pressing social problem of the 1960s both in America and in Africa. It was thought that although categories such as class and gender were important they were, nevertheless, not suitable instruments for struggle because they distracted attention from attempts to defeat racism. But this stance resulted in criticism from Latin American liberation theologians as well as from feminists. I cannot go into the details of this debate here for reasons of space. But I wish to note the fact that there is now in Black theology a significant number of black women rewriting Black theology, and thus in some ways even redefining blackness itself, in terms of their own experiences of oppression at the hands of black men.[19]

### The concept of blackness

Two questions are in order at this point: first, how is this notion to be construed? and second, does the qualifier 'black' and its cognates add anything to our understanding of theology? Cone's formulation of Black theology turns, in the main, upon the significance which he attaches to the symbol of blackness. That symbolism or at least this particular one is important for Black theology can be glimpsed in the way in which Cone justifies his use of blackness by arguing (following Tillich) that, as well as being contextual, all theological speech is symbolic in character. In Cone's thought, if humanity correctly understands the reality of God, and if therefore it correctly understands the nature of theological language, it will be driven to speak of Him (*sic*) through the mediation of symbols; symbols 'that point to dimensions of reality that cannot be spoken of literally'.[20] Therefore, Cone concludes, 'to speak of Black Theology is to speak with the Tillichian understanding of symbol in mind'.[21] By so fastening on to the symbolic character of theological language, Cone is enabled to appropriate blackness as a theological topos.

The notion of blackness is important for Black theology because in Western culture the contrast between black and white is morally significant. It marks the difference between evil and good and provides the analogical framework within which both good and evil are named in terms of their signifiers. Thus in Western culture black signifies evil and white signifies good. The representation of blacks as evil, ugly, dirty etc. in Western culture was, therefore, at least partly, predicated upon that contrast. In other words, it is this contrast which served as a metaphysical basis for justifying the oppression of blacks in the name of the good (read white culture and supremacy).[22]

For virtually all the advocates of Black theology, however, this negative function of blackness is of much more than just historical interest since it is still applicable today for the oppressor and oppressed alike; it delimits their perception of each other. For the oppressor, it intends his or her self-understanding of a given people as at least racially inferior and, therefore, as not deserving of equal human treatment.[23] Thus, Deotis Roberts draws attention to the fact that, even in contemporary culture, blackness signifies shame, ostracism and inferiority; he illustrates his point by referring to how the Webster dictionary has 'ugly', 'fiendish', 'evil', 'everything undesirable' as basic characteristics of blackness.[24]

It is this symbolism, with regard to both its historical as well as its present function(s), that Black theology has appropriated in order to enunciate the historical possibilities for the self-affirmation and/or negation of the black subject. These possibilities are the 'black condition' which constitutes the fundamental datum of human experience and, thus, so to speak, the raw materials of Black theology itself.[25] If, then, blackness in both its positive and negative aspects is concerned about structures of historical experience and with the social and cultural conditions for their realisation, it follows that, although its reference or meaning involves an element of skin colour, it is not reducible to this.

As the Taiwanese theologian Choan Seng Song has argued, 'blackness' as understood in Black theology embodies the whole history and culture built on the experience of slavery.[26] But more than a historical or cultural phenomenon, 'our blackness', says Desmond Tutu, 'is an intractable ontological surd'.[27] In other words, what is at stake when we talk about blackness is nothing other than the being or humanity of black people. If so, it is perhaps not too much to say that Black theology is, at one level, an attempt to work out a theological anthropology based on a conception of the self as a racialised subject. It represents a recognition that whatever race is, centrally involved in the different ways people define each other in modernity is a process of racialisation of identities.

It is true that Black theology has generally not worked out a precise relationship of the historical to the ontological claims of blackness. This, however, has not been its main aim: proponents of Black theology have not sought to define the nature and content of symbol as such but rather to identify the part played in the experience of blacks by a particular symbol. Indeed, even where both the 'external' and the 'internal' aspects of symbol have been assimilated, there is a predilection for the historical dimension. We may illustrate this by considering more specifically the way this symbol is employed in Black theology.

### The function of the symbolism of blackness

According to Cone, the symbolism of blackness performs a double function: first, it symbolises white oppression. Cone is here linking the character-istics 'ugly', 'fiendish', 'evil', 'dark' etc. (which we saw earlier are imputed to blackness in Western consciousness) with the fact that a particular people bearing the skin whose colour has been alleged to symbolise these very features 'have been the victims of white brutality'. The other role of black-ness is, paradoxically, to symbolise what blacks mean by liberation.[28]

Of course there is at once a problem here: how have we arrived at the harmonious juxtaposition of these apparently contradictory functions? Deotis Roberts has attempted to deal with precisely this problem. In his essay 'A Creative Response to Racism: Black Theology', he argues that the latter has salvaged, redefined and transmuted blackness into a basis for self-affirmation. As understood by Roberts, this process is analogous to the Christian transformation of 'the arch symbol of our faith, the Cross' whereby the 'curse' of the Cross has been made into the ultimate symbol of salvation.[29]

Although Cone insists that 'blackness' refers to both oppression and liberation, he nowhere offers a theory of symbols or of their relationship to paradox. While this is true, it is equally true that he supplies a different – though not systematic – explanation of the double function of the sym-bol which concerns us here and which, seemingly, enables him to evade the need for such a theory. His explanation is interesting because it also intro-duces us to another aspect of his thought; namely, Black theology's anthro-pology which, in an important sense, underlies his whole theological project. The key terms of this explanation are 'liberation' and 'freedom'. In A Black Theology of Liberation, Cone maintains that authentic human existence means 'being in freedom'.[30] But this is not freedom in the abstract. Freedom is genuine only if it is a concrete negation of oppression.[31] When Christians speak of the image of God in man (*sic*) as the grounding aspect of human nature, what they ought to stress is not the *analogia entis* side of the image, but image as *analogia relationis*. It is here that the 'divine–human encounter is made possible, it is here that human nature through liberation as a condition for its fulfillment is realized'.[32] In other words, since the image of God in man ultimately means liberation, and since liberation is achieved in relational rather than in ontological categories, man's real nature is revealed whenever man attempts to overthrow the powers that oppress him. Thus Cone asserts, '. . . the image is human nature in rebellion against the structures of oppression. It is humanity involved in the liberation struggle against the forces of inhumanity.'[33] This approach originates from Cone's belief in the existentialist dictum, 'existence precedes essence'. The subject and consequently the meaning of this existence is concrete humanity, 'the point of departure of any phenomenological analysis of human existence'.[34]

### Blackness as ultimate reality

Of course, terms such as 'freedom', 'historical' and the like do not in themselves describe in what way a given reality is concrete. But this hardly matters, since for Black theology, the emphasis is on 'blackness', and 'blackness' is what gives a particular set of experiences their historical specificity. Moreover, black people's consciousness of history is suffused with blackness itself, with the double experience of oppression and the struggle for liberation. Indeed, Cone has no hesitation in positing this experience as the ultimate determinative factor in his theology. He writes, 'The fact that I am black is my ultimate reality.'[35] Again, 'To put it simply,' says Cone, 'Black Theology knows no authority more binding than the experience of oppression itself. This alone must be the ultimate authority in religious matters.'[36] This, then, is 'the supreme test of truth'; the basic, non-negotiable datum which gives meaning to ultimate reality itself.[37] In making these contentious remarks Cone is fully aware that the 'Christian doctrine of God must logically precede the doctrine of man'.[38] He does not wish to subordinate the gospel to blackness. But is Cone being consistent? We shall deal with this question in a moment. First, it is necessary to point out that Cone's argument is that, even accepting the priority of God and of Christ, 'black people can view God only through black eyes that behold the brutalities of white racism'; their knowledge of Christ comes from their experience of his identification with them in the pain of oppression.[39]

Still, the two assertions that one's blackness is one's ultimate reality and that there is another reality (God) which must, or needs to, relate to blackness seem to us to contradict each other. If blackness is the ultimate reality how can there be another final frame of reference outside of this one unless some sort of metaphysical dualism is assumed, or unless both realities – the gospel and blackness, God and humanity – are reduced to or identified with each other? Adopting the former position would not seem to square with one of the basic tenets of 'orthodox' Christian belief, namely, that there is only One Almighty God; and identifying the gospel with our experience would seem to be tantamount to saying that God's Word is indistinguishable from human words. At this point we also meet up with the ever threatening problem of 'ideology', with all the difficulties of definition and application which it entails. Has Cone not made the gospel into an 'ideology' for a black political cause? Let us suppose, for argument's sake, that it is true that black people's experience of racism as a form of oppression and their struggle for liberation are the supreme test of truth. We must then ask: What objective content can be given to truth; what guarantee is there that even Black theology itself is not, in the end, nothing but the subjective musings (in the name of truth) of a disenchanted ethnic group? If there is nothing in the gospel which is 'independently' the matter of 'fact', there seems nothing to prevent whites, or anyone, from justifying racism or tribalism in the name of a truth created in their own image.

Cone, to be sure, is not unaware of questions such as these and his answer is as follows:

> In the struggle for truth in a revolutionary age, there can be no principles of truth, no absolutes, not even God . . . we cannot speak of him at the expense of the oppressed. . . . There is no way to speak of this objectively; truth is not objective. It is subjective, a personal experience of the ultimate in the midst of degradation. Passion is the only appropriate response to this truth.[40]

Because truth arises out of the historical situation of blacks, and because it is subjective, truth is black;[41] it has no objective content other than that given to it by blacks.

But here, again, we must draw attention to the ambiguity of Cone's position. Black theology, he says, (in spite of these strong claims) seeks a Christian lifestyle and proclamation which are not reducible to the values of the black community. But how is this to be achieved and how can we be sure that we have achieved it? Indeed, what criteria might we use to distinguish this proclamation from our irenic declarations? These are important questions, touching as they do, on the whole question of the relationship between gospel and culture; between human words and God's claim – in short between revelation and ideology.[42]

## The twofold structure of Cone's thought

### The dogmatic aspect

The question of truth which we have just been discussing enables us now to move on from the methodological to the dogmatic aspects of Cone's thought. Let us remind ourselves that this distinction between method and content, form and structure is not total, as is evinced by the interdependence of the concepts of revelation and contextuality in Cone's mind. Furthermore, it is Cone's conviction that the question of revelation controls the 'methodological procedure' or the 'epistemological justification' of the Christian truth and vice versa.[43] Perhaps the best way of approaching his understanding of revelation is through an investigation of what Cone considers to be the sources and norms of Black theology. He borrows his definition of sources from John Macquarrie's *Principles of Christian Theology* which defines them as 'formative factors' (p. 4) which shape (Cone would say determine) the character of a given theology. Cone also borrows Tillich's definition of 'norm' as the test or criterion against which the sources of theology are judged.[44] On this definition, the hermeneutical function of norms is to stipulate which sources are to be accorded priority and how they are used.[45] Thus, Cone concludes, the conjunctive relationship of source to norm and vice versa marks the place where the most important decisions in theology are made: in it are given those presuppositions out of which theological questions and answers are derived and correlated.[46]

Cone identifies two main sources of Black theology within which he then subsumes different moments of these sources: he distinguishes between black experience and Scripture, on the one hand, and Jesus Christ on the other, calling the latter the subject or essence of the former.

It is Jesus, the subject of theology, who is the condition of possibility of theology. At the same time, however, this theology which seeks to speak of Christ can only do so through certain sources and materials. It is, however, not clear in Cone's writings what the source of these sources is: is it human experience or is it the free gift of God so that we can speak of Christ only through the means of the self-revelation of God? Nevertheless, what is beyond doubt is that, as far as Cone is concerned, authentic talk about Christ, the subject of theology, presupposes talk about the sources of theology.

## The sources of Black theology

Thus before proceeding further we need to ascertain what these sources are.

(1) Black experience has already been mentioned; we have discovered that the content of this experience is the humiliation and suffering caused by racism. In this sense, black experience is the basic condition which justifies the need for Black theology. This condition is made up of three dimensions: (a) slavery, (b) rebellion, and (c) self-affirmation.[47]

(2) The second source noted by Cone is related to the first; he calls it 'the history of black people',[48] but what he means by this is not clear since he formulates it in terms of the three dimensions of experience just cited above, and does not, therefore, differentiate distinctly between the two.

(3) Third in the list of sources is culture, that is, the black community's self-expression in music, poetry, prose and other art forms. The search, or rather the struggle, for a new historical black subject engenders a new consciousness of racial and cultural identity, which brings in its wake a different set of theological problems. This appeal to various aspects of black culture links Cone to the Harlem Renaissance of the inter-war years in which black poets, novelists and artists sought to recover their traditions as an affirmation of their humanity.[49]

(4) Revelation proper occupies fourth place in Cone's scheme of theology's formative factors. Cone defines it as an 'event'; 'a happening in human history': he asserts,

> It is God making himself known to man through a historical act of human liberation. Revelation is what Yahweh did in the event of the Exodus ... Throughout the entire history of Israel, to know God is to know what he is doing in human history on behalf of the oppressed of the land.[50]

Certainly modern theology is correct to stress the self-disclosure of God as the most distinctive attribute of the concept of revelation. But it would be a mistake to reduce this self-manifestation to a kind of rational discovery, or to restrict its meaning to biblical propositions or yet again to the self-projection of the human consciousness. To be sure, some of these factors are involved, but their significance, that which makes them revelatory, derives from God Himself; more exactly, from God's personal relationship with humans. Even so, Cone is not satisfied since he considers that there is a further element to be added to the definition: which is that 'Revelation is God's self-disclosure to man in a situation of liberation.'[51]

So, then, to be in right relationship with God – and that means to know Him and to know His revelation – is to be properly disposed toward his activity of liberation for the poor. Emancipation from oppressive political structures is, for Cone, 'the essence of the biblical revelation'.[52] But, lest we conclude that this understanding of revelation can be appropriated legitimately by all, oppressor and oppressed alike, Cone grounds its specificity in blackness itself. Revelation, he asserts, 'is a black event, i.e. what black people are doing about their liberation'. And he adds, 'I have spoken of black experience, black history, and black culture as theological sources because they are God himself at work liberating his people.'[53] The black community is the locus of God's presence in twentieth-century America. The Christ event and the Black event are one and the same thing.[54] Thus, since 'meaning', 'truth', 'authenticity' and 'understanding' reside in particular communities; since they are referenced and indexed in terms of the experiences and the language the character of which is moulded by the consciousness of those very communities; it follows that the validity of the community's truth claims about who God is and His activity in history can only be tested by internal criteria; that is by the codes and indices of meaning which form the community's frame of reference. Consequently, any interpretation which is not in harmony with the self-understanding of the group, which seeks to break this structural circularity, is deemed to have failed the test of authenticity. In short, what a community says about God, itself and others is verifiable only in terms of the horizons of meaning which 'determine' the production of those claims.

This is the context in which Cone discusses the self-disclosure of God as a black event for the liberation of oppressed blacks. His conclusion is: 'Revelation then is the epistemological justification of a community's claims about ontological reality.'[55] But here again we must ask, if only in passing, whether this is not a very clear case of the ideological instrumentalisation of revelation.[56]

What, in Cone's view, are the implications of the above considerations? First, given that God's truth is only truly manifested in the suffering and pain of the people of colour, and second, given that the authenticity of revelation must be judged in terms of whether or not it is consistent with the perspective of blacks, it is difficult, if not impossible, to envisage any other valid (for our time) form of theological discourse than Black theology itself. In effect, Cone, at least in his early writings, denies the legitimacy of white theology because, as was remarked earlier, when slaves and slave masters engage in God-talk, they are not simply using different starting points or different languages about God, but they are also talking about essentially different things. Whites, in other words, cannot do Black theology; they cannot faithfully proclaim the good news of liberation precisely because they are the oppressors; or else their theologians represent them through active theological justification of racism and oppression as in the days of slavery, or through silence, as is generally the case today. Cone can say all this because, as far as he is concerned, the criterion for deciding the authentic character of Christian theology is whether any praxis which claims this identity is totally on behalf of those who are oppressed. There is, for Black theology, an essential relationship between the status of the poor and the nature of the gospel. It is this decisive connection between the poor and God's preference for them which enables the early Cone to exclude the oppressors from the possibility of understanding the truth of the gospel.[57] The social presuppositions constitutive of their (the oppressors') conceptual universe and consequently of their practice, and vice versa, is constrained and determined by certain interests which contradict the story of divine liberation. That is why white theology is not strictly Christian theology. Such is the place of the concept of revelation and its implications in Cone's theology. But revelation is more than a concept, or at least it cannot be sufficiently described in terms of a single, somewhat abstract notion. Revelation includes other dimensions, the most significant of which are Christ, the Bible and tradition.

(5) In fifth place, then, and still under Black theology's idea of revelation, the Bible is to be considered. As Cone sees it (and perhaps somewhat in the manner of Barth[58]) Scripture itself cannot be identified with God's revelation, the full embodiment of which has been given in Christ. The revelatory significance of the Bible inheres, rather, in its function as a witness to God's ultimate and personal self-disclosure, and is, therefore, a primary source for theological reflection.[59] As such, it accounts for Black theology's claim that God is unquestionably identified with the cause of the poor.[60] Put differently, Black theology is conceived through a basic confrontation with the Bible and within this with two paradigmatic events: the story of the Exodus and the life and deeds of Jesus Christ, both of which form, as it were, the 'objective core' of its hermeneutic and express God's concern for those in social and political bondage. The Exodus is the central focus of the drama narrated in the Old Testament. It furnishes the starting point of Israel's history, for it is here that Israel, because of her weakness and slave status, is chosen by God and destined for freedom. In the Exodus event, God's revelation is identical with His power to liberate the down-trodden. Hence deliverance and revelation dialectically presuppose each other.

The centrality of the Exodus for Cone can be seen in the way in which the theme recurs in virtually all of his writings.[61] In this he has a great deal in common with liberation theology, at least in its early forms. The Exodus is, of course, not the final act of God's liberation; it does not exhaust His dramatic intervention in history.[62] Black theology links the development of prophecy throughout Israelite history to God's original concern for justice as shown in the Exodus: prophecy and the David-Zion tradition, according to which it was the King's duty to protect the weak (Ps. 2.7, 72.12–14; Isa. 1.16), both show God's ongoing concern for the latter.[63]

(6) The sixth source of Black theology cited by Cone is tradition. There are two kinds of tradition referred to here: (a) the main Christian tradition which has come to us through both Eastern and Western versions of Christianity, and of which Black theology is highly critical; and (b) the tradition of rebellion, protest and self-affirmation characteristic of the black experience during and after slavery. 'Tradition', in the first sense, consists of the Church's cumulative self-interpretation and self-understanding as this is embodied in the totality of her history and practice so far. Its indispensability for Black theology (and indeed perhaps for all theology) lies in two closely related directions: first, it shaped the biblical witness, and second, it supplies access to that witness. Moreover, tradition partly controls 'both our negative and positive thinking about the nature of the Christian gospel'. While Cone does not really specify what this means it may not be amiss to suggest that what he intends to say is, at least, that because of tradition, we cannot construe the gospel any way we like if faithfulness to its claim is our objective. Tradition provides some guidelines for its own 'proper' and 'faithful' construal as well as for the 'proper' and 'faithful' construal of the Christian message itself. This does not necessarily mean that tradition has precedence over, say, Scripture, since the latter is not only part of the tradition but often contradicts the former. But here, as with much else in Cone's writings, this interesting question is not fully explored. Thus we are left wondering what the precise nature of the connection is between these two aspects of Christian experience.

Finally we may conclude the discussion of the sources of Black theology by noting that the sources belong to a threefold relationship between revelation, history and faith. We may summarily formulate this relationship by saying that revelation presupposes two foci: history as the location of its occurrence, and faith as the medium through which it is perceived, understood and appropriated.

This, then, is Black theology's understanding of its own sources and its conception of the doctrine of revelation. But how might we discover the putative Christianness of the discourse based on these sources; or what norm or criterion ought to be used in establishing that which makes Black theology's sources suitable material for Christian theological reflection? Finally, how might the validity of this reflection itself be ascertained and measured?

## The norm of Black theology

We are asking here about the norm to which Black theology and its sources are ultimately accountable. In one sense the question seems otiose since we have already seen Cone declaring blackness as the ultimate reality. But in another sense the question is crucial, because even when Cone sought to make absolute a particular ethnic experience he was aware, or so it appeared, of another reality alongside which he placed blackness.[64] We saw, for example, that for Black theology there is no more binding authority than the experience of oppression, and that at the same time Cone says Christ comes first.

This ambiguity has already been noted. Our purpose in mentioning it here is to introduce Cone's christology and the framework in which it is presented.[65] For our explication we shall turn to two of his books where this topic is most clearly dealt with: *A Black Theology of Liberation* which is a sort of single-volume attempt at a fully fledged black systematic theology and *Black Theology and Black Power*.

I propose to deal with a distinction which is fairly central to Cone's doctrine of Christ in these books: the distinction between the Jesus of history and the Jesus of faith; and with how the content of his christology is subsumed within this distinction. Secondly, I shall discuss the importance of the incarnation itself, for the contextuality of theological discourse as well as the grounds it furnishes for Cone's claim that Christ is black. Cone (notwithstanding the ambiguity noted above) is quite clear that Christ is the key to the identity of all genuinely Christian theological utterances. It follows, then, that since Black theology belongs to the latter, the truth of its identity, both as black and as Christian, is centred in the person of Christ.

Cone begins to formulate his christology by searching for the 'historical Jesus' because He is the guarantee against the gospel being reduced to a purely human project. Besides, the Christ of the kerygma cannot be understood without presupposing the historical one. In this emphasis Cone consciously follows Käsemann, Bornkamm, Fuchs and Conzelmann rather than Bultmann. He wishes to stress the historical Jesus because, in his own words, 'Focusing on the historical Jesus means that Black theology recognizes history as the indispensable foundation of Christology.'[66]

Christology would, of course be incomplete, if not irrelevant, were its meaning and significance to be of merely historical interest. Just as access to the Christ of the kerygma requires the Jesus of history, so too the latter requires the former. But this dialectical connection between these two approaches does not in itself give us a clue to the content of the christologies it represents. One way of trying to sketch this out is to enquire as to what constitutes the historicity of Jesus. In *Black Theology and Black Power* Cone's christology has a double content: a negative and a positive one. Negatively, he describes the form of the work of Christ in terms of conflict. Thus, in the Gospels, Christ is seen as conducting a battle against the forces of evil: the healing of the sick, the exorcising of demons, the denunciation of corrupt religious authorities. The temptation of Christ at the beginning of his ministry and, ultimately, the cross itself, are characteristic features of his conflict-ridden campaign.[67] If, however, the cross is the ultimate symbol of conflict, pain and death, the latter has no final hold on Christ. The death which he died did not mark the end of God's involvement with humanity, it did not spell the end of His redemptive project. That is why Easter exists. The resurrection acts in Cone's thought as the living proof of the enactment of the presence of God in Jesus Christ: it is that which discloses the moment of victory over death. It is in view of this victory that we are brought to the positive aspect of the twofold nature of Cone's understanding of the person of Christ. Here, again, he describes the essence of Christ's work in the language of liberation. In fact, the relation between the negative and the positive aspects of this understanding are, in a sense, an extension of the dialectic between the Jesus of faith and the Jesus of history. For example, in *A Black Theology of Liberation*, both conflict and liberation in the ministry of Jesus make sense only if we accept that, according to the New Testament, the historical image of Jesus which has precedence over all the others is that of Christ as the Oppressed One, and that his whole life and work centred in his identification with the poor.[68]

> The finality of Jesus lies in the totality of his existence in complete freedom as the Oppressed One, who reveals through his death and resurrection that God himself is present in all dimensions of human liberation. His death is the revelation of the freedom of God, taking upon himself the totality of human oppression; his resurrection is the disclosure that God is not defeated by oppression but transforms it into the possibility for freedom.[69]

This quotation brings out clearly the connection between what we described above as the negative and the positive poles of Black theology's christology.

That 'Jesus' identification with the oppressed is the distinctive historical kernel in the gospels'[70] derives, according to Cone, from the generative events of the faith. In particular, he mentions four items to buttress his point:

(1) Jesus' birth in the stable, the socio-political marginality of Mary, the visit of the shepherds and the wise men and Herod's hostility towards his birth.
(2) Jesus' baptism and temptation:
  (a) In being baptised Christ identified himself with sinners: this was a practice intended primarily for them;
  (b) when he refused to yield to Satan's temptation he was effectively rejecting the 'available modes of oppressive or self-glorifying power'.
(3) As we have already seen, Jesus' ministry was directed at the poor and was intended to inaugurate God's Kingdom on their behalf (Mark 1.14–15).[71]
(4) Finally, his death and resurrection are the fulfilment of his campaign for the poor.[72]

For Black theology all this adds up to the biblical evidence that Jesus is the oppressed man *par excellence* and the liberator of all who suffer and are exploited.

But to speak of Christ as the representative of the oppressed because he himself knew what oppression is, is in fact to comprehend his christological significance through the symbol of blackness for, as we have already had occasion to observe, blackness itself has historically been a symbol of oppression. Thus the christological question and its significance for blacks, as well as the experience of faith which evokes it in the first place, are rooted in the reality of this symbol; in the concreteness of the social context of black existence (the context of racism, slavery and rejection). The existence of this 'situation' is the basis for the need to recast the issue of christology. It is not enough merely to appropriate the biblical witness as to who Christ was, for we cannot be satisfied simply with repeating Scripture: we need to ask who Christ is for us today. We must continually move from the identity of Christ then, to his identity now, and back again without undermining either pole. In order for the pendulum to swing in this way Cone proposes three stages necessary for the process: (1) Scripture; the primary, transcendent, 'other' source, (2) tradition; the mediating link and (3) the social context of black people. These are the moments through which the reformulation of christology must go. What is the precise shape of this reformulation? Here, once again, we need to recall Cone's emphasis on the historicity of Jesus. This emphasis is necessary not simply for the sake of history, but also because on history itself depends the humanity of Christ. Jesus' humanity in the concreteness of its self-expression (that is, in the ethnic specificity of its Jewishness) provides, at least for the present version of Black theology, the theological grounds for remoulding christology through a hermeneutic of blackness. So, the particularity of Jesus' ethnic identity – this irreducible mainstay of his humanity – allows Cone to say that if the christological significance of Jesus cannot be affirmed in terms of blackness, his resurrection is of little consequence for the twentieth century. Thus: 'It is on the basis of the soteriological meaning of the particularity of his Jewishness that theology must affirm the Christological significance of Jesus' present blackness. He is black because he was a Jew.'[73]

We must be careful to note here that Cone is not claiming that Jesus was biologically black, although he sometimes appears to want to say this;[74] rather his point seems to be that the experiences which characterised his (Jesus') life, being born a Jew, of an oppressed and despised people, and into an insignificant family, as well as his suffering at the hands of both the religious and political authorities, are capable of being apprehended through blackness today. Hence, when Cone declares, as he frequently does, that Christ is black, it is the idea of Christ's identification with the suffering of blacks caused by racism which is in the foreground, and not primarily the racial category of blackness.

Cone is aware that 'blackness' as a christological title may not be universally appropriate, but he points out that this is equally true of New Testament titles such as 'Son of God', 'Son of David' etc. Therefore to say Christ is black is not only to recognise the Jesus of history in the Jesus of faith and vice versa; it is also an indication that Black theology stands in a long tradition of naming Christ in terms of historical experience.

To sum up, christology cannot be reconstructed without regard for the historical specificity of Jesus' humanity; without regard for the social context which establishes his racial identity and thus identification with those who are negated because of their own racial identities. But, in turn, the christological importance of Jesus' humanity can itself not be properly construed except within the context of the kerygma of liberation.

## NOTES

1 J. H. Cone, *Martin and Malcolm and America: A Dream or a Nightmare.* (Maryknoll, NY, Orbis Books, 1991). Also by the same author: *For My People: Black Theology and the Black Church* (Maryknoll, NY, Orbis Books, 1984). L. V. Baldwin, *To Make The Wounded Whole: The Cultural Legacy of Martin*

*Luther King, Jr.* (Minneapolis, Fortress Press, 1992). For a collection of primary materials on the relationship between Black theology and the protest movements which inspired it see the papers collected in J. H. Cone and G. S. Wilmore (eds.), *Black Theology: A Documentary History* (Maryknoll, NY, Orbis Books, 1993), 2 vols. Vol. 1 covers the period from 1966 to 1979 and vol. 2 the period from 1980 to 1992. In this chapter I use the first single-volume edition of this work which was first published by Orbis in 1979. The second edition has been revised and contains new materials which do not affect the exposition of Black theology contained in this chapter.

2 Notable exceptions are T. Witvliet, *The Way of the Black Messiah* (London, SCM Press, 1987), and Rufus Burrow, Jr., *James H. Cone and Black Liberation Theology*, foreword by William Hanna (Jefferson, North Carolina, Mcfarland & Co., Inc., 1994).

3 'Black Theology: A Statement by the National Association of Black Churchmen, June 13, 1969'. In Cone and Wilmore (eds.), *Black Theology*, vol. 1.

4 J. H. Cone and G. S. Wilmore, 'Black Theology and African Theology: Considerations for Dialogue, Critique and Integration', in Cone and Wilmore (eds.), *Black Theology*, vol. 1, p. 468.

5 A good discussion on these issues can be found in the following: David Theo Goldberg, *Racist Culture: Philosophy and the Politics of Meaning* (Oxford, Blackwell Publishers, 1993); Kenan Malik, *The Meaning of Race: Race, History and Culture in Western Society* (New York, New York University Press, 1996); E. Chukwudi Eze, 1997, 'The Color of Reason: The Idea of "Race" in Kants's Anthropology', in E. Chukwudi Eze (ed.), *Post Colonial African Philosophy: A Critical Reader* (Cambridge, MA, Blackwell Publishers Inc., 1997), pp. 103–40.

6 It can be claimed, following certain interpreters of Cone's thought, that such a regulative principle is perhaps not unlike Paul Tillich's method of correlation set out at the beginning of the first volume of his *Systematic Theology*. Two very useful attempts to evaluate Cone's method in relation to Tillich's notion of 'correlation' are C. F. Stewart, III, 'The Method of Correlation in the Theology of James Cone', *Journal of Religious Thought* 40(2) (Fall/Winter 1983/84), pp. 27–38, and B. R. James, 'A Tillichian Analysis of James Cone's Black Theology', *Perspectives in Religious Studies* 1(1) (Spring 1974), pp. 27–38.

7 J. H. Cone, 1975, *God of the Oppressed* (New York, Seabury Press, 1975), p. 39.

8 J. H. Cone, 'The Content and Method of Black Theology', *Journal of Religious Thought* 32(2) (Fall/Winter 1975), pp. 90–103, esp. p. 100.

9 J. H. Cone, Remarks in 'Excerpts from a Symposium of the World Council of Churches on Black Theology and Latin American Liberation Theology' held in Geneva, May 1973. Published in Cone and Wilmore, *Black Theology*, p. 514 (see note 1 above).

10 Cone, *God of the Oppressed*, p. 10.

11 Ibid.

12 On Black religion see G. S. Wilmore, 1983. *Black Religion and Black Radicalism: An Interpretation of the Religious History of Afro-American People* (Maryknoll, NY, Orbis Books, 1983).

13 In his essay 'The Content and Method of Black Theology' (1975) pp. 91ff., Cone makes a series of contrasts between white American theology and black religion

meant to highlight the sociological as well as theological differences between the two. Thus where white theology concerns itself with logical systems, black religion concerns itself with narrative, the telling of story; where whites forced a wedge between thought and practice and worship and theology, blacks united them; whilst white theology sought to demonstrate the existence of God, blacks took that existence for granted. All these differences were due to the social position of blacks as slaves. Their concerns were more urgent and more practical than those of their masters. Hence they had to produce a language commensurate with their situation.

14 Cone, *God of the Oppressed*, pp. 46ff.
15 Some of the biographical aspects which have shaped Cone's approach to Black theology can be found in his *My Soul Looks Back* (Maryknoll, NY, Orbis Books, 1986).
16 Cone, *God of the Oppressed*, p. vi.
17 Cone and Wilmore, 'Black Theology and African Theology', in Cone and Wilmore (eds.), *Black Theology*, p. 468.
18 On the effects of racism on the self-consciousness of blacks as blacks see Franz Fanon, 1990, 'The Fact of Blackness', in David Theo Goldberg (ed.), *Anatomy of Racism* (Minneapolis, University of Minnesota Press, 1990), pp. 108–26.
19 For example, Jacquelyn Grant, *White Women's Christ and Black Women's Jesus: Feminist Christology and Womanist Response* (Atalanta, Scholars Press, 1989); also Katie G. Cannon, *Black Womanist Ethics* (Atalanta, Scholars Press, 1988).
20 J. H. Cone, *A Black Theology of Liberation*, 20th Anniversary edn (New York, Orbis Books, 1990), p. 7.
21 Ibid. For a critical discussion of Cone's dependence on Tillich's use of the concept of 'symbol' see Witvlict, *The Way of the Black Messiah*, pp. 173–7.
22 Cf. John L. Hodge, 'Equality: Beyond Dualism and Oppression', in Goldberg (ed.), *Anatomy of Racism*, pp. 89–107.
23 See, for example, Floya Anthias, 'Race and Class Revisited: Conceptualizing Race and Racisms', *The Sociological Review* 38(1) (February 1990), pp. 19–42, esp. p. 20.
24 Deotis Roberts, 'A Creative Response to Racism: Black Theology', in Gregory Baum and John Coleman (eds.), *Concilium: The Church and Racism* (Edinburgh: T&T Clark, 1982), p. 38. See also his *Black Theology Today: Liberation and Contextualization*, Toronto Studies in Theology, vol. 12 (New York, The Edwin Mellen Press, 1983).
25 Cone, *A Black Theology of Liberation*, p. 84.
26 Choan Seng Song, 1979, 'The Black Experience of the Exodus', in Cone and Wilmore (eds.), *Black Theology*, p. 580. Cf. the NCBC statement of 1976 (1979), p. 343.
27 Desmond Tutu, (1979), 'Black Theology/African Theology', in Cone and Wilmore (eds.), *Black Theology*, pp. 483–4.
28 Cone, *A Black Theology of Liberation*, pp. 11–12.
29 Roberts, 'A Creative Response to Racism', in Baum and Coleman (eds.), *Concilium*, pp. 38–9.
30 Cone, *A Black Theology of Liberation*, pp. 159ff.

31 In *My Soul Looks Back* Cone speaks of freedom as a responsibility to liberate, something to be taken against the will of the oppressor.

32 Cone, *A Black Theology of Liberation*, pp. 165–8.

33 Ibid. See the second edition published in 1986, p. 94.

34 Ibid., p. 154.

35 J. H. Cone, *Black Theology and Black Power* (New York, Seabury Press, 1969), p. 32.

36 Ibid., p. 120.

37 Ibid.

38 Ibid., p. 117.

39 Ibid., pp. 117–18.

40 Cone, *A Black Theology of Liberation*, pp. 47–8.

41 Cone, *God of the Oppressed*, pp. 17–18.

42 The problem here is accentuated if we recall Thiemann's discussion in his *Theology and Revelation: The Gospel As Narrated Promise* (Notre Dame, IN, University of Notre Dame Press, 1985) in which the search for the prevenience of God is central. Compare the radicalism of Barth's idea concerning our knowledge of God. See *Church Dogmatics: The Doctrine of God*, ed. G. W. Bromiley and trans. T. F. Torrance (Edinburgh, T&T Clark, 1957), 2.1:40ff.

43 Cone, *A Black Theology of Liberation*, pp. 82 and 85.

44 Ibid., p. 50.

45 Ibid., p. 75.

46 Ibid., p. 52.

47 Ibid., pp. 54ff.

48 Ibid., pp. 57–60.

49 On the relationship between the Harlem Renaissance and Black theology see Roy D. Morrison II, 'Self Transformation in American Blacks: The Harlem Renaissance and Black Theology', in Lewis R. Gordon (ed.), *Existence in Black: An Anthology of Black Existential Philosophy* (New York, Routledge, 1997), pp. 37–47.

50 Cone, *A Black Theology of Liberation*, p. 64.

51 Ibid., pp. 90–1.

52 Ibid., p. 91. Cf. Cone and Wilmore, *Black Theology*, p. 467.

53 Ibid., p. 65.

54 Ibid., p. 24.

55 Ibid., p. 85. Cone has been taken to task by Preston Williams in his paper 'James Cone and the Problem of a Black Ethic', *Harvard Theological Review* 65, (October 1972), pp. 483–94. Williams says Cone's identification of God's intention for humanity with the black community is not based on empirical fact; its exclusivist claims invite us to jettison rational debate and argument because important aspects of Cone's thought are based on an arbitrary reading of God's acts in history. He urges that in Cone we should recover the universal dimension rather than place emphasis on exclusive loyalty to the black community: p. 488. Compare this with Dussel's remark, 'Totalization means the identification of the church with the temporal state or culture. All totalization is sin': E. Dussel, *Ethics and the Theology of Liberation* (Maryknoll, NY, Orbis Books, 1978), p. 65.

56 On instrumentalisation and ideology see J. L. Segundo, *Faith and Ideologies*, trans. John Drury (Maryknoll, NY, Orbis Books, 1984). According to Segundo '. . . the most common and perhaps primitive function of explicit and recordable religions has been "ideological" in my sense of the term . . . they have served as instruments for any and every class of values.' Religion, in other words, is used as a tool to attain values that are 'independent of the god who is adopted and adored': pp. 38ff.

57 In his later works Cone appears to have changed his mind somewhat for he now says: 'Also the white churches of Europe and North America have presented an enormous theological challenge to my understanding of the gospel. Although I have been critical of them, the criticism was meant to be prophetic and not cynical. I firmly believe that the gospel is available to all – including white people.' *My Soul Looks Back*, p. 13.

58 It must be remembered that Cone did his doctorate on Barth's theological anthropology. See *My Soul Looks Back*.

59 Cone, *A Black Theology of Liberation*, p. 66.

60 Cone and Wilmore, *Black Theology*, p. 467.

61 See, for example, *God of the Oppressed* and *Black Theology and Black Power*.

62 For a helpful philosophical critique of Cone's theology including his use of the Exodus see W. R. Jones, 'Theodicy: The Controlling Category for Black Theology', *Journal of Religious Thought*, 30 (1973–74), pp. 28–38.

63 Cone, *God of the Oppressed*, pp. 62–72.

64 Without recanting his earlier position Cone now says, 'It was this universalism in the gospel that prevented me from elevating the black experience or the African reality to an absolute norm in black theology . . . we must never absolutize a particular struggle (whether black, African, Asian or Latin) to the exclusion of others': *My Soul Looks Back*, p. 99. It is hard to believe that Cone's earlier remarks about the absoluteness of black experience did not have the effect that he is now trying to avoid here. If Cone was sufficiently convinced of the universality of the gospel it is strange that these qualifications were not introduced then. It is also strange that he does not discuss the way in which they relate to his earlier position.

65 Two interesting attempts at writing full-blown christologies using a Black theology paradigm are T. Mofokeng, *The Crucified Among the Cross Bearers: Towards a Black Christology* (Kok-Kampen, Uitgeversmaatschappj J. H., 1983) and Kelly Douglas Brown, 1994, *The Black Christ* (Maryknoll, NY, Orbis Books, 1994).

66 Cone, *A Black Theology of Liberation*, pp. 212–13.

67 Cone, *Black Theology and Black Power*, p. 40.

68 Cone, *A Black Theology of Liberation*, pp. 202ff.

69 Ibid., p. 210.

70 Ibid., p. 203.

71 Ibid., p. 205.

72 Ibid., p. 210.

73 Cone, *God of the Oppressed*, p. 134. Cf. A. B. Cleage, Jr., *The Black Messiah* (New York, Sheed and Ward, 1968).

74 In *God of the Oppressed*, for example, he writes: 'Christ's blackness is both literal and symbolic. His blackness is literal in the sense that he truly becomes One with the oppressed blacks, taking their suffering as his suffering and revealing that he is found in the history of our struggle, the story of our pain and the rhythm of our bodies' (p. 136). One suspects that behind this rather ambiguous racial biologisation of christology lies a crude notion of the nature of race and racism.

# 5

MARY GREY

# Feminist theology: a critical theology of liberation

Feminist theology is a global theology, or rather, a family of contextual theologies committed to the struggle for justice for women and the transformation of society. It is therefore a critical theology of liberation[1] engaged in the reconstruction of theology and religion in the service of this transformation process, in the specificity of the many contexts in which women live. Whereas in European and North American contexts the term 'feminist theology' is most frequently accepted, in other parts of the globe, in order to heighten visibility, recognise identity and respect the diversity of experiences and goals, the different theologies of Asian, African and Latin American women have acquired their own distinctiveness, together with Womanist theology (the theology of the United States black American women and women of colour),[2] and Mujerista theology (the liberation theology of Hispanic women).[3] Increasingly emergent is the spirituality of, for example, indigenous American Indian women and indigenous Indian women in Latin America, as well as of aboriginal women in Australia, New Zealand and the Pacific.

If there is a commonality of purpose in all this diversity, it is the liberation of humankind together with all sentient life. The words of the American poet Adrienne Rich are widely inspirational:

> My heart is touched by all I cannot save;
> So much has been destroyed
> I have to cast my lot in with those who
> with no extraordinary power
> re-constitute the world.[4]

Here, after charting the origins of such diverse theologies, I will describe feminist theologies in a four-pronged method, namely, as *new awareness*, *new academic discipline*, *new culture and ethic*, and *new spiritual quest*.[5]

## New awareness

The origins of feminist theology in the Northern Hemisphere are usually associated with the secular feminist movement which followed the Universal Declaration of Human Rights at the end of the eighteenth century with the struggle for equal rights for women.[6] It is generally maintained that the nineteenth-century movement lost its momentum after suffrage for women was achieved in 1920, became quiescent, and revived in the 1960s although many would dispute this analysis[7] which certainly does not fit the experience of women in the Southern Hemisphere. The early movement was strongly influenced by such works as Mary Wollstonecraft's *On the Vindication of the Rights of Women* (1792). This liberal feminist agenda had a twofold aim: it focused on the historical exclusion of women from the spheres where men, traditionally, held power – political, economic, educational and religious – and aimed, first, to dismantle the historical structures of patriarchal laws which denied women rights, and second, to achieve equal access for women to all these spheres.[8] This became the focus in the United States, and there, from the beginning, religious women were prominent in the leadership: especially active in the movement were such figures as Elizabeth Cady Stanton, author of the *Women's Bible Project*,[9] the Grimké sisters, Susan B. Anthony and Matilda Jocelyn Gage.[10] Though the struggle for the vote was achieved for white women in 1920, the fact that black women were not included caused a deep rift between black and white women which, sadly, is not yet healed.

Even at this early stage it was felt that the Equal Rights Agenda did not address the complexity of women's experience; the nineteenth-century split between public and private spheres of life also disguised hidden areas of oppression in the home. Thus *Romantic feminism* – characterised by the slogan 'The Rising of the Woman is the Rising of the Race' – focuses on a presumed superiority of women in the private sphere and the qualities of caring, tenderness and nurture which women are supposed to both symbolise and embody. (This tendency is frequently caricatured as the 'Angel in the House' symbol).[11] What is needed, says Romantic feminism, is for these qualities to transform public life, characterised as it is by a male, competitive and aggressive culture. Its most essentialist form appears as the 'eternal feminine', which attributes the above-mentioned qualities to women as part of a divinely-ordered creation.[12] Rosemary Radford Ruether classifies Romantic feminism in three types – as conservative, as reformist, (reforming society through 'feminine' attributes), and the radical/separatist strand, which repudiates male culture for the 'utopian world of the good female'.[13] Although this type is still manifested in feminist theology, it remains problematic in lacking an analytic framework for understanding women's place in the social structures, as well as resting on an essentialist understanding of gender.

*Radical or separatist* feminism, resting on the belief that the person is political, rejects the patriarchal culture of domination/submission, challenges traditional notions of family and romantic love as means to control the identity and lives of women for patriarchal ends, and develops an alternative woman-identified culture. Thus radical feminism has exposed the violent means used to control women – such as rape, pornography and domestic violence – and claims that the structure of the patriarchal family and motherhood as institution arose over the securing of inheritance rights. It celebrates women's culture and space and aims to liberate from male-controlled spaces. But in so doing it fails to address the many other oppressions from which both women and men suffer, for example, those of class, race and heterosexism.

Therefore socialist feminism insists on a class analysis and criticises radical feminism for its lack of attention to these factors. Not only does it challenge the equal rights agenda and seek to articulate a much more comprehensive analysis of women's oppression, but it focuses on the sexual division of work as its central but not as its exclusive lens. Socialist feminism asserts that *neither liberalism nor Marxism is enough*. The structural analysis of work conditions outside the home exclusively, renders the economic basis of women's *reproductive* work invisible. Women are productive and reproductive and the whole area of housework and child-rearing, of responsibility for the home and care for the elderly, should be taken into the struggle for juster structural relationships between women and men.

Feminist theologies reflect all these strands of secular feminism: indeed they are dependent on and in dialogue with the analyses of secular feminism. The growing realisation that the concept of the human subject, the familiar 'man', was gender-blind – now uncovered in anthropology, sociology, psychology, philosophy, literature and the sciences – was the catalyst for the development of feminist theology as a new consciousness and a new awareness.

It was an awareness that the religions, too, operated with this gender-blindness, and that the Christian churches failed to promote the full humanity of women in their structures of theology, and what was worse, legitimised the subordination and victimisation of women by recourse to Scripture and tradition to show that this was the part of God's plan for creation. Hence it is not enough, as Elizabeth Schüssler Fiorenza writes, for the work of feminist theology to *understand* the sacred texts in their historical settings. Tradition is also 'a source of untruth, repression and domination'.[14] Feminist theology's task is therefore twofold: to uncover the theologies and institutional practices which perpetuate the injustices inflicted on women and deny their full human subjectivity; and constructively, to create a *liberated and liberating* theology. Thus whether feminist theologians stay within the churches – and many women have a deep, abiding loyalty to and hope for the Church[15] – or choose to leave because, for them, the inherited patriarchal tradition is irredeemably sexist (the position of, for example, Daphne Hampson, Mary Daly and Carol Christ), there is a common focus on theology as the *praxis of transformation.*[16]

For many Roman Catholic feminists – such as Rosemary Radford Ruether, Elizabeth Schüssler Fiorenza, Mary Daly and Catherine Halkes – the dawn of the new consciousness coincided with the Second Vatican Council (1962–5). Mary Daly describes (in *The Church and the Second Sex*[17]) how the wind of change which the council documents inaugurated created enormous hope that the injustice inflicted on women through the centuries would be replaced by the just structural relationships between women and men in the Church.[18] The emphasis on the Church as the *people of God*, the emphasis on the mission of baptism for every Christian, the dignity of the lay apostolate, for example, raised the expectations of women. Correspondingly, the disillusionment which followed was the catalyst for many women leaving the Church. But for many other women – from all denominations – the consciousness-raising process began earlier and owes much to the ecumenical work of the World Council of Churches since its foundation in 1948.[19] Much of the early work was therefore achieved in the context for the struggle for the ordination of women[20] although built in from the beginning of the process were the wider issues of justice for women on a world-wide scale as the programme 'The Community of Women and Men in the Church' witnesses.[21] There was also from the beginning an awareness that context made a difference to the articulation of feminist theology, and serious attempts began to make the connections between feminist theology and liberation theology.[22] On a European level there are two networks where women theologians are active – in a more or less explicitly feminist way, although this is sometimes disputed – namely, the European Ecumenical Forum of Christian Women (EFECW), and the European Society of Women in Theological Research (ESWTR). The latter, which held its first Conference at Magliaso in Switzerland in 1985, now publishes a *Jarhbuch*, of which the first volume was devoted to *Feminist Theology in a European Context* (1993), and the second to *Ecofeminism and Theology*.[23] Its special focus is the struggle of women in theology both in academic institutions and working as independent scholars, and with that in mind the Society holds biennial conferences, the different regions organising their own networks.

There is an attempt to work in a broadly based manner beyond Christian theology, to include Jewish and Islamic scholars: for four years the Society had a Jewish vice-President, Dr Evelyn Goodman-Thau from Jerusalem. The Forum is more rooted in the Christian Churches of Europe: it holds an Assembly every four years, and maintains networks on a very wide scale across Europe. Since 1989 it has made valuable links with the women in the churches of Eastern Europe. The third networking is a European Synod of Women. The first event, which gathered more than a thousand women together, took place at Gmünden, Austria, and further events are planned.

But women from the Southern Hemisphere followed a different process which is usually associated with the development of the Ecumenical Association of Third World Theologians (EATWOT).[24] EATWOT's birth in 1976 had been preceded by a decade of heightening awareness of the common problems of 'Third World' countries, politically, economically and socio-culturally. The actual association, which began in Dar es Salaam in 1976, had as its aim, 'the continuing development of Third World Christian theologies which will serve the church's mission in the world and witness to the new humanity in Christ expressed in the struggle for a just society'.[25] Its theology was from the beginning contextual, liberational, and ecumenical and the primacy of praxis was its hallmark. But the real breakthrough for women did not come until EATWOT's fifth conference in New Delhi, in 1981. As Virginia Fabella relates, the women felt that their contribution was not taken seriously, that

> despite the supportive statements regarding women's equality and the declarations against sexism in all the past conference documents, the reality was different. Both disturbed and disappointed, the EATWOT women decided it was time to demand their rightful place not only in society but in the association as well. Oduyoye [Mercy Amba Oduyoye from Ghana, MG] referred to this as the 'eruption within the eruption' in her assessment of the Delhi event.[26]

This eruption had an influence on the final statement of the Delhi Conference. Clause 7 of the statement reads: 'Just as the experience of the Third World as a true source for theology must be taken seriously, so also must the common experience of women in their liberational struggle be taken seriously' (p. 30). In 1983 the EATWOT Women's Commission was born and a process of work in four phases inaugurated, from national, to continental, to intercontinental and to global in 1987. This final phase was envisaged as a dialogue between First and Third World women, a dialogue which finally took place at Costa Rica in December 1994.[27]

The women theologians from each regional group expressed the emphases of their theology distinctively: for example, the Latin American theologians characterised liberation theology from women's perspective as unifying, relational, free (with the freedom of those who have nothing to lose), marked by humour, joy and celebration and filled with a spirituality of hope. The Asian women began the characterisation of their theology by denouncing oppression of women as systemic sin, and accusing both theology and the churches as having contributed to the subjugation and marginalisation of women and of having 'blurred the image of God that we are'; further that the bias against women in the Christian tradition is buttressed by male-oriented Asian beliefs. But just as they uncovered the hidden realities of faith which oppressed women, so they rediscovered empowering elements of gospel faith and expressed solidarity with all oppressed peoples. Among the resolutions emerging from the two meetings of African women theologians in 1986 were the commitment to participate in the holistic human development to eliminate the life-denying developments in Church and society, and to work towards eliminating racism, abject poverty and the neglect of rural areas, in a theological framework in which men and women together image God and neither is complete without the other. After this historic development, feminist theology could not be articulated without the voices of Third World women. The awareness that 'the maps they gave us were out of date' (the phrase is Adrienne Rich's),[28] the need for new cartographies to map the categories of thinking about the human person, has evolved to a complex and continuing process as yet more pieces of the jigsaw come to light, as more of the suppressed voices are 'heard into speech'.[29]

Alongside Mujerista theology – the distinctive theology arising from Hispanic women in the United States[30] and their experience of being forced into being a permanent underclass – womanist theology continues to grow in stature as a powerful voice for the experience of black women in the United States. Owing its name to Alice Walker's phrase in *In Search of our Mothers' Gardens*, 'womanist' is defined as

> 1. From womanish (Opp. of 'girlish' i.e. frivolous, irresponsible, not serious). A black feminist or feminist of color. From the black folk expression of mothers to female children, 'you acting womanish' . . . Usually referring to outrageous, audacious, courageous or willful behavior. Wanting to know more and in greater depth than is good for one . . . Responsible. In charge. Serious. 2. Also: a woman who loves other women, sexually and/or nonsexually. Appreciates and prefers women's culture, women's emotional flexibility . . . Committed to survival and wholeness of whole people, male and female.[31]

Womanist theology has a double origin. It distinguishes itself from Black theology, because it claims that black men did not include black women in their analysis. But it also distinguishes itself from Euro-American feminist theology, which, it claims, ignores the realities of race and class in its agenda, reducing the oppression of women to sexism alone. White women, say the womanist theologians, do suffer from oppression *qua* women; but vis-à-vis black women they are privileged because of the benefits which whiteness, and often class privilege, bring in a racist, unequal society. Thus, writes Emilie Townes, 'the most common understanding of womanist is that she is a woman committed to an integrated analysis of race, gender, class ... Womanist thought is intentionally and unapologetically biassed. Its bias is for a diverse and faithful community of witnesses.'[32]

The second distinctive feature of womanist theology is its anchor in the Black Church. The social structure, the world-views of the people, the very life of the Church, 'all are resources and guardians of communal memory and accountability. Academic theological discourse is also a part of womanist reflection and thought.'[33] This is in sharp contrast with Western feminism, with its secular roots and the many situations of estrangement between women and institutional Christian Church.

## Academic discipline

Feminist theology as an academic discipline has a somewhat varied career. Like all theologies of liberation, it attempts to keep its anchor and roots in the grassroots struggle; as such it runs into the Scylla of being considered ephemeral, lightweight, of being a 'changeling in the academy',[34] substituting a biased kind of activism for solid theology; on the other hand it runs into the Charybdis of being accused of over-intellectualising, of losing touch with the grassroots, when it engages with feminist theory from such disciplines as psychoanalysis, literary criticism, philosophy, history and anthropology. But it is when the feminist theological analysis manages to keep in a creative tension both with feminist theory and with the many struggles of women against oppression, that it is at its most authentic. As a critical theology of liberation there is no discipline of traditional theology to which it does not make a contribution. This contribution has become sophisticated and diverse in the last twenty years, for example, in Biblical Studies. From a rather naive initial attempt to highlight the forgotten or hidden stories of biblical women, three distinct types of interpretations have emerged.

The first, which might be called the literary-critical approach (illustrated by, for example, Phyllis Trible[35]), focuses on the androcentric nature of individual literary units of the Bible, 'cleans them up' and tries to present them as liberating for women. Important as this may be, the approach ignores the androcentric, patriarchal and oppressive context in which the entire text was produced.

The second approach – characteristic of Rosemary Radford Ruether, Letty Russell, Carter Heyward, and many others – privileges a certain strand of the Bible over against others, namely the 'prophetic-messianic dimension' with which, so Ruether claims, the Bible constantly critiques itself, recalling itself to God's authentic purposes for humanity. Ruether places Jesus in this same prophetic tradition: Jesus is the *kenosis* of patriarchy: Christic personhood goes before us, constantly calling humanity to yet more liberating forms of relation.[36] This approach – with which I am in considerable sympathy – yet encounters the difficulty that it arbitrarily discounts large chunks of the Bible as not belonging to the inner 'liberating core'.

The third approach, of which Elizabeth Schüssler Fiorenza is the most famous exponent, simply assumes that the Bible is thoroughly androcentric in origin and production. Yet Fiorenza acknowledges the ambiguity of the Bible functioning in *both* oppressive and liberating ways in the lives of women. Using a criterion derived from the contemporary struggle of women for liberation, she identifies what is liberating in the Jesus movement of the first century as in its deepest intuition promoting the full humanity of women in Christian community as 'Discipleship of Equals'.[37] Although the patriarchal structure of the household was soon to stifle the leadership role of women in the first flowering of the Christian Church, Fiorenza claims that this basic intuition was never totally lost. It is the task of feminist biblical hermeneutics of liberation to recover and restore women to their egalitarian position within Christian community and society through a four-pronged method of a hermeneutic of *suspicion*, of *proclamation*, of *remembrance*, and of *creative actualisation*.[38] The crucial importance of reclaiming biblical traditions in the service of achieving just relations between women and men in the Church as a whole cannot be over-emphasised. Here the interface between feminist theology as an academic discipline and as a grassroots movement is abundantly clear for both feminist and womanist theology. For example, the figure of Miriam has become significant as reclaiming the lost prophetic leadership role of women.[39] But for womanist theology the person of Hagar is crucial, symbolising the woman who is rejected on the grounds of race, sex and class, yet at the same time is the recipient of a divine revelation.[40]

When it comes to the area of doctrine, the same dialectic is observed between the lives and experiences of women and the structures of systematic theology. Unsurprisingly, there has been much attention to the meaning of the person of Christ. Feminist theology stresses the fundamental importance of the incarnation of God in Christ as *human*, rather than Christ as male, although it has to be said that the maleness of Christ does not present the same problem for womanist theology, where the symbolic force of Jesus as *suffering brother in the struggle*, regardless of his gender, is a more empowering symbol. As the richness of the contextual diversity of feminist theology develops, the plurality of christologies is a rich resource.[41] Another focus is the revealing of the connections between central doctrines and the suffering of women. It is not the doctrines of redemption and atonement, or the cross of Christ as such which are seen as problematic, but their dominant interpretations which are seen as legitimating the suffering and expiatory role of women.[42] The method of feminist theology is twofold: a critique (Mary Daly's term is *castration*) of the patriarchal dualist categories of classical theology, and an alternative constructive movement built on anti-dualist, liberating, justice-making categories, which express the key notions of revelation in *embodied* terms, directly relating to the diverse experiences of women, as the poorest of the poor, and therefore the direct focus of the ministry of Jesus and the justice of the Kingdom of God. From the very beginning, the predominantly male categories of theology were felt to be a stumbling-block to the full humanity of women: not only the maleness of Jesus, but maleness as *constitutive of divinity*: 'If God is male, then the male is God', as Mary Daly proclaimed.[43] It is the link between privileging maleness as more intrinsically Godlike – witnessed to by the intransigent hanging on to exclusive language in the liturgy – and the legitimation of structures which dominate women, both domestically and in the societal structures, which has been consistently highlighted by feminist theology.[44] Elizabeth Schüssler Fiorenza even uses the term *kyriarchal* – which better expresses the rule of domination legitimated by patriarchy.[45]

But it would be false to suppose that feminist theologians simplistically replace a Father with a Mother God. Rather, the many strands of feminist theology tend towards imaging God as relational – the Trinity is conceived as a God in dynamic movement, as the archetype for just relationality[46] – as the power to make right relation,[47] as Sophia, Wisdom, and with a variety of titles, such as Mother, Friend, Lover, Sister.[48] The concept of a God who suffers with the pain of women and all broken people is very much to the fore: 'God weeps with our pain', as the Chinese theologian Kwok Pui Lan wrote.[49] Even when God is called Mother, this is not simply a new essentialising of the experience of motherhood: it is both a highlighting of this strand already present in the Christian tradition, a valorising of the embodied experience of women, calling attention to the role of mothers as culture bearers, as bearers of tradition, and also to the symbolism of the sorrowing mother: *God as mother cradles the pain of all generations.* It is the pluralism of images, metaphors and concepts of God which is most manifest in feminist theology, and particularly vital are the non-personal images derived from the mystical tradition and those images which call into being the becoming of women. 'I found God in myself, and I loved her, I loved her fiercely', was the famous line from Ntosake Shange's play which was so popular on Broadway.[50] This is not a call to self-indulgence, but a rediscovery of the immanent God: as Catherine Keller wrote, making the connections between the vital presence of the God within and the ethical project of theology: 'If we meet God in ourselves, we meet her at the molten core of heart's desire, energising our courage and our quest.'[51] In seeking this relational, inclusive, suffering God, beyond rigid, exclusive, masculinist conceptions, feminist theology unmasks the links between certain interpretations of the atonement and death of Jesus which serve to legitimate the suffering and victim status of women.[52]

## A new ethic and a new culture

Feminist theology as the search for a new ethic and a new culture resists the logic of domination/submission of patriarchy. Although there is a sharp focus on ethical issues which contribute to the oppression of women – in particular, the many forms of violence against women – there is a more profound project of transforming the culture of violence into a culture which affirms and celebrates life. Whereas there have been attempts to construct an ethics based on a rather essentialised view of female human nature, for example Carol Gilligan's 'ethic of care',[53] there is far more focus on an ethic transcending the dualisms of patriarchy. Sharon Welch calls this 'an ethic of risk', which refuses to give way to 'the culture despair of the middle classes' and which is able to celebrate limits, contingency and ambiguity.[54] The final statement of the Costa Rica dialogue called for an alternative anthropological discourse to ground this theo-ethical project and stressed its deeply spiritual nature:

> Resisting violence is a deeply spiritual work interwoven with the struggle for life. We must deconstruct theologies of the spirit that devalue physical life, especially life as symbolised in the bodies, and particularly in the sexuality, of women. Spirit/body dualism must be reconstructed toward a whole life energy of resisting, renewing, sustaining healing and growing. Such a spirituality of and for life is continually being renewed not only through our experiences of work and struggle, but also through those of prayer, contemplation, and communion in worship and action. [55]

This shows how the task of reconstructing the ethical basis of culture is deeply related to the fourth dimension of the feminist theological project, namely the spiritual quest.

## The spiritual quest

The very fact that the Costa Rica dialogue was titled 'A Spirituality for Life' indicates the crucial nature of the spiritual quest for feminist theology. Feminist spirituality, writes Katherine Zappone, 'may be simply defined as the *praxis of imaging a whole world*. Such praxis depends on the lived experience of mutually supportive relations between self, others, God and nature.'[56] The spiritual quest begins with the new, heightened awareness that, as I have written, *the maps they gave us were out of date*. It begins, Carol Christ has written, with an experience of *nothingness* . . . that women have no real identity, but simply reflect the identity which others have given them. Feminist spirituality (-ies) rejects all dualistic splits between matter and spirit which have dogged traditional spiritualities. It is an embodied spirituality, embodied in the specificity of the lived daily realities of women's lives, with all the diversity which this brings. Thus the spiritual quest is embarked upon across the world faiths, in Islam, Buddhism, Judaism, Hinduism, Sikhism and so on.[57] But it is also embarked on in what has been called a post-Christian direction. For example, goddess-based spirituality invokes the memory and active presence of the ancient earth-goddesses, in particular Isis, Cybele, Demeter, Astarte, Ceridwen, Aphrodite and so on. And these are merely to cite one tradition: African, Afro-Caribbean, Indian, Japanese, Chinese and Latin American women are actively reclaiming the goddess traditions of their own cultures as part of their own burgeoning spiritualities.[58] In addition, the Wicca or witchcraft movement, often associated with the name of Starhawk, evokes the power of the ancient goddess as inspiration for its rituals of healing, celebration of the seasons, and ethical lifestyle based on respect for the earth and bodily rhythms:

> 'Wicca' are the wise ones, the women priestesses, diviners, midwives, poets, healers and singers of power. Starhawk maintains that a woman-centred culture based on the worship of the Great Goddess underlies the beginnings of all great civilisations. For her and her followers, the old religion of witchcraft, or 'the craft of the wise', was handed down in the covens of Europe where the mythology and rituals of ancient, mother-centered times, were preserved through the age of persecutions.[59]

'The Goddess' has many meanings in feminist spirituality and is not unproblematic. Carol Christ, in a now famous article, has distinguished three dimensions of 'the Return of the Goddess'.[60] The first is the goddess as divine female, who really exists (in different cultural manifestations), and can be invoked in prayer and ritual. The next two interpretations see the Goddess primarily as symbol

> rather than metaphysical reality; she symbolises above all life, death and rebirth energy in nature and culture, in personal and communal life. The third view also understands the Goddess as a symbol, but reads it differently as affirming above all the legitimacy and beauty of female power, made possible by the new becoming of women in the women's liberation movement.[61]

This last interpretation makes clear why the Goddess movement has become crucial for many women in their search for identity and self-affirmation, as the already cited title of Ntosake Shange's play has made clear.[62] Criticism of the many goddess movements has been on the grounds of a 'lapse into neo-paganism' or accusations of nostalgia for a supposed Golden Age of matriarchy which possibly never existed,[63] or because the Goddess movement distracts attention from the social and political challenge of feminism, or even because it encourages self-indulgence, as 'women snuggle up into the arms of the goddess' (Elizabeth Moltmann-Wendel), or a trivialising of the (serious) feminist agenda. No doubt there is an element of truth in many of these criticisms, as there is also an element of hysteria and exaggeration. Starhawk, for example, has a very earnest ethical project for a peaceful, non-violent culture which emerges from her commitment to the Wicca movement.[64] The criticism of self-indulgence seems to me equally applicable to many of the current, narcissistic spiritualities of the 'me generation'. What is beyond dispute, is both that the quest for the Goddess can never be more than one dimension of an embodied, non-dualistic, justice-seeking spirituality for women, and that it has stimulated the search within the established religions – Christianity, Judaism, Hinduism, Buddhism and Sikhism – if not for actual goddesses, for traditions which affirmed the leadership and contributions of women which had been 'forgotten' or obliterated from 'mainstream' versions.

Of special significance in Christian feminism is the spirituality associated with the Women Church.[65] Rosemary Radford Ruether sees this as an exodus, not from the institutional Church, but from patriarchy. Women Church – a global movement of women seeking authentic ecclesial communities of justice – is in voluntary exile from patriarchy, is dynamic and speaks the prophetic word for our times. Mary Jo Weaver describes the movement's origin in 1983, when 1400 Catholic women met at Grailville in the USA and declared themselves to be Woman Church (later Women Church). Since then the movement has become global, ecumenical and interfaith in character.[66] Elizabeth Schüssler Fiorenza understands the roots of this *ecclesia of women* to be planted in the very origins of Christianity: in her reconstruction of the history of women in early Christianity, in a vision of the Church as *discipleship of equals*, she finds inspiration for a new praxis of ecclesial community today. Mary Hunt has defined her vision of Women Church as 'base-communities of justice – seeking friends who come together to share word and sacrament'.[67] In The Netherlands the grassroots movement *Vrouw en Geloof* (Women and Faith) functions as a Women Church movement, which either focuses on ritual and symbol, or is a more action-based group. I prefer the term *Beloved Community*, because I want somehow to recapture the sense of vision of early Christianity and combine this with recent justice-based movements – like that of Martin Luther King.[68]

Women Church is neither a new Church nor an exodus from the established churches and religions. It is both an attempt to make it clear, after years of being marginalised from church structures, that *women are church*, and to recover authentic inclusive, justice-based communities, responding to the reality that within the present structures, many women and men receive no nurture in faith: as Rosemary Radford Ruether wrote:

> Women in contemporary Churches are suffering from linguistic deprivation and eucharistic famine. They can no longer nurture their souls in alienating words that ignore or systematically deny their existence . . . Their call for new communities of faith and ritual assumes that existing institutional churches do not have a monopoly on the words of truth and the power of salvation.[69]

Again, the Women Church movement is only one expression of the contemporary spiritual quest of women. Whether this is expressed through the creation of healing, transforming rituals using new symbols, or recovering lost images (for example those of the female mystics); whether it is expressed through a new lifestyle, caring for and affirming the sacredness of the earth, its rhythms and seasons, as in many ecofeminist groups; whether its inspiration is 'a passion for justice-making' – the phrase is Carter Heyward's,[70] – attempting to speak the prophetic word in the face of global poverty and violence; or, finally, whether it is expressed through a new mysticism, God being experienced in the political struggle, in nature, as mother or Sophia – Wisdom – or through the female mystics of the tradition, there is a global awakening of women's spirituality which is a powerful response to secularism and to the fact that human spiritual hunger cannot be quenched. As the women in Costa Rica affirmed, spirituality in its basic meaning is *life itself*.

But these four dimensions which I have explored – new awareness, new discipline, new ethic and culture and spiritual quest – are not separable categories, capable of hard and fast definitions. Feminist theology's authenticity is its openness to the challenge of new contexts, its ability to resist foreclosure, and its commitment to the working out of the theological implications of new forms of oppression. (There will inevitably be an ongoing symphony of liberation but sadly, like Schubert's, it is unfinished.) The implications of contextuality, diversity, pluralism and the global need for justice mean that our work is only beginning.

## NOTES

1 This phrase is the title of a ground-breaking article in the definition of feminist theology and its method(s), namely, Elizabeth Schüssler Fiorenza, 'Feminist Theology as a Critical Theology of Liberation', in *Theological Studies* (1975), pp. 606–26; reprinted with new introduction in *Discipleship of Equals* (New York, Crossroads, 1993), pp. 53–79.
2 See Delores Williams, 'Womanist Theology: Black Women's Voices', in Ursula King (ed.), *Feminist Theology from the Third World, A Reader* (London, SPCK, 1994), pp. 77–86.
3 See Ada Maria Isasi-Diaz, 'The Task of Hispanic Women's Liberation Theology – Mujeristas: Who We Are and What We are About', in ibid., pp. 88–102. In the category 'Hispanic women' are included women whose cultural and historical roots are in Cuba, Puerto Rico and Mexico, but who at present live in the USA (ibid., p. 102).
4 Adrienne Rich, 'Natural Resources', in *The Dream of a Common Language* (New York, W&W Norton, 1977), p. 67.
5 I owe this analytic tool to two colleagues and friends, the Irish theologian Dr Anne-Louise Gilligan and the US-born – but active in Ireland – Dr Katherine Zappone.
6 The literature on the secular feminist movement is voluminous. Suffice it to cite Betty Roszak and Theodore Roszak (eds.), *Masculine/Feminine: Readings in Sexual Mythology and the Liberation of Women* (New York, Harper and Row, 1969); Germaine Greer, *The Female Eunuch* (London, McGibbon and Kee, 1970); Kate Millett, *Sexual Politics* (London, Jonathan Cape, 1970); Simone de Beauvoir, *The Second Sex*, tr. H. H. Parsley, 1949 (Harmondsworth, Penguin, 1972); Betty Friedan, *The Feminine Mystique* (New York, Norton, 1963).
7 It ignores, for example, the work of Dorothy Sayers and Vera Brittain in England, and the early efforts in the Congregational and other churches to achieve the ordination of women. The first Anglican woman priest, Florence Ti Oi, was ordained in Hong Kong in 1949.
8 Helpful for the origins of the different types of feminism and their relevance to theology is Maria Riley, *Transforming Feminism* (Kansas City, Sheed and Ward, 1989).
9 Elizabeth Cady Stanton, *The Women's Bible Project* (1895).

10 See Matilda Jocelyn Gage, *Woman, Church and State: the Original Exposé of Male Collaboration against the Female Sex* (Massachusetts (1893), Persephone Press, 1980).

11 For the 'Angel in the House' see Tillie Olsen, *Silences* (London, Virago, 1980), pp. 34–7, 213–17.

12 For the 'Eternal Feminine' see Gertrud Von Le Fort, *The Eternal Woman*, tr. Placid Jordan, (Milwaukee, Bruce, 1962).

13 Cited in Riley, *Transforming Feminism*, pp. 105–6.

14 Schüssler Fiorenza, *Theological Studies*, p. 62: 'Critical theory as developed in the Frankfurt school provides a key for a hermeneutic understanding that is directed not just towards an actualizing continuation and perceptive understanding of history but towards a criticism of history and tradition to the extent that they participate in the repression and domination that are experienced as alienation.'

15 I will discuss the theology and spirituality of Women Church in the final section of this Chapter.

16 See M. Grey, 'From Cultures of Silence to Cosmic Justice-making – a Way Forward for Theology?' Inaugural Lecture, Southampton University, 1993.

17 Mary Daly, *The Church and the Second Sex* (Boston, Beacon, 1968). In her original re-introduction to a later edition of the book Daly satirises the idealism of her early position. (Daly, 'autobiographical preface' and 'feminist postchristian re-introduction' (New York, Harper and Row, 1975).) See also the introduction to *Beyond God the Father: Towards a Philosophy of Women's Liberation* (Boston, Beacon, 1973).

18 For example, Pope John Paul XXIII in his encyclical, *Pacem in Terris*, wrote: 'Since women are becoming more confident of their human dignity, they will not tolerate being treated as mere material instruments, but demand rights befitting a human person both in domestic and public life.'

19 See Catherine Halkes, 'The History of Feminist Theology', in *Yearbook of the European Society of Women in Theological Research*, vol. 1, pp. 11–37.

20 For a selection of early writings on the subject, see E. Schüssler Fiorenza, *Priester für Gott* (Munster, Aschendorff, 1972); Emily C. Hewitt and Suzanne R. Hiatt, *Women Priests: Yes or No?* (New York, Seabury, 1973); Carter Heyward, *A Priest Forever* (New York, Harper and Row, 1976); Letty Russell, 'Women and Ministry', in Alice L. Hageman (ed.), *Sexist Religion and Women in the Church* (New York, Association Press, 1974), pp. 47–62. For a recent account of the struggle in England, see Monica Furlong, *A Dangerous Delight* (London, SPCK, 1993).

21 See Constance Parvey (ed.), *The Community of Women and Men in the Church – the Sheffield Report* (WCC, Geneva, 1983).

22 For example, Letty Russell, *Human Liberation in a Feminist Perspective: A Theology* (Philadelphia, Westminster Press, 1974); J. O'Connor, 'Liberation Theologies and the Women's Movement: Points of Comparison and Contrast', *Horizons* 2 (1975), pp. 103–13; Letty Russell *et al.*, *Inheriting our Mothers' Gardens* (Philadelphia, Westminster, 1988).

23 Volume I was edited by Annette Esser and Luise Schottroff (Kampen, Kok Pharos, 1993), and the second by Mary Grey and Elizabeth Green (Kampen, Kok Pharos, 1994). For the emergence of feminist theology in Europe and the

position of women in the churches, see Anne Brotherton (ed.), *The Voice of the Turtle Dove* (New Jersey, Paulist, 1992); M. Grey, 'Women in the Churches of Europe', in Sean Gill, Gavin Da Costa and Ursula King (eds.), *Religion in Europe* (Kampen, Kok Pharos, 1994).

24 For the following account I am dependent on Virginia Fabella, *Beyond Bonding: a Third World Women's Journey* (joint publication of the Ecumenical Association of Third World Theologians and the Institute of Women's Studies, Manila, Philippines, 1993).

25 Ibid., p. 16.

26 Ibid., p. 27.

27 45 women theologians from 25 countries met in San José, Costa Rica from 6 to 13 December on the theme, 'A Spirituality for Life: Women struggling against Global violence'. Panellists reflected on domestic, ecological, cultural, economic, and military violence as well as violence against women's health. The keynote speaker for the Third World was Professor Chung Hyun Kyung from Korea, and for the First World, Professor Ursula King, Bristol University, England.

28 Adrienne Rich, 'Twenty-One Love Poems', in *The Dream of a Common Language* (New York, W&W Norton, 1978), p. 31. The notion of redrawing the map, of reconceptualising categories of thought, has been a powerful motivator in feminist theology. Sara Maitland also used the image in *Map of a New Country; Women and Christianity* (London, SPCK, 1980).

29 The phrase 'being heard to speech' is an influential one for feminist method in theology. It is the invention of the late Nelle Morton, *The Journey is Home* (Boston, Beacon, 1986).

30 One of the strongest exponents of Mujerista theology is Ada Maria Isasi-Diaz. See *En la lucha: Elaborating a Mujerista Theology* (Minneapolis, Fortress, 1993).

31 See Alice Walker, *In Search of Our Mothers' Gardens: Womanist Prose* (San Diego, Harcourt Brace Jovanovich, 1983), p. xi. 'The names associated with the development of womanist thought in theology, ethics, biblical studies, sociology of religion and ministry are Jacqueline Grant, Delores S. Williams, Katie Cannon, Marcia Riggs, Kelly Brown, Emily Townes, Joan Speaks, Renita Weems, Clarise J. Martin, Cheryl Townsend Gilkes . . . Additional womanist voices are emerging every day.' Dolores S. Williams, *Sisters in the Wilderness: the Challenge of Womanist God-Talk* (Maryknoll, NY, Orbis, 1993), p. 243. There are parallel developments to the Christian in the Jewish, Islamic, Hindu and Buddhist religions which are not charted here. For Judaism, see Judith Plaskow, *Standing Again at Sinai* (San Francisco, Harper and Row, 1990). For a useful general study of the effects of feminism on world faiths, see Paula M. Cooey, *After Patriarchy* (Maryknoll, NY, Orbis, 1992).

32 Emilie Townes (ed.), *A Troubling in my Soul: Womanist Perspectives on Evil and Suffering* (Maryknoll, NY, Orbis, 1993), p. 2.

33 Ibid., p. 2.

34 I invented this phrase in Grey, 'From Cultures of Silence'.

35 Phyllis Trible, *God and the Rhetoric of Sexuality* (Philadelphia, Fortress, 1978); *Texts of Terror* (Philadelphia, Fortress, 1978). See now A. Loades, 'Feminist Interpretation' in J. Barton, *The Cambridge Companion to Biblical Interpretation* (Cambridge, Cambridge University Press, 1998), pp. 81–94.

36 See Rosemary Radford Ruether, *Sexism and God-Talk* (London, SCM, 1983). Cited critically in Rita Brock, *Journeys by Heart: a Christology of Erotic Power* (New York, Crossroads, 1988), p. 64.

37 Elizabeth Schüssler Fiorenza, *In Memory of Her: a Feminist Reconstruction of Christological Origins* (London, SCM, 1983).

38 See Elizabeth Schüssler Fiorenza, *Bread not Stone – the Challenge of Feminist Biblical Interpretation* (Boston, Beacon, 1984).

39 See, for example, Catherine Halkes, *Met Miriam is het Begonnen* (Baarn, Ten Have, 1980).

40 See Williams, *Sisters in the Wilderness*.

41 For example, Julie Hopkins, *Towards a Feminist Christology* (London, SPCK, 1994); Kelly Brown, *The Black Christ* (Maryknoll, Orbis, 1994); Jacqueline Grant, *White Women's Christ, Black Women's Jesus* (Atlanta, Scholars' Press, 1989); Elizabeth Schüssler Fiorenza, *Jesus, Miriam's Child, Sophia's Prophet* (New York, Continuum, 1994).

42 See M. Grey, *Redeeming the Dream: Feminism, Redemption and Christianity* (London, SPCK, 1989); J. C. Brown and R. Parker, 'For God so loved the world', in J. C. Brown and C. R. Bohn (eds.), *Christianity, Patriarchy and Abuse* (New York, Pilgrim, 1989), pp. 1–30.

43 Daly, *Beyond God the Father* (Boston, Beacon, 1978), p. 19.

44 In addition to the analysis of Daly, see Ruether, *Sexism and God-Talk*; Elizabeth Johnson, *She Who Is* (New York, Crossroads, 1993); Grey, *Redeeming the Dream*; Chung Hyun Kyung, *Struggle to be the Sun Again* (Maryknoll, NY, Orbis, 1990).

45 This term is used in many of her works, but was used as a category of elucidation in particular in her paper on domestic violence given at the Costa Rica dialogue already referred to, December 1994. See Mananzan, Oduyoe, Tamez, Clarkson, Grey and Russell, *Women Resisting Violence: A Spirituality for Life* (Maryknoll, NY, Orbis, 1996).

46 See M. Grey, 'The Core of our Desire – Re-imaging the Trinity', in *Theology*, vol. XCIII, no. 755 (September 1990), pp. 363–72.

47 See Carter Heyward, *The Redemption of God* (Washington, University of America Press, 1980); M. Grey, *Redeeming the Dream*; Catherine Keller, *From a Broken Web* (Boston, Beacon, 1986).

48 See Johnson, *She Who Is*; Sallie McFague, *Models of God* (London, SCM, 1987); *The Body of God* (London, SCM, 1993).

49 Kwok Pui Lan, 'God weeps with our Pain', in John Pobee and Bärbel Wartenburg-Potter (eds.), *New Eyes for Reading* (Geneva, WCC, 1986), pp. 90–5.

50 Ntosake Shange: *For Coloured Girls who Consider Suicide/when the Rainbow is not Enuf* (New York, Macmillan, 1976).

51 Keller, *From a Broken Web*, p. 215.

52 See Grey, *Redeeming the Dream*.

53 See Carol Gilligan, *In a Different Voice?* (Cambridge, MA, Harvard University Press, 1982).

54 Sharon Welch, *A Feminist Ethic of Risk* (Minneapolis, Fortress, 1990).

55 Final Statement, Costa Rica Dialogue, December 1994, p. 6.

56 Katherine Zappone, *A Hope for Wholeness: a Spirituality for Feminists* (Mystic, CT, Twenty Third Publications, 1991), p. 13.

57 For a comprehensive study of women's spirituality, see Ursula King, *Women and Spirituality: Voices of Protest, Voices of Promise* (London, Macmillan Educational, 1989).

58 See Rita Gross, 'Human Female Deities as a Resource for the Contemporary Rediscovery of the Goddess', in *Journal of the American Academy of Religion*, XLVI/3, pp. 291–9.

59 See King, *Women and Spirituality*, p. 133. For Starhawk, see *The Spiral Dance: a Rebirth of the ancient Religion of the Great Goddess* (San Francisco, Harper and Row, 1979).

60 See Carol Christ, 'Why Women need the Goddess: Phenomenological, Psychological and Political Reflections', in Carol Christ and Judith Plaskow (eds.), *Womanspirit Rising, A Feminist Reader in Religion* (New York, Harper and Row, 1979), pp. 273–87.

61 King, *Women and Spirituality*, p. 149.

62 See note 50.

63 See the famous discussion between Merlin Stone and Sally Binford on the presumed historical reality of the goddess: Merlin Stone, 'The Great Goddess – Who was She? in Charlene Spretnak (ed.), *The Politics of Women's Spirituality* (New York, Doubleday, 1982); Sally Binford, 'Are Goddesses and Matriarchies merely figments of Feminist Imagination?' in ibid., pp. 541–9. Rosemary Radford Ruether is also sceptical on the Golden Age of the Goddess as a historical reality, in many of her writings, for example, *Sexism and God-Talk*, ch. 2, *Gaia and God* (San Francisco, Harper, 1992).

64 See Starhawk, 'Ethics and Justice in Goddess Religion', in Spretnak (ed.), *The Politics of Women's Spirituality*, pp. 415–22.

65 The literature on Women Church is voluminous. See Rosemary Radford Ruether, *Women-Church, Theology and Practice* (San Francisco, Harper and Row, 1985); Schüssler Fiorenza, *In Memory of Her*; *Bread not Stone*; M. Grey, *The Wisdom of Fools* (London, SPCK, 1993), ch. 9.

66 Mary Jo Weaver, *New Catholic Women: a Contemporary Challenge to Traditional Religious Authority* (San Francisco, Harper and Row, 1985).

67 Mary Hunt and Dianne Neu together run WATER – Women's Association for Theology, Ethics and Ritual. Their Newsletter is a rich resource for the ritual of Women Church.

68 See M. Grey, *Beyond the Dark Night – a Way Forward for the Church* (London, Cassell, 1997), p. 19.

69 Radford Ruether, *Women-Church*, pp. 4, 5.

70 Carter Heyward, *Our Passion for Justice* (New York, Crossroads, 1984).

# 6

## MARCELLA MARIA ALTHAUS-REID

# Demythologising liberation theology: reflections on power, poverty and sexuality

There *is* no 'right' against the mass of the people! (What we need is) a material world for all, without borders and without frontiers. (What we need is) a common table covered with broad linen; a table that is for everybody like this Eucharist. (What we need are) *chairs for everybody.*

Fr Rutilio Grande, homily of 13 February 1977. El Salvador. (My italics)[1]

The mere existence of socio-sexual activists does not guarantee a radical and profoundly subversive thinking, but it makes it possible, which in itself is no small thing to do.

Susana Rostagnol (2004:43)

## Chairs for everybody: on inclusivity

Only a few weeks after giving what was going to be his last public homily, Father Rutilio Grande was assassinated by paramilitary troops in his native land, El Salvador. I am beginning this reflection on liberation theology and sexuality by paying homage to him and to the many Christian martyrs from Latin America in the twentieth century, as a way to ground my reflections on Liberation Theology in the twenty-first century. This is a debt of love and gratitude that we have for those pioneers who liberated the Gospel in that continent during the difficult political climate of the 1970s.

It is tempting to think that two different projects, theological as well as political, were symbolically confronted in Father Grande's assassination. One was the project of liberation theology, the project of the alternative Kingdom and integral salvation from private and structural sins such as hunger and political persecution. The other was the hegemonic project from the dictatorial regimes which flourished during the Cold War, which curiously mixed the national security doctrine with their own theological discourses. The project from liberation theology could be expressed in Father

Grande's idea of an inclusive church. The metaphor of a broad Eucharistic table, surrounded with enough chairs for everybody, is not just a fraternal image but an economic metaphor of inclusiveness concerned with the creation of an alternative model of a participatory society: that is, a society where bread and wine will not be the product of exploitative labour conditions, but, on the contrary, the fruit of the liberating work of communities in which bread and wine on the table will be a right. I have deliberately said before that it could be tempting to think in this way, affirming the idea of a liberationist project for an inclusive church and society. Yet, it may be that this was not the case. In a way, we can say that liberation theology has this message of inclusivity, but from another perspective, we may say that it does not. This is a hard comment to make, but let us consider the issue of 'chairs for everybody' in Latin America, with theological honesty.

In the same way that my years of experience working with poor communities taught me how many subtleties and nuances of the everyday realities of the liberationist Christian praxis cannot be expressed in theological discourses, the same can be said about the metaphors of inclusiveness. Liberationists from the seventies and eighties in Latin America[2] have a discourse which is sometimes lacking reality. In fact, the liberationist praxis in Latin America, from where the richness of doing a theology in community comes, has been and still is a contested area. Anyone who has sat in a militant church around a table, together with the poorest of the poor of our brothers and sisters, knows that the bad smell left in the room by those who never have a bath or access to clean clothes creates more opposition amongst the members of the parish than the idea of a politically involved theology. Alternatively, the mixture of races and cultures amongst those sitting around the table of the Lord on a Sunday can somehow prove more controversial for many churches than a radical sermon from James Cone on Black theology. There is a gap in liberationist discourse and it is, paradoxically, a gap between uncontested ideologies and critical reality.

## A theology without myths

My point is that, tempting as it sounds, and even conceding that in many cases inclusiveness was (and still is) a high priority in the discourse of militant churches, the liberation theology project was never concerned with finding chairs for everybody but only with providing chairs for some of the nobodies of church and theology, the poor. The underdogs of history (as Gustavo Gutiérrez called them), or the poor (*el pueblo pobre*), required a voice, but not just a voice amongst many others. The voices for those historically voiceless and silenced by the alliances of power in church and state in Latin

America demanded that the space of traditional voices of authority be vacated. Far from inclusiveness, this was a discourse of privilege, reflecting the precedence of the marginalised and poor in God's plans for the Kingdom. In the Kingdom of God, the nobodies have the prerogative, as Jesus himself is the historical option of a God who became human by becoming a marginal, humble man in a country under foreign occupation. Following Father Grande's metaphor will mean that God somehow demands from us, as a prophetic action, that chairs previously occupied by the powerful and the exploiters need to become vacant. Inclusiveness becomes a key liberationist concept but only to be seen in the diachronic dimension of the historical *Kairos* (or 'Hour, or moment, of God') amongst the poor. What I am claiming is that the key for an appraisal of the discourse of liberation theology in the last century is to consider the liberationist praxis as related not to inclusiveness, but to power struggles. Perhaps we can still speak about inclusivity, but only if we acknowledge that the militant churches have never been neutral, but took options (even unconsciously) supporting colonial, theoretical constructions in Latin America, such as the ideologies of gender, race and sexuality. Therefore, liberation theology did not set out chairs for poor women, or poor gays – or at least it never did so willingly. The inclusive project affirmed itself by exclusion policies which determined the identity of the poor. The poor who were included were conceived of as male, generally peasant, vaguely indigenous, Christian and heterosexual. In fact, militant churches would not have needed many chairs around the table of the Lord if these criteria had been applied. It describes the identity of only a minority of the poor. The poor in Latin America cannot be stereotyped so easily and they include urban poor women, transvestites in poor street neighbourhoods and gays everywhere.

Only when we begin to demythologise liberation theology as a naive theology, which attempts to harmonise in a hegemonic and authoritarian way the positive and revolutionary elements of difference and dissent in our communities, will we be able to continue the *caminata* (the walk) of theology. More than trying to affirm liberation theology as a theology based on a premise of equality, we need to understand that no theology can escape the epistemological characteristics of its time, even when it intends to oppose them. The excluded from the table of Father Grande were those marginalised from church and society, the Latin American *Other*, represented by the poor. What they required was grace (freedom/gratuitousness) in contrast to the project of the dictatorial regimes with their logic of exclusion and profit, rather than inclusion and divine grace. Emphasising this proclamation of grace as opposed to the profit theology of the dictatorial regimes, liberation theologians used contrasting metaphors, such as the 'theology of life against theology of death' or the 'God of Justice against idols'. However, the grace of the liberationists was not based on the absolute gratuitous love of Christ: it shared some of the understanding of the profit theologies from the Cold War. Some years ago, discussing the notorious lack of mentoring between the first wave of liberation theologians and the new generations, the late Guillermo Cook shared with me his conviction that, beyond the differences, liberationists had much in common with the military frameworks of the seventies. Consider, for instance, the contrast between the discourse of inclusion from Father Grande and the rigid hierarchical order of the militant churches. Or again, consider the idea of giving a voice to the voiceless and the exclusion of women in the churches and in theology. According to Cook, discrimination against women on grounds of a prioritisation of tasks in the liberationist churches obeyed a principle of military strategy, where responsibilities are normally distributed in order to minimise casualties and to be ready to act at short notice: grace is distributed according to a logic of profit. I have myself been involved in many discussions in the past concerning the prioritisation of the struggle in Latin America. Those who considered that the suffering arising from gender and sexual discrimination was of a second order failed to recognise that they shared the same logic which creates poverty in the first instance.

The fact is that military dictatorships gave way to our Latin American democracies; weak, fragile, dependent democracies but still democracies. Yet liberationists seem to continue to work in military mode, where rigidity and authoritarianism have not given way to difference and disruption. The dualist thinking of the Cold War has seldom been realist thinking, and dualist theologies (including liberation theology) hardly reached the definition of *realpolitik*. However, facts are more ambiguous and subversive than dogmas, which are fixed by definition. Latin American Liberation Theology, born of an ethos of authoritarianism (social, political and ecclesiastical), has missed the possibilities of theological *poiesis* which comes not from discourses on the idealised poor, but from the reality of the poor as people of different sexual and gender identities.

The point is that, in the distribution of the liberationist chairs, colonial patterns of identity and particularly Christian identity were imposed. The theology which promised an option for the poor also defined, ideologically, a Christian identity based on patriarchal, colonial identities.

## On sexuality as ideology

The supposed equality in liberation theology failed in terms of agency – that is, it failed in its practice. Simply, there were no structurally implemented elements for the empowerment required to exercise responsibilities in the church and in the nation, or to have all the voices of the voiceless heard. If we were to have a broad table with chairs for everybody in the twenty-first century, we should have to begin by addressing deep-rooted ideologies concerning the identity of believers in Latin American Christianity and in liberation theology. The poor come in many colours, cultural contexts and sexualities. Liberation theology – whose defining theme has been not just God, but love and loving attitudes which can transform our world – was never grounded in love at the margin of medieval European models of affective relationships, which were regulated by economic interest. Not surprisingly the Latin American poor have little to do with church patterns of sacralised, patriarchal families: they seldom marry, or live in monogamy, but in patterns of solidarity, characterised by accepting and mutually helping each other in a kind of affective network of extensive family relationships. Those who call the poor promiscuous ignore the bonding of the social and the spiritual that a less profitable loving relationship pattern can create amongst the marginalised. In these terms, promiscuity could mean grace, that is, love outside the logic of the law. I myself have, somehow, learnt more about poverty and sexuality, and the subversive power of solidarity and social transformation of the excluded of our societies, by reading the Argentinian social psychoanalyst Alfredo Moffat, than by volumes written on Christian Base Communities. Why? Because liberation theology knows more about dogmas than about people, and more about discourses on love than about love itself. Only a postcolonial analysis, suspicious of the alliance between European ideologies and Christianity in relation to the construction of people's identities and relationships, can introduce liberationists to new levels of hermeneutical suspicion. After all, liberationists never took seriously the patterns of love and relationship among the Latin American people.

This brings us to the specific issue of gender and sexuality in liberation theology. These are the two discordant notes in its discourse on freedom and liberation, a discourse which in reversing Biblical miracles and wisdom sayings has turned copious wine into water and abundant bread into stones. Liberationists, by a lack of reflection on their discourse on power, have systematically denied chairs around the table to the poor, be these women or non-heterosexual people. But even worse than that, they have succeed in theologically under-nourishing a whole generation of Latin American Christians who should have been well prepared to continue interrogating the influence of hegemonic ideologies of a political or gender nature on the continent.

## On sexuality and power

Allow me to continue this analysis by stating something that has been a key for my own reflections: every theology is a sexual act.[3] If we were to follow

Karl Barth's suggestion of taking both the newspaper and the Bible into the pulpit, then in these times of globalisation processes, poverty and exclusion, we should find it difficult to preach on anything except sexuality. And I am not referring here to sexual issues arising from the market society, which uses sexuality as part of a culture of consumption, but rather from the church. We are continuously confronted, not only from the Vatican but also from local parishes, by the church's obsessive preoccupation with sexuality, or, to be more accurate, by its preoccupation with controlling sexuality. This is exhibited in the high priority given to issues concerning the regulation and control of sexuality such as abortion, contraception, the use of condoms, artificial insemination, sex outside marriage, marriage and divorce. At the same time, paradoxically, issues concerning paedophilia within the ranks of the clergy receive more attention from the media than from the church itself. There are many documents and encyclicals on marriage and divorce or on abortion but none on paedophilia. Liberation theologians from the first generation, who knew very well the sexual identity crisis and affective dilemmas of the young men in their seminaries, curiously never reflected on this issue. Neither did they reflect on the fact that in Latin America the whole mission of the church was driven by a sexual enterprise, the sexual conversion of the Latin American people to patterns of accepted sexual behaviour and relations from medieval Spain.[4] Issues of monogamy, hetero-sexual marriage and gender codes, treated according to the European pre-valent fashion, had such a pre-eminence in the teaching of the church that, as some distinguished scholars have commented, the Christian mission seemed to depend on sexuality, in particular on the negative portrayal and under-mining of the sexual identity of the *Other* (the native). Still functioning as a colonial theology, liberation theology never challenged this imposed order on the poor, and love among the poor. The theology which promised an option for the poor also defined ideologically a Christian identity for them, based on European patriarchal colonial codes. This was a theology which ignored, for instance, the complex sexual construction of the natives of the Americas, reflected in their love lives and also in their economic commu-nitarian structures. There is a connection between monogamy, monotheism and multinational cartels, just as there is a connection between different Latin American family structures, bisexual deities and the Ayllus (the indi-genous economic and affective communities of Perú).

The problem is that, unfortunately, theological discourse in the church is not a reflexive discourse on sexuality or a truly theological reflection on issues of sexuality: for the most part it is merely an instrument of power. This is why I consider that issues of gender and sexuality are fundamental to the church. It is not because Christianity depends on who marries whom or when, but because the church in its discourse on sexuality is sustaining, in reality, a discourse on hegemonic power and control. Some years ago, Leonardo Boff reflected on the fact that the Roman Catholic Church had failed with regard to the liberation project. He perceptively claimed that the church would never commit class suicide. Specifically in our case, the church will not commit a sexual or gender suicide. What is at stake is not so much questions about sexual practice, but challenges to the whole underlying pattern of hierarchical thinking and its structures of power.

## Sexuality matters

Therefore, if we are talking about the liberation of theology, sexuality matters. It matters in a way similar to that in which the discourse from the socially excluded matters. That occurs in two ways. The first is by challenging ideological formations in the church and theology, and the second is by restoring the Gospel's true message through a praxis of justice amongst God's people. It is important, after all, that a poor gay sits with his/her community at the Lord's Table, but it is also important that the theological framework which supports alliances, between church and state or between church representatives and local oligarchies, is denounced and dismantled. It has been my concern to unveil issues of sexual ideology in liberation theology and to declare that no theology, not even liberation theology, can be considered sexually neutral. In my project, which I have called 'Indecent Theology', I have tried to dislocate the entanglement between liberation theology, the option for the poor and issues pertaining to sexual ideology. In the same way that gender is a social construct, subjected to cultural and historical changes, sexuality is not a given. Following Judith Butler in her influential book *Gender Trouble* (1990), sexuality has begun to be recognised as ideologically construed. That is, we have started to differentiate between sex (as biological) and sexuality as a cultural performance. Sex and sexuality, or sex and gender, do not need to match up. Moreover, from an epistemological perspective, it becomes crucial that we interrogate the politics of matching biological data with issues of another nature, such as love and relationality which are culturally mediated, and not with outside understandings of production and profit. Christianity should be based on grace and not on profit. But here is the paradox: on the one hand, the Gospel is now used to convert people by subjecting loving relationships to produce and gain, while on the other it is used to condemn relationships such as the LGBT (Lesbian Gay Bisexual Transgender) precisely in terms of non-productivity. In reality, we are confronted here by two economies: the economy of the gift (such as *el cariño* in Perú) versus the market economy of profit. Each of these economies has different presuppositions concerning relationships and loving exchanges. Latin American economies are nearer to the grace economy of the Gospel than to the church's actual sexual and economic understanding of community life. What liberation theology, preoccupied with the option for the poor, has forgotten are what Amartya Sen calls the 'constituent components' of development:[5] that is, the fact that economic development is not an end in itself, but the expansion of the project of human freedom is. Economy should not be thought to be apart from human rights, and these include the right of the poor in Latin America to develop their own sexual identity outside the hegemonic constructions of the church. These ideological constructions have sacralised heterosexuality to the point of not allowing it to be interrogated.

One of the problems has been that liberation theology confronted structures of hegemonic power without questioning which epistemology grounded such power. Sexuality is about more than who loves whom. This is a way of thinking, relating and producing many significant patterns of exchange amongst communities. Heterosexuality in particular is an ideological form of affective and economic production which, curiously, has never been the focus of the liberationist ideological suspicion. Moreover, heterosexuality has been sacralised as the only valuable sexual epistemology, when in reality Latin American cultures historically exhibit a great diversity on sexual and economic thinking. Anyone who has worked seriously with the poor in Latin America has found the presence of God within the diversity of its communities, which is racial, cultural but also sexual. When middle class theologians accuse the poor of being promiscuous they fail to see the presence of God in the solidarity of extended families. These families are made by affection if not by law, as the poor build communities around love and compassion rather than by legal ties. In the process of questioning colonial heterosexuality in Latin America, it is not simply that we discover a face of the poor that has been unknown or ignored: it is also a pedagogical process which can teach more about love at the margins and reveal a different face of God when freed from the patterns thought and practised in medieval Spain. We may even rediscover a different Trinity outside patriarchal relationships, an Ayllu trinity, or a trinity of women loving each other. Why should we, the people of Latin America, countenance the curtailing of the joy of finding novelty, or of being surprised by God – especially through the acceptance of the discourse and patterns of sexual ideologies which are not even from our cultures?

### Feminist liberation theologies and sexuality

There are only a few of us in Latin America raising questions about the sexual paradigm of liberation theology rather than about gender issues.[6]

Why is it that sexuality is a more important paradigm than gender for liberation theology? To begin with, gender is an unstable category which presents differences according to times, political economics and cultures. In a way this is what has divided Third World feminist theologies, the realisation of the multitude of genders and the different ways of being a woman, which cannot be defined in a universal, essentialised way. Anecdotes abound about occasional women theologians misunderstanding the gendered patterns of other women. For example, I remember being criticised for serving the *mate* tea, a traditional herbal drink from Argentina, to a group of family and friends. Women from another culture saw me as fulfilling the traditional role of a woman serving tea. I needed to explain that in my family, in my country, the tradition was that my father had the honour of passing the *mate* tea to the guests. In fact, by taking the initiative I was reversing the patriarchal custom. Although gender, as a behavioural pattern, needs to be challenged and it is important to keep doing so in our communities, it does not provide us with a sufficient basis for theological reflection. Gender is a surface discourse, while sexuality is deeper. Gender behaviour only fulfils the role of sustaining sexual identities; the facts that men do not use high heels or women do not shave their faces contribute to a gender sign system which defines who is a man, and who is a woman.[7] Heterosexuality, far from being given by God, depends on these little gestures of legislating how we use clothes or move our hips when walking in the street. In fact, sexual identity depends on gender codes. During the time of the Argentinian dictatorial regime there were laws to enforce gender codes. It was as if sexuality (and indeed the world order) depended on the length of boys' hair or girls wearing skirts instead of trousers. However, systematic theology is not simply sustained by gender. The discourse on God 'the father', or God as 'He', is not concerned with masculinity, in the sense of God's gender behaviour (what God does), but with (hetero)sexuality. This is a God who defines Godself as a 'husband' (or a Lord, to be more precise) but, specifically, this is a God who procreates with a virgin (or pubescent girl) and has a son. This is the kernel of Christianity, God's sexuality manifested in history in the incarnation of Jesus Christ the Liberator. However, heterosexuality, being a cultural and economic construction, subjected to many changes over the course of history, should not have been sacralised. Ideologies (political, sexual or religious) need to be discussed in order to open the way to liberating theologies and to finding a better understanding of God. To use the liberationist words, unveiling ideologies, including sexual ones, helps us to keep re-discovering the face of God amongst us. Heterosexuality has become an idol in liberation theology. It is time to rediscover the face of God amongst the Other as sexual dissidents, in the midst of other forms of loving relationships and sexual identities. Curiously, these dissident relationships may also come to throw light on different forms of economic relationships.

Theology of liberation has said that the Trinity is a society, but it does not need to be an economic relation of men in solidarity with each other, honest and important as that relationship could be. To introduce a gender change in the Trinity (such as a female Holy Spirit) is not enough, because then the Trinity is infiltrated by identity presuppositions. What is a female Spirit? A mother? A caring, nurturing person? Or an amazon, a fierce independent woman who loves women? There is more to being a woman than to love a man or be a mother, just as there is more to being God than being the head of a patriarchal tribe. Small wonder that liberation theology became stagnant: all its discussions about God are based on sexual, ideological stereotypes, from which the poor, as a concept, become a blanket category which erases sexual differences amongst them. So much for the principle of theology as a second act, when the Latin American reality is ignored. God has been reduced, has nothing else to say and nothing with which to surprise us anymore. The liberationists' understanding of the Trinity as a society has become what J. Severino Croatto called 'a fixed model', instead of a reservoir of meaning. Our theology then lacks revelation.[8]

It has been said that feminist liberation theology made a particularly important contribution to feminist theologies in the West. Although the claim has been at times exaggerated,[9] it is also true that Latin American women, conscious of the limitations of the liberationists' paradigms, produced an important contribution to a wider dialogue between race and culture, class and gender. Issues of sexuality have been more recent. The discourse from Latin American women which came from churches and communities may have been a crucial contribution to the praxis of Western feminist theologies but, paradoxically, it did not have any impact on liberation theology itself. Theology of liberation is not the homogenous discourse frequently presented (or misrepresented) by North Atlantic theologians. It is well known that liberation theology has a praxis which needs to be understood with respect to the cultural and historical differences of the continent, which include differences in church perspectives. It may be true that Argentinians, Chileans and Uruguayans have developed somehow a line of theological thinking around Human Rights, while Central Americans tended to place more emphasis on developing a political-cultural theology. However, Central and South America have been linked by their discourses in solidarity with each other, in spite of their different options. The same can be said about individual theologians, who in the past decade have stood in opposition to (or disillusion with) their own churches and also publicly disagreed amongst themselves. They were united by a sense of solidarity around the option for the poor. However, when we turn to gender and sexuality, apart from a few isolated voices giving occasional statements about theology and gender equality, there has never been any sustained solidarity.[10] None of the great names from the liberationist ranks has ever produced any nuanced, deep theology which could justify a claim that liberation theology has heard the voice of the voiceless when ideologies of gender and sexuality have been the cause of the suffering and marginalisation of the Latin American people.

## By way of a conclusion

It could be argued that the pioneer theologians were men and that women's issues needed to be developed by women. Yes, they were men, but they wrote about poverty without knowing poverty themselves, at least not the enforced poverty of the slums. They were mostly theologians of European descent and yet they wrote about the lives of the indigenous people in Latin America. They reflected on the lives of the coloured and black people of the continent, but they were white. If it were true that only women should undertake reflection on gender and sexuality – according to the simple and empty equalising formulae applied by many male liberationists – then, by the same logic, only the poor should develop a theology with an option for the poor. Unless we have theologians from the slums (not just living there as part of a church project), the liberationist argument of theological representatives contradicts itself.

The point is that the ideological construction of gender and sexuality in Latin American theology is very influential. As liberationists, we have been encouraged to doubt the legitimacy of church hierarchies and government, but never of who is who at the moment of determining sexual identities. In the compact, power-structured worlds of Latin American churches, more dependent on old colonial powers for their finances than they would like to be, women and gays are casualties of assaults instigated by many different interests, including economic ones. When issues of gender and sexuality appear, the hermeneutical circle of suspicion disappears.

These are serious, even controversial, charges. They arise from my sense of betrayal – betrayal not so much from a group of theologians, as from a church which set out on a *caminata*, a walk of liberation towards political and ideological freedom several decades ago. That risky *caminata* was undertaken in the company of many women and people whose voices continue to be ignored. This point must be made emphatically: the struggle was carried on in the company of women and gays. There were Queers amongst the revolutionaries and also amongst the members of our militant churches. As Revd Roberto Gonzalez from the Iglesia de la Comunidad Metropolitana de Buenos Aires has said, during the time of the struggle against dictatorial regimes there were other oppressions and concentration camps buried in many of our hearts.[11] As we have already said, the problem is that, although liberationists tried to do theology as a second act – that is, starting not with dogmas but, to paraphrase Marx, with the real actors of theological history – issues of gender and sexuality were always dealt with at the dogmatic (ideological) level. Therefore, for instance, the masculinist liberationist gazes upon the Virgin Mary and thereafter supports the submission of Latin American women's identities to colonial (medieval European) Christian patterns. The betrayal undermines affections and relationships and has consequences which go beyond issues of women and equality. It is a betrayal of the project of human freedom which encompasses any economic project of liberation in Latin America and it is a betrayal of the orthopraxis claimed by liberationists. I am calling on liberation theology to become once again an honest theology – that is, a theology which is able to reflect on the lives of the people and the manifestation of God in our communities, beyond the dogma of a sexual ideology such as heterosexuality. Without that, we risk continuing to betray the Gospel of Justice by making of God a prisoner of issues of sexuality and power in the church and by reducing the project of the Kingdom to an ideological apparatus. To keep unveiling the political and sexual masks and to keep re-discovering the true face of God in Latin America is a daring and risky project which still has not finished. It continues with every Christian person who claims his/her right to dissent from the imposition of political and (hetero)sexual identities upon the Latin American people. For that reason, I call for a jubilee and cancellation of all the external debts of the people of Latin America: the all-too-obvious debts of the many but also the debts incurred through gender and sexual ideologies, which continue to force people to pay with interest, with their own suffering, for the right to be different from a central hegemonic definition of identity which comes not from God, but actually from colonial structures of power. It is time to honour our name as liberation theologians and to liberate people, and also God, from the oppression of centuries of injustice and abuse towards those who do not partake of patriarchal, heterosexual ideologies. I call on the first generation of theologians, that courageous generation: 'Will you now honour your old pledge to stand by the poor and those marginalised by ideologies of oppression? Will you now risk your good name by opposing the homophobic, by publicly standing in solidarity against the marginalisation of and violence against women and Queers?' There is a new generation of theologians doing that already, proud to keep the *caminata* of liberation theology going, with all the risks that honesty to God and our theological vocation entail.

## NOTES

1. Quoted by Jon Sobrino in *Jesus in Latin America* (Maryknoll, NY, Orbis, 1989), p. 18.
2. I am referring here to the historical period in which the main corpus of the Latin American Liberation Theology was conceived and formed/informed by the praxis of the militant churches during times of political oppression in the continent. These discourses have produced the canon or normativity of liberation theology, or, to put it another way, they have made of liberation theology a dogma.
3. See Althaus-Reid's *Indecent Theology. Theological Perversions in Sex, Gender and Politics* (London, Routledge, 2000).
4. See the work done in this area by the Paraguayan theologian Graciela Chamorro, especially her book *Teología Guaraní* (Quito, Abya Yala, 2004).
5. Amartya Sen, *Development as Freedom* (Oxford, Anchor Books, 2000).
6. I would like to mention here some names from the new generation of Latin American theologians working on sexuality, such as the Brazilians Mario Ribas, Nancy Cardoso Pereyra and André Musskopf. Jaci Maraschin has been a pioneer on issues of the body from the perspective of a class and sexual analysis since the seventies, and the same can be said of Tomas Hanks and his work in Argentina. Amongst this new generation we can also mention the Argentinians Iván Petrella, Hugo Cordoba Quero in Queer Liberation Theology, and the pastoral theological reflections from Roberto González and Norberto D'Amico from the Metropolitan Community Church in Buenos Aires. For further readings, see Althaus-Reid, *Liberation Theology and Sexuality* (London: Ashgate, 2006).
7. For this point, see Judith Butler, *Gender Trouble. Feminism and the Subversion of Identity* (London, Routledge, 1990). Liberationists should consider the work from Butler together with that of Marx, Nietzsche and Freud, as what Paul Ricoeur called 'the masters of suspicion', for the hermeneutics of suspicion from Juan Luis Segundo.
8. J. Severino Croatto, 'A Modo de Presentación', in *Mito y hermenéutica* (Buenos Aires, El Escudo, 1973), pp. 7–11.
9. It is important to remember the work from Rosemary Radford Ruether, a pioneer feminist theologian from the USA, whose work has always been characterised by a strong class analysis and social consciousness. Radford Ruether exercised considerable influence amongst Latin American theologians from the first generation, by introducing issues of gender and race together with issues of poverty and marginalisation.
10. For instance, it has not been uncommon to see the odd article on the Virgin Mary written by a Latin American woman theologian in an edited book on liberation theology. Male theologians have also written on the Virgin Mary from their masculinish perspectives, without any informed analysis on sexuality and

ideology, thus creating more stereotypes and contributing more to the status quo than to revolutionary column inches. For further readings on this aspect, see Althaus-Reid, *Indecent Theology*, especially ch. 2, 'The Indecent Virgin'.

11. Roberto González and Norberto D'Amico, 'Love in Times of Dictatorships: Memoirs of a Gay Minister from Buenos Aires', in Marcella Althaus-Reid (ed.), *Liberation Theology and Sexuality* (London, Ashgate, 2006).

# PART II

# Aspects of Liberation Theology

# 7

ANDREW DAWSON

# The origins and character of the base ecclesial community: a Brazilian perspective

## Introduction

It seems that for every commentator who has put pen to paper or given voice upon the lecture circuit, there is set forth a different, and supposedly conclusive, definition of the base ecclesial community (*comunidade eclesial de base*). Ever since the emergence of this innovative and challenging ecclesial phenomenon within the Latin American continent, ecclesiologists and sociologists alike have fallen over themselves in an attempt to explicate the concrete, lived experiences of those within the base communities by way of their own preferred analytical vocabulary.[1] The precision with which etymological origins, epistemological status and theological significance is sought, whilst laudable in terms of theoretical rigour, often belies the haphazard, disjointed and sporadic nature of much of the actual pastoral practice and tangible experience of those engaged in the day-to-day struggle to survive at the base of Latin American society.

As the above intimates, it is not our intention here to understand the base ecclesial community by means of dissecting the words *comunidade*, *eclesial*, *de base*.[2] Rather, we shall explore the character of the *comunidade eclesial de base* (hereafter, CEB) by way of highlighting a number of landmark events and experiences which, over the course of at least a decade, played a constitutive part in the emergence of the CEB phenomenon. To this end, we seek to understand the CEB, not as a neatly definable entity, but rather as an ecclesial tool and lived experience which has emerged out of a prolonged series of pastoral crises, perceived threats, ecclesiological shifts, theological refinements, and historical exigencies born of a whole gamut of economic, political, social, and theoretical upheavals. In short, there can be no unilineal representation of CEB development, nor can there be given a singularly conclusive definition. The reality of the CEB experience is far too *ad hoc* and varied for any such exercise to be either honest or accurate. As such, the following material is offered only as one attempt, among many, to appreciate the origins and character of the *comunidade eclesial de base*.

Given the sheer size of the Latin American continent, not to mention its attendant socio-political and cultural diversity, it would prove fruitless to try and sketch the origins and character of the CEB through such a wide and varied panorama. Consequently, the following material will concentrate upon outlining the development of the CEB movement with Brazil as its major point of reference. At the same time, it should be noted that the Brazilian experience is taken by many to be both the arena in which the earliest CEBs emerged and broadly representative of the overall historical processes, forces and demands which combined to give rise to the base ecclesial community.[3]

With the above in mind, a four-stage periodisation is adopted as the historical framework within which the origins and character of the *comunidade eclesial de base* in Brazil is to be sketched. This historical periodisation comprises: (1) the years prior to 1962; (2) 1962–1968; (3) 1969–1974; and, (4) 1975 to the present.

## Pre-1962

The post-war years witnessed in Brazil, as in most other Latin American countries, a significant period of accelerated industrialisation and concomitant urban growth.[4] Rapid demographic shift from countryside to city, on top of an already hastily increasing population, did much to undermine the static and monotonal cultural milieu upon which the church had traditionally relied for the transmission and inculcation of those values giving rise to an adherence to the Catholic credo and participation within the Roman cultus. Alongside the implications of such hastening demographic change, the rapidity with which Protestantism was making headway within the elite and petit bourgeois strata, in addition (especially, post-Cuba, 1959) to the perceived encroachment of communism upon the ignorant and impoverished masses, gave rise to a heightened anxiety among the Roman Catholic hierarchy.[5]

Traditionally, a relatively short supply of ordained clergy had weighed heavily upon a church whose *modus operandi* encouraged a strong clerical dependency. Any clerical shortage, however, had always remained a manageable, though inconvenient, problem on account of the prevailing ethos of *desobriga*. *Desobriga* is a mode of ecclesial participation in which the faith content and activity of the laity revolves around the 'discharging of religious obligations' solely upon those infrequent visits of the clergy to meet the sacramental needs of the people. In effect, there are no baptisms, marriages or eucharists, etc., until the local cleric makes his rounds; in outlying areas, such might occur only once in every four months![6] Further to the challenges of rapid demographic shift, Protestant growth and a perceived communist threat, the escalating decline in priestly vocations and subsequent growth in priest-to-person disparity (increasing in Brazil from 1:5,714 in 1950 to 1:6,349 by 1960), engendered within a growing number of Roman Catholic prelates a distinct reluctance to regard traditional pastoral practices as in any way capable of staving off the seemingly inevitable dwindling of Catholic influence within the continent.[7] This crisis of confidence came to be known as the 'pastoral crisis'.

In addition to a sustained emphasis upon structural reform, the Roman Catholic church in Latin America responded to the challenges of the pastoral crisis by means of coopting the rural laity in an attempt to compensate for the endemic shortage of ordained personnel. One early example of such lay cooptation is that of the catechetical experiment at Barra do Piraí, Brazil. Barra do Piraí is worthy of note because it is regarded by many authors as initiating one stream of emphasis which would, upon the confluence of others, eventually give rise to the *comunidades eclesiais de base*.[8]

The catechetical experiment at Barra do Piraí was directed by Dom Agnelo Rossi, and emerged out of the search for an 'efficient and practical means of defending the faith' in the face of the increased 'protestant problem' and the ensuing 'avalanche of heretical propaganda in Brazil'.[9] This 'defence and preservation of the faith' began subsequent to Roman Catholic parishioners' complaints concerning the vibrant activity of the three local Protestant churches, whilst their church buildings remained closed and unused during the lengthy absence of any priest from the area. In response to these complaints, Rossi suggested that there exists some ecclesial activity that need not be confined solely to those times in which a cleric is available to commence and direct it. Consequently, and realising the sorry state of lay preparedness in the sphere of formal ecclesial participation, Rossi initiated a series of training programmes (October 1958), in which lay people already exhibiting signs of leadership in the wider secular community, were selected and trained as community catechists and animators.

The task of the newly trained *catequistas populares* was to gather together the members of the local religious community, two or three times a week, for the purposes of reading the Bible, praying together and singing hymns. On Sundays, the catechist would lead the people in Catholic worship which came to be known as a 'priestless Mass' (*missa sem padre*). These regular mid-weekly gatherings were eventually to be situated in meeting huts (*salões*) built to house such assemblies. Over time, however, these specially constructed buildings came to be used for more than straightforward religious meetings, being progressively utilised by the wider secular community as the location for food and sewing cooperatives, as well as other, non-religious, social gatherings. At the height of the catechetical experiment, there were some 475 meeting huts throughout the local dioceses.

Having accepted the above as an important step in the right direction, it is crucial, nevertheless, to note that the lay catechist of the Barra do Piraí experiment was by no means intended to have a free rein in following his own initiative. Rather, the lay catechist was called upon *only* to read material which had been specially prepared by the diocesan authorities. As Rossi maintained, 'the popular catechist reads, and does not speak. He is a reader, not a preacher nor an improviser', and is to transmit the teachings of Christ only 'in those modalities which do not demand the priestly function'.

Given the above, it can be seen that Rossi's utilisation of the laity in a formal, though highly qualified, pastoral capacity was characterised by two emphases. First, Rossi regarded the laity as no more than a stop-gap measure in the face of priestly scarcity. As the popular catechist could 'never add' to the material supplied by Rossi's team, 'nor make commentaries' apart from a verbatim reading, it is apparent that Rossi's concept of popular lay catechesis comprised no more than a strong lay subordination and strict clerical dependence, albeit once removed. As such, it is reasonable to surmise that Rossi would have favoured the rapid phasing out of lay catechists and their replacement by a traditional clerico-centricity should the priestly scarcity have ended. The second characteristic of Rossi's endeavour was its strong reactionary character to the perceived threats of non-Catholic religious movements in his area. Rossi considered the main cause of the growing 'propaganda of heresy' to be the people's 'religious ignorance' of Catholic moral teaching. The people chose other forms of religious practice simply because they did not know better. The catechist's task, therefore, was that 'of deterring and impeding the advance of heresy among us', by providing the necessary Catholic moral education to the people. Rossi's concept of catechetical endeavour and lay education was, thereby, driven by a negative desire not to lose ground in the face of perceived threats to Catholic influence, rather than any positive wish to promote lay insertion and catechesis on its own merits.[10]

The elitism and reactive character exhibited by the catechetical experiment at Barra do Piraí need not, however, detract from its early contribution to the later development of a trust in the laity to perform certain, though limited, pastoral tasks on behalf of their religious communities. In addition, mention might also be made of the important results of the proliferation of meeting huts in which both religious and non-religious events could take place. Such a move, along with the ecclesiastical appropriation of local secular community leaders, served to lay a foundation upon which the gradual breakdown of traditional sacred–profane barriers could later be promoted. In such a way, there would be engendered a distinctive growing together of the Christian faith and everyday social activity. Given these points, the catechetical experiment at Barra do Piraí can be adjudged to have played an important role as an incipient precursor of those later movements which, in the light of Vatican II's *Lumen Gentium*, included the laity on account of their shared charisms, and not simply as an obligatory last resort.

## 1962–1968

Responding to the promptings of John XXIII and building upon the momentum generated by the Second Vatican Council (Rome, 1962–5), the years 1962–8 witnessed in Latin America the increasing utilisation of the Pastoral Plan (*plano de pastoral*).[11] The pastoral plan was designed to maximise the use of limited ecclesiastical resources via a coordinated and informed approach to the pastoral terrain in which the church was seeking to work.[12] With regards to Brazil and our present purposes, the two most influential pastoral plans were the *Plano de Emergência* (Emergency Plan, 1962–3) and the *Plano de Pastoral de Conjunto* (Joint Pastoral Plan, 1966–70).[13] Making use of the latest sociological research undertaken in Latin America and Europe, and guided by the ongoing ecclesiological paradigm shift being effected at the Second Vatican Council, both pastoral plans endeavoured to adapt the Church in Brazil to its rapidly mutating context.[14]

In broad terms, both sociological and ecclesiological developments converged upon the theme of community. In relation to ecclesiological concerns, Vatican II's stress upon the Church as living organism and the pilgrim people of God (*Lumen Gentium*, 9–17) placed emphasis upon the mutual dependence of the different parts of the ecclesial community, as well as its assorted individual participants.[15] Consequently, the status and participation of the laity within the formal ecclesial arena became important, as the themes of interdependence, co-responsibility and equality were stressed (*Lumen Gentium*, 2, 10–12, 31–2, 37; *Ad Gentes Divinitus*, 21). Likewise, the significance of the local church as the point in which the individual is inserted into the ecclesial realm was underlined (*Lumen Gentium*, 13, 23, 26; *Ad Gentes Divinitus*, 4, 8, 22). In keeping with the above themes, the ecclesiastical hierarchy were concerned to ensure that the laity be given a greater role within and access to the liturgical rites of the Church. As such, Vatican II called for these rites to be simplified, chiefly in the language of the local people, and allowing for a greater variety more attuned to the needs of relevant cultural expression (*Sacrosanctum Concilium*, 19, 26–7, 30, 46).

Building upon recent sociological findings, and backed by anthropological and psychological research, the concept of the 'primary group' (characterised by face-to-face relations, the smaller number of persons involved and the intimacy thereby engendered) had begun to hold sway in certain sectors of the church.[16] Developing the idea that real community (i.e., true interpersonal relations) can be fostered only in small and intimate groups, there was formulated a critique of the prevailing large-scale parish framework. The conclusions reached were that any concept of the traditional (large-scale) parish as promoting community must be dismissed and such parish structures revised. Instead, a vision of the parish structure as comprising a collection of community-promoting, smaller 'cells' or 'organic communities' was proposed, existing within limits defined by demographic, geographical and administrative factors.

Responding to the above emphases, and with the need for lay cooptation still high on the agenda, both the Emergency Plan and the Joint Pastoral Plan set about championing the dual themes of community and participation by means of decentralising prevailing parish structures.[17] Whilst not dismantling existing parish boundaries as such, the creation of a growing number of 'pilot'/'local'/'base communities' within the broader parish structure was proposed, in which there might be fostered 'a communion of interpersonal life in Christ', along with an 'interpersonal relationship of love' (*Joint Pastoral Plan*, 27). The parish church thereby becomes the 'mother church' (*Igreja-Matriz*; *comunidade Mãe*), surrounded by any number of *comunidades de base* (*Joint Pastoral Plan*, 57–8). Within these 'base communities', 'Christians would not be anonymous persons seeking only a service or to fulfil an obligation [*re desobriga*], but would feel welcome and responsible, as well as playing an integral part in the communion of life with Christ and with all their brothers and sisters' (*Joint Pastoral Plan*, 39). To this end, the traditional large-scale parish is to be transformed 'into a confederation of small base communities', by which the parish structure becomes 'a community of communities, an overarching community that promotes, interlocks and supports the smaller or base communities'.[18]

Whilst the Joint Pastoral Plan neither fully defined its concept of the *comunidade de base*, nor elucidated its precise ecclesiological standing, this omission was subsequently amended by the Second General Conference of Latin American Bishops, held at Medellín (August 1968).[19] Adding little to the understanding of the base community as a micro-environment conducive to intimate contact, interpersonal affirmation and lay participation

(*Justice*, 7, 14, 20; *Peace*, 27; *Formation of the Clergy*, 21), Conference findings did, however, accord the 'Christian base community' formal and prominent ecclesial status. For those at Medellín, the Christian base community represented 'the first and fundamental ecclesiastical nucleus . . . the initial cell of the ecclesiastical structures and the focus of evangelization, and . . . [currently] . . . the most important source of human advancement and development' (*Joint Pastoral Planning*, 10).

With its ecclesiological credentials now established, and its pastoral effectiveness becoming increasingly evident, the base ecclesial community nevertheless had one more transformative development to make before it could be said to have reached adulthood. This transitional stage from adolescence to maturity took place within a context of heightening repression and economic exploitation, and comprised the shift from a primarily internal emphasis to one of a more balanced approach inclusive of an external orientation.

## 1969–1974

Subsequent to the military *coup d'état* (April 1964), the ending of democratic government in Brazil was succeeded by the gradual construction of a national security dictatorship; a dictatorship representing an ominous presage to later developments throughout Latin America. By no means indulgent of would-be detractors prior to 1968, from the December of this year the military dictatorship commenced a substantially bloodier and repressive regime. Effected via political purges, almost absolute censorship, countless arrests, tortures and deaths, and the proscription of every institution likely to harbour protest, the closure of Brazilian society left only a blanket of silence which cloaked an increasing abuse of human rights and the escalating economic exploitation of those at the base of the social pyramid.[20]

Encouraged by the challenges issued at Medellín, and in view of the closure of every avenue of protest and resistance besides those of an ecclesiastical nature, pastoral agents already working at the socio-economic base of Brazilian society were joined by increasing numbers (lay and ordained) making their way to the most impoverished neighbourhoods. The days of mass action along state or national lines were gone. Now, the only means of humanitarian action which could survive the national security onslaught was that organised along strictly delimited neighbourhood lines, and dependent on mutual trust and person-to-person contact.[21]

During this time of pastoral innovation and societal turmoil, there existed three overriding objectives on the part of many pastoral agents working among the poor. Living side by side with those at the base (*pastoral de convivência*), the primary concern of the majority of pastoral agents was that of encouraging a greater lay responsibility and participation within the formal ecclesial arena. Consequently, a growing number of leadership training courses were promoted with the aim of furnishing each locale with a core group of community 'animators' (*animadores*) who might assume greater responsibility, thereby engendering a lessening of clerical dependency whilst also acting as positive role models for other lay members.

Secondly, many pastoral agents were concerned to stimulate a new and more radical religious consciousness within those at the base. Rejecting the traditionally dualistic approach to the individual as a union of body and soul (with the Church being chiefly concerned with the latter), there was posited instead a more holistic approach in which the person is regarded as an indistinguishable psychosomatic unity. Utilising the concept of *o homem integral* ('the whole person'), developed within Catholic University Youth and the Base Education Movement, it was argued that one cannot talk of the spiritual welfare of an individual in isolation from that person's physical needs; physical needs which can be met only in relation to the prevailing economic, political and social environment in which s/he is enmeshed.[22] Thus, whilst engaged in day-to-day parish work with biblical circles, baptism and first communion classes, family catechesis, and marriage counselling groups, many pastoral agents used such opportunities to communicate their vision of the unified subject existing within a unified historical plane. Regarding the work of redemption as taking place within the warp and woof of historical processes, this view is well explicated in theological terms by the relatively early thoughts of Gustavo Gutiérrez:

> I emphasize that the work of building the earth is not a preceding stage, not a stepping stone, but already the work of salvation. The creation of a just and fraternal society is the salvation of human beings, if by salvation we mean the passage from the less human to the more human. Salvation, therefore, is not purely 'religious'.[23]

The third objective of those pastoral agents working at the base comprised the greater integration of the local ecclesial community within the broad expanse of surrounding neighbourhood affairs. Although undoubtedly influenced by the concept of *o homem integral*, increasing numbers of pastoral agents came to learn that it was not until the traditional practices of the church were linked with concrete activity concerned with food, clothing, finance distribution, and neighbourhood issues that the local Christian community began to make headway within its surrounding locale. Reflecting the perduring pragmatism born of poverty, it was only upon first demonstrating to the local community that the implications of the Christian gospel touch upon every dimension of human existence, no matter how seemingly mundane, that those at the base saw fit to invest both trust and effort within these novel ecclesial experiences.[24]

With all of the above in mind, pastoral agents came increasingly to incorporate reflection upon wider (i.e., non-religious) community events within the formal ecclesial arena. The methodological tool utilised for this conjoining of concerns was the See–Judge–Act method, previously used within Catholic University Youth and the Base Education Movement. The importance of this pastoral tool in overcoming the traditional chasm between the religion of the masses and their everyday experiences should not be underestimated; not least because the See–Judge–Act method continues to be the foundation upon which much of CEB success rests today. It is for this reason that the following example of how the See–Judge–Act method might work in action is given.[25]

Our typical mid-week CEB gathering, coordinated by a lay person or couple and possibly facilitated by a local priest or nun, is opened with the communal saying of a prayer, song or psalm. Following this formal commencement of proceedings, the next half-hour or so is given over to the recounting of the past week's events and concerns by each individual participating in the community gathering. Such concerns and events might include, for example, news of illness through lack of adequate sanitation facilities, proper housing or malnutrition, the sharing of hardships caused by redundancy or low pay, and information upon someone injured on account of dangerous working conditions. Often termed the *revisão de vida* (life review), this stage of open sharing represents the *seeing* phase of the See–Judge–Act method.

Following this review of the past week's happenings, a scriptural passage might be read aloud by all present, with each person then sharing any comments felt relevant to both text and context of the gathering. When the round is completed, the biblical text and shared comments are then drawn together in the form of a reflection delivered by a member of the community. Subsequent to this reflection, a further period of open discussion takes place, in which the scriptural passage is questioned in the light of present preoccupations and events, in the hope that it might shed light upon the situation at hand. In effect, the past week's life experiences provide the tool by which the biblical text is interrogated and made relevant to the life setting of the group. In such a way, the scriptural passage speaks in retrospect concerning recent events, whilst at the same time giving encouragement to those gathered concerning the week to come. As the God of the Bible is so evidently on the side of the poor and dispossessed, wrestling for the cause of justice and calling for a love which is realised in concrete acts of fairness and equality, must not this same God stand by our side and fight our corner?[26] Lasting for up to an hour or more, this time of reflection constitutes the moment of *judging* (evaluation) within the threefold methodology being utilised.

Upon being opened to the everyday concerns and events of the poor, it is within the formal ecclesial arena that the people find acceptance, resolve and encouragement from the knowledge and experience that God is not only on their side, but also calling for an end to the massively unjust and unacceptable conditions in which so many at the base spend their entire lives. Spurred on by the affirmation they have found, many involved in such community gatherings seek to work out what they have heard by way of a practical engagement with pressing neighbourhood (*bairro*) issues. The stages of *seeing* and *judging* thereby pass to a time of *action*; a time of action in which those empowered within the base ecclesial community immerse themselves within traditionally secular neighbourhood (*bairro*) concerns such as local community centres, women's groups, cooperative ventures, political parties and unions, youth clubs, and *ad hoc* campaigns in the pursuit of a local health clinic, sanitation facilities, school and public transport provisions.

Having originally been envisaged by the hierarchy as a means of including the laity within the ecclesial realm, in the face of a refusal by the people to concern themselves with a church divorced from their everyday experiences, and in view of the See–Judge–Act pastoral method, the CEB emerged as something more besides. By means of accepting the people within itself (centripetal movement) and then subsequently emboldening them to engage their surrounding milieu in the knowledge that this is what the gospel demands (centrifugal movement), the base ecclesial community reaches adulthood. The mature CEB thereby feeds into the local *bairro* a band of Christian believers no longer willing to be the passive objects of abuse and exploitation, but now determined to be active subjects, increasingly responsible for the construction of their own history. As such, the secular community is opened to the influence of the faithful, whilst in return the ecclesial community is progressively exposed to the ongoing preoccupations, struggles and aspirations of those at the socio-economic base of society. It is by means of this dialectical process of mutual ingression that traditional distinctions between the religious and the mundane are overcome; and it is via this overcoming of traditional distinctions that maturity is attained by the CEB. Thus, the mature CEB can be diagrammatically represented as follows:

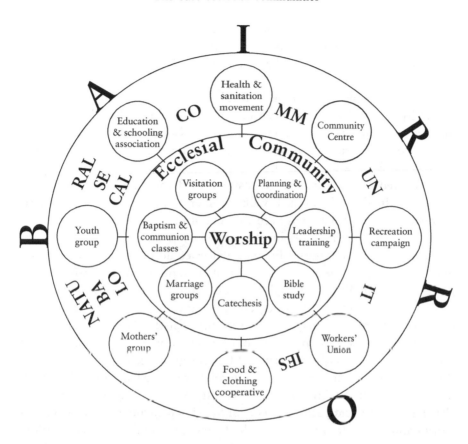

## 1975 to the present

For various reasons, the year 1975 represented an important landmark in the historical trajectory of the *comunidade eclesial de base*. In the first instance, 1975 witnessed the first national gathering (*encontro*) of the base ecclesial movement in Brazil. This national *encontro* heralded the beginning of a new collective moment in the life of the CEB. Second, it was from 1975 onwards that Brazilian president General Ernesto Geisel's policy of *distensão* ('decompression'/'liberalisation') started gaining momentum towards a gradualised return to normality (*abertura*) and full democratic elections by 1986. In addition, it might also be noted that 1975 saw the issuing of the first of a series of increasingly captious statements regarding the military government by the National Conference of Bishops in Brazil.[27] Over the course of the next decade these statements would be followed by a number of progressive documents, in which the Roman Catholic hierarchy in Brazil assumed a more prophetic stance regarding matters of justice, equality, land rights, and democracy.[28] As such, it was in a climate of growing hierarchical sympathy with matters pertaining to political and socio-economic conditions at the base that the first interecclesial gathering of the CEBs occurred.

Upon the lapsing of the Joint Pastoral Plan (1966–70), the ecclesiastical hierarchy in Brazil was keen to ensure that each of its subsequent biennial plans give prominence to CEB implantation.[29] Consequent upon such hierarchical encouragement, not to mention the increasingly fruitful labours of those already working at the base, there existed by the end of 1974 an estimated 40,000 Brazilian CEBs scattered throughout at least forty dioceses.[30] In the light of such CEB proliferation, a number of pastoral agents and bishops who had been influential in the early successes of the CEB in Brazil sought to organise a national forum by which previously disparate and often solitary CEB experiences could be shared and reflected upon. As a result, the first of a series of national CEB conferences took place at Vitória (Espírito Santo) between 6 and 8 January 1975.

With over seventy participants, comprising ordinary *cebistas* (members of a CEB), pastoral agents, bishops and intellectuals, the people at Vitória gathered under the *encontro* theme of 'A Church born of the people'.[31] For our purposes, the *encontro* event held two significant implications. First, the establishment of a national conference provided a forum in which previously isolated CEB experiences could be disseminated. Within such sharing, *cebistas* and pastoral agents alike gained encouragement from the stories and histories of other individuals and communities, found comfort in the news that they were not the only ones struggling to be church at the base, and were emboldened by the fact that the God of the poor was seemingly undertaking a new venture in which all of God's people are called to participate on an equal footing. Whether in formal conference proceedings or after sessions had closed, common experiences were reflected upon, divergent emphases explored and a wide variety of motivations, objectives and struggles argued over in the cause of mutuality and learning. It was in view of this critical interaction that the CEB movement as such was born, and continues today to generate common themes of study and programmatic action along diocesan, state and national lines.

The second major implication emerging from the interecclesial *encontro* was the provision of an environment in which theologians could begin to learn from and take stock of the voiced experiences of those living day in and day out at the socio-economic base. Attending in the capacity of *periti* (professional advisors) to the first conference, for example, were Leonardo Boff, Carlos Mesters and Eduardo Hoornaert; with the likes of João B. Libânio, Pedro A. Ribeiro de Oliveira swelling the ranks in later years and

Gustavo Gutiérrez and Thomas Bruneau attending as guests. Although inter-ecclesial CEB gatherings subsequent to the first at Vitória would increase in popular participation and progressively come under the organisation and oversight of *cebistas* themselves (rather than their clerical counterparts), the advisory role played by these theologians and sociologists would continue to be regarded as essential to the ongoing success of the movement itself.

Emerging from experiences gained via the *encontro* event, and growing out of a reflection upon a number of reports and histories furnished by various CEBs throughout Brazil, the second interecclesial gathering (again, at Vitória) saw the production of a number of papers by, among others, Eduardo Hoornaert, J. B. Libânio, Carlos Mesters, and Leonardo Boff.[32] Carlos Mesters' paper, 'Flor sem defesa: ler o evangelho na vida', would later form part of his highly influential book, *Defenseless Flower: A New Reading of the Bible*. Perhaps most noteworthy, however, is Leonardo Boff's 'Eclesiogênese: as ceb reinventam a igreja', the blueprint from which would be developed *Ecclesiogenesis: The Base Communities Reinvent the Church*.

Providing the initial grounding in issues and concerns of the base, the interecclesial gatherings acted as a springboard for various young thinkers who would later come to be recognised as the second generation of Brazil's theologians of liberation.[33] What is important to note, however, is that the experience of the CEB gained at these early *encontros* represented the impetus towards the later formulation of ecclesiological themes which subsequently formed an integral part of the theoretical bedrock upon which a more mature theology of liberation came to rest. Such ecclesiological themes also led to Vatican disapprobation and the subsequent censure and silencing of Leonardo Boff.[34] Although it can be said, therefore, that the majority of its theological and socio-political critique was in place prior to the mid-1970s, it was only via its engagement with the nascent CEB movement that Latin American liberation theology was fully enabled to root itself within the lived experiences of the masses at the base. Without this praxiological grounding, liberation theology would neither have been able to articulate the sufferings of the poor, nor been allowed to claim the representative status upon which so much of its credibility continues to rest.

By the late 1980s, the political and ecclesiastical climate in Brazil had undergone considerable change. Under the direction of president João Figueiredo, *distensão* was carefully nurtured into *abertura* (opening). In the face of increasing popular and middle-class mobilisation, the democratic party system was restored, direct gubernatorial elections in 1982 allowed and the first open presidential elections for over twenty years held in 1986.[35] On the ecclesiastical front, the conservative 'restorationist' programme set in motion by John Paul II was now fully up and running, and in the light of this traditionalist resurgence strong pressures were brought to bear upon any in Latin America espousing anything close to a liberationist line.[36] In view of this shift in climate, and although there existed an estimated 100,000 CEBs in Brazil alone at this time, there was much talk about how this once innovative and challenging ecclesial phenomenon was in danger of becoming no more than a depoliticised and spiritualised shell of its former self.[37]

As the only national institution which could face up to the military dictatorship and survive, and with no legitimate or effective opposition existing throughout the prolonged period of socio-political closure in Brazil, certain progressive sectors of the Roman Catholic church came to represent for many the only avenue through which democratic ideals and popular aspirations could be both espoused and pursued. Furthermore, given the repressive nature of the national security state and the timely emergence of many CEBs within neighbourhoods throughout Brazil, it was upon these small, intimate and local ecclesial communities that growing numbers of those at the base came to pin their hopes for a better future. It was, therefore, within the burgeoning number of CEBs that local pockets of popular organisation, previously channelled through unions, professional associations, state campaigns, and political parties, were enabled to survive.[38] Nurturing the democratic ideals of mutuality, participation and corresponsibility, which the military in Brazil had supposedly upheld by torturing and killing thousands, by the late 1970s the CEB movement was in a most advantageous position from which to exploit the growing benefits of *distensão* and organise the increasingly coordinated movements of popular protest which eventually drove decompression into full *abertura*.

With the onset of full democratic elections, however, those channels of popular organisation and expression previously closed to the masses were once again opened. As such, the need for the base ecclesial community to function as a space for the preservation and pursuit of many popular aspirations and concerns thereby ended, as did the *religious* motivations of a number of people who had attached themselves to the CEB movement throughout the years of dictatorship. To this extent, the CEB movement can be said to have undergone a certain degree of depoliticisation, as it handed back to the appropriate and ultimately more effective channels those tasks it had undertaken by virtue of its peculiar status within dictatorial Brazil.[39]

Already exerting concerted pressure upon the ecclesiastical hierarchy since 1983, Vatican-orchestrated forces took the democratisation of Brazil as their cue for a further push towards a comprehensive adoption of the restorationist line.⁴⁰ In view of recent events within the political arena, Vatican orthodoxy soon gained hegemony, with the church subsequently reverting to a pastoral concentration upon the middle classes and bourgeois elite as the principal bulwarks of its influence in Brazil. Concomitant with this rapprochement with the petite bourgeoisie and economico-political elite, the now powerful conservative lobby within the ecclesiastical institution took this opportunity to lessen the church's emphasis upon the popular pastoral. As they sought to eradicate all potential sources of compromise and embarrassment in the face of the new political regime, the CEB movement and its progressive agenda were regarded as one such likely well-spring of contention. Consequently, previously available personal and financial resources were gradually withdrawn and a growing number of prelates began to impress an increasingly traditionalist agenda upon a pastoral terrain which until recently they had been content to leave to the oversight of pastoral agents within their charge. Emphases upon ecclesial engagement with land, housing, health, and education matters were now played down in favour of an individualised spirituality based upon a passive, unquestioning deference to hierarchical authority and the privatised veneration of our Lady and the saints.⁴¹ It is to this extent that the CEB movement has undergone some form of spiritualisation.

Having acknowledged the processes of depoliticisation and push towards spiritualisation to which the CEBs have been subjected since the mid-1980s, it is not intended to create the impression that these pressures have left the CEB movement in Latin America altogether devoid of influence and relevance. Certainly, changes in the political and ecclesiastical climate have made it difficult for the CEB to continue in the same manner as before; but, where is it written in stone that this is what the CEB or any other movement of God must do? Rather, the fortunes and emphases of the CEB differ from country to country, diocese to diocese and even parish to parish.

Furthermore, it should be noted that talk of the depoliticisation of the CEB must not be allowed to mask the still significant continuity of pastoral practice and engagement between the pre- and post-*abertura* CEB. Whilst issues pertaining to party politics and unionisation, for example, may well have been gladly handed back to the proper channels, many CEBs continue to play an influential role within local campaigns for improved sanitation and health facilities, better educational and housing provision, and other ongoing struggles towards the improvement of life chances at the base. Within the contrasting political climates of national security and open democracy, however, the same actions can assume markedly different overtones and implications, as well as eliciting somewhat divergent responses from the powers that be. Having thereby acknowledged the transition from dictatorship to *abertura*, it can be seen that it is not necessarily the nature of all CEB activity which has changed over this period, but also the socio-political matrix in which the content of such activism is interpreted. What was regarded as political agitation in 1975, for example, might not be regarded as such today.

In addition to recognising the changing nature of the *political* in Brazil (and, therefore, the changing nature of what constitutes politicisation), the enduring pragmatism of the masses must also not be overlooked as an important guarantor of the CEB legacy. It should not be forgotten, for example, that one of the principal contributing factors towards the integration of the incipient ecclesial communities within their surrounding locale was the refusal of many at the base to concern themselves with any venture whose *raison d'être* stood divorced from those preoccupations, struggles and needs generated at almost every turn by life at the bottom of the social pyramid. It is upon this continuing refusal of the faithful to countenance any religious undertaking which has no relevance to the everyday experiences of poverty that much of the future hope of the base ecclesial community lies.

For the last decade, Brazil has continued down the road of democratic politics. It is, however, a politics of democracy which continues to rest upon the unbridled exploitation of the many by a small minority. High unemployment, low pay, poor working conditions, lack of job security, and myriad restrictions in health care, schooling and decent housing all conspire to prevent the impoverished masses from learning to strive for that which justice demands they have. Within a context such as this, the *comunidade eclesial de base* continues to have relevance and purpose. Yet, it is a relevance and purpose which has meaning only to the extent that the powerless assume a role, the voiceless are empowered to speak out, and the poor are enabled to seek the Reign of God by way of engaging in the transformation of our world towards that for which the God of justice calls.

## NOTES

1 For the great diversity in CEB definitions, see, for example: Mariano Baraglia, *Evolução das Comunidades Eclesiais de Base: Experiências Comunitárias na Cidade de São Paulo* (Petrópolis, Vozes, 1974), p. 54; Luís Fernandes, *Como se Faz uma Comunidade Eclesial de Base*, 5th edn (Petrópolis, Vozes, 1986), p. 47; Yves Congar, 'Os Grupos Informais na Igreja: Um Ponto de Vista Católica', in A. Gregory (ed.), *Comunidades Eclesiais de Base: Utopia ou Realidade* (Petrópolis, Vozes/CERIS, 1973), p. 127; Faustino L. C. Teixeira, *A Fé na Vida: Um Estudo Teológico-Pastoral Sobre a Experiência das Comunidades Eclesiais de Base no Brasil* (São Paulo, Edições Loyola, 1988), pp. 20–3.

2 The words *comunidade, eclesial* and *de base* are given individualised treatment in Marcello de C. Azevedo, *Basic Ecclesial Communities in Brazil: The Challenge of a New Way of Being Church*, tr. J. Drury (Washington, Georgetown University Press, 1987), pp. 57–117; Clodovis Boff, *Comunidade Eclesial, Comunidade Política: Ensaios de Eclesiologia Política* (Petrópolis, Vozes, 1978), pp. 51–63; Guillermo Cook, *The Expectation of the Poor: Latin American Basic Ecclesial Communities in Protestant Perspective* (Maryknoll, NY, Orbis, 1985), pp. 61–85; Jesús Andrés Vela, *Las Comunidades de Base y una Iglesia Nueva*, 4th edn (Buenos Aires, Editorial Guadalupe, 1971), pp. 150–3.

3 See, for example: Edward L. Cleary, *Crisis and Change: The Church in Latin America Today* (Maryknoll NY, Orbis, 1985), pp. 104–24; David Lehmann, *Democracy and Development in Latin America: Economics, Politics and Religion in the Postwar Period* (Oxford, Polity Press, 1990), pp. 126–41; Arnoldo Zenteno, *La C. E. B. en México* (Centro Antonio de Montesinos, Mexico City, 1983), pp. 171–89.

4 For developments in Latin America see Celso Furtado, *Economic Development of Latin America: Historical Background and Contemporary Problems*, 2nd edn, tr. S. Macedo (Cambridge, Cambridge University Press, 1976); for Brazil, Thomas E. Skidmore, *Politics in Brazil, 1930–1964: An Experiment in Democracy* (Oxford, Oxford University Press, 1967).

5 Protestantism and communism were listed by Pius XII among the 'four mortal dangers' to Roman Catholicism in Latin America; the other two were naturalism (including liberalism and nationalism) and spiritism. Hellmut G. Vitalis, *The Significance of Changes in Latin American Catholicism Since Chimbote 1953* (Cuernavaca, CIDOC, 1969), p. 3/1.

6 For *desobriga*, see Azevedo, *Basic Ecclesial Communities in Brazil*, p. 67. For an account of the pastoral overload generated by priestly scarcity in Brazil, see Alfredo Konz, 'A bcc in a rural setting: Morroas', in *Basic Christian Communities*, LADOC Keyhole Series, no. 14 (Washington, Georgetown University Press, 1976), pp. 30–4.

7 Gustavo Pérez, Alfonso Gregory and François Lepargneur, *O Problema Sacerdotal no Brasil* (Rio de Janeiro, FERES/CERIS, 1965), p. 15.

8 For example, Leonardo Boff, *Ecclesiogenesis: The Base Communities Reinvent the Church*, tr. R. R. Barr (London, Collins, 1986), p. 3; and, José Marins, 'Comunidades eclesiales de base en América Latina', in *Concilium*, 104 (April 1974), p. 30.

9 The following material draws upon: Agnelo Rossi, 'Uma experiência de catequese popular', in *Revista Eclesiástica Brasileira*, 17 (September 1957), pp. 731–6; and 'Os principais manuais de catequese popular', in *Revista Eclesiástica Brasileira*, 18 (June 1958), pp. 461–3.

10 For evidence that Rossi's clericalism was not out of step with the church either abroad or in Brazil at this time, see: Avery Dulles, *Models of the Church: A Critical Assessment of the Church in All Its Aspects*, 2nd edn (Gill and Macmillan, Dublin, 1988), p. 52, and Almir R. Guimarães, *Comunidades de Base: Uma Nova Maneira de Ser em Igreja* (Petrópolis, Vozes, 1978), p. 104, for Roman Catholicism in general; F. L. C. Teixeira, *A Gênese das Cebs no Brasil: Elementos Explicativos* (São Paulo, Edições Paulinas, 1988), pp. 67–72, and Sergio Bernal, *La Iglesia del Brasil y el Compromiso Social: El Paso de*

*la Iglesia de la Cristiandad a la Iglesia de los Pobres* (Rome, Editorial de la Pontificia Universidad Gregoriana, 1986), p. 69, for Brazil.

11 David Regan, *Church for Liberation: A Pastoral Portrait of the Church in Brazil* (Dublin, Dominican Publications, 1987), p. 153; Bernal, *La Iglesia del Brasil,* p. 25.

12 François Houtart, 'The Master Plan Arrives in Latin America', in J. J. Considine (ed.), *The Church in the New Latin America* (Notre Dame, IL, Fides, 1964), pp. 52–63.

13 The Emergency Plan was published in two parts, in *Comunicado Mensal,* 116 (May 1962), pp. 7–21 and 117 (June 1962), pp. 16–46; Conferência Nacional dos Bispos do Brasil, *Plano de Pastoral de Conjunto, 1966–1970,* 2nd edn (Rio de Janeiro, Livraria Dom Bosco Editôra, 1967).

14 For ongoing sociological developments in Latin America and Europe, see: David E. Mutchler, *The Church as a Political Factor in Latin America* (New York, Praeger, 1971), pp. 29–31; and Guimarães, *Comunidades de Base,* pp. 125–34. For ecclesiological developments, see Giuseppe Alberigo, Jean-Pierre Jossua and Joseph A. Komonchak, *The Reception of Vatican II,* tr. M. J. O'Connell (Burns and Oates, Tunbridge Wells, 1987); and J. Gremillion (ed.), *The Church and Culture Since Vatican II: The Experience of North and Latin America* (Notre Dame, IL, University of Notre Dame Press, 1985).

15 References to Vatican II documents are taken from Austin Flannery (ed.), *Vatican Council II: The Conciliar and Post-Conciliar Documents,* rev. edn (Dublin, Dominican Publications, 1988).

16 Dulles, *Models of the Church,* pp. 37–49.

17 Earlier, yet uncoordinated, attempts at parish decentralisation had been under way in Brazil since the late 1950s. Madeleine Adriance, *Opting for the Poor: Brazilian Catholicism in Transition* (Sheed and Ward, Kansas City, 1986), pp. 54–9.

18 Baraglia, *Evolução das Comunidades Eclesiais de Base,* p. 59; Paulo P. Koop, 'Lins: comunidades em renovação', in *Vozes,* no. 9 (September 1969), p. 799.

19 References to the Medellín documentation are taken from CELAM: *Second General Conference of Latin American Bishops: The Church in the Present-Day Transformation of Latin America in the Light of the Council: II Conclusions,* 3rd edn (Washington, NCCB, 1979).

20 See Thomas E. Skidmore, *The Politics of Military Rule in Brazil, 1964–1985* (Oxford, Oxford University Press, 1988).

21 Dominique Barbé, *Grace and Power: Base Communities and Nonviolence in Brazil,* tr. J. P. Brown (Maryknoll, NY, Orbis, 1987), p. 92.

22 For the Base Education Movement (MEB), see Luiz E. Wanderley, *Educar Para Transformar: Educação Popular, Igreja Católica e Política no Movimento de Educação de Base* (Petrópolis, Vozes, 1984); for Catholic University Youth (JUC): Luiz A. Gómez de Souza, *A JUC: Os Estudantes Católicos e A Política* (Petrópolis, Vozes, 1984).

23 G. Gutiérrez, 'Toward a Theology of Liberation' (July 1968), in Alfred T. Hennelly (ed.), *Liberation Theology: A Documentary History* (Maryknoll, NY, Orbis, 1990). p. 71.

24 For example, Raimundo Caramuru de Barros, *Comunidade Eclesial de Base: Uma Opção Pastoral Decisiva* (Petrópolis, Vozes, 1968), pp. 55–66.

25 See, for example: Frei Betto, *O Que é Comunidade Eclesial de Base*, 4th edn (São Paulo, Editora Brasiliense, 1981), pp. 29–44; and D. Barbé and E. Retumba, *Retrato de Uma Comunidade de Base: Prática e Teologia de Comunidade de Base* (Petrópolis, Vozes, 1970), pp. 25–34.

26 For a treatment of the pedagogical processes operative within the CEB, see: Antonio Alonso, *Comunidades Eclesiales de Base: Teología-Sociología-Pastoral* (Salamanca, Ediciones Sígueme, 1970), pp. 239–60; José Marins, *Metodologia Emergente das Comunidades Eclesiais de Base* (São Paulo, Edições Paulinas, 1980); Laura M. S. Duarte, *Isto Não se Aprende na Escola: A Educação do Povo nas CEBs* (Petrópolis, Vozes, 1983). With special emphasis upon the use of the Bible, Carlos Mesters, *Defenceless Flower: A New Reading of the Bible*, tr. F. McDonagh (Maryknoll, NY, Orbis/CIIR, 1989).

27 For the earliest of these comments, see: Thomas C. Bruneau, *The Church in Brazil: The Politics of Religion* (Austin, Texas University Press, 1980), p. 176; and Luiz G. de Souza Lima, *Evolução Política dos Católicos e da Igreja no Brasil: Hipóteses para uma Interpretação* (Petrópolis, Vozes, 1979), pp. 240–66.

28 For example: 'Subsídios para Puebla' (São Paulo, Edições Paulinas, 1978); 'Subsídios para uma Política Social' (São Paulo, Edições Paulinas, 1979); 'Igreja e Problemas da Terra' (São Paulo, Edições Paulinas, 1980); 'Reflexão Cristã sobre a Conjuntura Política' *Comunicado Mensal*, 347 (1981), pp. 733–41; 'Solo Urbano e Ação Pastoral' (São Paulo, Edições Paulinas, 1982).

29 Gervásio F. de Queiroga, *Conferência Nacional dos Bispos do Brasil: Comunhão e Corresponsabilidade* (São Paulo, Edições Paulinas, 1977), pp. 394–403.

30 Cook, *The Expectation of the Poor*, p. 68.

31 *Uma Igreja que Nasce do Povo* (Petrópolis, Vozes, 1975).

32 The theme of the second interecclesial gathering (29 July–1 August) was: A Church Born of the People Through the Spirit of God. 'Uma igreja que nasce do povo pelo espírito de Deus – relatório e conclusões do segundo encontro de Vitória', in *SEDOC*, 9, October/November 1976.

33 Brazilians Rubem Alves (*A Theology of Human Hope* (St Meinard, Abbey Press, 1969)) and Hugo Assmann (*Teología desde la Praxis de la Liberación: Ensayo Teológico desde la América Dependiente* (Salamanca, Ediciones Sígueme, 1973) can be counted among the first generation. Brazilians among the second wave of liberation theologians might include, for example, Leonardo Boff, João B. Libânio and Carlos Mesters. See Battista Mondin, *Os Teólogos da Libertação* (São Paulo, Edições Paulinas, 1980); and Christian Smith, *The Emergence of Liberation Theology: Radical Religion and Social Movement Theory* (Chicago, University of Chicago Press, 1991).

34 It was Leonardo Boff's application of basic democratic principles to Roman Catholic ecclesiastical structures in *Church: Charism and Power. Liberation Theology and the Institutional Church*, tr. J. W. Diercksmeier (London, SCM Press, 1985) which most alienated Vatican authorities.

35 Ronald M. Schneider, *'Order and Progress': A Political History of Brazil* (Oxford, Westview Press, 1991), pp. 267ff.

36 For an overview of the restorationist programme and the ongoing debate in Latin America, see J. O. Beozzo (ed.), *O Vaticano II e A Igreja Latino-Americana*, (São Paulo, Edições Paulinas, 1985), pp. 52–86.

37 J. B. Libânio, 'BECs in socio-cultural perspective', in *Transformation*, vol. 3, no. 3 (July/September 1986), pp. 7–11; and Scott Mainwaring, 'Grass-Roots Catholic Groups and Politics in Brazil', in S. Mainwaring and A. Wilde (eds.), *The Progressive Church in Latin America* (Notre Dame, IL, University of Notre Dame Press, 1989), pp. 151–92.
38 Vinícius C. Brant, 'Da Resistência aos Movimentos Sociais: A Emergência das Classes Populares em São Paulo', and Paul Singer, Movimentos de Bairro, in P. Singer and V. C. Brant (eds.), *São Paulo: O Povo em Movimento* (Petrópolis, Vozes, 1980), pp. 9–28, 85–92.
39 Betto, *O Que é Comunidade Eclesial de Base*, pp. 91–2.
40 Scott Mainwaring, *The Catholic Church and Politics in Brazil, 1916–1985* (Stanford, MT, Stanford University Press, 1986), pp. 237–53; Ralph Della Cava, 'The "Peoples Church", the Vatican and Abertura', in Alfred Stepan (ed.), *Democratizing Brazil: Problems of Transition and Consolidation* (Oxford, Oxford University Press, 1989), pp. 143–67.
41 W. E. Hewitt, *Base Christian Communities and Social Change in Brazil* (Lincoln, University of Nebraska Press, 1991), pp. 91–105.

# 8

GERALD WEST

# The Bible and the poor: a new way of doing theology

The question of the relationship between socially engaged biblical scholars and ordinary poor and marginalised readers of the Bible lies at the heart of this chapter. While it may seem strange to begin an essay on 'The Bible and the poor' with such a statement, liberation theologies in their various forms all emerge from the interface between socially committed theologians and ordinary Christians from poor and marginalised communities. The task of this chapter is to understand the contours of the interface more clearly.

As most of the readers of this volume are probably from the First World, we must begin by making it quite clear that liberation theologies are different from First World theology.[1] It is not just that liberation theologies have a different *content*, they are more profoundly different in that they have a different *methodology*. 'The established methodology of First World theology – often regarded as a universally valid norm – has recently been challenged. The challenge comes from different quarters in Africa, Asia, and Latin America, but it also comes from certain groups within the First World, e.g., from Christians within the feminist and labour movements.'[2]

Elaborating on this statement, Per Frostin defines the challenge posed by theologies of liberation with reference to five interrelated emphases: the choice of the interlocutors of theology, the perception of God, the social analysis of conflicts, the choice of theological tools, and the relationship between theology and praxis.[3] Of particular concern in this chapter is the first of these emphases, what Frostin calls 'the interlocutors of theology', because it is this emphasis that shapes each of the others.

Frostin notes that all conferences of the Ecumenical Association of Third World Theologians (EATWOT) have argued persistently for a new method of doing theology. The focus of this stress on methodology is expressed in a concern for epistemology. As early as 1976, the founding members of EATWOT declared that this new methodology was based on a 'radical break in epistemology'.

The theologies from Europe and North America are dominant today in our churches and represent one form of cultural domination. They must be understood to have arisen out of situations related to those countries, and therefore must not be uncritically adopted without our raising the question of their relevance in the context of our countries. Indeed, we must, in order to be faithful to the gospel and to our peoples, reflect on the realities of our own situations and interpret the word of God in relation to these realities. We reject as irrelevant an academic type of theology that is divorced from action. We are prepared for a radical break in epistemology which makes commitment the first act of theology and engages in critical reflection on the praxis of the reality of the Third World.[4]

This quotation makes two crucial points. First, in this methodology there is a stress on epistemology. When liberation theologians stress the question of epistemological issues, questions related to the origin, structure, methods, and validity of knowledge, 'the reason is obviously that they want to explain that their reflection cannot be assessed on the basis of established epistemology. In other words, they do not understand their own contribution as a mere reform within an existing framework but as a challenge to a basic consensus.'[5]

Second, in this new methodology the experience of oppression and of the struggle for liberation are fundamental. The opening phrases of one of the first reflections on liberation theologies, Gustavo Gutiérrez's A Theology of Liberation, emphasises the role of experience as the starting point for theological reflection: 'This book is an attempt at reflection, based on the Gospel and the experiences of men and women committed to the process of liberation in the oppressed and exploited land of Latin America. It is a theological reflection born of the experience of shared efforts to abolish the current unjust situation to build a different society, freer and more human.'[6]

In their emphasis on epistemology and the experience of oppression in the struggle for liberation and life, liberation theologies ask a question not usually asked in Western theology: who are the interlocutors of theology? Or, who are asking the questions that theologians try to answer? Liberation theologies not only pose this question, they also give a specific answer: the poor and marginalised.

Frostin compares liberation theologies with modern Western theology in two ways. He first compares the option for the oppressed as interlocutors of theology with the influential position of Schleiermacher, who addressed the 'cultured critics' of religion.[7] In an important contribution to the first EATWOT conference, Gustavo Gutiérrez interpreted modern Western theology in the light of Schleiermacher's approach. The chief interlocutor of even 'progressivist' Western theology, he maintains, has been the educated non-believer. Liberation theology, by contrast, has chosen 'nonpersons' as its chief interlocutors, 'the poor, the exploited classes, the marginalized races, all the despised cultures'.[8]

In a second comparison, Frostin argues that in Western theology the relation to the poor is usually an ethical question, not an epistemological question. But, he continues, 'such a distinction cannot do justice to the idea of the poor as interlocutors'. According to theologies of liberation, 'solidarity with the poor also has consequences for the perception of the social reality', and so 'an option for the poor' implies 'the epistemological privilege of the poor'. This penetrating expression suggests, argues Frostin, 'that cognizance of the experience of those defined as poor is a necessary condition for theological reflection'.[9]

In other words, theologies of liberation require that we not only make 'an option for the poor', but that we also accept 'the epistemological privilege of the poor'. This involves an epistemological paradigm shift in which the poor and marginalised are seen as the primary dialogue partners of theology. Theology begins with the reality, experience, needs, interests, questions, and resources of the poor and marginalised.

Implicit in my discussion of liberation theologies so far is some form of relationship between the theologian and the ordinary Christian from a poor and marginalised community. We must now probe the form of that relationship more carefully. In order to do this I will concentrate on the Bible and the poor.

## Biblical scholarship and the contribution of the common people

The Bible is and has been one of the basic sources of liberation theologies. This is certainly the case in South African and African American Black theology, Latin American liberation theology, African American womanist theology, and feminist theologies.[10] For the poor in particular, the Bible is not merely a strategic tool for liberation; the Bible is *the* source of 'God's project', which is a project of liberation. An anecdote and two recent pieces of research from South Africa illustrate this point.

The dilemma that confronts black South Africans in their relationship with the Bible is captured in the following well-known anecdote: 'When the white man came to our country he had the Bible and we had the land. The white man said to us "Let us pray." After the prayer, the white man had the land and we had the Bible.' This anecdote clearly points to the central position that the Bible occupies in the process of oppression and exploitation. The anecdote also reflects the paradox of the oppressor and the oppressed sharing the same Bible and the same faith. However, what is remarkable about this anecdote is that Desmond Tutu responded to it after one of its tellings by stating, 'And we got the better deal.' While Tutu's response would be and has been challenged, it does capture something of the reality of the Bible in South Africa (and elsewhere): it plays a central role in the lives of many, particularly the poor and marginalised. The Bible is a symbol of the presence of the God of life with them.

Two recent studies have clearly demonstrated this. In discussing the construction of an indigenous theology of work in South Africa, James Cochrane makes some penetrating comments on workers reading the Bible.[11] He argues that besides being 'the primary source of the Christian mythos', the Bible 'is probably the only source of theology for most members of our churches. It is, as some have said, the people's book par excellence.'[12]

Cochrane's argument is supported by the Institute for Contextual Theology's Church and Labour Project Research Group. The report of this group notes that perhaps 'the most interesting question of all, given the response to it, was whether or not the Bible had any significance for workers, and if so, what kind of a meaning it could have'. 'The answers are astonishing,' the report continues, 'at least to anyone who might have thought that the general picture of a relatively high level of alienation from the Church would be echoed in this question.' The research found that an effective 80 per cent of respondents regarded the Bible as significant, which, as the report notes, is 'a very high positive evaluation in the light of all the other generally more negative data' concerning, for example, the relevance of the Church. 'Overall,' the report concludes, 'the most important conclusion to be drawn from this question is that the Bible is a rich source of interpretation for the worker's life, certainly of much greater significance than the liturgical and pastoral operations of the Church.'[13]

In his research with the informal peri-urban shack community of Amaoti, Graham Philpott examines 'how members of that community use and re-interpet the symbol of the kingdom of God to make meaning of and communicate their reality of poverty and oppression, of suffering and hope'. He notes that '[t]he re-interpretation of this symbol has emerged from a particular Bible study group which has met regularly over a four-year period to reflect on their involvement in the struggles of their community *in the light of the God who is revealed in the Bible* and in their community life'.[14] Philpott goes on to argue that 'This reflection has equipped them better to *dialogue with and engage the oppressive reality* of their community, so that they can work against the forces of death and be involved in engendering life.' The Bible is central to the process.

But, and this is a significant 'but', having demonstrated the primary place the Bible has among the poor and marginalised and having argued that the experience of the poor is a necessary constituent of doing theology, what role do the biblical interpretations of the poor play in liberation theology?

There are two lines of response to this question, and at the core of each response is a different understanding of the relationship between the theologian and the ordinary poor Bible reader. In the Latin American context, for example, Jan Luis Segundo has analysed this question with remarkable clarity. In an important article Segundo outlines the shift within Latin American theology between 'two lines' of liberation theology, one foregrounding the categories and contribution of the theologian or biblical scholar and the other foregrounding the categories and contribution of 'the common people'.

Segundo looks at the history, aims, methods, and results of at least two theologies of liberation coexisting in Latin America. The first line of response has three characteristics: the solidarity of biblical scholars and theologians with the poor and marginalised; a methodological suspicion that Christian faith at all levels of society is ideologically distorted and thus serves the status quo; and finally, a commitment to provide 'the pastoral activities of the Church with a new and de-ideologized theology capable of speaking about the common themes of Christian faith'.[15] Because it is the social sciences that 'provide the theologian who wants to carry out a de-ideologizing task with valuable cognitive tools', and because these are 'tools which . . . are beyond the grasp of the majority of people',[16] the role of the theologian or biblical scholar is emphasised. An option is made for the poor, but the categories and contribution of their experience is subordinated to or translated into the terms of the intellectual trained in the social sciences.

However, the rise of popular movements either outside or inside the Church 'had shown that common people had neither understood nor welcomed anything from the first theology of liberation, and had actually reacted against its criticism of the supposed oppressive elements of popular religion'.[17] And so it appeared then that 'if theologians were still to be the "organic intellectuals" of the common people, that is to say useful as intellectuals charged with the understanding of popular faith, they were obliged to learn how oppressed people lived their faith'.[18] So theologians wanting to be in religious matters the organic intellectuals of poor and marginalised people, 'began then to understand their function as one of unifying and structuring people's understanding of their faith, as well as grounding and defending the practices coming from this faith'.[19]

Although Segundo, like other liberation theologians, empathises with much in this second position, he does not want 'to give up the first *critical* function which comes out of a suspicion that theology, like other all-pervasive cultural features, can and perhaps should be considered an instrument of oppression and, hence, as a non-Christian theology'.[20] He then goes on immediately to claim that '[f]acts point so obviously in that direction that theologians belonging explicitly to the second line cannot but raise the same central question.' But do 'facts point so obviously in that direction'? I do not think so. Let me explain.

The tension between these two positions can be found in every context in which there is a struggle for liberation and life, and at the centre of this difference, as I have already suggested, is the relationship between the socially engaged biblical scholar or theologian and the ordinary poor and marginalised believer. The emphasis tends to be either on the critical contribution of the trained reader or on the reading resources of the ordinary reader. Both emphases want the Bible to be a resource for liberation and life. But for this to be a reality one position argues the Bible must be read critically,[21] and so the ordinary reader must to some extent be dependent on the work of biblical scholarship, while for the other position the Bible must be read from the perspective of the poor and oppressed, and so the trained reader must to some extent be dependent on the readings of ordinary readers. In other words, for the Bible to be a resource of liberation and life there needs to be an appropriate relationship between the trained reader and the ordinary reader, but there are differing opinions on where to place the emphasis, on the trained reader or the ordinary reader. In order to analyse these differences in emphasis it will be useful to reconsider the dynamics and complexity of oppression and domination and to reconsider the role of the organic intellectual.

For Paulo Freire, among others,[22] 'the logic of domination represents a combination of historical and contemporary ideological and material practices that are never completely successful, always embody contradictions, and are constantly being fought over within asymmetrical relations of power'.[23] In other words, we find in Freire's work a discourse that begins to bridge the relationship between agency and structure, 'a discourse that situates human action in constraints forged in historical and contemporary practices, while also pointing to the spaces, contradictions, and forms of resistance that raise the possibility for social struggle'.[24] However, in Freire's analysis of domination, the poor and oppressed are not only oppressed by external structures and forces, they also internalise and thus participate in their own oppression. So Freire argues that oppressed people's accommodation to the logic of domination may mean that they actively resist emancipatory forms of knowledge.[25]

But in James Scott's study of domination and resistance we find a more nuanced analysis, arguing that theories of hegemony and false consciousness do not take account of what he calls 'the hidden transcript'.[26]

> Every subordinate group creates, out of its ordeal, a 'hidden transcript' that represents a critique of power spoken behind the back of the dominant. The powerful, for their part, also develop a hidden transcript representing the practices and claims of their rule that cannot be openly avowed. A comparison of the hidden transcipt of the weak with that of the powerful and of *both* hidden transcripts to the public transcript of power relations offers a substantially new way of understanding resistance to domination.[27]

The crucial point of Scott's detailed argument is that '[t]he public transcript, where it is not positively misleading, is unlikely to tell the whole story about power relations. It is frequently in the interest of both parties to tacitly conspire in misrepresentation.'[28] So social analysis which focuses on the public transcript, as most social analysis does, is focusing on the formal relations between the powerful and weak,[29] but is not attempting to 'read, interpret, and understand the often fugitive political conduct of subordinate groups'.[30] A focus on the hidden transcript, where it is accessible in the rumours, gossip, folktales, songs, gestures, jokes, and theatre of the poor and marginalised, or the more public infrapolitics of popular culture,[31] reveals forms of resistance and defiance. 'Unless one can penetrate the official transcript of both subordinates and elites, a reading of the social evidence will almost always represent a confirmation of the status quo in hegemonic terms.'[32]

But is there still not a case for the Italian social theorist Antonio Gramsci's notion of the dominated consciousness of the working class? For Gramsci hegemony works primarily at the level of thought as distinct from the level of action. Scott turns this around. He considers 'subordinate classes *less* constrained at the level of thought and ideology, since they can in secluded settings speak with comparative safety, and *more* constrained at the level of political action and struggle, where the daily exercise of power sharply limits the options available to them'.[33] So he argues that 'subordinate groups have typically learned, in situations short of those rare all-or-nothing struggles, to clothe their resistance and defiance in ritualisms of subordination that serve both to disguise their purposes and to provide them with a ready route of retreat that may soften the consequences of a possible failure'.[34] This is because most protests and challenges – even quite violent ones – 'are made in the realistic expectation that the central features of the form of domination will remain intact'. Consequently, '[m]ost acts of power from below, even when they are protests – implicitly or explicitly – will largely observe the "rules" even if their objective is to undermine them'.[35] He believes 'the historical evidence clearly shows that subordinate groups have been capable of revolutionary *thought* that repudiates existing forms of domination'.[36] However, because the occasions on which subordinate groups have been able to act openly and fully on that thought are rare, the conflict will usually take 'a dialogic form in which the language of the dialogue will invariably borrow heavily from the terms of the dominant ideology prevailing in the public transcipt'. So we must 'consider the dominant discourse as a plastic idiom or dialect that is capable of carrying an enormous variety of meanings, including those that are subversive of their use as intended by the dominant'.[37]

The picture that emerges from this brief overview of Freire's and Scott's analyses of domination and resistance is clearly complex. If we are to understand the meaning of liberation we must first understand the form that domination takes, the nature of its location, and the problems it poses for those who experience it as both a subjective and an objective force.[38] Because there is no 'average' ordinary reader and no 'average' context of poverty and oppression, trained readers committed to working with the poor and marginalised will have differing emphases depending on their analysis of the nature of domination and oppression within specific contexts. So, for example, in Albert Nolan's work with politicised and critically conscious workers in South Africa, he emphasises the possibilities and resources for self-emancipation.[39] In Mosala's work with members of an African Independent Church, a Zion Apostolic Church, who he believes have in certain respects internalised their own oppression, he emphasises the need for critical resources.[40] Although analyses may differ, as in the case of Mosala and Nolan, the starting point remains the same: the social and historical particularities, the problems, sufferings, visions, and acts of resistance of the poor and oppressed constitute the starting point for the committed intellectual.[41]

The contours of an appropriate relationship between socially committed biblical scholars and ordinary poor readers of the Bible are still complex, but some clarity is emerging. Whether biblical scholars are organic intellectuals, those fused organically with the culture and practical activities of the oppressed,[42] or intellectuals like myself, a white, middle-class male, who are not and cannot be *organic* intellectuals and yet who are committed to the struggles of the poor and marginalised, we can only inhabit the 'ongoing tension between avoiding the indignity of speaking for the oppressed and attempting to respond to their voices by engaging in social and political critique'[43] by moving beyond 'speaking for', and beyond 'listening to' the poor and oppressed, towards 'speaking to/[with]' the poor and oppressed.[44]

'Listening to' presupposes the speaking voice of a wholly self-knowing subject free from ideology, while 'speaking for' denies the subject status of the poor and oppressed altogether. In other words, the danger of 'listening to' is that we romanticise and idealise the contribution of the poor, while the danger of 'speaking for' is that we minimise and rationalise the contribution of the poor. Jill Arnott argues that Gayatri Spivak uses the phrase 'speaking to/[with]' to point to 'the need to occupy the dialectical space between two subject-positions, without ever allowing either to become transparent'. 'By remaining constantly alert to, and interrogative of, her own positionality and that of her subject, and ensuring that the mediating process of representation remains visible', the feminist intellectual 'may succeed in enabling a dialogue in which the "testimony of the [subaltern] woman's voice-consciousness" can be heard'.[45]

Clearly 'such a testimony would not be ideology-transcendent or "fully" subjective',[46] 'but it would not be misrecognised as such, and it would, at least, be heard'.[47] In other words, Arnott and Spivak are arguing that 'speaking to/with' takes seriously the subjectivity of both the intellectual and the subaltern, and all that this entails for their respective resources, categories, and contributions. However, the power relations in the interface between the subaltern (or what I call the 'ordinary reader') and the intellectual (or what I call the 'trained reader') cannot be obliterated, and they must not be ignored. They must be foregrounded.

Postmodern feminists like Arnott and Spivak emphasise the creative and constructive potential of 'a genuinely dialectical interaction between two vigilantly foregrounded subject-positions'.[48] Provided the unequal power relations between ordinary and trained readers are acknowledged and foregrounded, provided the trained reader is willing to serve and to learn 'from below', and provided the poor and marginalised continue to empower and be empowered, there is hope for something truly transformative emerging from the interface between trained and ordinary readers of the Bible.

## Models of contextual Bible study

Within contexts like Brazil and South Africa such an interface between an engaged biblical study with its socially committed trained readers of the Bible and ordinary poor readers of the Bible is developing. The *contextual Bible study* interface functions within four commitments, which have emerged from the reading practice of the interface: first, a commitment to begin with reality as perceived by the organised base; second, a commitment to read the Bible in community; third, a commitment to read the Bible critically; and fourth, a commitment to socio-political transformation through Bible reading.[49] Two examples of what we call 'contextual Bible study' will illustrate many of the points I have made, and will also serve to offer examples of the contextual Bible study process and product as it took place in an actual series of Bible studies in South Africa.

In a research project with a range of Anglican Bible study groups in Pietermaritzburg, South Africa, a colleague and I noted that almost all the readers, irrespective of their different contexts, understood Mark 10.17–22 as a story about individual sin.[50] In this story the sin was putting wealth/possessions before following Jesus. This was the sin of the man in the story (in the time of Jesus), and this was a potential sin for present-day readers. The challenge to the wealthy man (then) and to the participants (now) was to make sure that wealth was not an idol, that possessions did not come between them and Jesus.

In one or two groups, significantly groups from poor and oppressed communities, there was some discussion of 'structural sin'. In other words, participants in some groups argued that the problem was not only one of individual sin but also one of structural or systemic sin. However, only one group pursued this reading with any persistence.[51] But it was this possible reading which provoked a series of Bible studies, particularly as 'structural sin' was a key concept at that time in the struggle against apartheid.[52] A series of workshops which I was invited to facilitate provided a useful opportunity to develop a contextual Bible study on Mark 10.17–22.

The Bible studies were conducted during seven workshops with people from a number of different contexts, the majority of whom were from poor and marginalised communities. A common feature of all workshops was that most of the participants were politically conscientised. For each of the groups the Bible was a significant text and Bible study a serious religious experience.

My commitment to a process of 'speaking to/with' required that I acknowledge and foreground my own contribution to the process of 'reading with'. As I will describe in more detail below, my contribution to the reading process was limited to constantly encouraging and facilitating a critical reading of the text. The substantive contribution came from the resources, categories, concepts and experiences of ordinary readers.

There was considerable continuity between workshops in that my own contribution had been shaped extensively by the previous workshop(s). In addition, I would also share the comments and questions of previous workshops with subsequent workshops. This enabled a form of dialogue to develop between successive workshops. In a sense, therefore, there was a 'speaking with' through me with the participants who had shaped my speaking.

In each workshop I was acutely aware of the power dynamics implicit in my presence. My training gave me power in the context of Bible study. There were, of course, other locations of power in each Bible study group. Like Michel Foucault, I recognise that there are multifarious points of power.[53] The ordinary readers in the Bible study groups also had power, particularly those who came from communities of the poor and oppressed. They had power because they are the privileged voice of the poor and oppressed in the contextual Bible study process and in the process of 'reading with'.

Recognising these particular locations of power, I was especially concerned that ordinary readers did not simply defer to my reading/interpretation, that they did not offer the 'expected', 'orthodox', reading, and that they did not opt for 'a fundamentalism of the Left'. So I was determined to foreground my own contribution to the reading process, and also to assist ordinary readers in *reading the text*. For a variety of reasons,[54] the critical mode of reading I chose enabled a close and careful reading of the text. I therefore concentrated my contribution on certain aspects of the text, specifically the link between the commandments (v. 19) and the link between these commandments and the command to the man to sell all that he possesses and to give to the poor (v. 21). Because ordinary readers tend not to read the text carefully,[55] one of my roles as a facilitator was to constantly return their reading to the text.

When ordinary readers in these workshops read verse 19 carefully, prompted by questions on the commandments,[56] there was general agreement that these commandments were concerned with social relationships (in contrast to the omitted commandments which referred to the human-to-God relationship). Once ordinary readers realised this, they then began to explore *why* Jesus chose these commandments, and concluded that there was obviously something wrong in the area of the man's social relationships. This realisation in turn led to considerable discussion and debate as the readers probed for a more precise understanding of the problems in the man's social relationships.

As ordinary readers began to explore and probe these questions, they were constantly driven *to reread the text*. For example, many readers went back to the questions concerning the challenge of Jesus,[57] and then back to the text to reread it more closely and carefully. Verse 22, with its reference to 'much property',[58] became a key verse in their attempt to understand this man's wealth.

The more critical reading process did not prevent readers from drawing on their own experience and resources. Their rereading of the text generated at first a certain amount of frustration, because the text did not seem to give many clues concerning the man's social relationships. However, by drawing on their own South African experience some readers argued that the man probably obtained his 'much property' through exploiting others. There were other ordinary readers who argued that this was not the only possible reading, and that this man could have worked hard for or inherited his 'much property'. Through most of this discussion and debate I attempted to facilitate discussion on as broad a basis as possible, encouraging all participants to share their views. But as I have already stated, my contribution was to pose specific questions which would return readers to the text. So when some readers themselves recognised the social and structural dimensions of 'owning much property', I focused their reading on the relationship between the commandments (v. 19), the command to the man to sell all he possessed and to give to the poor (v. 21), and the statement that he owned much property (v. 22), encouraging them to explore the internal relationships within the text.

Once again my contribution led to a return to the text. Those ordinary readers who had argued that the man had probably obtained his 'much property' by exploiting others, based on their own South African experience, now found textual evidence to support this argument. Gradually others began to see this argument, and so a reading of Mark 10.17–22 which included a concern for social and structural sin began to emerge.

In exploring the relationship between the commandments (v. 19), the command to the man to sell all he possessed and to give to the poor (v. 21), and the statement that he owned much property (v. 22), we understood that the text (and Jesus)[59] made a connection between the socially orientated commandments, the wealth of the man, and the poor. We argued that Jesus chose these commandments because he knew that the man had gained his 'much property' by exploiting the poor, whether or not the man himself had done so consciously or personally. In other words, we argued that there might have been social structures which produced wealth for the man and exploited the people, in the same way that the social system of apartheid empowered white South Africans to become wealthy and pushed black South Africans into poverty. So even if the man had worked hard for his property or had inherited his wealth, he was still part of sinful social structures.

Given this reading, the challenge of Jesus to the man (v. 21) to sell all he possessed and to give to the poor made sense. The man could not follow Jesus until he had repented of, and made restitution for, his social and structural sin. As the Third World document *The Road to Damascus* argues,[60] following Jesus requires structural repentance and conversion.

The commandments in verse 19 also took on a new meaning in the light of this reading. The man thought that he had kept the commandments, but he was thinking only on an individual level. While he himself might not have murdered anyone, or committed adultery, or stolen, or given false testimony, or defrauded, or dishonoured his parents, he was a part of and perpetuated a system that did all of these things. The ordinary readers in the workshops, most of whom were black, gave countless examples of how the apartheid system had resulted in murder, adultery, theft, legal injustice, unjust wages, and the destruction of black family life. For example, an inadequate health system for black people, impoverished 'homelands' and townships, and biased and brutal security forces murdered black people every day. The migrant labour system, pass laws, the group areas act, and single-sex hostels all generated adultery and destroyed family life. Forced removals, no minimum wage, and education for inferiority were forms of theft and fraud. The discriminatory legal system and the state-controlled media constantly disseminated false and biased testimony.

The challenge of Mark 10.17–22 was clear to us. The man, and those who are like him today, must repent and make restitution before they/we could be reconciled to God. This text (and Jesus) seemed to say that there could be no reconciliation with God, and no membership in the community of Jesus, without repentance and restitution. So while we must be constantly alert to wealth as an idolatrous danger, we must also be constantly critical of our social location in sinful structures and systems.

A further example might also be useful, particularly as it demonstrates the growing awareness in our work that critical resources are already present in poor and marginalised communities. The Institute for the Study of the Bible (ISB) was invited by a women's group in Umtata, a rural town in South Africa, to facilitate a workshop on 'liberating ways of reading the Bible as women'. The group consists of a majority of black women, most of whom are from Umtata, with a few from rural areas, and a few white women from Umtata.

Although the theme of the workshop was determined by the Umtata women's group, as well as the programme, the ISB was asked to suggest some texts for Bible study. Mark 5.21–6.1 was one of the texts used. The text was chosen because two of the main characters are women. Besides this, there was no clear sense of where the Bible study group might go with the text. No exegesis was done in preparation, and only three questions were used to facilitate the Bible study process.

Question 1: Read Mark 5.21–6.1 and discuss in small groups what this text is about.

Question 2: If this text is about women, what is it saying?

Question 3: In what way does this text speak to us today?

Question 1 was designed to encourage participants to read the text carefully and closely. Question 2 had a similar purpose, but also invited readers to probe behind the text to the society that produced the text. The final question, question 3, drew text and the readers' context together in an act of appropriation.

My role as facilitator was to provide what Cornel West calls 'enabling forms of criticism'.[61] In this case the process entailed first, encouraging participants to read the text fully, carefully, and closely, and then, when asked, providing some resources for reflection on the type of society that produced the text. The resulting discussion, first in groups and then in plenary report-back, produced the basic elements of form and content that constitute the reading that follows below. There is nothing in the final form of the reading that did not have its beginning in that first Bible study group among ordinary African women readers.

But the process of the reading's production did not end there. Subsequent to the Umtata women's workshop, a local Anglican church asked me to preach on the subject of 'Compassion and women'. I declined to preach, but offered to do a short workshop instead. The same format was used as with the Umtata women's group, but this time the ordinary readers were mainly white, about 60 per cent women and 40 per cent men. Their responses too have shaped this reading, just as the responses of the Umtata women's group shaped the responses of the local church participants.

I then did the workshop with a Master's class in the School of Theology, University of Natal, Pietermaritzburg. This time the responses of trained readers were allowed to shape the Bible study, but only in ways that were 'accountable' to the shape that had emerged 'from below'. This was not difficult or forced because most of the responses of these trained readers, half of whom are women and half of whom are black, supported and strengthened the reading of the ordinary readers. The readings of the trained readers might have been more systematic, but the contextual Bible study process produced substantially similar responses.

The final stage in the development of the reading presented here included some systematic structuring and further textual and sociological support for the reading that had already emerged from the contextual Bible study process. It was remarkable to discover how, for example, reference to the

Greek text reinforced and supported a reading that had initially emerged from ordinary poor African women readers.

Initial responses to the first question concerning what Mark 5.21–6.1 is about included the following: healing, compassion, faith, love, hope, despair, suffering, power, and other similar themes. When the groups had reported back with these reponses, I then asked the plenary group as a whole whether they thought the text could also be about women. There was an immediate buzz as participants began to explore this option with each other. I therefore asked them to go back into their small groups to discuss the question more fully and to support their discussion with careful reference to the text.

Participants argued that a careful reading of the text did indicate that the story is about women. The groups supported this reading in the following way. First, the story of the two women is a literary unit, delimited by the geographic shifts in verses 5.21 and 6.1. Second, although the central character appears initially to be a man, Jairus, the central characters in the story are in fact two women. Jairus does initiate the action, but is then ignored as first the woman with the flow of blood and then Jairus' daughter move to centre-stage. The actual absence of the first woman, Jairus' daughter, emphasises her narrative presence. The plot depends on her presence. Similarly, the woman with the flow of blood, the second woman, is foregrounded even though she seeks to be self-effacing. And while Jesus is still speaking to the second woman, the first woman is again presented (verse 35). It is almost as if the narrator himself (herself?) is interrupted – the narrative certainly is – by the unnamed woman with the flow of blood. The careful narrative introduction of Jairus, a named male with power (verse 22), is first interrupted, and then deconstructed, by the unnamed woman with no power.

Third, that the plot and sub-plot are carefully connected is stressed by the repetition of 'daughter', in verse 34 with reference to the second woman and in verse 35 with reference to the first woman. The ambiguity of 'your daughter', referring to Jairus and possibly to Jesus, in verse 35 reinforces this connection. The women, and so their stories, are also linked by repetition of 'twelve years' (verses 25 and 42). It has also been suggested by some readers that 'twelve years' may, in the case of the young woman, be an allusion to the onset of menstruation and so the beginning of fertility. The flow of blood for the younger woman meant life was possible, but the flow of blood for the older woman meant that life was no longer possible. The young woman of twelve years of age is a narrative reminder of the child(ren) that the older woman has not been able to bear. Here is another link between the two stories. There is also a parallel structure to each episode. In each case the woman is defined by her social location; in each case the woman is in need; in each case Jesus responds to her need; in each case the woman is unclean; in each case there is contact, touching, between Jesus and the woman; in each case Jesus speaks to the woman; in each case there is healing and restoration of the woman to the community.

We agreed, then, that this text is about women. This does not mean, of course, that the text is not also about other things as well. But it is clearly, and probably primarily, about women.

At this point in the workshops we moved on to the second question: If this text is about women, what is it saying? Small group discussion and report-back on this question generated a clear understanding of the issues involved but also many questions of a historical and sociological nature, so I offered historical and sociological resources as they were requested. Participants then returned to their small groups before the final plenary report-back.

Participants argued that both women in the story are initially identified in terms of patriarchal social systems, and not in their own right. They are not named, they are described in terms of their location within two central social systems. The first woman is defined by the patriarchal system of first-century Palestine. She is defined in terms of her relationship to a male, her father. The second woman is defined by the purity system of first-century Palestine. She is defined in terms of her uncleanness, her flow of blood. Both women, in other words, are situated in social systems that determine how the world in which they live relates to them.

But Jesus responds differently. Having heard the story of the second woman, he embraces her uncleanness by affirming her faith and healing. Her twelve years of uncleanness and social alienation are ended when she is healed and restored to the community. The acceptance and affirmation of Jesus, together with her faith, bring freedom from her religious, economic (verse 26), sexual and social suffering. The nameless, self-effacing woman has become a part of the Jesus movement; has become 'daughter'. Jesus has literally empowered her! (verse 30)

There will still be times when this woman will not be able to worship in the temple, when she will not be able to be touched, when she will be unclean, when she will be marginalised by the patriarchal purity system. But that system has been challenged by her story.

Similarly with the first woman. Not only does Jesus touch her unclean dead body (verse 41), he also refers to her in her own right rather than as the property of her father. Her father and 'some men' (used by certain English translations) refer to her in the patriarchal genitive (verses 23 and

35). Jesus relates to the young woman as a subject, not as an object (verses 39 and 41). Significantly, the narrator adopts Jesus' subject designation in verse 40, in his (her?) implicit refusal to relate to the young woman as the property of her father, rather than the patriarchal language of Jairus and his men. He even goes so far as to reverse the genitive of possession. Instead of defining the young woman as possessed by her father, as an object (see verse 23 where Jairus refers to her as 'My little daughter'), the narrator now designates her as a subject, possessing her father and mother (verse 40).

There will still be times when this young woman is defined in terms of her social location within a patriarchal household, when she will be described with the possessive case, when she will be treated as an object by the patriarchal system. But that system has been challenged by her story.

The final question related text and present context: In what way does this text speak to us today? There were a variety of responses to this last question. In one group, for example, women began to explore ways of lobbying the new government to make health care for women a priority. In another group, the women decided to design a series of Bible studies that would make men in their congregations more conscious of structures and attitudes that oppress women. Overall, women experienced the Bible study as empowering. In the words of one woman, 'This Bible study has stopped me from throwing my Bible into the toilet and flushing it away.'

As I have already indicated, this workshop did not produce the above reading 'as is'. This reading in its final form is the product of a longer process, but the basic shape and substance of the reading emerged from this group.

We can now return to our earlier discussion by reflecting on these examples. The contextual Bible study process that produced these readings is suggestive in a number of respects. Contextual Bible study begins with the needs and concerns of poor and marginalised communities. The question or questions that shape the Bible reading emerge from below, not from above. So, for example, in actual contextual readings of Mark 5.21–6.1 the life interests of the participating group determined the theme, in each case the theme focused on 'women'. In the three workshops in which this text was used the theme was related to the needs and concerns of women. Trained readers did not dictate the theme, it emerged from the life experience of ordinary readers.

The ISB is committed to working with organised communities or groups who can 'talk back' and who have the identity, structures, and resources to 'own' the workshop process. In other words, the ISB deliberately chooses to work in those contexts in which it is possible for the subject positions of both the ISB staff and the community participants to be vigilantly fore-grounded. The relationship between trained and ordinary reader is subject to subject and not subject to object. The trained reader reads the Bible 'with' and not 'for' ordinary readers.[62]

Within such a framework of accountability to Bible study groups of ordinary readers, trained readers can participate fully in the Bible study process. For example, in the workshops on the two women in Mark 5, I as a trained reader suggested that this text, along with a number of other texts identified by the groups, might be relevant to the chosen theme of 'women'. The advantage of a text like Mark 5.21–6.1 is that is not usually perceived as a text primarily about women. Consequently, reading this text in this way 'surprises' the readers, and facilitates a more critical reading of the text. The danger with well-known texts is that we think we already know what they mean; we 'domesticate' and 'tame' them. The disclosive power of the 'untamed' and 'undomesticated' text is a contribution that trained readers can make to the contextual reading process. And this was the effect. On an initial reading most readers did not consider that the text was primarily about women. But once this was suggested and supported from a careful reading of the text there was great excitement and expecta-tion. Women were no longer incidental to christological concerns; the text was about women.[63]

In any reading of the Bible in the interface between trained and ordinary readers there is a great deal that ordinary readers can discover and recover in texts using their own resources, provided there is some facilitation of this process. So in the workshops the Bible was read communally, in small groups. My role was to facilitate a more critical reading, by bringing to the reading process additional critical resources. For example, instead of me providing evidence from the text to support the suggestion that the text was about women, it was usually sufficient to give one or two examples from the text and then to ask the groups to find additional examples. My task was then to summarise and systematise their arguments. Contextual Bible study, then, is committed to corporate and communal reading of the Bible in which the trained reader is just another reader with *different* resources and skills, not *better* resources and skills.[64]

As already indicated, the contextual reading process is also committed to critical readings of the Bible. While ordinary readers do have critical resources, these are not the specific critical resources of biblical studies. Ordinary readers, by definition, read the Bible pre-critically, while trained readers read the Bible critically (or post-critically).[65] Once again, creative facilitation can enable ordinary readers to read more critically than is their usual practice, and this seems to be what poor and marginalised readers want with the resources of biblical scholarship. In the readings of both texts in Mark I concentrated on providing resources for two critical modes of reading. A close and careful (literary) mode of reading was used in order to support the suggestion that Mark 10.17–22 was about structural sin and that Mark 5.21–6.1 was primarily about women. The use of narrative transitions to delimit the literary unit, the reading of the whole text to discern its structure, the careful and close reading of the component parts, the return to reread the text as a whole in the light of the reading of the parts, and the continual attention to the internal relationships within the text, including reference to plot, character, theme, repetition, and other literary devices, are elements of this mode of reading.[66] And while ordinary readers are not familiar with these literary resources for reading in any systematic way, they are able to recognise and appreciate their usefulness and integrate these resources into their own modes of reading.

A historical and sociological mode of reading was also used to situate these texts in their first-century contexts. The implicit use of historical-critical tools to delimit the text, and to locate it historically, and the reconstruction of aspects of the sociological setting of the text, including reference to the patriarchal and purity systems, are elements of this mode of reading.[67] Once again, while ordinary readers are not familiar with these historical and sociological resources, they are able to recognise and appreciate their usefulness and integrate these resources into their own modes of reading. As with the literary resources used, the historical and sociological resources were not used as ends in themselves, as is usually the case in biblical scholarship, but as resources for interpretation in the fullest sense. I will say more on this below.

It must be stressed again that these critical resources were not used as the way into the text. The Bible study began with a life interest of the participants. The generative theme determined by the group, in the second example the theme of 'women', provided the initial mode of reading. This mode of reading is similar to what I have called 'reading in front of the text',[68] although as practised by ordinary readers it is usually not a critical mode of reading. But a thematic approach does provide a useful way into the text, particularly as it draws on the needs and questions of the participants. The role of the other modes of reading is then to develop and elaborate what is initiated through this thematic approach to the text.

The range of experience that groups of ordinary readers bring to their reading of the Bible is various and vast. Creative facilitation, including asking questions instead of simply providing information, can draw on the resources of ordinary readers and in so doing empower them to construct their own critical and contextual readings.

Our task as biblical scholars in the contextual Bible study process is not to do the reading for ordinary readers, nor to simply uncritically accept their readings. Rather, our task is to read the Bible *with* ordinary readers. This requires that we vigilantly foreground our respective subject positions, and that we become explicit concerning the power relations implicit in the reading process.[69]

The key contribution of critical resources to the contextual Bible study process is that it enables ordinary readers themselves to articulate 'the hidden transcript' and not only 'the public transcript', both in the Bible and in their own traditions of interpretation. Critical tools and skills provide ordinary readers with a means for articulating what is incipient and subjugated.[70] While the first response in many Bible study groups is often the 'missionary response' or the dogmatically 'correct' response – the public transcript – critical modes of reading enable ordinary people from poor and marginalised communities to begin to articulate readings and theologies that are incipient and even perhaps elements of readings and theologies that are deliberately hidden from public view. The latter is clearly dangerous; what is hidden from the dominant is hidden for good reason, and can and should only be openly spoken in a context of trust and accountability. But within such a context, the intersection of contextual and critical resources enables the recognising, recovering, and arousing of dangerous memories, subjugated knowledges, and hidden transcripts.

The more systematic, critical, reading process of contextual Bible study provides ordinary readers with the resources to situate the text within its literary and linguistic context and within its historical and sociological context and in so doing enables the text to be appropriated more critically. Situating the text in these ways also prevents a simple correspondence between text and present context and so facilitates a more critical appropriation which takes seriously a structural 'reading' of both text and context.[71] By beginning with and foregrounding the questions, needs, experiences and resources of ordinary poor readers the contextual Bible study process belongs to and is owned by them. Their culture, categories, and concepts constitute the core of the reading process.

Reading the Bible with ordinary readers also challenges the trained reader. The trained reader is not only challenged to take seriously the experiences, categories, and concepts of the poor, but also to complete the hermeneutic cycle and risk appropriation, albeit a critical appropriation. In the contextual Bible study process trained readers cannot be content to remain with 'what it meant', we must move on to risk asking 'what it means', for our communities, ourselves, and those poor and marginalised communities who are our primary interlocutors. Historical-critical resources, together with sociological resources, are no longer sterile tools for reconstructing the past; they are resources for interpretation in the fullest sense, which includes the risk of appropriation for liberation and life. Similarly, literary resources must not only produce 'interesting' readings; they must provide resources for interested readings – readings that matter.

It is important to recognise that in the process of contextual Bible study it is quite legitimate for ordinary readers and trained readers to emerge from the reading process with different challenges. The readings produced in this interface affect ordinary and trained readers differently, and this is not surprising because we come to the text from different places, and after the reading encounter return to our different places. Our subjectivities as trained and ordinary readers are differently constituted, and so the effect that the corporate reading has on our subjectivities will be different. However, and this is extremely important, we will have been partially constituted by each other's subjectivities.[72] And this should always be a constituent element of the contextual Bible study process: a desire to be partially constituted by those from other communities. For me, this means choosing to be partially constituted by working with poor and marginalised communities.

Reading the Bible with ordinary readers is a creative and challenging process. From the perspective of liberation hermeneutics there is no choice. If we are to do theology in situations of struggle for liberation and life then the readings of the poor are a necessary resource. If we are serious about 'an option for the poor' we must read the Bible *with them*.

## NOTES

1 Of course there is no one such thing as 'First World theology', even though proponents would like to think there is. First World theology is really a cluster of theologies with often hidden sets of interests and agendas.

2 P. Frostin, *Liberation Theology in Tanzania and South Africa: A First World Interpretation* (Lund, Lund University Press, 1988), p. 1.

3 Ibid., pp. 6–11.

4 S. Torres and V. Fabella (eds.), *The Emergent Gospel: Theology from the Underside of History* (Maryknoll, NY, Orbis, 1978), p. 269.

5 Frostin, *Liberation Theology in Tanzania*, pp. 3–4.

6 G. Gutiérrez, *A Theology of Liberation: History, Politics and Salvation* (London, SCM, 1974), p. ix.

7 Cited in Frostin, *Liberation Theology in Tanzania*, p. 6.

8 'The main issue between progressive Western theology and its interlocutors, has been whether God exists or not, while the central problem in Third World countries is not atheism but an idolatrous submission to systems of oppression' (ibid., pp. 7–8).

9 Ibid., p. 6.
10 Of these theologies, those that find the Bible most problematic are feminist theologies. See L. E. Cady, 'Hermeneutics and Tradition: The Role of the Past in Jurisprudence and Theology', *Harvard Theological Review*, 79 (1986), pp. 439–63.
11 Here, and throughout this chapter, I use the term 'reader' and 'reading' to include the hearings, retellings, and interpretations of the many poor and marginalised who are illiterate.
12 J. R. Cochrane, 'Already, But Not Yet: Programmatic Notes for a Theology of Work', in J. R. Cochrane and G. O. West, *The Threefold Cord: Theology, Work and Labour* (Pietermaritzburg, Cluster Publications, 1991), pp. 177–89, esp. p. 181.
13 ICT Church and Labour Project Research Group, 'Workers, the Church and the Alienation of Religious Life', in ibid., pp. 253–75, esp. p. 272.
14 G. Philpott, *Jesus is Tricky and God is Undemocratic: The Kin-dom of God in Amawoti* (Pietermaritzburg, Cluster Publications, 1993), p. 15, my emphasis.
15 J. L. Segundo, 'The Shift Within Latin American Theology', *Journal of Theology for Southern Africa*, 52 (1985), pp. 17–29, esp. p. 22.
16 Ibid., p. 28.
17 Ibid., p. 23.
18 Ibid.
19 Ibid., p. 24.
20 Ibid. (my emphasis).
21 Although the predominant critical methods used are historical and socioligical, other critical methods are also used: see G. O. West, *Biblical Hermeneutics of Liberation: Modes of Reading the Bible in the South African Context* (Maryknoll, NY, Orbis, 1995), pp. 131–73.
22 See especially S. D. Welch, *A Feminist Ethic of Risk* (Minneapolis, Fortress, 1990) and M. Foucault, *Power/Knowledge: Selected Writings and Other Interviews 1972–1977* (New York, Pantheon, 1980).
23 H. A. Giroux, 'Introduction', in P. Freire, *The Politics of Education* (London, Macmillan, 1985), pp. xi–xxv, esp. p. xii.
24 Ibid., p. xviii.
25 Ibid., p. xix. Frostin makes a similar point when he argues that 'when oppressed people live in silence, they use the words of their oppressors to describe their experience of oppression' (Frostin, *Liberation Theology in Tanzania*, p. 10). For a detailed account of this phenomenon see A. Memmi, *The Colonizer and the Colonized* (London, Souvenir Press, 1965).
26 J. C. Scott, *Domination and the Arts of Resistance: Hidden Transcripts* (New Haven and London, Yale University Press, 1990), pp. 85–90.
27 Ibid., p. xii.
28 Ibid., p. 2.
29 Ibid., p. 13.
30 Ibid., p. xii.
31 Ibid., p. 198.
32 Ibid., p. 90.
33 Ibid., p. 91.
34 Ibid., p. 96.

35 Ibid., p. 93.

36 Ibid., p. 101.

37 Ibid., pp. 102–3.

38 Giroux, 'Introduction', in Freire, *The Politics of Education*, p. xx.

39 A. Nolan, 'A Worker's Theology' (1991), in Cochrane and West (eds.), *The Three-fold Cord*, pp. 177–89.

40 West, *Biblical Hermeneutics of Liberation*, pp. 157–61.

41 Giroux, 'Introduction', in Freire, *The Politics of Education*, pp. xx–xxi.

42 Ibid., p. xxiii.

43 S. D. Welch, *Communities of Resistance and Solidarity: A Feminist Theology of Liberation* (Maryknoll, Orbis, 1985), p. 44; see also M. Foucault, *Language, Counter-memory, Practice: Selected Essays and Interviews* (Ithaca, NY, Cornell University Press, 1977), p. 209.

44 G. Spivak, 'Can the Subaltern Speak?', in G. Nelson and L. Grossberg (eds.), *Marxism and the Interpretation of Culture* (London, Macmillan, 1988), pp. 271–313; J. Arnott, 'French Feminism in a South African Frame?: Gayatri Spivak and the Problem of "Representation" in South African Feminism', *Pretexts* 3 (1991), pp. 118–28. Spivak uses the preposition 'to', but I prefer the preposition 'with'.

45 Arnott, 'French Feminism', p. 125.

46 Spivak, 'Can the Subaltern Speak?', p. 297; Arnott, 'French Feminism', p. 125.

47 Arnott, 'French Feminism', p. 125.

48 Ibid., p. 127.

49 See G. O. West, *Contextual Bible Study* (Pietermaritzburg, Cluster Publications, 1993), and West, *Biblical Hermeneutics of Liberation*, pp. 174–80.

50 J. A. Draper and G. O. West, 'Anglicans and Scripture in South Africa', in F. England, F. Paterson and T. J. M. Paterson (eds.), *Bounty in Bondage* (Johannesburg, Ravan, 1989), pp. 30–52, esp. 42–3.

51 Draper and West, 'Anglicans and Scripture', p. 43.

52 A. Nolan, *God in South Africa: The Challenge of the Gospel* (Cape Town, David Philip, 1988); *The Kairos Document: Challenge to the Church*, 2nd edn (Braamfontein, Skotaville, 1986).

53 Foucault, *Power/Knowledge*; see also Welch, *Communities of Resistance and Solidarity*.

54 G. O. West, 'The Relationship Between Different Modes of Reading and the Ordinary Reader', *Scriptura* S9 (1991), pp. 87–110.

55 Draper and West, 'Anglicans and Scripture', pp. 41, 45.

56 Why do you think Jesus talked about the commandments? Why do you think Jesus used these particular commandments? What do you think the commandments that Jesus used have in common? Why do you think keeping these commandments was not enough to gain eternal life? Which do you think is more important to Jesus, to keep the commandments or to give to the poor?

57 Why do you think Jesus told the man to sell his possessions and give to the poor? Why do you think Jesus told the man to do this before he could follow him? Why do you think the young man did not obey Jesus? What do you think Jesus meant by 'treasure in heaven'?

58 No one translation was used during these Bible studies. Participants used various translations. I am using the New American Standard translation here and below.

59 Ordinary readers did not distinguish between 'the text' and 'Jesus'. The ideological perspective of this particular text was not the concern of these Bible studies, although some participants did raise the question when referring to the synoptic parallels (see also Draper and West, 'Anglicans and Scripture', p. 41).

60 *The Road to Damascus: Kairos and Conversion* (Johannesburg, Skotaville, 1989). This document was produced by Third World Christians from South Africa, Namibia, South Korea, Philippines, El Salvador, Nicaragua, and Guatemala.

61 C. West, *Prophetic Fragments* (Grand Rapids, MI, Eerdmans, 1988), p. 210.

62 G. O. West, 'Difference and Dialogue: Reading the Joseph Story with Poor and Marginalized Communities in South Africa', *Biblical Interpretation* 2 (1994), pp. 152–70, esp. 154–5.

63 The work of Third World feminist and womanist scholars demonstrates a similar shift. See for example: T. Okure, 'The Will to Arise: Reflections on Luke 8:40–56', in M. A. Oduyoye and M. R. A. Kanyoro (eds.), *The Will to Arise: Women, Tradition, and the Church in Africa* (Maryknoll, NY, Orbis, 1992), pp. 221–30; M. R. A. Kanyoro, 'Daughter, Arise (Luke 8:40–56)', in M. A. Oduyoye and M. R. A. Kanyoro (eds.), *'Talitha, Qumi!' Proceedings of the Convocation of African Women Theologians* (Ibadan, Nigeria, Daystar Press, 1990), pp. 54–62; E. Amoah, 'The Woman Who Decided to Break the Rules', in J. S. Pobee and B. van Wartenberg-Potter (eds.), *New Eyes for Reading: Biblical and Theological Reflections by Women from the Third Word* (Geneva, WCC, 1986), pp. 3–4; R. Cochrane, 'Equal Discipleship of Women and Men: Reading the New Testament from a Feminist Perspective', in D. Ackermann, J. A. Draper, and E. Mashinini (eds.), *Women Hold Up Half the Sky: Women in the Church in Southern Africa* (Pietermaritzburg, Cluster Publications, 1991), pp. 21–36. For a First World feminist perspective see M. A. Tolbert, 'Mark', in C. A. Newsom and S. H. Ringe (eds.), *The Women's Bible Commentary* (London, SPCK and Louisville, KY, Westminster/John Knox Press, 1992), pp. 263–74.

64 'Different, not better' requires some form of conversion experience. Postmodernism can provide, I would suggest, resources for this conversion; see G. O. West, 'No Integrity without Contextuality: The Presence of Particularity in Biblical Hermeneutics and Pedagogy', *Scriptura* S11 (1993), pp. 131–46.

65 The term post-critical is not usually used to mean 'anti-critical', rather it is used to indicate modes of reading which move beyond historical-critical methods.

66 West, *Contextual Bible Study*, pp. 30–6.

67 See ibid., pp. 25–30.

68 Ibid., pp. 36–40.

69 West, 'Difference and Dialogue', p. 154.

70 For a discussion of what he calles 'incipient theologies' see J. R. Cochrane, 'Conversation or Collaboration?: Base Christian Communities and the Dialogue of Faith', *Scriptura*, 57 (1996), pp. 103–24.

71 This is Mosala's concern; see I. J. Mosala, *Biblical Hermeneutics and Black Theology in South Africa* (Grand Rapids, MI, Eerdmans, 1989), p. 32.

72 G. O. West, 'No Integrity without Contextuality: The Presence of Particularity in Biblical Hermeneutics and Pedagogy', *Scriptura*, S11 (1993), pp. 131–46; Welch, *A Feminist Ethic of Risk*, p. 151. For a detailed discussion see G. O. West, *The Academy of the Poor: Towards a Dialogical Reading of the Bible* (Sheffield, Sheffield Academic Press, 1998).

# 9

CHARLES VILLA-VICENCIO

# Liberation and reconstruction: the unfinished agenda

Liberation theology – an umbrella term embracing a number of particular movements, including African, black, feminist, and womanist theologies – is self-consciously contextual. While having certain characteristics in common, specific liberation theologies need to be understood in terms of their particular contexts. In this chapter attention is first given to the broad and inclusive tenets of Latin American liberation theology. The second part explores some of the challenges facing liberation theologians in the wider context defined by the post-cold war period; in particular, the situation of the poor in the changing contexts of debate. Specific attention is given to the changing South African context within which the present writer is located.

There is, of course, no *one* prevailing context in any particular Latin American country or in South Africa. Divisions of class, race, gender and choice continue to ferment the liberation theology debate, and each of these is, in turn, profoundly affected by the changes that have taken place in different regional contexts since the 1960s. The Medellín and Puebla conferences of 1968 and 1979 gave formative expression to Latin American liberation theology, which formed part of the revolutionary milieu that swept South and Central America during this time. In Europe 1968 was the year of the Prague Spring. In North America the 1960s were the time of the Black Power movement. In South Africa, Black theology and liberation theology were born in the late 1960s,[1] reaching their highwater mark with the publication of the *Kairos Document* in 1985, while Black theology regained a sense of prominence in the debate at more or less the same time.[2] The divide between the forces of resistance and liberation, throughout this period, was crisp, clear and relatively uncomplicated.

Things have since changed. Latin American dictatorships in Argentina, Brazil, Chile and elsewhere have fallen. The iron curtain dividing Eastern and Western Europe has come down. In South Africa a democratically elected government of national unity, under the presidency of Thabo

Mbeki, is governing the country. Yet many of those out of whose oppression liberation theologies were first born, are still oppressed. They remain without houses. They are still denied adequate educational and health resources. Massive unemployment rages on. Grinding poverty, exploitation and unnecessary deaths are daily realities. Yet despite the marked lack of clear winners in these negotiated revolutions, changes experienced in Latin America and South Africa are indeed momentous.

Because political liberation in Latin America and South Africa is not 'evenly distributed', it is likely that the fissures and ferment that have always been part of liberation theology will become more pronounced in the future.[3] Some Christians who were hitherto part of the revolutionary struggle have joined government. Others have chosen to leave politics to the politicians. Still others have refused to concede the extent of the acknowledged changes, standing aloof from the politics of negotiation. They have resisted engagement in the frustrating complexities of political transition.

Ironically those who uncritically embrace the new age *and* those who sullenly resist it both fail to exploit the opportunities of renewal that exist at the political, economic and spiritual interface where the 'old' is dying and the 'new' is agonising to be born. The former baptise the revolution into complacency. The latter fail the revolution in not forcing it to deliver on its own agenda. Neither group grasps the opportunity to contribute theologically and *ethically* to the nation-building and reconstruction process.

Can liberation theology liberate the liberated – from both complacency and cynicism? Is liberation theology indeed a vehicle for liberating the poor not only when liberation is on the distant horizon but also when it is within grasp? Can liberation theology be more than a theology of resistance? In what follows I argue that it can. It will, however, need to take its contextual nature seriously, continuing to respond creatively to the actual contexts within which it is located. In so doing it is likely to tear open ideological and contextual cleavages that liberation theologians have, to a significant extent, hitherto been able to hold together. That is part of the price to be paid for taking context (contexts within contexts) seriously.

### Naming the dialectic

'When God saw that the rich Christians, who possessed ninety percent of the thousand riches of humanity, had not done with those riches what they should have done ... God allowed socialists the enterprise of dignifying the poor of Latin America who are the immense majority.' These words, spoken by Guatemalan Juan David Garcia Vaca, capture the double identity of Latin American theology.[4] They locate the economic agenda at the heart of the Latin American revolution. They also give expression to a popular belief that the God of history is at work in the Latin American social revolution.

This piety is often ignored by Western critics of Latin American liberation theology, who reduce it to little more than a Christian facade behind which is found a Marxist agenda. Such attacks unabashedly ignore the insistence of Gustavo Gutiérrez's formative study *A Theology of Liberation* that liberation theology is 'critical reflection on Christian praxis in the light of the Word'.[5] Gutiérrez's critical analysis of the Latin America situation is, at least in its early stages, poignantly Marxian.[6] His theology has at the same time always been grounded in a biblical hermeneutic and a spirituality of liberation, while more recently Gutiérrez has given increasing emphasis to popular Christian belief.[7] A similar double emphasis, and in several instances a shift towards piety and popular belief can, in turn, be found in other Latin American theological writings. Juan Luis Segundo speaks of 'a new context for theologizing: the common people' with which theologians were obliged to come to grips in the Latin American struggle. He refers to it as a painful conversion which intellectuals need to undergo – a kind of self-negation within which they give expression to the theology of the poor.[8] Enrique Dussel came to speak of the 'discipleship of the poor', and Leonardo Boff of a new 'ecclesiogenesis' which came to expression in the 'church of the poor'.[9] It must however be noted that this affirmation of 'the common people' has been severely criticised by Latin American women as failing to take the concerns of women seriously.[10] Indeed it has also been criticised by black theologians for failing to give sufficient attention to race as a category of exploitation.[11] This concern is addressed elsewhere in this volume.

When confronted with this (albeit truncated) focus on popular religion, the critics of liberation theology respond by suggesting that the earlier formative works of liberation theologians gave *proportionally* more attention to the critique of structural capitalism than to this popular religion. This, they argue, shifted the liberation theology debate away from the earlier theological concerns of the Medellín Conference (which included sin, conversion and reconciliation) to socio-economic concerns of a Marxian kind. The counter-argument is that the emphasis on social analysis and the promotion of socialism is a logical consequence of the application of the theological concerns of Medellín to the broader Latin American context. In the words of Enrique Dussel: 'It was Christian praxis and faith, and criteria fundamentally spiritual and pastoral (the fact that Christians were becoming involved in politics in order to fight injustice, together with the social teaching of the church) that made adequate analytical categories necessary.'[12]

'Proportion' aside, deep-rooted spirituality, liturgy and theological debate constitute an inherent part of the Latin American Church. To suggest that this ethos can be ignored or played down in an assessment of Latin American theology is absurd. The extent to which a Marxian understanding of class struggle influenced liberation theology in the 1970s and the early 1980s needs, in turn, to be understood in relation to the growing power of Latin American dictatorships during this period. Often bolstered by the ideology of the national security state (promoted by the United States as a means of saving the region from alleged communist aggression), Marxian rhetoric and socialist ideals existed as an ideology of resistance to a state-imposed ideology of militarism and exploitative capitalism.[13] Reflecting on the relationship between liberation theology and Marxism, Dussel is adamant in stating that liberation theologians had painstakingly adopted a '"certain" Marxism, one compatible with a Christian faith received from the prophets, from Jesus, and from church tradition immemorial . . .'[14]

We turn now to a consideration, first, of the socialist ideal of liberation theology and to the spirituality inherent to this theology. We then evaluate the nature of the relationship between the two as a basis for judging possible future developments in liberation theology in Latin America and South Africa.[15]

## Socialism

The socialist agenda of Latin American liberation theology is expressed nowhere more clearly than in the meeting of the Group of Eighty Priests in April 1971 in Santiago, Chile. The priests declared themselves to be in unequivocal support of socialism and the 'peoples' revolution'. The bishops in Chile responded to the eighty priests both directly, warning them to keep out of politics, and indirectly, in a document entitled 'The Gospel, Politics and Socialism'.[16] The bishops rejected both Marxist socialism and capitalism as materialist ideologies that favoured the few at the cost of the many. The next important step in a series of documents relevant to liberation theology came with the publication of Pope Paul VI's encyclical *Octagesima Adveniens*, issued in celebration of Pope Leo XIII's labour encyclical, *Rerum Novarum*. It affirmed the familiar third-option economic policy of the Vatican. When the Second General Synod of Bishops met in Rome later that same year, it supported the rights of the poor – carefully drawing on the language of the Medellín Conference, while avoiding the Marxian underpinnings included in the Latin American theology debate at the time.

In April 1972 the eighty priests went a step further, forming the Christians for Socialism Movement. The final document of its founding (and only) meeting advocated the 'takeover of power by the exploited masses'.[17]

By the time the bishops met to respond to this document, their condemnation was of little avail. Chilean President Allende had been removed from power in a military coup, and the Christians for Socialism Movement was prohibited and its leaders driven into exile.

When Pope Paul VI published *Evangelii Nuntiandi* in 1975 he was ready to appropriate the essential ideas of liberation theology, while couching them strictly in terms of New Testament teaching. The encyclical recognised that liberation 'cannot be contained in the simple and restricted dimension of economics, politics, social or cultural life; it must envisage the whole man, in all aspects, right up to and including his [*sic*] openness to the absolute, even the divine absolute'.[18] In the words of Paul Sigmund, 'liberation had ... become theologically respectable'. An attempt was being made to break its association with Marxism. 'Henceforth the argument would be over the theological content of the term [i.e. "liberation"] ...'[19]

Generally speaking, liberation theologians rejected the Vatican initiative (Rubem Alves had earlier warned against what he called the 'cultural imperialism' of the First World church[20]) and continued to engage questions concerning salvation (liberation), the preferential option for the poor and social justice (at the material level) through the promotion of socialism over against capitalism.[21]

Few theologians seriously engaged the writings of Marx directly.[22] Marxian undertones were, however, present in the writings of most liberation theologians with some affirming a more uncritical espousal of Marxism than others.[23] Gustavo Gutiérrez rejects what he calls 'naive reformism', insisting that the Church in Latin America needed to 'break its ties with the present order', making itself 'one with the poor', and dedicating itself to the 'revolutionary cause'.[24] Indeed he later writes that 'only by overcoming a society divided into classes ... by eliminating the private appropriation of wealth created by human toil, can we build the foundation of a more just society'.[25] When asked in 1985 whether liberation theologians could support a welfare-oriented capitalism as a basis for a preferential option for the poor, Gutiérrez replied: 'I don't know any who do.'[26] And still later he wrote in the *New York Times* (27 July 1988): 'I don't believe the capitalist system as we know it today is good for the poor. But theoretically, if it is a way out of poverty, I have no problem. My question is not about capitalism. My question is about poverty.'[27]

Similarly rejecting 'dogmatic Marxism', Mìguez Bonino emphasises the place of 'a strict scientific-ideological analysis, avowedly Marxist' as a way of unmasking 'enslaving political options' which include such 'third options' as promoted by the Vatican.[28] Hugo Assmann, in turn, rejects the notion of capitalist development, urging its exposure as 'the lie that it is'.[29] He insists that the biblical notion of truth involves working for the liberation of humanity, which action he defines as being served by 'a sociological analysis derived from Marxism, and a strategy that will lead to a form of socialist society'.[30] Juan Luis Segundo acknowledges the limitations of socialist revolutions that have promoted 'the role of the party and of government repression', but insists that the socialist ideals incorporated in historical materialism are not undermined in the process.[31] In his meditation on the Lord's Prayer, Leonardo Boff, in turn, defines 'the evil one' as the one 'embodied in an elitist, exclusivist social system that has no solidarity with the multitudes of the poor. He has a name; he is the Capitalism of private property and the Capitalism of the state.'[32]

Liberation theologians clearly sought a radical alternative to structural capitalism as well as to 'third way' economics. At the same time, it would be claiming too much to say that any prominent Latin American liberation theologian showed an unequivocal dogmatic commitment to Marxian-based socialism. Indeed, Gutiérrez repeatedly insists that it is not any intellectual elite (Marxist or otherwise) that constitutes the vanguard of the struggle, but the poor. For him, the poor of the base Christian communities are inspired by a spirituality that is grounded in a sense of God's impending rule which will be to the social benefit of the poor. 'Conversion', says Gutiérrez, requires us to centre our lives on 'the neighbour, the oppressed person, the exploited social class, the despised race, the dominated country. Our conversion to the Lord implies conversion to the neighbour.'[33] The exaltation of the poor, which is part of Christian liberation, is grounded in this centre. It is a centre which Gutiérrez sees as both radicalising the revolution and preventing it from betraying its ultimate purpose.

Mìguez Bonino warns against the radical 'monism' of liberation theology. This he sees occurring when 'the history of divine revelation is [viewed as] secondary, merely exemplary, or even dispensable'. His concern is that either wittingly or unwittingly 'history' and 'struggle' could themselves be deified in the process. Insisting that this is not the intention of liberation theology, he nevertheless exhorts his fellow theologians to a self-critical stance: 'We must ask ourselves whether the formulations we have worked out so far do enough to rule out that possibility.'[34] Likewise Leonardo Boff insists that *all* theology needs to be subjected to ideological critique.[35] And yet, liberation theologians were not prepared to mask or deny unequivocal support for the poor. Mìguez Bonino accuses First World theologians of claiming solidarity with the poor while 'hover[ing] above the right and the left as if that choice did not have anything to do with the matter'.[36] This too, Mìguez Bonino insists, is an ideological stance. Jon Sobrino approvingly quotes a Peruvian bishop at the Puebla Conference: 'Let him who is without ideology cast the first stone.'[37] Indeed for liberation theologians it has been a matter of choice: Which ideology for which side? It has forced all theologians to face this question with radical honesty. The dialectic between ideology and popular praxis has been at the centre of the liberation theology debate.

John Coleman, among others, has accused liberation theologians of insufficiently critiquing socialist ideology in their concern to promote the interests of the poor. They have been insufficiently 'discriminating [in their] judgements about alternative economic and political choices with which we are faced'.[38] Peter Moll has, in turn, criticised liberation theologians for failing to grapple in a critical and serious manner with the contemporary debate on Marxian economics. The difficulty, Moll insists, is that liberation theologians have accepted dependency theory as axiomatic of Marxism while failing to consider alternative ways of reading Marx. In so doing, he suggests that liberation theologians are guilty of the very critique they level against traditional theology, namely, living in bondage to specific cultures, philosophies or political systems.[39] Moll has probably overstated his case. Ignacio Ellacuría suggests that while Latin American liberation theologians have inclined towards socialism rather than capitalism, they have been mindful of the limitations of both systems.[40] Gregory Baum's spirited response to Moll's article (while downplaying the influence of Marxism on liberation theology) offers alternative (non-Marxian) critiques of exploitative capitalism which liberation theology would do well to explore.[41]

The shift from resistance to reconstruction in liberation theology needs to be rooted here – in theological critique of *all* economic theory and praxis. In this regard Segundo's observation is salutary. He insists that theologians '[should] not be able to take the easy way out . . . setting aside the great problems of today on the pretext that they belong to other fields or disciplines'.[42] Karl Rahner argues that in addressing the concrete problems of the day the Church 'can be wide of the mark in its imperatives and directives' in much the same way as any other organisation. 'But this', he (like Segundo) urges, 'is a risk that must be taken if the church is not to seem pedantic, to be living in a world of pure theory, remote from life, making pronouncements that do not touch the stubborn concreteness of real life.'[43]

## Popular religion

The socialist ideal and the struggle to give material content to liberation in Latin America has never been isolated from popular religion. Liberation theologians have repeatedly recognised the need for a spirituality capable of driving the social revolution. To quote Gutiérrez: 'The project of crafting a new and different society includes the creation of *new human persons* as well, who must be progressively liberated from whatever enslaves them.'[44] This demands more than intellectual or ideological ideals. It involves an inward and spiritual understanding of what it means to 'proclaim God as father in a world that is inhumane'.[45] This is a spirituality grounded in the lived experience (historical praxis) of the poor in Latin America. It involves what Gutiérrez defines as 'the fundamental hermeneutical circle'. In a memorable passage he relates this as a process of moving:

> . . . from humanity to God and from God to humanity, from history to faith and from faith to history . . . from the love of one's brothers and one's sisters to the love of the Father and from the love of the Father to the love of one's brothers and one's sisters, from human justice to God's holiness and from God's holiness to human justice.[46]

This, he further stresses, involves 'an understanding of the faith from the point of departure in real, effective solidarity with the exploited classes, oppressed ethnic groups, and despised cultures in Latin America'.[47] It involves empowering the poor through liturgy, prayer and Bible studies – which constitute the life-blood for many within rural villages and *favelas* that exist cheek by jowl with the cities of Latin America. In the words of Leonardo and Clodovis Boff: 'It is in prayer and contemplation, and intimate and communitarian contact with God, that the motivations for a faith-inspired commitment to the oppressed and all humankind spring.'[48] It involves what Segundo Galilea has defined as the linking of the mystic and the militant. For him, spiritual contemplation not only results in engagement in the world, it *is* engagement. It is not withdrawal from the world, in order to participate later. It is reflective, spiritual participation in the struggle for justice.[49]

Few question the power of the spiritual resources of base Christian communities in Latin America. Indeed Cardinal Ratzinger has identified these communities as providing 'a new consciousness of Christian existence and the opportunity for the real renewal of the church'.[50] What distinguishes *this* spirituality from what is often the individualistic and privatised spirituality of the First World is its material base in the Latin American struggle of the poor against oppression.

In a manner that many Western theologians cannot begin to comprehend, the Bible has empowered the poor in their commitment to create a just society. In the words of Carlos Mesters, 'the principal object of reading the Bible is not to interpret the Bible but to interpret life with the help of the Bible'.[51] Indeed this method of understanding the written text in relation to the lived text of poverty and oppression constitutes a hermeneutic that has energised local Christian communities well beyond the shores of the Latin American continent.[52]

The Latin American spirituality of liberation has also involved the emergence of a religio-cultural encounter between Roman Catholic spirituality and the Afro-Brazilian religions such as *Umbanda, Quimbanda, Macumba* and *Candomblé*. Not all those who laud Latin American spirituality approve of these developments. They do, however, provide African Brazilians, many of whom are alienated and excluded from the Latino culture of Brazil and other Latin American countries, with a symbolic universe that empowers and sustains. Revering traditional African divinities alongside Catholic saints, Brazilian followers of African-Christian religions give expression to a cultural reimaging of traditional Christian spirituality that has profoundly influenced the character of popular religion in Latin America.[53]

Gutiérrez's *We Drink from Our Own Wells* describes a spirituality born in the midst of the struggles of the Latin American poor.[54] It is a spirituality that arises out of an encounter with God within the community of the poor. It is communal rather than individualistic in character in response to God's gracious activity within the world. This response constitutes a conversion to a life of obedience to Jesus, which integrates those areas of life normally associated with spirituality, such as prayer and meditation, with those which are traditionally excluded from spirituality, such as politics, economic systems and material well-being. This is a spirituality that gives rise to hope in the midst of suffering – a hope grounded in the resurrection which carries the promise of liberation. Finally, this spirituality can only be experienced in solidarity with the poor. Donal Dorr's publication *Integral Spirituality* provides a useful description of this all-embracing, holistic spirituality.[55] This is a spirituality which empowers people to deal with the challenges of poverty and political exploitation. In brief, it is a spirituality which undergirds the social mission of the Church.

Jether Ramalho, who has been part of the base Christian communities movement in Brazil for the past two decades, identifies four different phases of this mission within the base Christian communities (BCC) in Brazil:[56]

> *The encounter between laity and priests.* 'This first phase', he observes, 'was essentially ecclesial and theological. It involved establishing a new relationship between the clergy and the people. BCCs constituted a process of the people themselves becoming the church.'

> *The relationship between the oppressed and the oppressors.* 'The second phase of the BCCs was the level of social and economic analysis. This involved class struggle between the rich and the poor. As a basis for this we sought to understand the political and economic

structures that made for this exploitation. This became a basis for our strategic participation in the struggle for transformed political and economic structures.'

*The encounter between the church and popular organisations.* 'This had to do with a realisation by Christians that they did not control the political struggle. In the process we learned of our theological vulnerability as church. We were buffeted by various political forces, but resisted absorption by any political party. We at the same time underwent a shift away from "pastoral" ministry to direct "political" engagement . . .'

*The post elections period.* With the first democratic elections in Brazil behind them, the BCCs faced yet a further challenge. Ramalho explains:

> This new phase has to do with religion and culture and the grappling with contemporary problems, such as sexuality, gender questions, leisure, unemployment and so forth. We are seeking to work out a practical, theological way of enabling people to realise their full God-given potential. We are at the same time seeking to understand what it means to give expression to the Christian faith in different cultural forms. . . . By addressing these issues we believe we are freeing people to stand up, to be themselves and to participate more vigorously in the creation of a compassionate society. The real struggle for renewal in Brazil has only just started. All that democracy does is give people an opportunity to share in the creation of their future. People need to be empowered to do so. That is the task of the church.

Five points emerge from the above brief analysis:

(1) Context provides the agenda.
(2) The suffering of the poor requires radical questioning of the capitalist system.
(3) This questioning must be from the perspective of and serve the interests of the poor. This requires that contextual and ideological critique be employed to assess the benefits for the poor of both capitalist and socialist options for addressing specific economic problems.
(4) The participation by the Latin American poor in the struggle for liberation is grounded in popular religious culture. Elitist theological, ideological and intellectual ideals do not drive the popular revolution.
(5) Liberation theologians (who are mostly well-educated and not without social and economic power) have a complex role to play in the revolution of the poor.

## Facing the new challenge

The themes of economic justice and the spiritual empowerment of the poor continue to be relevant to the period of reconstruction in South Africa, Eastern Europe, Latin America and elsewhere. These situations require, however, that these themes be developed in relation to the contextual changes that have taken place within these situations.

Such developments will, in addition to engaging the particular demands of each context, also need to respond creatively to four historic shifts that have taken place within the global context:

(1)  The failure of the economic and political structures of Eastern Europe.
(2)  The collapse of a widespread belief in utopian socialist ideals in Third World countries.
(3)  The failure of Western-based capitalism to meet the needs of the poor.
(4)  A new-found appreciation that even under the most adverse conditions, the poor rise in rebellion in demand of their rights.

These changes are central to the consideration of economics and spirituality in the post-1990 South African context that follows.

### Towards an economic alternative

Gar Alperovitz, president of the National Center for Economic Alternatives in Washington DC, has captured the mood prevailing in the wake of the global changes of the last decade of the twentieth century: 'Perhaps the most important lesson of recent developments in Eastern Europe and the Soviet Union is that fundamental problems in society, despite misleading appearances of superficial calm, are very difficult to "paper-over" forever.'[57]

Theologically there is nothing sacrosanct about *any* economic (or theological) system. The call for an alternative economic system, which rejects the failed ideologies of Marxian socialism and laissez-faire capitalism, has at the same time frequently been rejected as no more than a quest for Vatican-style 'third option' reformism. It does little more than point to the weaknesses inherent to both systems – while effectively promoting the status quo.[58]

Karl Polanyi's observation in relation to early twentieth-century developments in economic change is, however, a pertinent one. He reminds us that major economic change is often born in compromise and reformism. 'Not for the first time in history,' he observes, 'have makeshifts contained the germs of great and permanent [revolutions].'[59] He identifies social legislation, ranging from the prohibition of child labour to health laws and statutory pensions, as having emerged from incomplete (partial) responses to the demands of industrial workers.[60] It is thus in industrial struggle (with all its ambiguities) that the cause of the poor is promoted, rather than by the intellectual pitting of one ideological system against another.

The shift in South Africa – from a doctrinaire Marxist-Leninist type socialism, often promoted by trade unions, the South African Communist Party and some other liberation movements prior to 1990, to a more pragmatic demand for a market economy that addresses the needs of the poor – took place precisely within the ambits of compromise and make-shift adjustments.[61] There is more at stake in the South African struggle for economic justice than a carefully balanced 'third option' economy. With sufficient political incentive the partial victories gained by workers in recent years could mark the beginning of a historic compromise between the dis-possessed, workers, bankers, business and government. There is at the same time a growing realisation by all concerned that the solutions to the eco-nomic woes of the population are likely to be worked out within a market economy[62] – a market economy within which the rights of workers are protected and advanced. This, needless to say, involves a major structural undertaking. The 'nuts and bolts' of an appropriate economy cannot be debated here. It is not likely to be Marxist, socialist or capitalist in any 'pure' essence – raising the question how useful the continual employment of these categories are in contemporary economic debate.[63] It is also not the task of theology to provide the detail of economic practice, although certain theological observations are appropiate:[64]

(1) Theology is about the well-being of God's creation. This means that neither the human race nor the natural order must be made subservient to unnecessary material gain or the domination of commodities. At least this much must be theologically affirmed: the infinite dignity of humanity, fair access by all people to material resources, communal solidarity, and the protection of the natural order. It must be further recognised that women are more exploited in the marketplace than are men. This puts gender high on the theological agenda for human equality and the fair distribution of resources.[65] Simply stated, labour (women and men) and natural resources (the environment) must not be reduced to commodities.

(2) The theological ideals of this economic vision need to be realised within the context of a commitment to a balanced budget – although one that favours the poor. This will require reassessment of the lifestyles of the middle-class and the wealthy, as well as budget expenditure on the military, the salaries of government officials and what is often a bloated civil service.

It will also require the poor, where possible, to contribute to reducing the deficit.[66] Further, this vision also needs to be realised within the context of a growth-oriented economy – which at the same time accepts the need for fair distribution. For theologians to fail to address these directives is to fail to take reconstruction and national independence seriously.

(3) The Church is obliged to work with concerned economists, political activists and the exploited poor in seeking to redress a situation within which the market is influenced by transnational corporations, monopoly businesses, labour-saving technology, the International Monetary Fund, the World Bank and the imposition of trade agreements that benefit the rich.[67] For the Church to fail to give concrete economic and political content to its ethical values is for it to fail to take its own ethic seriously enough to incarnate it in a given time and place.

(4) The Church is obliged to ask anew whether the concerns of the poor are in fact being promoted within any particular economic order. It is one thing to raise certain ethical concerns *within* the context of a particular economic or political system, in an attempt to improve the lot of the poor in a partial manner. It is another to question the ethical nature of an economic system itself. The essential question that needs to be asked of market capitalism, suggest Duchrow and Gück, is whether it is capable of serving the interests of the poor.[68] Liberation theologians have traditionally answered this question in the negative. The loyalty of some liberation theologians to doctrinaire socialism is, however, not as strong as it used to be.

The challenge facing theology concerns the nature of a possible economic alternative to exploitative capitalism as well as the dysfunctional forms of socialism practised in Eastern Europe and elsewhere. It nevertheless needs to be recognised that whatever the nature of any future economic development, it will need to be worked out in relation to existing economic structures. A consideration of reconstruction programmes in Eastern Europe, Latin America, Africa and other Third World regions points to the nightmarish fact that the struggle for the 'new' inevitably occurs under the drag of the 'old'. The possibility of a radical overthrow of the existing global economic order to be replaced by a radically *new* alternative is an unlikely option in the foreseeable future.

(5) Specific models of economic growth and distribution to the benefit of the poor and disadvantaged – within the broad ambit of what is outlined above – are at times seen in local, community-based and regional initiatives.[69] It is important that small business initiatives, informal trading and

agricultural cooperatives be protected against absorption and destruction by big companies. Legislation and possible fiscal measures may need to be developed to ensure the survival of small and medium-size businesses. Economic growth and Third World development will, however, require more than this. For southern African regional development to succeed, fair trade agreements between southern African nations are necessary. For the South to counter the domination of the North, South–South development projects are required. For free trade to become a reality, global regulations and tighter control of transnational capital markets are necessary. The role of the World Bank, the International Monetary Fund and international trade agreements will need to be renegotiated to serve the needs of poor nations, i.e., in ways that assist local production, distribution and economic viability.[70]

(6) Threats to the environment by an industrial economy need to be seriously addressed. It is not sufficient to impose a 'green' agenda on the existing industrial order essentially because the source of the present ecological crisis is not merely a result of our more unfortunate management miscalculations. It involves the indiscriminate human assertion of self over the natural environment. This is a reality that has deep cultural roots, requiring that the theological borderline between dominion and domination (Genesis 1.28) be investigated.[71] This places theological concern with ecology at the centre of the theological encounter with economics. It demands a programme of environmental accounting that takes into account not only current production but also long-term health costs and future productivity, as well as natural and cultural interests.

(7) The Church (because it is church) is obliged to discern the practical implications of theological work on the struggle for a just (alternative) economic system within the Hebrew Bible and Jesus movement.[72] The pertinent question concerns the formative values and ultimate goals of the people of Yahweh in the Hebrew Bible and in the early Christian messianic community of the New Testament. Both these societies were driven by an understanding of a God who takes sides with the poor and destitute (Leviticus 25), with those whose basic needs are not satisfied (Matthew 25.31f.), with the empowerment of the weak and the judgment of the strong (Luke 1.46f.). Differently stated, the biblical God is never revealed in a neutral place (whether in the mind of intellectuals or among the counsellors of the Pharaohs or high priests), but among the slaves (Exodus), the peasant farmers (Amos), the widows and orphans (New Testament).[73]

(8) The Church is obliged to note the legitimate objection of economists to this biblical affirmation. 'Theology', economists insist, 'does not produce grain, nor does it build houses!' Indeed, the theological task is not to construct specific economic models for society. It is rather to bring the basic social impulses of the liberating biblical tradition to bear on the economic struggle of the poor and the oppressed in contemporary times. This requires the Church to ensure that the economy is not left to unfettered market forces (individual and corporate) that serve the interests of the powerful.[74] While conceding the disastrous consequences of statist controls in Eastern Europe, the task of theology is to promote such forces within the economy that allow for democratic intervention by ordinary people (including the poor) to ensure that their needs are addressed. For all the virtues of the market system, history shows that market-minded people strive primarily to satisfy their own need for survival, scarcely that of others. Theologically it is imperative to stress that life consists of more than money and consumer goods. The 'proper functioning of the market'[75] necessarily includes the recognition of the intrinsic value of human life, which includes health, beauty, community, conviviality, moral integrity and spiritual well-being. An economy that is driven by profit alone requires the strongest theological critique.

Christian theology is about community. It is about people living 'in Christ' one with another. The role of the economy in community-building has motivated Douglas Meeks to entitle his book *God the Economist*,[76] precisely because of the way in which the economy is inextricably bound up with how people coexist. It is this that causes liberation theologians to instinctively lean in the direction of socialism – whether in the form of social democracy, democratic socialism or socialism of a more doctrinaire kind. The democratic impulse of liberation theology, grounded in the empowerment of the poor, should, at the same time, militate against statist-type (non-democratic) forms of economic control.

Suffice it to say, the demands for economic justice have shifted from the ideological debates of the 1970s and 1980s to a more pragmatic struggle with economic realities – to which there appear to be no simple or quick solutions. For liberation theology to meet this challenge it must build on the pragmatism, social critique and the democratic impulses that have permeated this theological debate from its inception, rather than its ideological, doctrinaire dimensions. This means that the quest for an economy that promotes the welfare of all, and more specifically the well-being of the poor, is to be democratically pursued in relation (albeit in competition) with the views of those who reject these initiatives. Bluntly stated, a utopian notion of an exclusive socialism that politically excludes those who promote the interests of rich and powerful is not a viable option. Democracy demands the recognition of difference and the right of dissent. This requires theologians to concern themselves with matters of constitutionalism, the rule of law, human rights and free elections as a basis for addressing the economic problems of the poor.[77]

In summary: The quest for an economic alternative to exploitative capitalism constitutes the point of continuity between the theological agenda prior to the 1990s and that of the present. Given the global realities of the present, the vision of the alternative order is not finalised. There is at the same time a certain confidence that pervades the struggle of the poor. It is grounded in what Jorge Pixley calls a 'natural majority' within most countries that favour radical economic reform.[78] The pertinent question is how to mobilise this constituency. Ultimately it is about how to mobilise people to project goals and to realise these in quest of the common good.

### Empowering the poor

The common good and national reconstruction is about jobs, houses, health care, education and democratic structures that empower people. Empowerment, however, includes cultural renewal and a spirituality that draws on religious, social and historical resources that provide a sense of personal and communal self-worth. In the words of Franz Fanon, culture is 'the action through which [a] people creates itself and keeps itself in existence'.[79] Culture that empowers is born where people suffer, where hope emerges from defeat and life out of death. Spirituality is that exercise by which people reach beyond themselves to draw on what Max Weber calls the 'life forces' of existence.[80] It is story, memory, symbol, language, poetry, song and places. It is the soil, the blood and the history which constitutes our identity. It is the experience of the *mysterium*, the poetic, the holy – of God, in the midst of life. It is that within which we live, move and have our being. It is the food of the soul. As such it involves more than ecclesial reliance or priestly dependency. Indeed Leonardo Boff provocatively argues that the poverty of an empowering spirituality needs to be explained in relation to priests having 'expropriated the spiritual means of production from the laity'![81] A people's spirituality can of course be facilitated by ecclesial structures, but it involves more than the internalisation of traditional Christian devotional practices.

This organic, people-based spirituality is more than one option among others for discovering our worth and giving expression to our identity. It is more than a light coat that rests on our shoulders, to be discarded at will.

Spirituality is being. It is religion and belief. It is culture. It is life. To the extent that a person is alive, responding to new challenges and ready to engage the other in dialogue, spirituality is an irrepressably dynamic reality. It unites, synthesises and brings difference into creative harmony.

Africans instinctively understand this. Traditional African understandings of *ubuntu* affirm the organic wholeness of humanity – a wholeness realised in and through other people. The notion is enshrined in the Xhosa proverb: *umuntu ngumuntu ngabantu* (a person is a person through persons). This is a belief that recognises within other people the presence of the divine through which a person attains full humanity. *Ubuntu* involves the realisation that for better *and* worse we are shaped by a host of others with whom we share our lives. Meaningful relationships, whether 'by blood', 'by marriage' or even 'by association', are dearly cherished by traditional African culture.[82] Primarily the sense of belonging involves kinship within one's own clan. One can, however, also discern a sense of belonging with 'personal strangers' – people with whom one grows in his or her humanity, whether through affirmation or conflict. In sum, an African sense of community *includes* and *unites*.

Theologians have, however, with few exceptions, failed to provide the kind of systematic reflection on this encounter that is required. Liturgists and priests have, in turn, been too timid in plumbing the depths of African identity to glean from it spiritual resources for the Church.

H. Richard Niebuhr has reminded us that:

> ... where common memory is lacking, where men [sic] do not share in the same past there can be no real community, and where community is to be formed common memory must be created ... The measure of our distance from each other in our nations and our groups can be taken by noting the divergence, the separateness and the lack of sympathy in our social memories. Conversely, the measure of our unity is the extent of our common memory.[83]

South Africa still awaits a unifying memory which incorporates provincial memories and partial pasts. This struggle, for symbols that unite and stories that bind, has only just begun. A new genre of theology is waiting to be born, one that draws on song, dance, poetry and art. It will need to look to the spoken and unspoken word, often so deep within the human psyche that it cannot be adequately articulated. Where seers, prophets, priests of the people and poets have scarcely succeeded in uncovering the mysteries of the past, academics will need, however, to tread warily! They will need to remove the shoes from their feet. They will be on holy ground.

If spirituality is what creates and sustains a people, in South Africa it is urgently needed. For it to succeed in this task it is obliged to deal with difference – accentuated not only by generations of apartheid, but also by centuries of religious conflict, proselytisation and war.

Again it is Niebuhr who assists us. He speaks of revelation in a broad and inclusive sense. For him revelation is recorded in all life's stories that encapsulate an event or events that give life its purpose and meaning.[84] Rosemary Radford Ruether reminds us of a growing repertoire of such events that provide new insights into life – contemporary stories and events. New liberating experiences in life, she suggests, continually empower us 'to write new stories, new parables, new *midrashim* on old stories'.[85] These new (contemporary) stories, both oral and written from within the heat and passion of lived experience, function every bit as powerfully – if not more powerfully – than the stories of traditional religious texts in the shaping of our identities.

The parochial memory of a battle won, of a defeat suffered, of a celebration or a funeral, of an engaging event or bitter conflict often does more to unite and motivate a people than the most sacred events of established religion. At times these stories override the importance of established sacred symbols; at times they give established religious stories new vitality and contextual meaning. The memory of the Great Trek, Blood River and the suffering of Boer women and children in English concentration camps are memories that unite many Afrikaners. Sharpeville, the 1976 Soweto rebellion, Umkhonto we Sizwe (for some) and Apla (for others) have equally united blacks. And yet these same stories, memories, symbols and culture are at the same time at the root of the alienation that exists between most whites and most blacks. Thus nation-building of the inclusive kind that underpins the goals of the present era of South African politics, requires that in affirming these memories, we also transcend them. We need to share memories as a basis for the emergence of new unifying memories.

Storytelling, in one form or another, is part of all traditions, cultures and civilisations. 'If you cannot understand my story, you do not accept me as your neighbour,' Ellen Kuzwayo once told me. 'I am an African woman. I've tried to share my soul, my way of seeing things, the way I understand life. I hope you understand.' We continued to speak at some length. 'Africa is a place of storytelling,' she continued. 'We need more stories, never mind how painful the exercise might be. This is how we will learn to love one another. Stories help us to understand, to forgive and to see things through someone else's eyes.'[86]

Gustavo Gutiérrez speaks of the need for people to drink from their own wells. Nation-building in South Africa demands more than this. It requires us to discover the subterranean rivers on which the different wells draw. The discovery of this unifying source which affirms rather than denies the *particular* wells that constitute the multicultural reality of South Africa could unleash a source of spiritual energy capable of uniting and empowering the nation to face the challenges that await it. It is a source where the different religions, traditions, cultures and memories of South Africans encounter one another. It is a *common* source (allowing that all cultures and religions are not necessarily inherently the same) to the extent that it constitutes a common human quest for inspiration and a universal set of values and ideals that provide purpose and hope.

## Freedom is forever unfinished

Eric Foner, the Columbian University historian who delivered the 34th T. B. Davie Memorial Lecture at the University of Cape Town shortly after the South African election, reminded us that 'freedom is not achieved in a day, or once and forever'. Taking as his topic 'The Story of American Freedom', he then quoted Eric Wolf, a previous T. B. Davie lecturer: 'Freedom is a process that is forever unfinished.'[87]

Finally, the South African liberation struggle is personified in the person of past-President Nelson Mandela. It is therefore appropriate to conclude this chapter with a quotation from his autobiography:

> When I walked out of prison, that was my mission, to liberate the oppressed and the oppressor both. Some say that has now been achieved. But I know that is not the case. The truth is we are not yet free; we have merely achieved the freedom to be free, the right not to be oppressed. We have not taken the final step of our journey, but the first step on a longer and more difficult road.[88]

## NOTES

1 See Basil Moore, *An Introduction to Black Theology* (London, C. Hurst and Co, 1973).

2 The *Journal of Black Theology in South Africa* was launched in May 1987.

3 The divisions within the South African liberation theology debate are seen nowhere more clearly than in Simon S. Maimela's review of Albert Nolan's *God in South Africa* (Cape Town, David Philip, 1988) in the *Journal of Black Theology in South Africa* 3:1 (May 1989), pp. 50–2.

4 In Alberto Espada-Matta, *Church and State in the Social Context of Latin America* (New York, Vantage Press, 1985), p. 41.

5 Gustavo Gutiérrez, *A Theology of Liberation* (Maryknoll, NY, Orbis Books, 1973), p. 13.

6 In his early formative work, Gutiérrez argues that Marxism is simply the best theory available for ensuring that theology is adequately contextual (ibid., pp. 9–10). In the decade of the 1980s a shift is discernible in Gutiérrez, away from ideological structuralist critique to a more pragmatic approach to poverty, grounded in participatory involvement. In his 1984 essay, 'Theology and the Social Sciences', published in *The Truth Shall Set You Free* (Maryknoll, NY, Orbis Books, 1990) he affirms the use of dependency theory in liberation theology, while arguing that this does not imply a 'permanent commitment to it'. He continues: 'In the context of theological work, this theory is simply a means of better understanding social reality' (p. 61).

7 Gustavo Gutiérrez, *We Drink From Our Own Wells* (Maryknoll, NY, Orbis Books, 1984); *On Job* (Maryknoll, NY, Orbis Books, 1987).

8 Juan Luis Segundo, 'The Shift in Latin American Theology', published, *inter alia*, in *Journal of Theology for Southern Africa*, 52 (September 1985), pp. 17–29.

9 Ibid.

10 See, *inter alia*, E. Tamez, *Against Machismo* (Oak Park, Meyer Stone, 1987) and *Through Her Eyes: Women's Theology From Latin America* (Maryknoll, NY, Orbis Books, 1989). Also Ana Marìa Tepedino and Margarida L. Ribeiro Brandao, 'Women and the Theology of Liberation', in Ignacio Ellacuría and Jon Sobrino (eds.), *Mysterium Liberationis: Fundamental Concepts of Liberation Theology* (Maryknoll, NY, Orbis Books, 1993), pp. 221–31.

11 See S. Torres and J Eagleson (eds.), *Theology in the Americas* (Maryknoll, NY, Orbis Books, 1976).

12 Enrique Dussel, 'Theology of Liberation and Marxism', in Ellacuría and Sobrino (eds.), *Mysterium Liberationis*, p. 86.

13 See Franz J. Hinkelammert, *The Ideological Weapons of Death: A Theological Critique of Capitalism* (Maryknoll, NY, Orbis Books, 1986).

14 Dussel, 'Theology of Liberation and Marxism', in Ellacuría and Sobrino (eds.), *Mysterium Liberationis*, p. 88.

15 See Enrique Dussel, *A History of Liberation Theology* (Grand Rapids, MI, Eerdmans, 1981); Paul E. Sigmund, *Liberation Theology at the Crossroads: Democracy or Revolution* (New York, Oxford University Press, 1990); Deane William Ferm, *Latin American Liberation Theology: An Introductory Survey* (Maryknoll, NY, Orbis Books, 1985).

16 John Eagleson (ed.), *Christians and Socialism: Documentation of the Christians for Socialism Movement in Latin America* (Maryknoll, NY, Orbis Books, 1975).

17 Ibid.

18 Michael Walsh and Brian Davies (eds.), *Proclaiming Justice and Peace: Documents From John XXII to John Paul II*, par. 33 (London, Collins Liturgical Publications, 1984), p. 217.

19 Sigmund, *Liberation Theology at the Crossroads*, p. 50.

20 In *Christianity and Crisis*, 17 September 1973.

21 McGovern's careful study of liberation theology concedes that 'most liberation theologians favor some form of socialism ... I have yet to find any liberation theologians who do not favor some form of socialism.' Arthur F. McGovern, *Liberation Theology and Its Critics* (Maryknoll, NY, Orbis Books, 1989).

22 A notable exception was José Miranda. See, for example, his *Marx and the Bible* (Maryknoll, NY, Orbis Books, 1974); *Marx Against the Marxists* (Maryknoll, NY, Orbis Books, 1980). Also Hinkelammert, *The Ideological Weapons of Death*.

23 Hugo Assmann's *A Practical Theology of Liberation* (London, Search Press, 1975) is an example of the former. Clodovis Boff's *Theology and Praxis: Epistemological Foundations* (Maryknoll, NY, Orbis Books, 1987), on the other hand, adopts a more nuanced usage of Marxian hermeneutics.

24 Gustavo Gutiérrez, 'Notes on a Theology of Liberation', *Theological Studies*, 31, no. 2 (June 1970), pp. 254, 260–1.

25 Gustavo Gutiérrez, *The Power of the Poor in History* (Maryknoll, NY, Orbis Books, 1983), p. 46.

26 At a Georgetown University Conference on Liberation Theology, 10 June 1985. Quoted in Sigmund, *Liberation Theology at the Crossroads*, p. 238, footnote 3.

27 Ibid.

28 José Míguez Bonino, *Doing Theology in A Revolutionary Situation* (Philadelphia, Fortress Press, 1975), p. 73.

29 Hugo Assmann, *Theology for a Nomad Church* (Maryknoll, NY, Orbis Books, 1976), p. 49. Such developmentist ideas include for him state capitalism, revolutionary nationalism and 'third option' economics as promoted by the Vatican.

30 Ibid., pp. 76, 116.

31 Juan Luis Segundo, *Faith and Ideologies* (Maryknoll, NY, Orbis Books, 1984), p. 199.

32 Leonardo Boff, *The Lord's Prayer* (Maryknoll, NY, Orbis Books, 1983), p. 119.

33 Gutiérrez, *A Theology of Liberation*, pp. 204–5.

34 Míguez Bonino, 'Historical Praxis and Christian Identity', in Rosino Gibellini, ed., *Frontiers of Theology in Latin America* (Maryknoll, NY, Orbis Books, 1979), p. 263.

35 Leonardo Boff, *Jesus the Liberator* (London, SPCK, 1980), p. 265.

36 Ibid., pp. 147–8.

37 Jon Sobrino in J. Filochowski (ed.), *Reflections on Puebla*. See Christopher Rowland, *Radical Christianity: A Reading of Recovery* (Oxford, Polity Press, 1988), p. 128.

38 In Torres and Eagleson (eds.), *Theology in the Americas*, p. 385.

39 Peter Moll, 'Liberating Liberation Theology: Towards Independence from Dependency Theory', *Journal of Theology for Southern Africa*, 78 (March 1992), pp. 34–5.

40 Ignacio Ellacuría, 'Utopia and Prophecy in Latin America', in Ellacuría and Sobrino (eds.), *Mysterium Liberationis*, pp. 318–19.

41 Gregory Baum, 'Correspondence', in *Journal of Theology for Southern Africa*, no. 81 (December 1992), pp. 72–4. For Moll's response to Baum, see pp. 74–7.

42 Juan Luis Segundo, *The Liberation of Theology* (Maryknoll, NY, Orbis Books, 1976), p. 237.

43 Karl Rahner, *The Shape of the Church to Come* (London, SPCK, 1974), p. 79.

44 Gutiérrez, *The Power of the Poor*, p. 192. Italics are added.

45 Ibid., p. 57.
46 Ibid., p. 60.
47 Ibid.
48 L. Boff and C. Boff, *Introducing Liberation Theology* (Tunbridge Wells, Burns and Oates, 1987), p. 64.
49 Segundo Galilea, *Following Jesus* (Maryknoll, NY, Orbis Books, 1981).
50 Quoted in Rowland, *Radical Christianity*, p. 121.
51 Quoted in ibid., p. 131.
52 See, for example, Ernesto Cardenal, *Love in Practice: The Gospel in Solentiname* (London, SPCK, 1972).
53 I acknowledge the work of Neil Whitehouse, 'Images of God in the Favelas of Rio de Janeiro', unpublished manuscript, 1992. See also R. Bastide, *The Afro-Brazilian Religions* (Baltimore, Johns Hopkins University Press, 1978).
54 See Gutiérrez, *We Drink from Our Own Wells*, and *A Theology of Liberation*, pp. 203–8.
55 Donal Dorr, *Integral Spirituality* (Maryknoll, NY, Orbis Books, 1990), p. 1.
56 In an interview conducted at CEDI (the Ecumenical Centre for Documentation and Information) in Rio de Janeiro in January 1993.
57 Gar Alverovitz, 'Building a Living Democracy', *Sojourners*, July 1990, p. 21.
58 Pope Paul VI's explanation is different. He sees it not as putting 'forward a solution which has universal validity' but one designed to help 'Christian communities analyze their situation . . . to shed on it the light of the Gospel . . . and to draw principles of reflection, norms of judgment and directives for action'. *Octogesima Adveniens*, no. 4 (London, Collins Pubications, 1984). See Bernard F. Connor, 'The Church's Ministry in the Economic Field', *Praxis*, 4 (1994), p. 6.
59 Karl Polanyi, *The Great Transformation: The Political and Economic Origins of Our Time* (Boston, Beacon Press, 1967), p. 251.
60 Ibid., p. 150.
61 See, *inter alia*, Joe Slovo, *Has Socialism Failed?* (London, Inkululeko Publications, 1990). Shortly before he died, Slovo expressed the regret that he did not have the time to undertake a second study entitled, *Has Capitalism Succeeded?*
62 It must immediately be recognised that the notion of a contemporary 'market economy' is a complex reality that is not likely to disappear easily. It involves both international finance and trade agreements as well as an interweaving of 'checks and balances' negotiated between the workers and owners of business. When Adam Smith first used the concept England was to a significant degree a 'nation of shopkeepers'.
63 A survey conducted among businesses, NGOs, liberation movements and trade unionists in South Africa in 1988 (at the height of political conflict) showed that even then the economics debate was increasingly of a non-ideological kind. Although names were not disclosed in order to preserve confidentiality, the person conducting the survey indicated that big business was often suggesting socialist solutions (more government intervention), while supposedly 'left-wing' liberation movements were talking about encouraging business and private enterprise to play a more significant role in the proposed reconstruction process.
64 See, *inter alia*: *Christian Faith and the World Economy. A Study Document from the World Council of Churches* (Geneva, WCC Publications, 1992); Ulrich

Duchrow and Martin Gück, *Economic Alternatives: Responding to the Fifty Years of the Dominant Financial Systems Established at Bretton Woods* (Heidelberg, Kairos Europa, May 1994); Robert Archer, *Markets and Good Government: The Way Forward for Economic and Social Development* (Geneva, UN Non-Governmental Liaison Service, 1994).

65 *Christian Faith and the World Economy*, pp. 25–6.

66 In South Africa a programme of *Masakhane* (social responsibility) has been introduced, with the personal support of President Mandela, requiring people who had under the apartheid regime refused to pay for services such as rent, to now make these payments.

67 United Nations Development Programme (UNDP), *Human Development Report* (New York and Oxford, Oxford University Press, 1992). See also *Christian Faith and the World Economy*, pp. 18–20. For the escalating global debt crisis within which poor nations become increasingly dependent on rich nations see Susan George, *The Debt Boomerang: How Third World Debt Harms Us All* (London, Pluto Press, 1992).

68 Duchrow and Gück, *Economic Alternatives*, p. 9.

69 See Duchrow and Gück, *Economic Alternatives*; Wolfgang Thomas, 'The Dynamics of Unemployment and Job Creation in South Africa: Looking Behind Doomsday Projections' (Cape Town, Institute for Theological and Interdisciplinary Research, August 1994); see also Connor, 'The Church's Ministry in the Economic Field', *Praxis*, 4 (1994), pp. 8–10.

70 Duchrow and Gück show that this was the intention of the Bretton Woods Conference in 1944. This goal was contradicted by the United States, which promoted a policy that favoured the economically stronger countries at the expense of weaker nations (*Economic Alternatives*, p. 7).

71 Graeme Cowley is undertaking important theological work on depth ecology. See his Honours dissertation 'God Reborn: Towards a Theology for an Ecological Age' (Department of Religious Studies, University of Cape Town, 1994).

72 See, *inter alia*, Norman Gottwald, *The Tribes of Yahweh* (Maryknoll, NY, Orbis Books, 1979); Gerhard Lohfink, *Jesus and Community* (Philadelphia, Fortress Press, 1984); Richard A. Horsley, *Jesus and the Spiral of Violence: Popular Jewish Resistance in Roman Palestine* (San Francisco, Harper and Row, 1987), pp. 167f; Michael Zweig (ed.), *Religion and Economic Justice* (Philadelphia, Temple University Press, 1991). Also *Christian Faith and the World Economy*, pp. 8–10.

73 Duchrow and Gück, *Economic Alternatives*, p. 12.

74 For the relationship between democracy, Christianity and the market, see John W. de Gruchy, *Christianity and Democracy* (Cambridge, Cambridge University Press, 1995).

75 *Christian Faith and the World Economy*, p. 35.

76 Douglas M. Meeks, *God the Economist: The Doctrine of God and Political Economy* (Minneapolis, Fortress Press, 1973).

77 See my *Theology of Reconstruction* (Cambridge, Cambridge University Press, 1992), pp. 76–196.

78 Jorge Pixley, 'Reimaging God's Kingdom After the Crisis in Socialism.' A paper read in the Department of Religious studies, University of Cape Town, March 1995.

79 Franz Fanon, *Wretched of the Earth* (London, Penguin Books, 1983), p. 188.
80 Talcott Parsons, 'Introduction', in Max Weber, *The Sociology of Religion* (Boston, Beacon Press, 1964), pp. xxxiiif.
81 See Leonardo and Clodovis Boff, *Liberation Theology: From Dialogue to Confrontation* (New York, Harper and Row, 1986), pp. 84–8; 'Doctrinal Congregation Criticises Brazilian Theologian's Book', *Origins*, 14, no. 42 (4 April 1985), pp. 683–7. Also Harvey Cox, *The Silencing of Leonardo Boff* (Oak Park, IL, Meyer Stone, 1988).
82 Gabriel Setiloane, *African Theology: An Introduction* (Johannesburg, Skotaville, 1986), pp. 9–16.
83 H. Richard Niebuhr, *The Meaning of Revelation* (New York, Macmillan, 1986), p. 115. I am grateful to Dirkie Smit, who in his 'Die Waarheid en Versoeningskommissie – Tentatiewe Kerklike en Teologiese Perspektiewe' (an unpublished paper), has drawn on Niebuhr to stress the importance of story-telling in the South African context.
84 Niebuhr, *The Meaning of Revelation*, p. 109.
85 Rosemary Radford Ruether, *Women Guides: Readings Toward a Feminist Theology* (Boston, Beacon Press, 1985), pp. xii, 247.
86 In personal conversation with Ellen Kuzwayo, 16 October 1994. See also her book, *Call Me Woman* (Johannesburg, David Philip, 1985).
87 Eric Foner, 'The Story of American Freedom', 34th T. B. Davie Memorial Lecture, 20 July 1994, University of Cape Town.
88 Nelson Mandela, *Long Walk To Freedom* (Randburg, Macdonald Purnell, 1994), pp. 616–17.

# PART III
# Analysis and Criticism

# 10

PETER HEBBLETHWAITE[1]

# Liberation theology and the Roman Catholic Church

## Medellín and the aftermath of the Second Vatican Council

It was from a situation of dependence on Europe that liberation theologians sought to free themselves. In so doing, they could call upon original tradition worth reviving. But the awareness of the tradition grew slowly. In 1968, the conventional date for the start of 'liberation theology' in the modern sense, the stress fell on what was *new*. The Latin American bishops, meeting at Medellín,[2] made the crucial move. How was the Christian doctrine of 'salvation' to be presented in terms that would be intelligible to the suffering peoples of Latin America? 'Salvation' always implies a metaphor, whether of restoration to health after sickness or 'redemption' from slavery. The Latin American bishops decided that the best translation of 'salvation' for their oppressed peoples was *liberation*. To be meaningful, however, they would have to stand with their oppressed peoples. The phrase 'option for the poor', first used in a letter from Pedro Arrupe to the Jesuits of Latin America in May 1968, expressed this truth.

'Liberation theology'[3] came into being to expand on and explain these two insights. Its originality consisted in the fact that it was not just a theology *about* liberation, as the theology of 'grace' was about grace. It was *for* liberation, promoting and propagating it. Likewise, it was not just a theology *about* the poor, it was theology *for* the poor. So it would be an active practical theology intended to make a difference in the real world: the Marxist concept of *praxis* indicated that. The stress of liberation theology lay as much on orthopraxis (right action) as on orthodoxy (right thinking). But despite these claims to practical effects, liberation theology could only qualify as serious *theo-logos*, discourse about God, if it spoke relevantly of God.

The Second Vatican Council (or Vatican II) had such momentous consequences for the Catholic Church. Yet Latin American theologians admit that in many respects the agenda of Vatican II did not concern them. The more progressive bishops, like Helder Câmara from Recife, Brazil, were committed to the idea of the 'Church of the poor', but they were a minority among Latin Americans. The Council was in danger of passing Latin America by. There was little cohesion at Vatican II between the Latin American bishops. Yet the Conference of Latin American Bishops (CELAM), the body designed to bring them together, had been in existence for ten years. In 1955 they had met for a 'conference' during the Eucharistic Congress in Rio de Janeiro. This was a novel type of meeting, unprecedented in Church history. It was summoned by the Holy See, presided over by a Cardinal Legate, Adeodato Piazza, named by Pope Pius XII, and its conclusions were revised by Rome before being published. This meeting of seven cardinals and ninety bishops was devoted to a 'new pastoral programme'. Four questions prevailed: the priest shortage, religious education, social problems, and the plight of the Amerindian population.

Towards the end of Vatican II Pope Paul VI delivered a substantial 'pastoral exhortation' to the Latin American bishops on the tenth anniversary of the foundation of CELAM. It was devoted to the need for pastoral planning *on the continental level*. Paul VI was briefed by the president and vice-president of CELAM, Manuel Larrain, Bishop of Talpa, Chile, and Helder Câmara.

Paul VI had measured the problem of two models of the Church. In the triumphalist model the Church was the unabashed ally of the established order which it sanctioned. In Chile and Colombia Our Lady, Mary the mother of Jesus, was regarded as honorary commander in chief of the armed forces. In Brazil the arch-reactionary Cardinal Sigaud equated modest proposals for land reform with 'atheistic communism'.[4] Paul VI warned that the gap between rich and poor was widening, and that Catholics had to become sensitive to social justice otherwise what he called 'the social messianism' of Marxism would prove attractive and promote 'violent revolution'. The remedy, Paul VI averred, was not sterile anti-communism but that integration of life and faith which *Gaudium et Spes*, the Council's pastoral constitution recently promulgated, had so strongly asserted: 'The Christian who neglects his temporal duties, neglects his duties towards his neighbour and towards God, jeopardising his eternal salvation.' This was the starting point for the denunciation of any false 'dualism' that would lead Christians to shirk action here below on the pretext of otherworldly spirituality. That was decidedly not the wave of the future.

Pope John XXIII spoke frequently of the need to 'discern the signs of the times'.[5] Pope John used this idea to draw attention to 'what the Holy Spirit is saying to the Churches'. What this meant in practice was that the Holy

Spirit speaks through the people and movements of our time. Grace does not come merely through institutional channels. Speaking of the concern for human rights and where the impulse to defend them comes from, *Gaudium et Spes* says: 'God's Spirit, who with a marvellous Providence directs the unfolding of time and renews the face of the earth is present to this development (*adest huic evolutioni*). The ferment of the Gospel arouses in men's hearts a demand for dignity that cannot be stifled' (GS26). This 'demand for dignity' is another sign of the times, another appeal of the Holy Spirit. Moreover, the magnificent opening chord of *Gaudium et Spes*, declaring the solidarity between the 'hopes and the fears, the griefs and the anxieties of the people of our time' and those of the Church, added the all important clause '*especially those who are poor or in any way afflicted*'.

1971 was the *annus mirabilis* of liberation theology. In May *Octogesima Adveniens*, marking the eightieth anniversary of *Rerum Novarum*, admitted that social situations were so diverse that no one teaching could be given to cover them all. 'Such is not our intention, nor our mission', Paul VI admitted. He meant that the task of 'discerning the signs of the times' would henceforward have to be done on the level of the local church. He could provide some guidelines, as he did in presenting a discriminating approach to variants of 'socialism'. It could take the form of sociological analysis, a strategy for radical change, a commitment to the class war, or a totalitarian philosophical system atheistic in character. There was much argument about whether it was possible to make such distinctions. The Jesuits, in the person of Pedro Arrupe, thought it might be possible to use Marxist analysis while rejecting its philosophical positions.

Liberation theology scored an even greater success in October 1971 when the Synod of Bishops declared the 'proclamation of justice' to be 'a constituent part of the preaching of the gospel'. It was not an afterthought or postscript to be tacked on when the spiritual message was complete: it was integral to the gospel. However this victory was challenged at the next Synod in 1974. The Brazilian cardinal Alfredo Scherer, a papal nominee, complained that liberation theology was provoking grave dissension in the Church. More menacing was the challenge from Alfonso López Trujillo, then auxiliary bishop of Medellín and secretary of CELAM. Trujillo charged that liberation theology was unduly influenced by Marxist thinking, identifying the poor of the Gospels with Marx's proletariat and thus encouraging the class war. This anticipated later CDF (Congregation of the Doctrine of the Faith) criticisms. But its only immediate effect was to make Paul VI very cautious in *Evangelii Nuntiandi*, the synthetic document in which he tried to resolve the contradictions of the 1974 synod. Cautious – but not negative. Base communities were all right, provided they were ecclesially based. On the central question, the link between evangelisation and liberation, Paul VI laid down two conditions:

(1) It cannot be limited purely and simply to the economic, social and cultural spheres, but must concern the whole person in all dimensions, including the relationship to an 'absolute', and even to *the* Absolute, which is God.

(2) It is based, therefore, on *a conception of human nature*, an anthropology, which can never be sacrificed to the requirements of some strategy or other, or to practice, or to short-term effectiveness.

## Pope John Paul II at Puebla

Just when liberation theology seemed poised for its greatest expansion, a pope appeared who was hostile to it. As a Pole, Pope John Paul II had seen the bankruptcy of Marxism and could not understand why Christians should feel they had anything to learn from it. The Latin American enthusiasm for borrowing some Marxist concepts seemed like the height of naiveté. At the first available opportunity, namely his visit to the CELAM conference in Puebla, Mexico,[6] in 1979, he declared roundly that 'the idea of Christ as a political figure, a revolutionary, as the subversive man from Nazareth, does not tally with the church's catechesis'. He also said it was wrong to identify the Kingdom of God with a political realm, and scotched the notion that Catholic social doctrine was out of date.

Did Pope John Paul condemn 'Liberation Theology' at Puebla, and so disappoint the hopes of the Latin Americans? Many reports suggested that he did, and that there was a contrast between the public acclaim given by the Mexican people and his reception at Puebla. Others have reacted against this interpretation and attributed the alleged rejection of 'liberation theology' to hasty misreporting of random remarks made on the plane out. The Pope's speech was well received at Puebla, and theologians of liberation, present in large numbers, welcomed it.

A careful reading of the full text of the speech will alone enable us to solve the puzzle of contradictory interpretations. It seems that the questions above are badly posed. It was assumed *either* that the Pope would endorse the 'conservative' line *or* that he would endorse the 'liberation' and 'progressive' line. In fact he did neither. He did something else. He changed the level on which the questions were to be asked. He revealed his 'pastoral solicitude' by inviting the Latin Americans to see their problems in a wider theological perspective. What he did in effect was to present, 'as a brother to very beloved brothers' but also 'with the solicitous care of a pastor and the affection of a father', *an alternative form of the theology of liberation*. This has two consequences – but they *must* be taken together, dialectically, otherwise the meaning of the speech will be distorted. First, liberation theology, as developed in Latin America is critically scrutinised and found gravely wanting. But at the same time, second, the concern for social justice expressed by liberation theology is validated and confirmed.

The criticism of liberation theology is acute and shows a good knowledge of the literature. John Paul II asserts, as a central principle, that the primary mission of pastors is to 'be teachers of the truth, not a human and rational truth, but the truth that comes from God'. This runs counter to one of the main theses of liberation theology which claims that 'truth that comes from God' cannot be discovered *outside* the political and social world in which they are embroiled. Hence their criticism of Maritain's expression 'the primacy of the spiritual'. They are for the primacy of *praxis*. A separated spiritual truth has no meaning for them. It is not enough to proclaim the gospel faithfully, it must be lived: or rather you cannot truly proclaim the gospel faithfully unless you live according to it (by identifying with the oppressed). But the Pope remarks: 'Over and above unity in love, unity in truth is always urgent for us.' The Pope also reacts against the tendency of liberation theology to say that the starting point of theology is the *situation*.[7] Against this 'source' of theology, the Pope reasserts the traditional 'sources', Scripture and tradition.

Just as emphatic is his rejection of the 're-interpretations' of the gospel that have been proposed. They are the result, he says, 'of theoretical speculations rather than an authentic mediation of the Gospel' (1,4). Liberation theology proposes that we read the Gospels from 'a class point of view', and this vantage point results in seeing Jesus as a political liberator, 'as one involved in the class struggle' as the Pope says. But 'this idea of Christ as a political figure, a revolutionary, as the subversive man from Nazareth, *does not tally with the Church's catechesis*'. Note the mildness of this formulation. He might have said 'is totally misleading' or 'is unfounded in Scripture'. Note, too, the 'unequivocal rejection of violence' which the Pope finds in the New Testament. However, one should also notice that John Paul II hints at the end of this section that Jesus is indeed a 'revolutionary' but in a far deeper sense: the claims of what he calls 'a transforming, peace-making, pardoning and reconciling love' are extremely demanding. Human values are turned upside down. Though John Paul does not say so, it is open to call that attitude 'revolutionary'.

Liberation theology has consequences over the whole field of theology. The Church becomes the unrealised union of all those who are committed in the struggle for human liberation, whether they happen to call themselves

Christians or not. The Pope rejects this account of the origin of the Church. 'The Church is born', he says, 'out of our response in faith to Christ' (1,6). It is not, or not primarily, born out of a response to political situations.

Pope John Paul II recalls that in his first ever speech as Pope he said that a concern for *sound ecclesiology* would be central in his pontificate. That is why he attacks as erroneous the position which suggests that a distinction can be made between the 'institutional' or 'official Church' – which is judged and condemned – and a new church, 'springing from the people and taking concrete form in the poor', which is said to be emerging. Preaching the gospel, he explains, is not an individualistic activity, and 'it is not subject to the discretionary power of individualistic criteria and perspectives' but to that of 'communion with the Church and her pastors' (1,7). Unity within the Church is a condition of the effective preaching of the gospel. This runs counter to the affirmation, sometimes found in liberation theology, that the 'unity of the Church' is often a sham. The dream of the harmonious collaboration between social classes, which is found in papal encyclicals, is still upheld by Pope John Paul II. It is at times denied by liberation theology.[8] Pope John Paul has an explanation for these deviant views. They are the product, he suggests, of 'familiar forms of ideological conditioning'. In his vocabulary that means Marxism, which does lead people to see everything in class terms, though he does not mention it by name (1,8).

So far, the most fundamental principles of liberation theology are challenged by John Paul II. *However* all that has been said so far must be qualified by the final and positive part of his speech. The Pope's fundamental *Christian humanism* comes out in his second part. Though the Christian message is primarily about God and his action in the world, it *says something correlatively about humanity*. To use his own words it enshrines an 'anthropology'. The paradox is that we live in an age which has poured forth endless rhetoric about humanity and about liberation, and yet in practice never has humanity been so enslaved, abused, tortured etc. John Paul II has no doubt about the answer. 'Humanism' requires a 'more than human' dimension to protect humanity against tyranny. 'Atheistic humanism' leads directly to this paradox: 'It is the drama of humanity deprived of an essential dimension of its being, namely its search for the infinite, and thus faced with having been reduced in the worst way' (1,9). The clear implication is that 'liberation' understood in a secularist context, leads straight to its contrary: enslavement. Against this the Pope sets 'Catholic social doctrine' which insists on the dignity of every human person: 'The complete truth about the human being constitutes the foundation of the church's social teaching *and the basis of true liberation*' (1,9).

This, for John Paul II, is what is *specific* about the Church's contribution to the debate about 'what is to be done'. John Paul II is in no doubt (3,1). In asserting the dignity of human persons, and therefore providing the basis for political commitment, the Church does not have to have recourse to political ideologies. He says: 'The Church does not need to have recourse to ideological systems in order to love, defend and collaborate in the liberation of humanity: at the centre of the message of which she is the depository and herald she finds inspiration for acting in favour of brotherhood, justice and peace, against all forms of domination, slavery, discrimination, violence etc.' (3,3).

The rest of the speech develops this idea, and shows its practical application. If so far, John Paul II has been delivering a shot across the bows of liberation theology, he now delivers blows against the military dictatorships. He denounces a situation in which 'the growing wealth of a few parallels the growing poverty of the masses' (3,4). He is aware of the problem of the redistribution of wealth (3,4). He recognises that the world is interdependent: 'Internal and international peace can only be secured if a social system and economic system based on justice flourishes' (3,4). The assertion of the 'right to private property', if understood in the context of his references to Aquinas and Vatican II, presupposes 'the universal destination of all the world's goods'.

The positive 'theology of liberation' sketched out by John Paul II occurs in 3,6. It offers, moreover, criteria for distinguishing true from false liberation (very close to the Gospel criterion of 'by their fruits you will known them). In *content*, you cannot 'liberate' except in the full truth of the gospel. In *attitudes*, there must be union with the bishops, and a *real* concern for the poor, the sick etc. (3,6). There is, penultimately, a passage on 'the Church's social doctrine' which is more controversial than it may appear. Briefly, the contrast is between a 'social doctrine' which offers a complete blue-print for society, and is presented as an alternative to say, Marxism, and 'social teaching', which is more modest in its claims, and which seemed to be the last word of Paul VI in *Octogesima Adveniens* (cf. 4: 'In view of the varied situations in the world, it is difficult to give one teaching to cover them all or to offer a solution which has universal value. *This is not our intention or our mission*'). John Paul II seems to go back on this disclaimer of Paul VI which he evidently finds too feeble and weak-kneed.

Early in his speech John Paul II says that Medellín will be the point of departure, and remarks that there were many 'incorrect interpretations at times' of its statements. But the 'retreat from Medellín' should not be interpreted as a *withdrawal* of the Church from the sphere of politics, or a simple return to inner church concerns and prayer. Medellín unleashed forces which have become alarming because they have been taken unilaterally. It never said that all sin was 'social sin' and continued to assert that human egoism was responsible for many social evils. In reminding the Latin American Church of fundamental principles, John Paul II is not 'clamping down' on what is good in their aspiration for social justice, he is doing his duty as supreme pastor in recalling that though the transformation of society is the supreme question for Latin America, it must be a *Christian* transformation of society. Though he did not speak of a 'third way', somewhere between capitalism and Marxism, that is evidently what is in his mind.

His hope, clearly, is that Latin American society will be changed in the direction of greater fraternity, pacification and justice, without violence and in the light of the gospel, undistorted by ideological manipulation. His intention is to hold the drifting away of Latin American Catholics – who will be half the Catholic population of the world by the year 2000 – and to ensure that the 'revolution' when it happens, will be a Christian revolution.

### Instruction on Certain Aspects of the 'Theology of Liberation'

From this point on, liberation theology went on the defensive. This was not because liberation theologians accepted the charge of Marxism or the papal account of what they were doing, but because so many of them were under direct attack from the CDF. A special assembly of the Peruvian bishops was summoned to Rome in September 1984 for the express purpose of condemning Gustavo Gutiérrez. Despite intense pressures, the Peruvian bishops held firm, knowing that in condemning Gutiérrez they would have been condemning their own past. Religious were dealt with by their superiors. Father Peter-Hans Kolvenbach, who had succeeded Pedro Arrupe as General of the Jesuits, managed to keep his men out of the direct line of fire. The Franciscans were less successful. Leonardo Boff was summoned to Rome for what was called by Cardinal Joseph Ratzinger a 'colloquy' and by everyone else a 'trial'. At issue was his book *Church: Charism and Power*. Authority and ministry, Boff maintained, could come from below in the Church. In the communion-of-persons that was the Trinity, there was no subordination or hierarchy. The Church was modelled on the Trinity, and so hierarchy and authority could only be allowed provided they were for the service of the whole. This was regarded as 'subversive'. Boff was silenced for a year.[9]

Two instructions were issued by the Congregation for the Doctrine of Faith in successive years, a more negative one in 1984 and a 'positive' one in 1986.

Read with discrimination, the Congregation for the Doctrine of the Faith's *Instruction on Certain Aspects of the 'Theology of Liberation'*[10] is one of the most radical documents ever to emanate from the Vatican. In its anxiety to refute liberation theologies (the plural is correctly insisted upon), it is obliged to borrow their clothes.

Here is the aspiration of the oppressed as a 'sign of the times':

> Humankind will no longer passively submit to crushing poverty with its effects of death, disease and decline. It resents this misery as an intolerable violation of its native dignity. Many factors, and among them certainly the leaven of the Gospel, have contributed to an awakening of the consciousness of the oppressed.                                                        (I,4)

This is the theme of 'consciousness-raising' of 'the wretched of the earth' that was historically at the origin of liberation theology in the 1960s. The Instruction then tackles a complementary theme: the scandal of inequality:

> The scandal of the shocking inequality between the rich and the poor – whether between rich and poor countries, or between social classes in a single nation – is no longer tolerated. On the one hand people have attained an unheard of abundance that is given to waste, while on the other hand so many live in such poverty, deprived of such basic necessities, that one is hardly able to count the victims of malnutrition.                          (I,6)

The Congregation for the Doctrine of the Faith's Instruction contains this ringing commitment:

> More than ever, the Church intends to condemn abuses, injustices and attacks against freedom, wherever they occur and whoever commits them. She intends to struggle, by her own means, for the defence and advancement of the rights of humankind, especially of the poor.                              (Introduction)

Liberation theologians should rejoice that the gist of their message has got across to the universal Church, and that what they have been saying for a decade and a half has now been accepted by the CDF. Its purpose is differently explained, however:

> To draw attention . . . to the deviations, and risks of deviations, damaging to the faith and to Christian living, that are brought about by certain forms of Liberation Theology which use, in an insufficiently critical manner, concepts borrowed from various currents of Marxist thought.                (Introduction)

Unlike earlier condemnations in this century, there is no talk of 'errors' still less of 'heresy', but merely of 'deviations' or the possible threat of them. To 'deviate' means to go astray, to get on a wrong track: it is not to be irremediably lost. Moreover, the risk of deviation afflicts only 'certain forms of Liberation Theology' – not presumably all of them. Its target is only those who use Marxist concepts 'in an insufficiently critical manner'. That suggests – though later this idea seems to be rejected – that provided one retains one's critical faculties, some Marxist concepts might be useful. Moreover, 'Marxism' itself exhibits great diversity, as Ratzinger, the Prefect of the Congregation for the Doctrine of the Faith, recognised. So we are dealing with a warning, not a condemnation; and right from the start the warning almost 'dies the death of a thousand qualifications'. It will be difficult to find a liberation theologian who owns up to an insufficiently critical use of Marxist concepts.

The second and negative part of the *Instruction* makes a powerful case against some Marxist assumptions. The first concerns the relationship between sin and social structures. It makes a concession: 'To be sure, there are structures that are evil and which cause evil and which we must have the courage to change' (IV,15). This is important because at the 1983 Synod some conservatives tried to throw out the concept of 'structural sin' altogether. Here it is redefined: 'Structures, whether they are good or bad, are the result of human actions, and so are consequences more than causes.' So one has to try to convert the people while changing the unjust structures. This also disposes of those who claim that morality has to be postponed until after the revolution on the grounds that 'you cannot draw straight lines in curved space'. The *Instruction* seems to be very much influenced by the East European experience when it points out how many crimes have been perpetrated in the name of liberty:

> This shame of our time cannot be ignored: while claiming to bring them freedom, these regimes keep whole nations in conditions of servitude which are unworthy of humankind. Those who, perhaps inadvertently, make themselves accomplices of similar enslavement betray the very poor they mean to help. (XI,10)

This pessimism is not entirely unjustified. The exact meaning of the *Instruction* remains unclear. Does this scepticism about revolutions rule out all possibility of the 'just revolution', envisaged in *Populorum Progressio*? Is the kind of 'violence' displayed in, say, the Warsaw uprising of 1944 and recently praised by Pope John Paul, never to be allowed? Is not the Congregation for the Doctrine of the Faith aware that liberation theologians – there are no exceptions to this rule – do not regard the Soviet Union as a model instance of Marxism in practice, and that most of them regard it on the contrary with abhorrence? For that reason, they fail to see why it should be dragged into a discussion of Latin America where, anyway, pro-Soviet Communist parties are weak.

The heart of the *Instruction* is reached in Section VII. It deals with 'Marxist Analysis'. Scholars have distinguished three elements or levels in Marxism. It can be seen as a would-be scientific analysis of the state of things, a strategy for transforming it, or an all-embracing philosophy or world-view. Many liberation theologians have suggested that the Marxist analysis was separable certainly from the world-view, and perhaps also from the strategy. The *Instruction* simply denies the possibility of making any such distinctions within Marxism. It is all one. It sees Marxism as a package deal in which you begin by buying class struggle and find you have embraced atheistic materialism. The denial that the 'analysis' can be separated from the world-view also involves the rejection of another favourite liberation theology thesis (borrowed from the French philosopher Louis Althusser): that Marxism is a science.[11] This rouses Ratzinger's special wrath. There are plenty of reasons for feeling indignant, he concedes, 'in certain parts of Latin America'. But this instinct, he believes, goes awry: 'The recognition of injustice is accompanied by a pathos which borrows its language from Marxism, wrongly presented as though it were scientific language' (VII,11). Marxism does not deserve the name of science, says Ratzinger. It is merely a set of unverified hypotheses. Marxism is not a neutral science. You cannot pick and choose among its tenets. If the class struggle determines all thinking and action, then it invades the Church itself (IX,2). Thus the magisterium will not be listened to because, embodying the class positions of the oppressors, it is discredited in advance (X,1).

More grievously, God and History are identified:

> There is a tendency to identify the Kingdom of God and its growth with the human liberation movement, and make history itself the subject of its own development, as a process of the self-redemption of humanity by means of the class struggle. (IX,3)

The secularisation of Christian concepts and sacraments is complete. Faith, hope and charity are transformed into 'fidelity to history', 'confidence in the future' and 'option for the poor' (IX,5), though liberation theologians will defend themselves by saying that they have 'translated' the theological virtues in this way, not transformed them.

The gravest and key accusation is that 'the theologians of liberation' are said to make a

> disastrous confusion between the poor of the Scripture and the proletariat of Marx ... In this way they transform the rights of the poor into a class fight

within the ideological perspective of the class struggle. For them the 'Church of the Poor' signifies the Church of the class which has become aware of the requirements of the revolutionary struggle as a step towards liberation and which celebrates this liberation in the liturgy. (IX,10)

It is true that many of them have drawn a parallel between the *anawim* or poor of the gospel and the proletariat in Marx. But that is not the same as identifying them. In any case, the dispossessed, landless peasants of Latin America do not fit easily into Marxist theory: far from being a working class bearing in themselves the meaning of history, they are more like the *Lumpenproletariat* that Marx thought useless for the revolution. The liberation theologians do not consign anyone to 'the scrap-heap of history'. Linked with the charge that liberation theologians identify the poor of the gospel with Marx's proletariat is the accusation that they have set up a 'popular Church' at odds with the hierarchy (IX.13).

## Instruction on Christian Freedom and Liberation

The *Instruction on Certain Aspects of the 'Theology of Liberation'* makes no claim to completeness. It says that another document is being prepared which will 'detail in positive fashion the great richness of this theme (namely Christian Liberation) for the doctrine and life of the Church'. The *Instruction on Christian Freedom and Liberation*, published on 5 April 1986, does little to correct the negative emphasis of the September 1984 *Instruction*.[12] It says on the contrary that its warning about 'deviations, or risks of deviations damaging to Christian faith and the Christian living', 'far from being outmoded ... appear ever more timely and relevant' (Introduction 1).

Yet there is a great difference between them: Pope John Paul has been involved in the production of this second *Instruction* to a far greater extent than in the last one. The ideas and the style are his throughout. For all practical purposes this second document can be considered as an encyclical: it has the style, sweep and scope of an encyclical. It is an essay in Catholic social doctrine, to be placed in the line of *Mater et Magistra, Pacem in Terris, Populorum Progressio*, and *Octogesima Adveniens*. Chapter 5 is significantly called: 'The Social Doctrine of the Church – towards a Christian Praxis of Liberation'. Social teaching develops, says the Pope, in accordance with the changing circumstances of history. He goes on to tell us how to read his document:

This is why, together with principles that are always valid, it also involves contingent judgements. Far from constituting a closed system, it remains constantly open to the new questions which constantly arise; it requires the contribution of all charisms, experiences and skills. (para. 72)

This marks an important shift. For in practice Catholic social doctrine had come to mean 'what Popes taught'. They undoubtedly thought of themselves as summing up the thinking of the whole Church. The return to Catholic teaching which the new document both urges and exemplifies, should also be seen as the recovery of a terrain which Pope Paul VI had abandoned. In *Octogesima Adveniens* – published in 1971, the eightieth anniversary of *Rerum Novarum* – Paul confessed: 'In the face of such widely varied situations it is difficult for us to utter a unified message and to put forward a solution which has universal validity. Such is not our ambition, nor is it our mission' (4). Where the Pope felt incompetent, the local churches had to take over and try to discern the signs of the times for their own place. This revivified the local churches and, incidentally, the episcopal conferences. The result in Latin America was liberation theology.

Pope John Paul deals with the question – who can teach Catholic social doctrine? – in the following way:

> The present document limits itself to indicating the principal theoretical and practical aspects. As regards applications to different local situations, it is for the local Churches, in communion with one another and with the See of Peter, to make direct provision for them. (para. 2)

The Pope recognises that this can be done:

> A theological reflection developed from a particular experience can constitute a very positive contribution, in as much as it makes possible a highlighting of aspects of the work of God, the richness of which had not yet been fully grasped. (para. 70)

The next remark however, suggests that the Latin Americans cannot pass this stringent test:

> But in order that this reflection may be truly a reading of scripture and not a projection onto the word of God of a meaning which it does not contain, the theologian will be careful to interpret the experience from which he begins in the light of the experience of the Church herself. This experience of the Church shines with a singular brightness and in all its purity in the lives of the saints. (para. 70)

The generalised 'experience' of sanctity in the Church looks merely like another way of imposing authority, as indeed the next sentence confirms: 'It pertains to the pastors of the Church, in communion with the Successor of Peter, to discern its [i.e. the experience's] authenticity.'

In the mind of the Pope the most dangerous threat to the Church comes from Marxism. Though it is never named in the document, its shadow is omnipresent. The particular version of Marxism he has in mind is radically atheistic, and not just atheistic by chance. Karl Marx did indeed once say that 'The human person is the supreme being for humankind.' John Paul refers to this:

> For many more, it is God himself who is the specific alienation of humanity. There is said to be radical incompatibility between the affirmation of God and human freedom, by rejecting belief in God, they say, humankind will become truly free.                                                   (para. 18)

This false dilemma – having to choose between God and humanity – is for John Paul the great tragedy of the modern world and the lesson of modern history:

> Why does this history, in spite of great achievements, which also remain always fragile, experience frequent relapses into alienation and see the appearance of new forms of slavery?                                       (para. 19)

Where God and humanity are seen in competition with each other, the denial of God leads straight to tyranny. Atheism is fundamentally immoral because it is idolatrous. It places the creature in the place of the Creator. It supplants the Creator, and usurps his role.

The result is this:

> When men and women wish to free themselves from the moral law and become independent of God, far from gaining their freedom, they destroy it. Having lost any criterion of truth, they fall prey to the arbitrary; fraternal relations between people are abolished and give way to terror, hatred and fear.                                                                        (para. 19)

In the early, and more philosophic, part of the document, John Paul traces a continuous line from Martin Luther to the eighteenth-century Enlightenment and the French Revolution. 'Since that time', he says, 'many have regarded future history as an irresistible process of liberation inevitably leading to an age in which humanity, totally free at last, will enjoy happiness on earth' (para. 6). To this anarchic individualism Pope John Paul opposes the Christian view of freedom: 'Freedom is not the liberty to do anything whatsoever. It is the freedom to do good, and in this alone is happiness to be found. The good is thus the goal of freedom' (para. 26).

If freedom really is the freedom to do good, then it represents an inner treasure that no one can take away. The Pope explains: 'Thus it is not liberation which produces human freedom. Common sense, confirmed by Christian sense, knows that even when freedom is subject to forms of conditioning it is not completely destroyed' (para. 31). 'People who undergo terrible constraints succeed in manifesting their freedom and taking steps to secure their own liberation.' Saint Maximilian Kolbe was freer than his Nazi executioners. However oppressed, the poor have always had this sense of inner freedom, the Pope claims.

> The 'poor of Yahweh' know that communion with God is the most precious treasure and the one in which men and women find their true freedom. For them, the most tragic misfortune is the loss of this communion. Hence their fight against injustice finds its deepest meaning and its effectiveness in their desire to be free from the slavery of sin.                    (para. 47)

This systematic 'spiritualising' of the theme of poverty is the chief difference between John Paul and liberation theologians. His interpretation of the Beatitudes, for example, is politically pessimistic: they 'prevent us from worshipping earthly goods and from committing the injustices which their unbridled pursuit involves, and they also divert us from an unrealistic and ruinous search for a perfect world' (para. 62). He never seems to allow that one might want to make it a slightly better place.

John Paul feels so strongly about this, that he says of the Magnificat, especially Luke 1.52:

> [the Magnificat] sings of the mystery of salvation and its power to transform. The *sensus fidei*, which is so vivid among the little ones, is able to grasp at once all the salvific and ethical treasures of the Magnificat.        (para. 48)

Granted that what the Pope says is true, is the Magnificat *only* about the mystery of salvation? Is it not *also* about the concrete lifting up (i.e. liberation) of the oppressed? John Paul seems to rule out this possibility.

This can be seen again in the crucial passage on the 'preferential option for the poor' as defined by Medellín in 1968 and confirmed by Puebla in 1979. John Paul interprets this to mean one should be charitable towards the poor:

> Those who are oppressed by poverty are the object of a love of preference on the part of the Church, which since her origin and in spite of failings of many of her members had not ceased to work for their relief, defence and liberation. She has done this through numberless works of charity which remain always and everywhere indispensable.        (para. 68)

The papal version of the option for the poor is as follows:

> The Church shows her solidarity with those who do not count in society by which they are rejected spiritually and sometimes physically. She is particularly drawn with maternal affection toward those children who, through human wickedness, will never be brought forth from the womb to the light of day, as also for the elderly, lonely and abandoned... The special option for the poor, far from being a sin of particularism or sectarianism, manifests the universality of the Church's being and mission. This option excludes no one. (para. 68)

Christians about to embark on a 'just revolution' need to take time to consider this grave warning:

> Those who discredit the path of reform and favour the myth of revolution not only foster the illusion that the abolition of an evil situation is in itself sufficient to create a more human society; they also encourage the setting up of totalitarian regimes. (para. 78)

The Pope says very firmly: 'Systematic recourse to violence put forward as the necessary path to liberation has to be condemned as a destructive illusion and one that opens the way to new forms of servitude' (para. 76).

Marx may have believed that force was the midwife of history, but the 'just revolution' tradition has always held that one should use the minimum of violence compatible with achieving the goal in view. The angriest statement in the *Instruction* again alludes to the Magnificat and declares: 'It would be criminal to take the energies of popular piety and misdirect them toward a purely earthly plan of liberation, which would soon be revealed as nothing more than an illusion and a cause of new forms of slavery' (para. 98).

The Exodus experience, so central to liberation theology, is re-interpreted. The Congregation for the Doctrine of the Faith cannot deny that it has a political aspect, but it is subordinated to a spiritual purpose. 'The Exodus', declares the second *Instruction*, 'has a meaning which is both religious and political' (para. 44). God sets the people free and gives them descendants, a land and a law, but within a covenant and for a covenant.' So the Exodus is ordered to the Covenant. The conclusion is: 'One cannot isolate the political aspect for its own sake: it has to be considered in the light of a plan of a religious nature within which it is integrated.' The assumption being made here was that liberation theologians had isolated the political aspect of the Exodus. Yet their whole point was that forms of dualism which separated the 'spiritual' and the 'political' religious should be avoided. So at the heart of the quarrel was a different experience of liberation, a semantic quarrel, and in the end a misunderstanding. This was masked because the two *Instructions* made it seem that the real issue was the 'Marxism' of liberation theologians. All would be well, if only liberation theology were purged of its 'Marxist' elements. John Paul, indeed, wrote a letter to the Brazilian bishops which they received at Easter, 1986, with Alleluias and tears of joy. John Paul wrote that liberation theology was 'not only timely, but useful and necessary'.

## Santo Domingo and after

These words have proved a false dawn. The theoretical attacks on liberation theology may have ceased. They were no longer needed: everything that could be said had been said. From now on the attacks on liberation theology used administrative means: the appointment of reactionary bishops, intense pressure on religious superiors to oust liberation theologians, the decapitation of CLAR (the Latin American Conference of Religious), the encouragement of right-wing movements hostile to liberation theology, control of the position-paper for Santo Domingo and the vetting of those who could go. The outcome of the Santo Domingo conference,[13] the fourth conference of Latin American bishops in 1992, was not the disaster for liberation theology that was predicted. Called to coincide with the five hundredth anniversary of Columbus' landfall in the Americas, the conference's theme was evangelisation, human development and Christian culture. In the Pope's opening address there were key markers of the spirit of the age with the call for 'interior renewal', to 'judge the signs of the times'. There was a clear call for continuity with Medellín and Puebla, however:

> In continuity with Medellín and Puebla conferences, the church reaffirms the preferential option on behalf of the poor, though that option is not exclusive or excluding, since the message of salvation is intended for all. It is an option, moreover, that is based essentially on God's word, and not on criteria provided by human sciences or opposed ideologies, which often reduce the poor to abstract socio-political and economic categories. But it is a firm and irrevocable option.[14]

The Pope then goes on to talk about

> the genuine praxis of liberation [which] must always be inspired by the doctrine of the Church as set forth in the two instructions by the Congregation for the Doctrine of Faith . . . which must be kept in mind when the topic of liberation theologies comes up for discussion. However, the Church can in no way allow any ideology or political current to snatch away the banner of

justice, for it is one of the primary demands of the gospel, and at the same time, a fruit of the coming of God's kingdom. (para. 16)

Similarly in the conclusions of the Conference the importance of the base ecclesial communities is stressed but their ecclesial character is underlined:

'...the leaders must be in communion with their parish and bishop...' When they lack a clear ecclesiological foundation and are not sincerely seeking communion, such communities cease being ecclesial and may fall victim to ideological or political manipulation. (para. 61f.)

The continuity with Medellín and Puebla is reaffirmed in the conference's conclusions – though with a subtle twist echoing the sentiments of the Pope's opening address:

Evangelising means doing what Jesus Christ did in the synagogue when he stated that he had come to 'bring glad tidings' to the poor. He 'became poor although he was rich, so that by his poverty you might become rich'. He challenges us to give an authentic witness of the gospel poverty in the way we live in our church structures, just as he gave it. (para. 178)

Such is the basis for a commitment to a *gospel-based* and preferential option for the poor, one that is firm and irrevocable but not exclusive or excluding, as was solemnly affirmed at the Medellín and Puebla conferences.

This emphasis on the 'gospel preferential option for the poor' is a theme which runs throughout the Santo Domingo conclusions and resonates with the Papal address and the themes of the *Instructions*, whose intent is to affirm the resources of the Christian tradition for the true understanding of liberation. For all the ecclesial tone of the Conclusions the central features which have marked so much Latin American theology over the last thirty years are nevertheless reaffirmed.

From the point of view of the Vatican the fortunes of liberation theology have continued to wane. In 1997 the Sri Lankan theologian, Tissa Balasuriya, was excommunicated for deviating from the Catholic faith because of 'errors' in his book *Mary and Human Liberation*, an action resembling but exceeding in its severity earlier penalties imposed on Leonardo Boff and others.[15] Liberation theology is in a less friendly theological and ecclesial climate. Indeed, the Prefect for the Congregation for the Doctrine of the Faith, Cardinal Joseph Ratzinger, seems to believe that he has put a stop to liberation theologians' attempts 'to turn religion ... into the handmaiden of political ideologies'. But reports of liberation theology's demise have been exaggerated. Even if bishops sympathetic to liberation theology may be less numerous than they once were and the particular theological ethos of the immediate aftermath of the Second Vatican Council less apparent, the influence of the liberation theologians on the theological positions of the Roman Catholic Church is everywhere apparent in its official statements. However vociferous the critics of liberation theology may have become, the pressing needs of the majority of men, women and children in our world only add force to the challenge to Catholic theology from Jon Sobrino: 'If those doing liberation theology are not doing it well, let others do it and do it better.'[16]

## NOTES

1 At his death in December 1994 Peter Hebblethwaite was a third of the way through this article. With the help of Margaret Hebblethwaite I have been able to incorporate material that he might have used. All but the final section were written by Peter. What appears here is, inevitably, only a shadow of what Peter would have finally offered on the subject, but it is included in this collection because it reflects the wisdom of one of the foremost Catholic commentators of our day on a matter on which he was uniquely equipped to comment.

2 For the final documents see *Medellín Conclusions* (New York, US Catholic Conference, 1973), also in A. T. Hennelly (ed.), *Liberation Theology: A Documentary History* (1990). The basic texts relevant for understanding evangelisation are to be found in the collection *Proclaiming Justice and Peace*, eds. M. Walsh and B. Davies (London, CIIR/CAFOD, 1984); particularly relevant is the encyclical *Evangelii Nuntiandi*.

3 A survey of important source material may be found in Hennelly (ed.), *Liberation Theology*, e.g. p. 64.

4 P. Hebblethwaite, *Paul VI: the First Modern Pope* (London, Harper Collins, 1993), p. 448.

5 John XXIII's treatment of 'signs of the times' was first seen in *Humanae Salutis*, the solemn apostolic constitution which convoked Vatican II. On the social teaching of Vatican II see Walsh and Davies (eds.), *Proclaiming Justice and Peace*.

6 *Puebla Conclusions* (London, CIIR, 1973).

7 Cf. Hugo Assmann quoting a 'committed Christian': 'The Bible? It doesn't exist. The only bible is the sociological bible of what I see happening here and now': *A Practical Theology of Liberation* (London, Search Press, 1975), p. 61.

8 Cf. G. Gutiérrez: 'It is a class option, deceitfully camouflaged by a purported equality before the law': *A Theology of Liberation*, rev. edn (London, SCM, 1988), p. 275.

9 H. Cox, *The Silencing of Leonardo Boff* (London, Collins, 1989) and on Tissa Balasuriya see p. 196.

10 Reprinted in Hennelly, *Liberation Theology*, pp. 393ff.

11 See the discussion in C. Boff, *Theology and Praxis* (Maryknoll, NY, Orbis, 1987).

12 Reprinted in Hennelly, *Liberation Theology*, pp. 461ff.

13 *Santo Domingo Conclusions*, tr. P. Berryman (London, CIIR, 1993).

14 Ibid., p. 13. There is a reference to an address to the Roman curia of December 1984.

15 The issues are summarised in *The Tablet*, 11 January 1997, pp. 50f.

16 J. Sobrino, *Companions of Jesus. The Murder and Martyrdom of the Salvadorean Jesuits* (London, CIIR, 1990), p. 51.

# 11

DENYS TURNER

# Marxism, liberation theology and the way of negation

I

In 1984 the Vatican's Congregation for the Doctrine of the Faith published an *Instruction on Certain Aspects of the 'Theology of Liberation'*, known from the first two words of its Latin text as *Libertatis Nuntius*. The intention of this document was, it says, 'limited and precise', which was

> to draw the attention of pastors, theologians, and all the faithful to the deviations, and risks of deviation, damaging to the faith and Christian living, that are brought about by certain forms of liberation theology which use, in an insufficiently critical manner, concepts borrowed from various currents of marxist thought.[1]

The issue, then, was Marxism, or the use of it within some versions of liberation theology. The document is careful to point out that it offers no general criticism of liberation theology as such, at any rate insofar as liberation theology is defined by its response to the 'preferential option for the poor'; nor, it adds, should its criticisms of liberation theology on the score of its Marxism 'serve as an excuse for those who maintain an attitude of neutrality and indifference in the face of the tragic and pressing problems of human misery and injustice'.[2] The Apostolic See, it goes on, has a good record of denunciation, for it 'has not ceased to denounce the scandal involved in the gigantic arms race',[3] nor does it any longer tolerate 'the shocking inequality between rich and poor'[4] the injuries of which to the poor, it notes, are aggravated by 'the memory of crimes of a certain type of colonialism'.[5]

The Church's 'yearning for justice' requires, however, to be submitted to a 'discernment process' in respect of both its 'theoretical and practical' expressions, for 'the aspiration for justice often finds itself captive of ideologies which hide or pervert its meaning',[6] even if, 'taken by itself, the desire for liberation finds a strong and fraternal echo in the heart and spirit of Christians',[7] and even if, 'in itself, the expression "theology of liberation"

is a thoroughly valid term', which designates 'a theological reflection centred on the biblical theme of liberation and freedom, and on the urgency of
its practical realisation'.[8]

In the process of discernment, the *Instruction* goes on, it is necessary to
begin from biblical foundations in the Scriptures, which, it insists, offer a
'radical experience of Christian liberty' which consists in the first instance
and fundamentally in liberation from 'that most radical form of slavery'
which is 'slavery to sin', for all 'other forms of slavery find their deepest
root in slavery to sin'.[9] For this reason 'the full ambit of sin, whose first
effect is to introduce disorder in the relationship between God and man,
cannot be restricted to "social sin" ',[10] nor 'can one localise evil principally
or uniquely in bad social, political, or economic "structures" as though all
other evils came from them so that the creation of the "new man" would
depend on the establishment of different economic and socio-political structures'.[11] 'To be sure', the document admits, 'there are structures which are
evil and which cause evil', but 'structures, whether they are good or bad,
are the result of human actions and so are consequences more than causes';
for which reason 'to demand first of all a radical revolution in social relations
and then to criticise the search for personal perfection is to set out on a
road which leads to the denial of the meaning of the person and his transcendence, and to destroy ethics and its foundation which is the absolute
character of the distinction between good and evil'.[12]

*Libertatis Nuntius* then proceeds to an analysis and critique of what it
calls 'a new interpretation of Christianity'. According to this ill-defined
and unreferenced congeries of theological opinions, there are 'some', who
'are tempted to put evangelisation into parentheses . . . and postpone it till
tomorrow: first the bread, then the Word of God';[13] there are 'some' to
whom 'it seems that the necessary struggle for human justice and freedom
in the economic and political sense constitutes the whole essence of salvation' and for whom 'the Gospel is reduced to a purely earthly gospel';[14] and,
in a more explicitly targeted comment, it rather curiously describes 'the
different theologies of liberation' as being 'situated between the *preferential
option for the poor* forcefully reaffirmed without ambiguity after Medellín
at the Conference of Puebla on the one hand, and the temptation to reduce
the Gospel to an earthly gospel on the other'.[15] These corruptions of 'whatever was authentic in the generous initial commitment on behalf of the
poor' it ascribes to an uncritical borrowing by such liberation theologians
'from marxist ideology and recourse to theses of a biblical hermeneutic
marked by rationalism'.[16]

There is scarcely a word of all this with which any published liberation
theologian writing before 1984 would not fully agree, still less any since.

On the other hand, any liberation theologian would note with some irony the Vatican's enthusiasm for the 'preferential option for the poor', since if there is any source for this theological principle upon which the Vatican could draw it would be the writings of liberation theologians; few would deny the Vatican its right to claim some credit for its recent record of denunciation of the exploitation of the poor, though all would want to add a comment on the Catholic Church's history of studied ambiguity (to say the least) on this score within Latin American history. All would concede the need for theological discernment between authentic and inauthentic expressions of the option for the poor, and most Catholic liberationists would concede the Vatican's right to some role in the processes of that discernment. All would heartily endorse the insistence upon the need, within those processes, to return to the biblical sources, though again they might note wryly that it is liberation theology itself which has been the agent chiefly responsible for a return to biblical sources for the construction of a Catholic social theology and away from the largely non-biblical 'natural law' traditions of the markedly 'Euro-centred' papal teachings of this century. None would deny the centrality of personal sin; all would deny that 'structural' sin is principally, even more emphatically they would deny that it is 'uniquely', the cause of personal sin; all would affirm the impropriety of severing the links of mutual interaction between the personal and social dimensions; all would reject any attempt to reduce the gospel to an 'earthly gospel', or to translate out the 'whole essence of salvation' into the 'necessary struggle for human justice and freedom in the economic and political sense'; none accepts 'uncritically' any relation with Marxism, and none offers a 'rationalist hermeneutic' of the Bible. In short, thus far, liberation theologians either anticipated all that the Vatican endorsed in *Libertatis Nuntius*, or else had no reason to dissent from its analysis except insofar as it was intended to target them. Only on one issue of principle need some liberation theologians engage in *substantive* disagreement with the Vatican, namely in the matter of the place of Marxism within the construction of a theological 'option for the poor'.

2

What, then was the issue about Marxism? The issue may be briefly stated. Marxism, the Vatican asserts, is a reductivist form of social analysis; as such, it is intrinsically and so inseparably connected with a praxis of class hatred and struggle, which offends against Christian norms of charity, and with the denial of God and of the human person, which strikes at the core of Christian belief about God and the human.[17] Liberation theologians, it

concedes, propose to ally themselves only with Marxism as to an instrument of the 'analysis' of the structures of oppression in the Third World;[18]
but in this they are multiply deceived. For Marxism is a totalising ideology
of materialism and its 'ideological principles come prior to the study of
social reality and are presupposed to it'.[19] Thus, insofar as it is truly Marxism that these liberationists ally themselves with, they are inviting a theological cuckoo into the nest; insofar as Christian faith and praxis can truly
live with a 'scientific' analysis of society and praxis for social change, that
analysis must cease to be Marxist.

The consequences of ignoring the theologically subversive character of
Marxism are a wholesale deformation of the Christian response to poverty
and exploitation. Marxism defines truth in general as inseparable from
praxis, the partisan praxis of engagement in the class struggle:[20] all and
only that which contributes to the success of the oppressed classes within
that struggle is 'true' and this class struggle 'is presented as an objective,
necessary law. Upon entering this process on behalf of the oppressed, one
"makes" truth, one acts "scientifically". Consequently, the conception of
the truth goes hand in hand with the affirmation of necessary violence, and
so, of a political amorality.'[21]

Worse still, the all-embracing character of this class analysis inevitably
requires its application to the Church as institution and to its core beliefs.[22]
Therefore, if liberation theologians accept class analysis in principle, they
will, whether they like it or not, have to accept the consequence that 'the
class struggle divides the Church herself, and that in the light of this
struggle even ecclesial realities must be judged'[23] – and the *Instruction*
clearly implies that at least some liberation theologians are none too un-
happy to accept this consequence. What is more, the totalising and deter-
ministic nature of Marxism entails wholesale consequences of a reductivist
sort for Christian faith as such.[24] Liberation theologians may not accept
that this is so, but the logic of Marxism requires it: for any alliance with
Marxism is an alliance with a system of thought for which religion as such
is merely a phenomenon, expressed in misleading and mystifying terms, of
real material – that is social, political and above all economic – forces
which are the true engine of history. Inevitably, then, a Christianity wed to
Marxism will lead to what the *Instruction* calls 'historicist immanentism'
which will tend 'to identify the Kingdom of God and its growth with the
human liberation movement, and to make history itself the subject of its
own development, as a process of the self-redemption of humanity by
means of the class struggle'.[25] Along these lines, the *Instruction* adds,
'some go so far as to identify God Himself with history and to define faith
as "fidelity to history"' and, '. . . as a consequence faith, hope and charity

are given a new content: they become "fidelity to history", "confidence in the future" and "option for the poor". This is tantamount to saying that they have been emptied of their theological reality'.[26]

No doubt there are scarcely any liberation theologians in any part of the world who would recognise themselves in this caricature. And for sure, as an account of what conclusions liberation theologians themselves accept as following from such accommodations with Marxist thought as they would admit to, the analysis is thoroughly inaccurate and grossly unfair. But it is only one part of the *Instruction*'s argument which can be so easily rebutted. For to the authors of this document, at least as important as the detailed critique of the actual texts of liberation theologians, is the critique of the inevitable dynamic of a theological association with Marxism. It raises a general point of theological principle: can a theology in search of an *analysis* of the social, political and economic structures of exploitation find one in a general theory of society and history which is *ideologically* committed to atheism, materialism and reductivism? And is Marxism a theory of such a kind that the analysis and the ideology cannot be separated so as to permit the instrumental use of the analysis detached from the ideology? The Vatican's argument is that it cannot: that being so, it will not for the authors of the *Instruction* be any more than a partial and weakly inadequate response even if one can demonstrate that liberation theologians do not *in fact* accept the logical consequences of their alliances with Marxism. For that simply means that they are the less able to identify the fundamental inconsistencies and incoherences which vitiate the very project of a liberation theology itself. And if it amounts to anything by way of *prima facie* support for this Vatican view of the matter, it would be worth mentioning that nearly every mainstream Marxist would thus far be in entire agreement with its view of the inseparability within Marxism of the class analysis, the atheism and the historical materialism.


3


But before considering how far this view of the logic of the relationship between Christianity and Marxism can be sustained, let us turn from the view that liberation theology dances too intimately with Marxism to one which maintains almost exactly the opposite. This is the view that liberation theology fails as an adequate theological project because it is not Marxist *enough*. Most systematically and thoroughly explored by Alistair Kee in his *Marx and the Failure of Liberation Theology*,[27] the starting point is, in one crucial respect, similar to that of the Vatican's: for Kee argues that Marxism cannot, at the eclectic whim of the theologian, be exploited for a merely empirical analysis of the structures of class exploitation and oppression, leaving aside as dispensable and 'ideological' components, the critique of religion itself. Moreover, insofar as liberation theologians have been prepared to acknowledge the force of Marx's critique of religion, they have done that too in an inconsistently selective fashion. For, as Kee points out, that critique of religion contains two inseparable but distinct elements, the first (and generally accepted by liberationists as legitimate) being the empirical, historical critique of the actual role of Christianity within society as normally reactionary, and the second (generally ignored by liberationists), the more radical and comprehensive critique of Christianity as involving *in principle* an 'ideological reversal', involving a falsification therefore of the real relations of class and domination and a mystification of them.[28]

Now Kee argues – and in this he is surely right – that these two elements of the generalised critique of religion cannot be separated one from the other. For particularly as regards Christianity, Marx's hostility was universal and directed at it as a form of religion *in principle*. It is sometimes supposed that Marx's criticism of Christianity as an historical phenomenon was culturally limited in its focus upon the German Lutheranism in which his father, a convert of convenience from Judaism, brought him up. This is not true. Certainly he identified early Lutheranism, with its individualistic emphasis on the 'authority of faith' as against the Roman Catholic feudal emphasis on 'faith in authority' as the natural ally of emergent sixteenth-century capitalism. But this was not because he regarded Roman Catholicism as any better placed to offer a theological critique of capitalism just because it was more distanced ideologically from it; on the contrary, he regarded Roman Catholicism, to which he admittedly paid scant attention, as still less capable of taking up the concerns of revolutionary socialism, since it stood even further back down the line of reactionary doctrines, a hopelessly stranded medieval survival from a world which pre-dated even capitalism.

Moreover, it is not true even that Marx thought all forms of Christianity necessarily make explicit alliances with reactionary politics: in fact he very well understood the mechanisms inherent in the religious formation of ideology which would lead to episodic recurrences of politically radical Christianity, and in addition to his scornful dismissal of Christian socialism in *The Communist Manifesto*, his friend and colleague Friedrich Engels made a detailed study of one such episode in his *Peasant War in Germany*.[29] There Engels analysed the peasant revolt in the early Reformation period in Germany, paying attention not only to the increasingly reactionary stance of Luther, but also to the increasingly radical communism of the neo-Anabaptist leader, Thomas Muentzer – the latter, on paper at least, a prototypical communist. But a 'communist by fantasy' is how Engels describes Muentzer, for, in Engels' view, the radical political programme which Muentzer proposed was inspired by utopian Christianity and as such 'went beyond the directly prevailing social and political conditions'.[30] Being a theologically inspired idealism unrooted in real history, Muentzer's communism could, therefore, hope to succeed only by virtue of violent imposition, and so inevitably degenerated into the tyranny in which all utopianisms must end. Thus, commented Marx himself, 'the Peasant War, the most radical event in German history, came to grief because of theology'.[31]

Empirically, therefore, Marx allows no exceptions to the proposition that *religiosity as such* has ever proved an obstacle to revolutionary progress, a claim which he thought was sufficiently demonstrated by the fact that, even when allied to politically revolutionary programmes, that alliance with religion had always in practice blunted the revolutionary edge of the politics, by converting a concrete historical practice of class struggle into idealistic utopianisms. Moreover, this empirical claim is supported by his analysis of religion itself – and here Kee's contention comes to the fore – because on Marx's account religion in principle involves an 'inversion' of reality and therefore must always be a source of alienating illusion. And if that is true of religion in general, it ought to be true of the 'radical' Christianity of the liberation theologians. Why must this be so?

4

Marx and Engels did, it is true, concede that there are stages at which the role of religion can be positive in the revolutionary process, for its very idealism can at least offer a standard from which to criticise the prevailing, unideal, conditions – it was after all something, Engels suggested, that Muentzer's revolutionary Christianity enabled the revolutionary masses in Germany to envisage alternatives to those conditions, even if those alternatives were in the end only visionary, apocalyptic and fantastic. In the last resort, however, both felt that there was no place for religion in any genuinely revolutionary outcome. And this is at first glance strange. For both there is an ideological politics but also a revolutionary politics, and for both there are revolutionary forms of the economic, intellectual, artistic, and even, perhaps, moral struggle, as well as their ideological forms. Why, then, did they regard religion, even politically radical religion, as irretrievably ideological?

The answer to this question seems to be that Marx and Engels saw Christianity as caught on the horns of a dilemma which, put simply, amounts to this: that insofar as Christianity is true to itself as religious, it must be alienating politically, and insofar as it engages genuinely with the revolutionary critical programme of socialism, it must cease to be genuinely religious. John Maguire argues that in posing this dilemma for Christianity, Marx and Engels 'put religion on trial before a rather Kafakaesque tribunal: insofar as religion is sincerely religious, it is a set of abstract platitudes, at best useless, at worst harmful to the advancement of humanity; insofar as it says anything about the social and political reality of its time, it has ceased to be religion'.[32] Luciano Parinetto contends that this dilemma on which Marx and Engels impale Christianity is but a version of another, more theological, predicament in which, for them, Christianity is irretrievably implicated. For Marx, Parinetto asserts, Christianity must always pose the question of God in opposition to the question of humans, for 'what one gives to God one must take away from humans'.[33] Given that choice – between God and the human, between the transcendent otherworldly and the this-worldly and historical, between religion and politics, between the projection of an alien being and the doctrine of the self-creation of the human by human beings – Marx, Parinetto says, 'saw no choice but to opt for humanity'.[34]

There are, as we shall see, good reasons to believe that this account actually misconstrues Marx's position on Christianity, though it probably does more justice to Engels'. Maguire's comment is particularly relevant to Engels' *The Peasant War* in which Christianity is hardly allowed to state its case at all. But before dismissing this characterisation of Christianity's relation with the secular political realm, it is worth noting a curious coincidence between (at least) Engels' view and that of many conservative Christians today, for whom even if Christian belief may have some incidental and contingently derived political *consequences*, the belief-system itself is quite devoid of any political *content* of its own. Thus, the notable Christian conservative, Edward Norman, argues that the 'politicisation' of Christianity involves the denial of its transcendence, of its otherworldliness, as if the affairs of this world and the affairs of the next could not coincide without the destruction of either the one or the other:[35] and in so arguing, Norman exhibits many of the same theological instincts exemplified not only in Engels, but also, paradoxically, in *Libertatis Nuntius* – namely that to claim 'political content' to Christian belief is *eo ipso* to lapse into 'historicist immanentism'. Now those shared instincts, we might very well conclude, present the obverse and the reverse of one and the same form of peculiarly nineteenth-century reductivist atheism, that of Ludwig Feuerbach, for it was Feuerbach who convinced the left-wing atheists of the nineteenth-century that the 'essence' of Christianity lay in its otherworldly projection of the immanent, historical human upon the transcendent, otherworldly, divine, thus evacuating the human of its this-worldly, historical, human content. It is, however, but the mirror-image of this Feuerbachian dichotomisation of the sacred and the secular if one merely responds in kind, as fideistic forms of Christianity commonly do: that is to say, by urging the distinctiveness of a Christianity whose essence as transcendent and otherworldly necessarily entails the denial of its this-worldly, secular, historical content – to argue, in short, that insofar as a theology accepts a 'politicisation' of its central message, it necessarily lapses into an 'historicist immanentism', as *Libertatis Nuntius* believes liberation theology does and must necessarily do.

There is, perhaps surprisingly, a residual element of this inverted Feuerbachianism in the Vatican document's critique of liberation theology, which vitiates the quality of its own theological response. But even before that, this Feuerbachianism infects its reading of Marx whose criticism of religion, as I have argued elsewhere, it consistently and wrongly confuses with Feuerbach's.[36] It was Feuerbach, not Marx, who argued that what is affirmed of God must necessarily be denied of the human; it is therefore the neo-Feuerbachian Christian who responds that the affirmation of God invokes a 'vertical' relation with the transcendent which must necessarily and *as such* be exclusive of simultaneous 'horizontal' relationships with the social and the historical. But this Feuerbachian dialectic is not Marx's. As early as 1844, in the *Economic and Philosophical MSS*, Marx had called down a plague on the houses *both* of a Christian theism *and* of a Feuerbachian atheism which but replicated in antithetical forms the same essentialist and abstract account of the 'sacred' and the 'secular':

> ...since for socialist man *the whole of what is called world history* is nothing more than the creation of man through labour, and the development of nature for man, he has therefore palpable and incontrovertible proof of his self-mediated *birth*, of his *process of emergence*. Since the *essentiality* ... of man and nature, man as the existence of nature for man and nature as the existence of man for man, has become practically and sensuously perceptible, the question of an alien being, a being above nature and man – a question which implies an admission of the unreality of nature and man – has become impossible in practice. *Atheism*, which is the denial of this unreality, no longer has any meaning, for atheism is a *negation of God*, through which negation it asserts the *existence of man*. But socialism as such no longer needs such mediation ... It is the *positive self-consciousness* of man, no longer mediated through the abolition of religion.[37]

A more decisive rejection of the Feuerbachian problematic is scarcely possible, and Parinetto's account of Marx's critique of religion as entailing the Feuerbachian reconquest of the territory of the secular human via the denial of God simply cannot survive the impact of this, an exceedingly early, and utterly explicit statement of Marx's true position.

For Marx's critique of religion is at once quite different from and vastly more challenging than Feuerbach's. Marx did not oppose 'religion' in the name of 'the human', oppose 'the sacred' in the name of 'the secular', oppose 'theology' in the name of 'politics': Marx first and foremost *opposed the oppositions* between all these 'essentialistically' defined abstractions and he opposed both Christian theism and Feuerbachian atheism because they were, he thought, irretrievably trapped within the antitheses of their opposed essentialisms. Both, therefore, were equally forms of 'idealism', forms of ideology through which social agents lived out their real relations with the human world in the medium of an 'unreality'; moreover, for Marx, the *opposition itself* between religion and the human was only superficial, for the atheism of a Feuerbach was implicitly as theological as the theology of the fideistical theist was implicitly atheist: for both shared the same essentially theological problematic, since for both *everything* turns on the question of the existence or non-existence of God. Whereas for Marx, *nothing* turns on it, since for 'socialist man' *the question of God cannot arise.*

## 5

In this strategy of, as I have put it, *opposing oppositions* between 'the sacred' and 'the secular', there may appear to be afforded some consolation for the liberation theologian envisaging an alliance with Marxism. For there is no doubt that this same strategy lies close to the heart of the project of most representatives of that movement. *Libertatis Nuntius* is superficial to the point of vulgar crassness in its characterisation of liberation theology as 'historicist immanentism', at any rate insofar as one can rely on the *intentions* of its theological project. If anything characterises the theology of Gustavo Gutiérrez, for example, it is the intention of reintegrating the transcendent with the historical, the eschatological with the immanent, the individual with the social, the personal spiritual with the pursuit of social justice. It is precisely in its resistence to these antitheses that the sharpest critique of 'northern' theological traditions, construed as they are upon these 'Feuerbachian' foundations, is to be found. Yet it is possible to acknowledge these intentions of liberation theology, as well as the mis-readings of it by critics of the Vatican school, and still entertain doubts about the coherence of its alliance with Marxism. For it is still possible to doubt, as Kee doubts, whether liberation theology has sufficiently understood the force of Marx's critique of religion, in particular, whether it has sufficiently understood the radical nature of Marx's atheism and the inseparability of that atheism from Marx's critique of economy and society. *Libertatis Nuntius* may very well have misconstrued that atheism by confusing it with Feuerbach's; but in doing so it entirely missed the point. For Feuerbach's atheism is easily rebutted, and convincingly so, by the arguments of the liberation theologians themselves. But Marx's atheism is less easily disposed of and here liberation theologians are on less secure ground, insofar as they too are easily misled by the confusion of Marx's with Feuerbach's atheisms into supposing that in dismissing what in fact is the latter's they can easily separate off Marx's analysis of economy and society – utilisable in their critiques of 'idolatrous' ideologies – from an atheism they deem equally 'ideological'.

In this view of the relationship between an adequate critique of idolatry and Marx's atheism I fear those liberation theologians are mistaken on more than one count: they are mistaken about Marx where *Libertatis Nuntius* is right, in particular about the inner connectedness of his social critique with his atheism; they are wrong where *Libertatis Nuntius* is wrong in that they neglect crucial differences between Marx's atheism and Feuerbach's; and because of both they are misled into a too superficial dismissal of Marx's atheism; hence, Kee is right where *Libertatis Nuntius* is most wrong, for it is not in being *too* Marxist that liberation theology fails of theological adequacy, but in not being Marxist *enough*.

## 6

The analysis of this relatively superficial treatment of atheism within liberation theology leads us back into the specific contextuality of liberation theology itself: its geographical – and religious-cultural – origins lie within a distinctly and very traditionally Catholic society, whose historical memory is fraught with the ambiguities of the Church's relationship with, first, directly colonial and, subsequently, indirectly neo-colonial forms of oppression and political and economic dependence. The historical crises to which Christian theology has had to respond in Latin America have been quite different from those which have afflicted the theologies of the North, whether in the last century or this: Northern theologies have been worked out in response to the phenomena of industrial development, forced urbanisation, rapid secularisation in the realms of politics and society, the dizzying pace of technological change, the ravages of two total wars on the European mainland and perhaps above all that nightmare, to which those theologies have yet to find a theological response of any degree of adequacy, the racial murder of six million Jews which we call, today, the Holocaust.

From the standpoint of Third World theologians, these events, which form the 'contextuality' of the theologies of the North, have, except incidentally, passed them by, for through the neo-colonial relations of dependence and marginalisation enforced upon them by the capitalist and post-capitalist economies of the North, their own development in these connections has been very largely arrested. And just as the economies of the South have failed to share the crises of the North because they have been denied a place within the history of Northern economic development, so their theologies have had to respond to quite different features of contextuality. For something like these reasons, atheism and disbelief have never been the central theological issues within Third World theologies that they have become within Northern theologies, just as, naturally enough within the hegemonic, imperialist societies of the North, revolution and liberation have not since the pre-imperial age been the central preoccupations which they have become in the South. Consequently, even if Marxism can appear as an attractive 'oppositional' import from Northern ideologies, utilisable *as analysis* within the critiques of colonial and neo-colonial economic oppression and exploitation – and to some degree within the critique of religious complicity with that exploitation – the issue of Marx's atheism has often been seen by liberation theologians as a problem for the North, not one raising critical questions about the construction of a theology contextually grounded in the experience of the South. It is therefore the very 'contextuality' of liberation theology, its sense of the necessity to work within its own context of issue and crisis, which leads it into what appears to a Northern theologian, an irenical and inconsistent appropriation of a selective Marxism.

It is for this reason too that for all the sharpness of its leading-edge of social critique, liberation theology can often look, as to its foundations, oddly 'pre-critical' to the Northern theologian, unproblematical and fundamentalist in its appropriation of Scripture, and strangely silent on issues of theodicy, which the Northern, in particular the European, experience of total evil in the twentieth century has pushed to the forefront of theological concern. In fact it is not merely in the politically naive optimism of the early liberation theologians about the prospects of revolution in Latin America that the Northern theologian can identify an excessive cheerfulness, but more fundamentally in the very prospect of constructing a theology of any kind at all, given the absence from their theologies of that generalised epistemological and theological self-doubt which afflicts Northern theology, casting it in so tragic and negative a mould.

Liberation theologians do not, as a consequence, regularly engage in that flirtation with atheism which is so characteristic of Northern theologies;

on the contrary, they are rather more inclined to dismiss the problematic as just a bit of Northern ideological baggage, along with all the paraphernalia of issues about secularisation, pluralism and relativism. In short, one might say that liberation theology lacks an apophaticism, a 'negative theology', a theology of the 'absence of God' and so lacks the impulse, so urgently pressing within the dynamics of Northern theologies, to distinguish the theology of God's 'absence' from the anti-theology of God's non-existence.

And yet, for all that so little can be said about it in an essay of this brevity, it is worth noting just how significant for any theological project is the prior engagement with the atheism of Marx. For, as we have seen, Marx's atheism is no mere inversion of Christian theology, as Feuerbach's is: and until we see this, Christian theology is very likely to remain trapped within a simple re-inversion of Feuerbach's atheism. It is Marx, not Feuerbach, who truly challenges the Christian, for it is Marx, not Feuerbach, who rejects as illusory in principle any vision of the world seen in theological terms, whether through the affirmation or through the negation of God.

For, as we have seen, Marx saw through this Feuerbachian atheism as being as firmly rooted in the theological conception of the universe as is its mirror-image, a theism which affirms God only via the negation of the human. Since Marx's atheism consisted not in the negation of God as such, but in the *negation of the negation* between God and the human, it is not possible to derive even a humanism, not even a post-theistic humanism from that atheism, because to negate the antithesis is to negate that whole intellectual and cultural world for which the abstraction 'the human' exists; namely, that world in which 'the human' is invented to stand in polar opposition to God. As much as anything else, Marx's opposition to Feuerbach resided in his hostility to this abstract, de-historicised and fraudulently culture-, gender- and class-neutral conception of the species-being, which only existed for Feuerbach via the negation of God – a conception which, given the negation of God, had to exist to be the bearer of the one, common, theological essence of things. Thus it was that in the name of actual populations of men, women and children – history's real agents and products – Marx protested equally against both a theist and an atheist ideology; for both theism and atheism crushed those real historical agents out of existence, either beneath the weight of an overwhelmingly dehumanising God or by their subsumption under the Feuerbachian abstraction, the 'species-being'. It was for this reason that Marx invokes a plague upon the house both of God and 'man'.

It is therefore with some sense of the irony of it, that one may welcome Quentin Lauer's comment on Marx's atheism both as a description of that atheism and as an unconscious debunking of a Feuerbachian Christianity: for Marx, Lauer says, 'there is no conceivable God that would be acceptable, for any being in any way superior to man is simply inconceivable'.[38] Here, albeit unconsciously uttered, is captured the true irony of Marx's atheism, its character of a radical negativity. To assert that no God as a being superior to the human is conceivable is at once to reject those idolatrous theisms for which God is all too conceivably top-being – a *super* human – and those atheisms which all too conceivably negate them. Taken strictly for what it says, therefore, this is a proposition with which any good Christian theologian should heartily agree, for no Christian who has absorbed the lessons of a negative theology has any business affirming a conceivable God superior to human beings. For the apophatic theologian denies that there is any scale of superiority and inferiority to which both God and creatures belong. So there cannot be any being in any knowable degree of superiority to human beings: or, if you admit angels, who would be measurably superior to humans, any beings measurably superior to humans *eo ipso* could not be God.

In this denial, therefore, lies the radicalism of Marx's atheism, which denies equally any theism which purports to identify a God in relations of opposition to the human and any atheism which can identify the human only through its negation of God. It is, therefore, in the radicalism of that atheism that Marx truly challenges the Christian theologian to construct a theology which is at once, and equally, post-theistical and *therefore*, post-atheistical, a theology which, being dispossessed of its language of affirmation, dispossesses the atheist of their language of denial; a theology therefore which joins hands with the radicalism of the *via negativa*, and so paradoxically, with the theological radicalism of the apophatic mystical traditions of classical theology; for in the denial that there is any kind of thing which God is, no essence to be affirmed or negated, as the pseudo-Denys says,[39] is contained the negation of that essentialism which unites, in common problematic, the Feuerbachian atheist and the neo-Feuerbachian Christian; in the insight, therefore, that God is beyond every possibility of affirmation and negation[40] and so beyond the possibility of being in a relation of 'either/or' with anything whatsoever, is contained a doctrine of God which transcends that Feuerbachian problematic. For as the pseudo-Denys says again, 'He does not possess this kind of existence and not that.'[41] Hence, there is nothing we can say which God is and there is nothing we can say which God is not. Hence, too, God cannot enter into relations of identity or difference with anything at all: for God is at once too transcendent to lack total immanence, and too immanent to be anything but utterly transcendent.[42]

7

But, it will be objected, is not this just playing with words? For obviously theists affirm God and Marx denies God. And if the relation between Christian apophaticism and Marxist atheism is so close as all that, if they are united in the radicalism of their denials, what is it that distinguishes them? To which objection a question may in turn be posed: *just what is it* that the theist affirms which, like the Marxist, the theist must not also deny?

It seems to me that Christians seem almost neurotically compelled to believe that they have, and must have, a ready answer to that question; to whom it may seem worth saying that they *ought* rather to have a problem distinguishing their position from that of good atheists like Marx; it *ought not* to be easy to see the difference; because gods do not come naturally to the Christian mind, because Christians do not, as some of the ancient pagans did, live in a world heavily populated by familiar deities or even, as some Christians appear to think, in a world very obviously populated by just one very big God; because Christians ought to feel more comfortable within the prophetic traditions of the ancient Hebrew world, which feared idolatries more than it feared divinities. And these things being so, they should not seek, actively, a solution to the problem of how the apophatic, mystical theology is to be distinguished from the more radical forms of atheism; at any rate, they should not seek that distinction prematurely; which is what they do who can tell you *a priori*, in advance of the debate with the atheist, what it is that one is affirming in saying there is a God; and so they can easily tell you what it is that distinguishes those who affirm this from those who deny it.

Which is why, I should say very briefly, any contemporary critique of the idolatries and ideologies of society ought to take a greater interest than is generally supposed necessary in the negative traditions of Western mysticism, in the pseudo-Denys, Marguerite of Porete, Eckhart, the author of *The Cloud of Unknowing* and in John of the Cross. For they, paradoxically, block another route to what might as well be called 'cheap theism' – the route of experience. Those writers speak of a spiritual path across unmapped territory, 'a land without ways', as John of the Cross called it; one in which, as the Meister Eckhart says, we must 'live without a why'; as if in a 'cloud of unknowing' as said another in the fourteenth century. This God of the mystics is no God met with in some supposed experience beyond language, but one before whom not only language but even experience itself fails; so that the bearing of the mystic's apophaticism is upon that same point at which the apophaticism of the pseudo-Denys intersects with the atheism of Marx.

For what Marx and the Christian traditions of negative theology have in common is their rejection of a describable God; all deny essentialism whether in theistic or atheistic forms since for none is there any common essence of the divine, the human or the natural which can be appropriated in language, social order or personal experience. All, as it were, demand that we should love in divine darkness, in a world deprived of any ultimate meaning which is at our disposal, for either, as in Marx, there is no such transcendent meaning, or as in the mystic, there is, but it is not at our disposal. And if at this point the charge is repeated that it is simply perverse to ignore the difference between the theist apophaticist and the atheist Marx; since manifestly what for the one is mystery is for the other mystification; then it would be possible to say this much, speaking for myself: I do not, of course, deny the importance of this distinction between the Marxist and the Christian, howsoever apophatic. But to produce that distinction requires a doctrine of God which is post-Marxist, a theology which has been unnerved by the closeness of the engagement in which it must associate with Marx's atheism and has thereby problematised its own very possibility as a discourse. This, as I suggest, it is in any case the instinct of some of our best theologies to do; and I do not limit this instinct to Christian mysticisms in the 'negative tradition'. Unfashionably, as it happens, I do not even deny the possibility of a natural theology, the possibility of demonstrating the existence of God. I would only note that what might in a general way commend Thomas Aquinas' arguments is that they are simultaneously the demonstration that God exists and that we could not possibly know what it means to say that God exists. And so it will follow from a natural theology of this sort, one which, as it were, is undertaken within the constraints of the apophatic, that the difference between atheism and theism will lie not in different ways of seeing the world, for both have radically demystified it. For in the same way that no language in particular speaks God, but only all language collectively, so there is nothing in particular which God's existence explains, as if there were some things it did not explain: just everything whatsoever. Consequently theism stands together with a radical atheism jointly opposed to that conception of things which loads an ultimate significance disjunctively either upon a fundamentalist God who would be a knowable 'something-in-particular' or upon the hegemony of a promethean human. Neither apophatic theism nor Marxist atheism, therefore, can offer us more consolation of meaningfulness than is to be found in a radically de-centred world, a world in which God and man no longer compete to give it meaning, because there is no centre from which either is in a position to do so.

8

I offer four points by way of conclusion and summary. The first is that it is a pity that most liberation theologians fail to take seriously the implications of Marx's atheism, dismissing the question of atheism itself, and of natural theology in general, as the preoccupation of a tired old European culture. Thereby they forgo the potential of this atheism's radicalness for their own critiques of idolatry. It is for this reason that, from the standpoint of the problematics of Western theology, liberation theologies can look so oddly pre-critical, even epistemologically complacent.

Second, the Vatican and some Western critics are superficially right in detecting a potential reductivism in some liberation theology – 'superficially', because generally they misidentify that potential as deriving from Marxism. Very far from it, indeed, if I am right, quite the opposite: if liberation theology is vulnerable to reductivist temptations, the source lies in a residual Feuerbachianism, curable by a stiffer dose of Marxist atheism. Finding a spirituality which de-mystifies religious experience; finding a non-disjunctive logic of religious language within the apophatic traditions of theology; these, for me the authentic energies of Christian mysticism, help us to see the theological necessity of a truly radical engagement with atheism. But then again, liberation theologians run the risk of neglecting this resource by virtue of what seems to me to be an irresponsible neglect of natural theology.

The third point is that I have, in response to the inadequacies both of liberation theology and of the Vatican's critique of it, been but sketching the case for a line of theological exploration. In this connection I should explain that nothing follows from what I have argued in support of some synthesis or other, still less any identity, between a negative theology on the one hand and Marxism on the other: nothing remotely so fanciful. They possess no common direction of thought and I have implied none. The point is, rather, to capture each movement of thought in our contemporary reception of them at a fleeting moment, as it were, of their intersection with one another, to retrieve them for purposes of our own and to take advantage of them as we address our own theological agenda. And I offer you the thought that it is not mere whimsicality, as one explores within Marxism the potentiality for a Christian critique of global exploitation and injustice, to take a theological interest also in that point of intersection between the negativity of the mystic and the negativity of Marx, for that coincidence occurs deep within the heart of any Christian spirituality, indeed of any theistic spirituality – and perhaps even of any spirituality whatever. Which brings me to my fourth and last point.

This is the Christian truism that atheism is in any case a crucial dimension of faith. This, though a truism, is, for all that, true. It is not, however, the mere platitude that atheism is a good exercise for muscle-bound Christians to try out their strength on. It is the requirement that at the heart of any authentic spirituality is the means of its own self-critique, an apophatic putting into question of every possibility of knowing who God is, even the God we pray to. In the heart of every Christian faith and prayer there is, as it were, a desolation, a sense of bewilderment and deprivation, even panic, at the loss of every familiar sign of God, at the requirement to 'unknow' God – as the Meister Eckhart put it, for the sake of the 'God beyond God'. For it is somewhere within that desolation and negativity that the nexus is to be found which binds together the Christian rediscovery of justice with the poor and the rediscovery of the God who demands that justice. For in that bond of action and experience – 'praxis' – is the discovery that, as the liberation theologians say, 'knowing God is doing justice'.

## NOTES

1 Introduction to the Congregation for the Doctrine of the Faith's *Instruction on Certain Aspects of the 'Theology of Liberation'* (Vatican City, 1984), reprinted in A. T. Hennelly (ed.), *Liberation Theology. A Documentary History* (Maryknoll, NY, Orbis, 1990), pp. 393–414.
2 Ibid.
3 Ibid., I, 9.
4 Ibid., I, 6.
5 Ibid., I, 8.
6 Ibid., II, 1–4.
7 Ibid., III, 1.
8 Ibid., III, 4.
9 Ibid., IV, 2.
10 Ibid., IV, 14.
11 Ibid., IV, 15. Note that, at least in this English translation, there is a failure of consistency between two parts of this argument. It is one thing to say that the full ambit of sin cannot be *restricted to* 'social sin'; no liberation theologian I know of maintains that it can. It is quite another to say that liberation from sin does not *depend upon* liberation from sinful structures. The second does not even follow from the first, let alone are they synonymous. For it is perfectly consistent to say that liberation from sinful structures is a *necessary* but not *sufficient* condition of full liberation from sin: as most liberation theologians do say.
12 Ibid., IV, 15.
13 Ibid., VI, 3.
14 Ibid., VI, 4.
15 Ibid., VI, 6.
16 Ibid., VI, 10.

17 Ibid., VII, 9.
18 Ibid., VII, 2.
19 Ibid., VII, 6.
20 Ibid., VIII, 2.
21 Ibid., VIII, 7.
22 Ibid., IX, 2.
23 Ibid.
24 Ibid., IX, 1.
25 Ibid., IX, 3.
26 Ibid., IX, 4.
27 Alistair Kee, *Marx and the Failure of Liberation Theology* (London, SCM, 1990).
28 Ibid., pp. 41–68.
29 See *Marx and Engels On Religion* (Moscow, Progressive Publishers, 1957).
30 *On Religion*, p. 98.
31 Karl Marx, *Contribution to the Critique of Hegel's Philosophy of Right, Preface*, in *Karl Marx, Early Writings*, tr. R. Livingstone and Gregor Benton (London, Penguin Books, 1975), p. 252.
32 John Maguire, 'Gospel or Religious Language: Engels on the Peasant War', *New Blackfriars*, 54, p. 350.
33 Luciano Parinetto, 'The Legend of Marx's Atheism', *Telos*, 58, p. 15.
34 Ibid.
35 Edward Norman, *Christianity and the World Order* (London, Oxford University Press, 1977).
36 See my 'Marx, Feuerbach and Reductivism', in Brian Davies O. P. (ed.), *Language, Truth and God* (London, Chapman, 1986), pp. 92–103.
37 *Karl Marx, Early Writings*, pp. 357–8.
38 Quentin Lauer, 'The Atheism of Karl Marx', in H. Aptheker, ed., *Marxism and Christianity* (New York, Humanities Press, 1968), p. 48.
39 *Divine Names*, 817D, in *Pseudo-Dionysius, The Complete Works*, tr. Colm Luibheid (New Jersey, Paulist Press, 1987).
40 Ibid., 641A.
41 Ibid., 821D.
42 See my *The Darkness of God* (Cambridge, Cambridge University Press, 1995), especially chapter 2 for an extended discussion of these themes in the theologies of the late antique and medieval periods.

# 12

VALPY FITZGERALD

# The economics of liberation theology

## Introduction

Economics – in the general sense of the critical study of production, distribution and consumption of wealth in human society – is a central theme of liberation theology. Although liberation theologians do not address the technical questions that constitute modern economic theory, they are concerned with the broader issues of the way in which economic organisation relates to the historical experience of humanity in general and to the 'infinite value' of the poor to God in particular.[1] These issues of economic organisation and social justice are similar to the agenda of European political economy until the end of the last century, and still central to debates on sustainable development strategies in poor countries. But a concern for life itself as the criterion for judging economic institutions can be considered to be a specific contribution from liberation theology. Further, this theology is probably unique in being located within the broader context of debates in poor countries on the origins of underdevelopment and the condition of poverty – mainly but not exclusively in Latin America – which themselves have a major economic dimension. In consequence, the 'economics of liberation theology' has had a considerable impact beyond church structures, ranging from grassroots social movements throughout the developing world to influential non-governmental organisations in industrialised countries.

The persistence of poverty in Latin America is morally unacceptable by any standard. In 1980, after a period of rapid income growth before the debt crisis, and at the outset of the decade in which most liberation theology has been written, 40 per cent of the population of the region were officially classified as living in poverty, and nearly half of these in extreme poverty – that is with incomes insufficient to purchase the food required to meet the United Nations' minimum nutritional standard for a healthy life.[2] The extent of poverty in any developing country is the result of two factors: the average level of income in the country as a whole, which may be quite low; and the gap between the rich and poor within that country. The former factor depends, broadly, upon the level of industrialisation and the relationship with richer countries; it reflects a long-term historical process, the consequence of both the colonial heritage and the style of development pursued since independence. Shorter-term economic factors such as debt repayment, export prices and macroeconomic policy can also be critical in determining average per capita income. The latter factor depends on institutional factors such as the pattern of ownership, asset yields, labour skills, unemployment, wage levels, taxation and social security provision which determine income distribution within the country. The wide differences between poverty levels in different Latin American countries, and the fact that income distribution is so much worse there than in Africa or Asia, show that this poverty is not inevitable and is largely the outcome of specific institutional structures.

The point of departure for the economics of liberation theology is thus a situation where the historical pattern of economic development and the present plight of the poor in Latin America – particularly the 'marginalisation' of half or more of the population in insecure, unskilled and poorly paid jobs – is clearly the result of cumulative decisions over many generations by powerful elites responsible for both public administration and private enterprise.[3]

## The economic dimension of liberation theology

In liberation theology, the anticipated economic order of Christian utopia (that is, the Kingdom) is not just derived from a prophetic vision. This utopia is firmly anchored in a historical reality – that of Latin America in this case – and is to be based on a 'civilisation of poverty' which is to replace the current 'civilisation of wealth'.[4] The ethical origins of this view are clearly biblical, but in modern times would correspond to a 'civilisation of labour' as opposed to the present 'civilisation of capital'. Capitalist civilisation has created a modern world quite different from that of Ancient Palestine, but the productive benefits of the civilisation of wealth have been accompanied by increasing social evil.

Liberation theologians are quite clear that the Kingdom belongs to the poor (Luke 6.20) and the rich as such have no part in it (Luke 6.24 *et seq.*; Luke 16.19–31; Mark 10.23–5)[5] because money is an idol which becomes an absolute value: we cannot serve God and Mammon (Matt. 6.24) – private property is by definition exclusive. However, Jesus does not idealise the poor, because poverty is the consequence of the sin of exclusive possession. Rather, his aim is for abundance for everyone – expressed symbolically by the banquet of the Kingdom – so that this can be possible. He teaches us to abandon the goods of this earth (Matt. 6.25–33) and invites us to share what we have with the poor (Luke 12.14 *et seq.*).

In contrast, the present civilisation of wealth is seen to be based upon the private accumulation of capital by individuals and firms with the support of the capitalist state, in the search for ever greater personal wealth and corporate power. Liberation theologians recognise that this historical process has brought beneficial technical progress, but argue that these benefits have not been put at the disposal of society as a whole, and that they have been achieved at the cost of massive human and environmental destruction. To an extent, therefore, liberation theology can be seen as a positive extension of the Roman Catholic tradition in encyclicals such as *Laborem Exercens*. But it also constitutes a radical departure insofar as an idealist solution to the material problems of humanity is firmly rejected. What is needed is not just the correction of the errors of capitalism but rather its replacement by the civilisation of poverty. Jesus insisted that wealth must be replaced by poverty in order to enter the Kingdom.

In common with the long tradition of Latin American dependency theory,[6] liberation theologians regard the relationship between the rich countries of the 'North' and the poor countries of the 'South' – home to three quarters of humanity – as profoundly unjust. They regard the modern world economy as intrinsically involving increased poverty and cultural domination, arising from unequal exchange in international trade (cheap primary products from mines and farms exported to pay for expensive machinery imports) and the dominance of multinational corporations (based in the US, Europe and Japan) over investment, employment and cultural decisions in poor countries. The technical advances of the North are recognised as valuable in themselves, and a return to the pre-colonial isolation of the South is recognised to be neither possible nor desirable. This unequal relationship was explicitly criticised, of course, by Vatican II in *Gaudium et Spes*, underlined in *Populorum Progressio* and repeated subsequently in *Sollicitudo Rei Socialis*. Liberation theology goes beyond this critique to denounce 'prophetically' the dependency of poor on rich countries as a real obstacle to the Kingdom.

The most dramatic example of this dependency is the Latin American foreign debt situation, which reached its height in the 1980s and thus became part of theological praxis, involving national political leaders and international agencies as well as the poor themselves. Liberation theologians consider that this debt was contracted under conditions of complicity between the rich and governments, and not used to help the poor. None the less, the burden of repayment (both the taxes required to service the debt owed to banks, and the cuts in social expenditure demanded by the international financial institutions) falls almost entirely on the poor – thereby contradicting one of the basic principles of Christian faith.

'Humanist materialism' as opposed to 'economic materialism' is to be the ethical foundation of the Christian civilisation of poverty which will make the universal satisfaction of the basic needs of ordinary people and growing solidarity between them its central aims. The civilisation of poverty is thus counterposed against the civilisation of wealth not as a form of 'universal pauperisation', but rather as a manifestation of the gospel tradition – a tradition firmly rooted in Jesus' own teaching and continued by the Christian saints. Moreover, poverty in this sense is traditionally required of institutions (particularly the Church itself) as well as of individuals. The dialectic between poverty and wealth defines our world as sinful, and can only be overcome salvifically.

According to the liberation theologians, the construction of this new civilisation is to be initiated in our own time by an economic order based on the satisfaction of 'basic needs' as a fundamental human right. If the basic needs of ordinary people are not met, then whatever the legal and political institutions there is no real respect for human dignity and world peace is endangered. Allowing for cultural differences, the nature of these basic needs does not admit of much debate in practice: the minimum requirements of nutrition, health, education, housing and employment are self-evident to the poor. The satisfaction of these basic needs is thus the necessary condition for any model of true economic development based on human dignity, and thus must be achieved as a right and not as charity ('crumbs from the rich man's table'). Once these basic needs are satisfied institutionally in the first stage of the process of liberation, humanity is free to become what it wants to be – so long as what it desires does not become a new mechanism of domination.

The theological notion of the civilisation of poverty proposes as a dynamic principle the 'dignification' of labour in explicit contrast to the accumulation of capital. The aim of work would no longer be the production of private wealth (as it is under capitalism) but rather the perfection of humanity, individually and collectively, as the basis of a new society. The Christian response to the civilisation of wealth thus cannot be to abandon the world and reject it in prophetic protest, but rather to enter this world in order to renew it and transform it – the long-run objective being the utopia of the 'new land'. Progress is made in this direction in our own time ('on earth') to the extent that one of the fundamental characteristics of the civilisation of poverty is strengthened – that is, shared solidarity in contrast to the closed and competitive individualism of the civilisation of wealth. This solidarity is held to be central to the early Christian inspiration as well as to communitarian movements throughout modern history. It appears once more in the new social movements[7] in Latin America – social unity and communion on the one hand, and the common use of common goods on the other.

The private appropriation of common goods upon which the market economy is based is not logically necessary in order to enjoy these goods. None the less, the economic doctrine of the Catholic Church since Aquinas suggests that private property may be the best way *in practice* to maintain economic production and social order. However, for Aquinas this situation is the result of human selfishness arising from original sin. In consequence liberation theologians argue that this sinful selfishness will be overcome as the 'new land' is approached. For instance, natural resources such as land and water are considered by economists as essentially public goods, and constitute the first step in the recovery of common ownership (the basis for peasant life in Latin America until the present century) dismantled by the civilisation of wealth. Moreover, the objective of Christian economics would not be to promote the private accumulation of wealth even after basic needs have been satisfied and personal development made possible.

According to liberation theology, capitalism has clearly been incapable of satisfying basic needs in Latin America, despite the fact that government and business leaders are professed Christians. Socialism in practice has not provided a satisfactory solution either: although advances have been made in basic needs provision – particularly in communist Cuba and in Nicaragua under the Sandinistas – socialist countries have been incapable of sustained technological creativity or of political freedom. None the less, the socialist *ideal* is more suitable than capitalism as an economic model for the 'new land' – as the traditional social teaching of the Church tacitly admits.

## Economics, life and structural sin

The relationship between theology and economics is thus seen by liberation theologians as reflecting the fundamental historical contradiction between death and life in Latin America.[8] This historical contradiction obviously has social, political, cultural, anthropological, ethical and spiritual dimensions as well; but economics is fundamental because it defines wealth and poverty. 'Life' in this context has a clear meaning: it is tangible human life expressed by work, land, house, food, health, education, family, participation, culture, environment, and even *fiesta*.[9] Basic needs thus go beyond essential physiological necessities because the realities of life are not merely economic – although they are not simply spiritual either. This concept is frequently illustrated by the observation that for Amerindian peasants (*campesino indigena*) 'land' is simultaneously an economic, social, political, cultural and spiritual reality – indeed it defines their own nature and that of their community, as well as providing for their survival in a world where the material and moral aspects of life are necessarily communitarian. When basic needs are discussed in Latin America – particularly by the poor themselves – no philosophical distinction between 'infrastructure' and 'superstructure' exists: there is only a single reality of life or of death. When in the Third World a person loses their job or their land they lose life itself. Marginalised people risk their lives daily in the search for work and food for their families, without any possibility of education or political participation. None the less, the poor affirm their option for life – and above all their hope for a better life – in the community *fiesta* and in shared joy.

Thus ethics and spirituality are expressed through this concrete human experience: access to work, land, housing, or health are not only economic requirements but also clearly ethical imperatives. They reflect the ethics of life, where the defence of specific human lives is the fundamental moral imperative. Death is immoral: unemployment, hunger, and illiteracy are economic problems but also forms of death and thus a perverse ethical reality. So real life as it is lived by the poor becomes the criterion by which good and evil can be distinguished. Life, work, and land are both economic *and* spiritual realities. In sum, although spirituality is clearly not just a matter of the bodily life or death of a human being, adequate provision of basic needs for all is the crucial criterion for distinguishing between authentic and false spirituality – or rather between a spirituality of life and a spirituality of death.

In Latin America the notions of the 'logic of life' or the 'logic of the majority' are widely used in both theological and radical political discourse – that is, human life is assumed to be the essential criterion for economic logic or rationality. That all should have life is the most logical or rational position: unemployment, illness, hunger, and illiteracy are illogical and irrational. Those whose lives are mainly threatened are the poor and oppressed, of course. This logic of life is opposed to the logic of the dominant economic system where the rationality is based on maximising corporate profits and private wealth. Life for all, especially for the poorest, can become illogical for the profit-maximising system. Unemployment, concentration of wealth in a few hands, marginality – and even the death of the poor – can become rational within the dominant economic system.

The satisfaction of basic needs – life for all – is therefore not seen by liberation theology as a goal, a programme, an ideology or a development model as it might be by a national economic policy maker or an international development agency. It is anterior to and more fundamental than economic policy. It is the *only* logical basis for an economic ideology or development model, because it is concerned with the choice between human life and profit maximisation.

All that liberation theology has to say about life as the fundamental 'mediator' in economics can also be applied to reflections on the nature of God – and is summed up by the expression 'the God of Life'.[10] For this theological purpose 'life' must be seen as something human and tangible, otherwise it evaporates into an abstract and purely spiritual theology. God is the God of Life because His will is essentially that all men and women should have life and life in abundance (John 10.10). The poor believe in the God of Life because He guarantees real human life for all, and particularly for them. God is the God of Life because He assumes human life as absolute truth, goodness and beauty – *gloria Dei vivens homo* in the words of Saint Irenaeus. The glory of God is manifested in specific human life – so this glory is at stake in the life or death of historically specific human beings. The economic dimension of life (work, land, house, health, food, education etc.) becomes the expression of the glory of God. Equally, the glory of God is dimmed in every person who suffers hunger, misery and oppression. Economy (i.e. life) and theology are thus inseparable in theory and practice.

One of the most characteristic contributions of liberation theology has been the concept of 'structural sin' or sinful structures[11] – which includes the systematic violation of civil rights but where economic injustice holds a central place. For 'Western' (liberation theologians would say 'Northern') theology in the tradition of Cartesian individualism and an individual relationship to God, this is a problematic notion. The concept of sinful structures – which includes the market economy in practice – shows how personal evil can be simultaneously strengthened and disguised by social relationships. A particular economic structure (a historical system of relations between people) can easily create a series of situations which make necessary – and thus apparently reasonable – that conduct which favours one's own greed or that of one's family at the expense of the life and dignity of many others. Usually, the consequences for the poor of such greed are not immediately visible to the sinner (as they would be in an isolated rural community, for instance) because they are diffused through the market economy. As a personal sinner, an individual is seen as both responsible for and as a victim of these oppressive social structures.

In effect, liberation theologians are attempting to recuperate a fundamental New Testament notion, that of the 'sin of the world' which renders the world incapable of understanding the Truth (John 17.25). Contemporary economic structures form a central part of the sin of the world; this is not just a matter of specific economic injustices which can be rectified by appropriate public or private action by good Christians. Despite considerable criticism from traditional theologians in general and the Vatican in particular, these concepts were implicit to the central arguments of both Puebla and Medellín.

Liberation theology has thus always used concepts of political economy in its analysis of both the real world and ideological discourse. None the less, a 'theology of the economy' as such has not yet been fully worked out. One fruitful approach is to start from the sacral nature of 'bread' – that is, the product of work within specific social relations. In this way, present or proposed economic arrangements can be related to the construction of the Kingdom or its negation.[12] Another approach is to start from a reformulation of the Marxian critique of commodity fetishism in terms of the biblical view of idolatry, which leads by extension to the valuation of 'real life' by the poor as opposed to the abstractions of the oppressors.[13] In both approaches, the analytical tools of Marxism (as opposed to its philosophical model) are used from a Christian perspective – in much the same way as Aquinas used Aristotle. The task of translating theological analysis of concepts such as social relations, alienation, work, commodities ('bread') or value ('blood') into a form that would be comprehensible to ordinary people as well as intellectually convincing, is still pending.

Fortunately perhaps, a considerable part of liberation theology is done 'from below' in Latin America; that is by base communities discussing the relevance of Scripture to their own lives. It is largely unrecorded, but no less real for that.[14] Popular hermeneutics takes much of its inspiration from the fact that the language and socio-economic circumstances of the Old and New Testaments are of direct and immediate relevance to the lives of the poor in Latin America. A biblical world of peasant farming, avaricious merchants, oppressive landowners, tax collectors, agricultural labour, and impoverished widows seems not dissimilar to life in Brazil or El Salvador. Indeed, it is perhaps unsurprising that the Apocalypse is the favourite book of the popular movements because there they find inspiration for resistance to persecution which can then be applied directly to contemporary society; similarly, the discourse in John does not seem abstract to them at all, as they can identify with the Christian struggle against the Roman Empire.[15]

## Liberation theology and economic theory

A frequent criticism of liberation theology – not least from the Vatican itself – is the influence of Marxism revealed by its stress on economic relationships and social conflict. However, the necessary stages of economic development in Marxist theory and the changes in class relationships they bring about are not the basis for the liberation theologians' view of history: the economic actors are 'the poor' and 'the rich' rather than capitalists and the proletariat, while the driving force of history is the relationship between God and His creation. Thus, the eschatological view of history in liberation theology is clearly opposed to that of historical materialism. None the less, liberation theologians explicitly regard Marx as an important source of analytical method which helps them look beyond the apparently objective nature of market forces; and thus to identify power with property, relate poverty to labour control and identify the intrinsic contradiction between the market economy and an egalitarian society.[16] Moreover, it is also clear to the informed reader that the implicit inspiration for their economic views is derived from the early 'Hegelian Marx' concerned with alienation and exploitation, rather than from technicalities of surplus value and industrial progress in *Das Kapital*. The economic nature of the transition to socialism/Kingdom is basic needs provision and the inclusion of the marginalised, rather than the over-accumulation of capital and the proletarianisation of the workforce in Marx.

Economic theory is underpinned by 'theories of value' which explain the way in which markets set prices and distribute income as a manifestation of the value which a society collectively places on a particular commodity or skill. The classical economists (including Smith and Ricardo as well as Marx) developed a 'labour theory of value' based on the amount of labour required to produce a commodity or skill, directly through the work involved or indirectly through the equipment or education needed in the production process. The modern theory of value is quite different: based on the utilitarianism of Mill and Bentham, it sees the market as expressing the social utility of goods and services as revealed by the spending decisions of consumers – who 'vote with their money', so to speak. Liberation theology is clearly directly opposed to the utilitarian view, not least because it privileges the choices of the rich, but more fundamentally because it converts human beings into commodities. There is more sympathy with a labour theory of value insofar as it recognises the origins of wealth, but the concept of value based on 'blood' clearly goes far beyond the ideas of Ricardo and Marx.

In fact, liberation theologians' views on the origins of poverty in Latin America and the economic relationship between rich and poor countries are firmly located within a long Latin American tradition of progressive thought – much of it specifically non-Marxist – which stresses the concentration of ownership, undemocratic economic policies, and unequal relationships within the world economy as constituting a 'crisis of capitalism in the region'. This tradition has strong roots in both popular discourse and the declarations of national leaders. It encompasses both the 'structuralist economics' associated with the UN Economic Commission for Latin America and the 'dependency school' of political thought in the region.[17] Indeed it might be argued that the communitarian and redistributive nature of the economic 'project' of liberation theology owes more to the radical populism of Proudhon than to the state power of Lenin. In practice, moreover, liberation theologians have always worked with social movements whose political position is highly critical of orthodox communist parties – particularly the revolutionary movements of Central America but also trade unions in Brazil and 'base communities' throughout the region.

If the economic content of liberation theology is compared to the analytical framework of modern economics as applied to developing countries, its shortcomings become evident. There is a measure of agreement as to the institutional roots of poverty, and an admission by the latter that the Pareto conditions for a free market equilibrium to correspond to a social welfare maximum may not hold in the presence of an unequal prior distribution of financial assets or human skills. Basic needs provision and poverty elimination have become accepted as central elements in formulating economic strategy in developing countries; and although these ideas clearly antedate liberation theology, its support for them has undoubtedly been influential – particularly among non-governmental development agencies. However, the central issues of economic development theory are not addressed by liberation theology: the balance between industry and agriculture, the best way to finance social expenditures, improving trade relationships between industrialised and industrialising countries, incentives for private producers, how to create jobs and the trade-off between the incomes of this generation and the next, and so on. This agenda might well seem too much to demand of theologians but the neglect of these more practical issues has serious consequences.

On the one hand, this neglect means that the orthodox prescriptions of macroeconomic policy have gone largely uncontested except by general denunciations of capitalism. Widespread unemployment, reduced wages and cuts in health expenditure are justified by democratic governments and international financial agencies in terms of the increased production efficiency and private investment they will generate, which will later result in greater income growth and employment for the poor. Whether this trade-off is feasible or desirable is one of the central issues in current economic debate at all levels of society in Latin America today:[18] 'structural adjustment' is defended by its proponents in ethical terms as 'good for the poor in the long run', while its opponents argue that there are sound reasons for believing that macroeconomic stability can be combined with poverty reduction.[19] On the other hand, in the one case where liberation theology did have a strong influence on the economic policy of a progressive government – the case of Nicaragua during the 1980s which attempted to implement a direct attack on poverty through large-scale land reform and massive basic needs provision to the poor[20] – the lack of a coherent response to the problems of national and international economic management turned out to be a fatal weakness in the attempt to implement the vision of a 'new land'. In sum, the critique of observed economic injustice can lose its force unless it is accompanied by some idea as to what would constitute a just economy in practice.

A more appropriate basis of comparison might therefore be the more specific topic of welfare economics,[21] which reflects not only the commitment to solidarity within a particular national economy but also the fact that a range of social services – such as health and education – has a positive return to the economy in the long run due to increased productivity and less communicable disease, but which the individuals concerned cannot afford and the private sector is unwilling to provide for the population as a whole. Indeed, this limited definition of the 'common good' appears to be emerging as the basis for basic needs provision in industrialised societies unable to achieve the political support required for the tax burden that existing levels of welfare entitlements imply. This is clearly far more limited than the commitment to the elimination of poverty as the central focus of economic strategy which liberation theology implies.

However, the basis for modern welfare economics is the notion of *social citizenship* (also termed the 'citizenship of entitlement') which consists of the rights to a modicum of economic welfare and security, to share fully in the social heritage of the community, and to live a civilised life according to the standards prevailing in society.[22] This is not, therefore, an argument from compassion, which focuses on the point of view of the *donor* as citizen and where the recipients are perceived as recipients of largesse rather than as citizens with entitlements to benefits and rights of participation in decisions which affect them. A depersonalised relationship based on entitlement is essential if recipients of social benefits are to be citizens rather than subjects. Social citizenship also 'depersonalises' the function of giving, converting it from a voluntary act by a few 'good citizens' to a duty on the part of all citizens who can afford to do so to pay tax so that the needs of the body of the citizenry are met as of right. Social citizenship thus implies not only entitlements to welfare payments, but also the obligation of better-off citizens to pay tax in order to finance them if the system is to be something more than social insurance. This is an agenda which liberation theology has not addressed but where it would have much to offer if it were to speak to the problems of economic development under democracy.

### Liberation theology and the theory of economic justice

Although liberation theology has a limited engagement with economic theory as such, there is a much clearer correspondence with notions of economic justice in political philosophy. A good basis for comparison is the modern theory of justice, based on liberal political theory and in particular the contractarian ideal of 'fairness' as a characteristic of the just economy. The contractarian theory of justice suggests that a set of economic institutions can be judged as fair if behind a 'veil of ignorance' all citizens are prepared to accept any position in that economy they might be allocated at random.[23] In other words, there is rigorous equality of economic opportunity and acceptable welfare provision, as opposed to equality of outcomes. Clearly all the Latin American economies would fail this test and thus can be judged 'unjust'. From a completely different ethical point of departure, liberation theology comes to a not dissimilar position; although the logic would derive from the relationship of people to each other in a community rather than in a social contract with the state.

Another philosophical approach to the problem of poverty is based on the idea that economic welfare is derived from the 'entitlements' possessed by individuals or households.[24] These entitlements can be market-based (e.g. income from economic assets or marketable skills) or social entitlements derived from legal or traditional rights to welfare, including access to common property resources such as water or grazing land; the loss of these entitlements – due to economic dislocation or social collapse – causes poverty and their restoration can eliminate it. The value of a specific 'bundle' of entitlements is judged by the extent to which they provide the conditions for the good life under the relevant circumstances. This powerful analytical concept, which has a deep influence on modern economic development theory, could also add some depth to the liberation theologians' view of the origins of poverty in marginalisation. None the less, like contractarian theories of economic justice, entitlement theory has little to say about the power structures which lie behind the institutions of the market economy.

In the global context, one of the key characteristics of poverty is the country in which people are born – in other words the citizenship of the poor. The traditional economists' response to this problem is that the potential economic benefits of migration in terms of increased employment and higher wages can be achieved just as well by labour-intensive exports and international investment in developing countries. None the less, citizenship is still the single most important asset most people possess in developed countries as it represents a claim on the accumulated social capital of the relevant country and its place in the world economy. In this case, the appropriate test in liberal political theory would presumably be whether a rational person would be willing to be born into the world irrespective of his citizenship. Clearly the answer is negative – in which case the present international economic arrangements can be properly judged as unjust[25] – as liberation theology would argue from quite different premises.

In a single global economy, the poorest countries and vulnerable groups who do not possess the resources to compete effectively have become more vulnerable to exogenous shocks and fall further behind in the race for technological competence.[26] From this point of view, development cooperation ('aid') can be seen as part of an international social safety net which reflects not only the global ethical responsibilities of the rich for the poor, but also the claim of the poor upon the rich as members of the same global community. This is not just a question of making international markets work more efficiently, so that the welfare of both donors *and* recipients is increased; the ethical argument for aid derives from the obligation to relieve human suffering when this can be done at little personal cost, which is a universal Kantian obligation in relation to all humans simply by virtue of our shared humanity. This obligation requires that resources be transferred to the poor, irrespective of state or national boundaries, to provide them with the means of survival. However, it is difficult to establish any clear philosophical argument for aid beyond this basic 'human entitlement' because the Aristotelian notion of redistributive justice is usually applied to individuals within an identifiable community. To apply it internationally poses two problems: first, whether the contractarian responsibility of individuals extends beyond state boundaries; and second, whether states can properly be considered as moral agents in the international sphere.[27] This issue is also one to which liberation theology may have more to offer than liberal moral philosophy.

## Conclusion

Economics – in the broad 'political economy' sense in which I have used it in this chapter – has a central place in liberation theology. Despite the fact that this theology does not really address the central questions of modern economic theory, it has undoubtedly had a significant influence on the way in which the economics of poor countries has developed in practice. In particular, liberation theology has changed the way in which social movements, non-governmental organisations and international aid agencies view economic policy – addressing such pressing problems as external debt and structural adjustment. Moreover, the inclusion of the prophetic critique of the market economy within ethical discourse through concepts such as the 'right to life' and 'structural sin' is clearly an important step forwards in a radical theology – not least because it permits a popular hermeneutic derived from the everyday experience of the poor.

In consequence, the 'economics of liberation theology' is very different from other traditions in the Christian approach to economics. On the one hand, there is the 'mainstream' Roman Catholic tradition of social responsibility established by Aquinas with its modern expression in *Rerum Novarum* and *Populorum Progressio*. This tradition, which stresses the mutual responsibility of labour and capital (and poor and rich countries) to work in harmony, is the economic equivalent to Christian Democracy in politics and has been particularly influential among reforming elites in Latin America during this century. In marked contrast, liberation theology not only considers capital and labour (the 'civilisation of wealth' and the 'civilisation of poverty') to be essentially in conflict by their very natures, but also that historical struggle between them will eventually lead to the construction of the Kingdom as promised in the Beatitudes. The difference between the two theological positions is most clear in the notion of 'sinful structures' where the poverty and exclusion in a competitive market economy as experienced by poor societies lie at the core of the *peccatum mundi*. It is this prophetic challenge, rather than association with Marxism or with revolutionary movements, that has made the liberation theologians the target of the Vatican.

On the other hand, there is a long-standing Protestant tradition of approaching the economy from the standpoint of the duties and obligations of the Christian towards one's fellows in the market.[28] The duty of charitable giving to the poor is accompanied by the obligation of responsible stewardship of wealth for the common good, a concept which can be usefully extended to the prudent use of natural resources on behalf of future generations. The emphasis on fairness and individual responsibility in this approach to economics can be seen as reflecting a greater concern with justice on earth, so to speak, than the dominant Catholic tradition. None the less, the liberation theologians' emphasis on the historical nature of class conflict and the essentially communitarian nature of the just economy as a precursor of the Kingdom is very different from the essentially individualist Protestant approach to the Christian economy, which takes the market and its institutions as a fact of nature rather than a sinful construct. However, in Latin America, many Protestant theologians in the evangelical tradition have been deeply influenced by (and contributed to) liberation theology – and this influence is particularly marked in the approach to economic questions.

In the late 1990s, although economic conditions in Latin America are not much better than before, there has been a major change since the 1970s and 1980s in the sense that democracy and human rights are now better established throughout the continent. This opening up of the political sphere has probably diverted popular protest against economic conditions away from the temple towards the forum, so to speak. Combined with steady pressure from Rome to exclude liberation theologians from bishoprics and seminaries, the public voice of liberation theology on economic questions may become less audible in years to come.

Meanwhile, poverty is still a central problem for the global economy in the post-cold war world:

> ...the number of absolute poor, the truly destitute, was estimated by the World Bank at 1.3 billion in 1993, and is probably still growing. One fifth of the world lives in countries, mainly in Africa and Latin America, where living standards actually fell during the 1980s. Several indicators of aggregate poverty – 1.5 billion lack access to safe water and 2 billion lack safe sanitation; more than 1 billion are illiterate, including half of the rural women – are no less chilling than a quarter-century ago.[29]

So in the economic sphere at least '... this theology is not a passing fashion. Its corollary – oppression – is unfortunately not a fashion but rather a growing problem. The theology of liberation is thus still very necessary, because Christian faith must today respond with credibility – and theological rationality – to the oldest and newest question as posed by Gutiérrez: how to tell the poor that God loves them.'[30]

## NOTES

1 See Phillip Berryman, *Liberation Theology: the Essential Facts About the Revolutionary Movement in Latin America and Beyond* (New York, Pantheon, 1987), chapter 3.
2 United Nations data cited in V. Bulmer-Thomas (ed.), *The New Economic Model in Latin America and its Impact on Income Distribution and Poverty* (Basingstoke, Macmillan, 1996), p. 6. 'Poverty' is defined as including some non-food essentials (e.g. clothing) as well as minimal nutrition, and is roughly equivalent to one US dollar per person per day (Organisation for Economic Cooperation and Development, *Shaping the 21st Century: the Contribution of Development Cooperation*, Paris, OECD, 1996, p. 9).
3 See V. Bulmer-Thomas, *The Economic History of Latin America since Independence* (Cambridge, Cambridge University Press, 1994).
4 Ignacio Ellacurìa, 'Utopía y profetismo' in I. Ellacurìa and J. Sobrino (eds.), *Mysterium liberationis: conceptos fundamentales del la teología de liberación* (Madrid, Editorial Trotta, 1990), vol. I, pp. 393–442.
5 Carlos Bravo, 'Jesús de Nazaret: el Cristo liberador' in ibid., vol. I, pp. 551–74.
6 See Cristobal Kay, *Latin American Theories of Development and Underdevelopment* (London, Routledge, 1989).
7 These 'new social movements' include groups of peasants, slum-dwellers, women etc. They are quite different from traditional political parties insofar as they do not seek state power, nor are they organised on a hierarchical basis. Liberation theology has been strongly influenced by (and has in turn contributed to) the growth of these movements throughout Latin America and even world-wide.
8 Pablo Richard, 'Teología en la teología de liberación', in Ellacurìa and Sobrino (eds.), *Mysterium liberationis*, vol. I, pp. 201–22.
9 The Spanish word *fiesta* is inadequately translated by the pallid English 'party'; it contains a strong sense of community and also of celebration – almost equivalent to *agape*.
10 See Berryman, *Liberation Theology*, chapter 2.
11 José Ignacio González Faus, 'Pecado' in Ellacurìa and Sobrino (eds.), *Mysterium liberationis*, vol. II, pp. 93–106.
12 Ricardo Antoncich, 'Teología de la liberación y doctrina social de la Iglesia', in ibid., vol. I, pp. 145–68.
13 Franz Hinkelhammert, *Crítica a la razón utópica* (San Jose de Costa Rica, DEI, 1984).
14 Berryman, *Liberation Theology*, chapter 3.
15 Gilberto da Silva Gorgulho, 'Hermenéutica bíblica', in Ellacurìa and Sobrino (eds.), *Mysterium liberationis*, vol. I, pp. 169–200.
16 See Enrique Dussel, 'Teología de la liberación y marxismo' in ibid., vol. I, pp. 115–144; and also Berryman, *Liberation Theology*, chapter 9, 'Using Marxism'.
17 As well as Kay, *Latin American Theories*, see C. Furtado, *Economic Development of Latin America* (Cambridge, Cambridge University Press, 1970) and R. Prebisch, 'A Critique of Peripheral Capitalism', *Cepal Review No. 1* (Santiago de Chile, United Nations Commission for Latin America and the Caribbean, 1976).
18 Bulmer-Thomas, *The New Economic Model*, 'Introduction'.

19 E. V. K. FitzGerald, *The Macroeconomics of Development Finance: a Kaleckian Analysis of the Semi-industrial Economy* (Basingstoke, Macmillan, 1993).

20 E. V. K. FitzGerald, 'Stabilization and Economic Justice: the Case of Nicaragua', in K. S. Kim and D. F. Ruccio (eds.), *Debt and Development in Latin America* (Notre Dame, IN, University of Notre Dame Press, 1985).

21 N. Barr, *The Economics of the Welfare State*, 2nd edn (London, Weidenfeld & Nicolson, 1993).

22 D. Rile, 'Citizenship and the Welfare State', in J. Allen, P. Barham and P. Lewis (eds.), *Political and Economic Forms of Modernity* (Cambridge, Polity Press for The Open University, 1992), pp. 179–228.

23 J. Rawls, *A Theory of Justice* (Oxford, Clarendon Press, 1972).

24 J. Dreze and A. K. Sen, *Hunger and Public Action* (Oxford, Clarendon Press, 1989), chapter 2.

25 C. Beitz, *Political Theory and International Relations* (Princeton, NJ, Princeton University Press, 1987).

26 United Nations Research Institute for Social Development, *States of Disarray: The Social Effects of Globalization* (London, Earthscan, 1995).

27 B. R. Opeskin, 'The Moral Foundations of Foreign Aid', *World Development* 24.1 (1996), pp. 21–44.

28 See Donald A. Hay, *Economics Today: a Christian Critique* (Leicester, Apollos, 1989).

29 Commission on Global Governance, *Our Global Neighbourhood* (Oxford, Oxford University Press, 1995), p. 139.

30 Ellacurìa and Sobrino, *Mysterium liberationis*, p. 12 (author's translation).

# 13

## OLIVER O'DONOVAN

# Political theology, tradition and modernity

Dated from the Medellín Conference, liberation theology is not yet thirty years old. Political theology, by contrast, has many centuries behind it. To define a High Tradition the period 1100–1650 suggests itself: at one end the Gregorian Reforms bring the conflict between papacy and secular rule to the centre of theological discussion; at the other the Moral Science of the early Enlightenment lifts political theory out of the purview of theology. The dates are especially happy as they coincide with two striking contributions to the genre. From the turn of the twelfth century the anonymous York Tractates argue with theological urgency for the sacral character of monarchy, discredited by the new papalism. From the midpoint of the seventeenth century Hobbes' *Leviathan*, a work with considerably more theology in it than philosophy, seals the case, as early modernity understood it, for politics as an autonomous theoretical discipline. In between lie the great peaks of political theology, scholastic and reformed. But the High Tradition itself did not spring from nothing, but drew on thinkers and ideas of the patristic and Carolingian ages. Augustine is rightly taken as a founding figure; but before him there were Ambrose, Eusebius of Caesarea (notoriously), and from the pre-Constantinian period Lactantius. And why not mention the second-century Letter to Diognetus, which, in turn, was only building on ideas in 1 Peter and Philippians . . . ?

But the relation of contemporary political theology to the High Tradition can be summed up in a single bleak word: ignorance. The feeling of invigorating new departure is due in considerable measure to the loss of antecedents from our view. Occasionally our contemporaries seize on moments in the tradition and identify their importance: Boff has written on St Francis; and the authors of the South African *Kairos Document* used the doctrine of tyrannicide from John of Salisbury and St Thomas. But by and large the tradition, with all its wealth of suggestive theo-political debate and analysis, has been eclipsed by the shadow of the modern period. The purpose of this essay is not to criticise liberation theology for this fact (in which, arguably, it merely shares the fate of a great deal of twentieth-century theology), nor to engage in close interpretation of it; but simply to *locate* it on a rather wider stage of theological history than it is used to locating itself on, and to show how the occluding preoccupations of modernity have constrained its understanding of its own agenda. For liberation theology, like all other political theology of our time, stands in a double relation to modernity, both highly critical and highly dependent.

'Modernity' can be described in many different ways. For our purposes one way is enough. It is characterised by a *twofold tradition of radical suspicion* directed against the classical political theology. Both suspicions were derived from that theology; but the early-modern consciousness radicalised them and combined them in a way that undermined the theo-political project as a whole.

(1) The first suspicion is voiced in a famous pronouncement of Kant: 'I can actually think of a moral politician, i.e. one who so interprets the principles of political prudence that they can be coherent with morality, but I cannot think of a political moralist, i.e. one who forges a morality to suit a statesman's advantage.'[1] Kant meant, of course, ironically, that he *could* think of a statesman forging a pseudo-morality to his advantage, but could not think of anything *else* 'political morality' might mean! There is the decisive statement of a troubled *motif* which has recurred throughout the long tradition of Christian political reflection: distrust of a 'forged' morality, a mere 'legitimation', as our current idiom would express it, for an arbitrary grip on power by given individuals or classes. Politicians are corruptors of moral discourse. Their moral sentiments are like bad coinage pumped into the currency, which can only lower its value and destroy it. This unmasking of political morality is what sets a distance between the Christian West and the Aristotelian conception of ethics as a subdivision of politics.

There are two sides to Kant's objection to the political moralist. In the first place it is a forgery, this morality which serves the convenience of the political order, when a true morality would dictate its terms to the politicians. This claim bears its theological ancestry on its face; there is a *true* morality to reckon with, not forged from within the political system but compelling it from above; and there is a *true* order which endures no matter who finds it inconvenient. In the second place, the political order itself should not be treated with too much solemnity, for it is, after all, only a 'statesman's advantage', a certain constellation of benefits and disbenefits of power which happens to suit one person rather than another. Politics is historically contingent, and therefore arbitrary. Only when subordinated to morality can its claims carry weight with us.

This second claim was of ancient Cynic origin, but long naturalised into Christian thought. When Augustine rhetorically denied the difference between kingdoms and 'large-scale criminal syndicates', he took his inspiration from a popular story about what a pirate said to Alexander: 'Because I use a small boat I am called a robber; because you use a large fleet you are called an emperor!' What raised this quip to the dignity of a political principle was the theological point of view. Augustine was in a position to belittle the political culture of antiquity; he could dismiss its achievements as 'the fragile splendour of a glass which one fears may shatter any moment'; he could do this without turning his back on society as the Cynics did, simply because he could point to a divine authority and a more lasting social order.[2] Unmasking supposes a theological point of vantage, essentially an eschatological one. Christ has led captivity captive; he has disarmed the principalities and powers; the Kingdom of Heaven is at hand. When we claim to have seen through the appearances of political power, we act, as King Lear says, 'as if we were God's spies'.[3]

So Kant disposes of the political moralist. But it is evident that the political moralist is one and the same as the political theologian. Kant's idea of morality, modelled on the thought of conscience as a form of divine revelation, makes it precisely a surrogate for theology. So we may say that we can think of a theological politician, who interprets the principles of political prudence in a way coherent with God's will, but we cannot think of a political theologian, who forges a theology to suit a statesman's advantage. (Or, again, we can *think* of one all too easily, but not as a figure who commands authority.) Theological forgery came to the notice of the Christian Church directly from its contest with the religious ideology of the Roman empire. The actual expression 'political theology' can, it has been suggested, be taken back to the *civile genus theologiae* of the Roman philosopher Marcus Varro, which Augustine dismissed as 'mendacious'.[4] 'Civil religion' is the title under which such forgeries are usually discussed today. More circumspectly, but with increasing conviction, Augustine seems to have found the same mendacious tendency in those historians of his time who made the conversion of Constantine and the dawning of the 'Christian epoch' an irreversible step in the unfolding of God's purposes.[5] But to the moralist of modernity, wielding the inner criticism of reflective consciousness rather than the public criticism of the Church's theology, this critique is directed categorically against all postures which unite theological and political judgments. The suspicion has become total.

(2) The second suspicion is apparently opposite: not the corruption of morality or theology by politicians, but the corruption of politics by theology.

This fear was voiced by the imperialist theologians of the fourteenth century, based on a classicising account of political authority (uniting elements of Aristotle, Roman law and feudalism) which derived it from the will of the people. The anxiety was: could divine authority intervene in politics in any way without overwhelming the authority of political structures? Revelation seemed to pose a threat to political freedom. The experience of confronting Islam, and in later centuries of inter-confessional war in Christendom itself, no doubt made this anxiety worse; but, once again, it was an early-modern philosophical development that extended its scope beyond theocratic hierarchs to reject every kind of political morality or theology.

In the seventeenth century philosophy came to lose confidence in the objectivity of final causes. Political communities, even when created from below, had been believed to be ordained by providence to serve the end of earthly perfection; but now there arose a tradition of explaining societies entirely by reference to efficient causes, focusing these in a notional compact whereby each individual was supposed to have surrendered sovereignty over his own person in return for certain protections. Individual agents had their ends; but objective structures only had their origins. Moral purposes and goals, questions of human virtue and fulfilment, seemed intrusive, another form of theocratic temptation. The internalising of morality, then, led modernity once again to radicalise its suspicions.

In the popular imagination of late-modern liberalism these twin suspicions have broadened and fused together. It is no longer the statesman who stands alone, uniquely suspect. All of us have our political interests, especially class interests, so that all fine public sentiments may be unmasked, from whatever source. Principles of morality, though not denied all claims to truth, may never shape the deliberations of a self-ruling people which determines its will in response to certain recognised and universal pre-moral interests. They are relegated to the status of 'ideals'. The original incompatibility of the two reasons for separating politics and morality (or theology) has been left behind. We still occasionally see old-fashioned sideshows, in which churchmen accuse statesmen of the blasphemous invocation of God's name – the Thatcher era in Britain, replete with atavistic moments, staged one or two of these – and others in which statesmen accuse churchmen of deploying 'the power of the crozier' – Ireland, forever resistant to fashion, continues to replay this popular medieval morality play. But what has really happened is that the division has become internalised. Each of us has a mind partitioned by a frontier, and accepts responsibility for policing it. It was said of Harold Wilson, preacher and politician, that he would go through the drafts of his speeches removing every echo of the biblical inflections that came too naturally to him. That is the paradigm for late-modern liberal culture.

Liberation theology, then, is the most effective, though not the only, twentieth-century challenge to this late-modern liberal consensus on the separation of theology and politics. But in framing its challenge, it drew help from secondary currents within late-modernity itself. For epochs are characterised not by positions but debates; it is the way they state their disagreements rather than their agreements that binds the thinkers of any age together. If the primary thesis of modernity has been the liberal one, there have been counter-theses which attempted to put together what liberal convention put asunder. Most notably, the idealist tradition, deriving through Hegel, has reasserted the old Aristotelian claim that morality is a sub-species of politics. This has been reconciled with the modern tradition of suspicion by way of a uniquely modern idea of history. The critical viewpoint was absorbed into the historical process. 'History' is the history of society, which embraces *both* the patterns of social order and of social right *and* the moments of unmasking in which these patterns are seen through and overthrown. The Enlightenment consensus itself, with its attempt to establish a pure ethics (whether theological or rational) in the light of which all political dynamisms can be seen through, can itself be seen through. Criticism can be turned back upon the critic *ad infinitum*. For criticism, too, is the strategy of some actor within the socio-historical polyphony, the representative speech of some historical grouping. With this move the two strands of suspicion in the liberal tradition are safeguarded; but they are woven back into a greater harmony in which ethics and politics are one again. But the matrix is political, not ethical. For it is the *social* dynamisms of history that provide a context in which moral commitments become intelligible. The autonomous self-justifying character of politics is thus preserved; so is the critical role of moral thought. The philosopher is licensed to go on being sceptical of every claim to authority; but this no longer seems to imply a perpetual distance from the political process; rather, it seems to make a useful contribution to it.

But for this attempt to reintegrate politics and ethics modern idealism paid a fearfully high price. The historical processes of society, offered as the matrix which would unify them, does not, apparently, leave either of them intact. Ethics, on the one hand, is deprived of authority when it is made to serve merely as a reactive critical function. It degenerates into little more than a rhetoric of scepticism. We can see this from the characteristic dilemma which besets the favourite causes of liberal idealism: how to claim moral licence for themselves without licensing their opposites. Each movement of social criticism draws in its train a counter-movement; and there is no ground in logic for paying more or less respect to the one than to the other. So black consciousness, for example, requires (logically),

invites (historically) and licenses (morally) a movement of white consciousness; feminism entails male chauvinism; homophilia entails homophobia,
and so on. Our intuitions tell us that some of these movements are worth
more than their shadows, but our intuitions are allowed no way of justifying themselves, and we are compelled, by the logic of historical dialectic,
to give away whatever it is we think we may have gained. Each generation
of God's spies has to settle for being spied upon by the next. No one can
have the last word. There is, therefore, no end in sight to any issue of
contention, except its replacement by some other more urgent one or its
collapse from exhaustion. The law of historical process is contingency, and
that gives us no space to object when our liberal arguments attract redneck
free-riders.

On the other hand, social process, which is supposed to fill the place
assigned to politics by Aristotle, is not the same thing as politics at all. The
account of society that it yields we call (non-technically) 'sociology'; and
though sociology was obviously a *classicising* movement of thought in its
eighteenth-century origins, it was never a *classical* one. It could not recover
the classical innocence which had once conceived as one object of study
both the natural ordering of society and the art of government. It had to
take into its system the critical deconstruction of the art of government;
and that meant that the society in which it hoped to reunite politics and
ethics was conceived headless, shorn of its decision-making capacities,
an organism that blundered forward undirected save by the unconscious
dynamics at work within it. Hence the recurrent charge that sociology
was, in fact, anti-political. A politics that does not encompass the direction
of society ceases to be a politics at all. But there is no room for direction
in a society ruled by the imperative of universal suspicion.

All this goes some way to explain the difficulties faced by the renewed
advocacy of political theology in our own time. The primary concern of
this advocacy was to break out of the *cordon sanitaire* in which late-
modern liberalism had imprisoned theology. When it has been at its clear-
est, it has insisted that theology is political simply by responding to the
dynamics of its own proper themes. Christ, salvation, the Church, the
Trinity: to speak about these has involved theologians in speaking of society, and has led them to formulate normative political ends which are very
much more than 'a statesman's advantage'. Theology turns out to know
about the ends of politics, and perhaps something about the means, too,
without being told. It is not a question of adapting to an alien demand or
subscribing to an external agenda, but of letting theology be true to its
task and of freeing it from a forced and unnatural detachment. Political
theology must recover for Christian faith in God, Christ and salvation

what scepticism surrendered to mechanistic necessity. Theology must be political if it is to be evangelical. Rule out the political questions and you cut short the proclamation of God's saving power; you leave people enslaved at points where they ought to be set free from the power of sin – their own sin and other people's.

A theologian who begins from the political discourse of the Kingdom of God will need to prove *bona fides* by demonstrating how it illumines all the topics that responsible theology attends to: repentance and forgiveness, the incarnation, the sharing of the life of Godhead in the Spirit, justification and adoption, creation and the renewal of the world, the life of the Church and its ministry of word and sacraments. The *regula fidei* does not prescribe a single starting point for theology; but it warns against making any starting point the stopping point. This is the test of theological seriousness which when any theologian fails to meet, he or she may be charged with arbitrariness. In the High Tradition of political theology such interpenetration of political and doctrinal concerns could be taken for granted. One may think of Grotius' theory of the Atonement, or of James of Viterbo's exploration of the offices of Christ. The liberation theologians, too, have proved their seriousness in this way, not least by bringing back into circulation theological themes for which liberal modernism had no use: judgment, original sin, demon-possession, for example.

Of course, no major movement of thought is unambiguous, especially not a movement of reaction. It is therefore quite possible to see this movement, as some influential liberal critics have seen it, as the dog's return to the vomit of 'legitimation'. In place of the statesman's advantage, it is said, there is the class advantage of the poor. How does that improve matters? But, though this line of attack may find its targets, it fails to recognise the character and inspiration of the movement, which is to take up the cause of the poor *as a theologically given mandate*. If the question of the poor is, quite specifically, the question of the Latin Americans because it arises in their context, it is at the same time a question for us all, because it arises from scriptural warrants to which we must attend as carefully as they. The excitement which accompanied the reassertion of political theology in the Latin American context was, as we should not forget, very evidently an excitement about reading the Bible.

But neither does the liberal attack identify the true points of weakness in the movement, which arise from its dependence on historicist idealism. We may notice three of these.

First, there is the question of epistemology. The liberationist critique of depoliticised liberal theology starts from a classic argument within the modern idealist tradition: does knowledge, which is by definition knowledge of history, arise retrospectively, as an aftermath, as Hegel's famous 'owl of Minerva' metaphor suggests? Or does it arise *mediis in rebus*, in the heat of action, as Marx maintained? The critique identifies liberal theology with an encyclopedic conception of theology, organising various departments of knowledge which function on their own terms; and in place of this it looks for a theology which makes its own discoveries on the ground. But can it do this without making 'the ground', i.e. the chosen field of social action, absolutely determinative for valid theological knowledge? Must theology be *parti pris* – and to that extent closed against criticism?

Consider the familiar epistemological programme: 'reflecting upon praxis'. It can be taken to suggest certain features of good practical theology:

- that action demands its own proper form of reasoning – 'practical reasoning' the tradition used to call it, though 'deliberation' is perhaps a better term;
- that as well as practical reasoning *towards* action we need reflection *upon* action that can situate our practical engagements within a vision of the world;
- that practical engagement is prior in experience to reflection, so that occasions for understanding open up to us only as we first give ourselves to action.

These three suggestions are all true, and important. But in the space between reflection and deliberation, as it were, is a moment of transcendent criticism, a moment of obedient attention to God's word; and that is squeezed out by the collapsing of the two, the backward and the forward glance, into one moment, 'reflection upon praxis'. Our practical engagements now seem to yield all the understanding that we need. We have snatched a knowledge of the world that is *fait accompli*, stolen from God by getting in first. So our action becomes the predetermining 'matrix' for anything which God may wish to say to us, ensuring that we hear nothing from him but the echo of our own practical energies. And with that we are deprived of the freedom which lies at the root of all freedoms, the freedom to repent.

Exponents of reflection upon praxis have turned in two directions when elaborating the context, which turns out also to be the content, of their theological knowledge. On the one hand, they have spoken of knowledge won in action: the act of 'transforming' the world gives a privileged viewpoint on the world, a thought which was once meant to be conveyed by the term 'praxis', now flabby from fashionable over-use. On the other hand, they have sometimes turned to knowledge won from suffering, making solidarity with the oppressed a primary category of epistemology. In fact, neither of these turns could give political theology the epistemological freedom that it sought. The one steered it in a technological direction, opening it to the influence of Western doctrines of progress, the worst possible platform from which to urge the cause of classes marginalised by progress. The other turned it towards the romantic, world-renouncing strands of the European tradition and cut its nerve for action. What it needed, but only sometimes seemed to achieve, was a concept of knowledge gained *in obedience*. But obedience is a concept which historicist idealism finds it difficult to make room for, because of its transcendent reference.

Gustavo Gutiérrez seems to me to have articulated this point with perfect clarity: 'The ultimate criteria come from revealed truth, which we accept in faith, and not from praxis itself. It is meaningless – it would, among other things be a tautology – to say that praxis is to be criticised "in the light of praxis". Moreover, to take such an approach would in any case be to cease doing properly theological work.'[6] 'Meaningless', possibly – if one can describe the whole Promethean self-positing of mankind against God as meaningless – and 'tautological', in the sense that all founding axioms are generated from tautology. And most certainly untheological. Yet I doubt whether Gutiérrez's repudiation of self-justifying praxis can accommodate the characteristic factitive and transformative language of liberationist epistemology. Take, for example, an earlier statement from the same author: 'Truth is something *verified*, something "made true". Knowledge of reality that leads to no modification of that reality is not verified, does not become true.'[7] Would it have made any difference to the force of these words if he had not highlighted 'verified' as a term of art, and had glossed it, more conventionally, as 'proved true'? Or if he had not spoken of 'modifying', but of *acting into* reality? Is it only rhetoric, that suggestion, supported from Vico and Marx, that praxis is more than the *condition* of knowledge, but in fact determines what there *is* to be known? How can a 'knowledge' by which human beings 'recreate the world and shape themselves' distinguish itself from a naked exercise of will?

Second, by relying on the deconstructive *cui bono?* question to empower its rejection of liberal secularism, liberation theology finds itself with an unsustainable combination of political affirmation and universal suspicion. It becomes tied in to the eternally inconclusive exchanges of historicism: allegations of sectional interest volleyed to and fro across the net, never to be ruled out of court, never to land beyond reach of return. In a political theology which hopes to be constructive about politics, the *cui bono?* question has a distinct but strictly limited usefulness. It alerts us to the fact that political theories are related to the actual political commitments of those who hold them. But it does not tell us whether those commitments are good or bad, generous or mean-spirited, true or false. It does not entitle us to think that no theory ever looks beyond the interest of its proponents. It is therefore useful as an interpretative tool, to test the scope and integrity of any theory; but it cannot provide a vision of reality which could direct or encourage anyone. One cannot gain a truer understanding of the world by criticism alone, any more than one can make mince with a grinder and no meat. Once totalised, criticism evacuates itself and turns into a series of empty gestures. Totalised criticism is the modern form of intellectual innocence; but it is not harmless innocence, unhappily, as it destroys trust and makes it impossible to learn.

We may put the same point theologically by challenging the metaphor in King Lear's invitation, to 'take upon's the mystery of things as if we were God's spies'. God has no spies. He has prophets, and he commissions them to speak about society in words which rebuke the inauthentic speech of false prophets. But true prophets cannot speak *only* of the errors of false prophets. Their judgment of the false consists precisely in what they have to say of God's purposes of renewal, his mercy towards weak and frangible societies on which the fate of souls depends. Christian theology must assume the prophets' task, and, accepting history as the context within which politics and ethics take form, affirm that it is the history of God's action, not sheer contingency but consistent purpose. The prophet is not allowed the luxury of perpetual subversion. After Ahab, Elijah must anoint some Hazael, some Jehu.

Third, what positive cause, then, shall the prophet anoint? A broad answer can be given in wholly theological terms: the poor. As a theological starting point this has proved a strong answer, capable of opening the way to serious biblical and theological explorations that have captured the imagination of the Church in the Northern as well as the Southern hemisphere. Yet in developing it into more detailed policy, liberation theologians have needed to call on analyses of political events and structures from outside theology. Typically these have been described as 'social scientific' analyses, a reference not to the empirical social sciences as they are usually studied in the English-speaking world, but to the more philosophical tradition of social theory that has emerged from Germanic strands of idealism. The problem with this answer does not lie with the strategy of borrowing conceptual assistance as such. Theology has often done this to its benefit; the important question is how well such borrowed material from secular disciplines has been metabolised into its own system of theological intelligibility. (There are instances both of successful and unsuccessful borrowings in liberation theology. To my mind the use of class-conflict analysis remains wedged in the theological oesophagus like an undigested bolus, whereas dependency-theory has yielded authentic theological nourishment.)

The problem is that the choice of such guidance is a restrictive one, closing off the possibility of a fully political conceptuality. As we have observed, in speaking of 'society' we abstract from questions of government. This abstraction can serve as a useful ascetic preparation for thinking about politics; it can correct the blight of formalism to which theories of government are exposed; it can remind us that society is a vital dynamism that controls its leaders as much as it is controlled by them. Yet the societies we actually inhabit are *politically formed*. They are dependent on the art of government; they are interested in the very questions which the study of society abstracts from. We know that is the case whenever we see a society slide into the dreadful abyss of sub-political disintegration. The epithet 'social', however, forecloses the agenda against these vital questions, often narrowing it to economic matters which are only a fraction of what a living society cares about.

These three weaknesses can be focused in one. Building itself on an acephalous idea of society, dissolving government in deconstructive scepticism, lacking a point of view which can transcend given matrices of social engagement, liberation theology has lacked a concept of *authority*. I say 'a' concept, because it would be inauthentic to make advance stipulations for what kind of concept of authority it might derive from the reading of Holy Scripture. But it is proper to say to liberation theologians that, just as poverty was their issue first but also ours, so authority is our issue first, but also theirs. Authority is the nuclear core, the all-present if unclarified source of rational energy that motivates the democratic bureaucratic organisations of the Northern hemisphere; but it is also a central theme of the High Tradition (their tradition, as well as ours) which sought to derive criteria from the apostolic proclamation of the Gospel to test every claim upon authority made by those who possessed, or wished to possess, power. To form a critical concept of authority, contemporary political theologians need also to revisit that tradition.

The question of authority, when raised, has often been met with a massive deployment of suspicion by political theologians. Some have rejected the idea outright: Dorothee Soelle, for example, thinks that political theology is concerned with 'the conditions under which authority can be seen through, controlled and ultimately destroyed'.[8] But those who take this ground are fewer than those who simply keep their silence, not knowing how to address the subject without relapsing into 'legitimation'. Historical dialectic has made the category seem unusable; and the result is a *political* incoherence at the heart of contemporary politico-theological aspirations.

This explains in part why Northern admirers of liberation theology have had such little success in deploying its approach in relation to questions faced in their own hemisphere. Can democracy avoid being corrupted by mass communications? Can individual freedom be protected from technological manipulation? Can civil rights be safeguarded without surrendering democratic control to appointed courts? Or stable market conditions without surrendering control to appointed bankers? Can punishment be humane and still satisfy the social conscience? Can international justice be protected by threats of nuclear devastation? Can ethnic, cultural and linguistic communities assert their identities without denying individual freedoms? Can a democracy contain the urge to excessive consumption of natural resources? Can the handicapped, the elderly and the unborn be protected against the exercises of liberty demanded by the strong, the articulate and the middle-aged? Should the nation-state yield place to large market-defined governmental conglomerates? The peculiar forms of oppression experienced by a daily commuter in a large Northern conurbation, a check-out assistant in a supermarket, or a democratic politician hoping to avoid deselection by the party: these characteristic dilemmas and experiences have attracted astonishingly little notice from the political theologians of our generation.

For the Northern experience has been shaped in all its aspects by what became of the notion of authority in the modern era. Its technological imperative, its mass consumer culture, its democratic forms of distributing and denying power, all spring, in ways which cannot be gone into here, from the wasting away of authority as it was understood and witnessed to by the High Tradition, authority derived from and responsible to the just rule of God. In speaking of God's rule in a political context the tradition did not refer to the *potentia absoluta* underlying the bare fact of creation itself, but to the *potentia ordinata* which gave itself in covenant through the creation. To speak of the authority of God's rule is to speak of the fulfilment promised to all things worldly and human; and to measure the exercise of political power in its light is to make its world-affirming and humane character a test for all that is authentically political in human communities. The questions that confront the Northern democracies require a careful scrutiny in this light of the claims to authority on which their dominant social practices rest. And it is not political theologians who have made a start here, but those philosophers who address the criticism of modernity, especially those who have concentrated on the philosophical character of technology and the distinctive features of late-modern political and moral thought. (We might mention Jacques Ellul, George Grant, Leo Strauss and Alasdair MacIntyre as a representative selection.) Not that this collection of diverse thinkers has been without its own theological seriousness, however. If a new generation of political theologians nourished on liberation theology were to effect a meeting with this tradition, they might discover some surprising echoes of their own concerns.

However that may be, political theology needs also to regain a purchase on its own forgotten tradition, which derived, and critiqued, all exercise of authority from the rule of God. This proposal should not be misunderstood. It is not meant to suggest that the proper goal of political theology is to describe an ideal set of political *institutions*; for political institutions are anyway too fluid to assume an ideal form. The assimilation of the idea of authority to that of office and structure was a cardinal mistake which happened as Western politics turned its back on its theological horizon. Offices and structures are important, certainly, but as a secondary expression of authority. The primary object of attention should be a certain type of human (also, humane) *act*: the 'political act' we may call it. This occurs when God authorises the action of one or few to be performed on the part of many. It is representative, effective, and it constitutes the society in which and for which it is done as a political society that acts in and through it. How is this act authorised by God, so that members of society are represented in it, whether they choose to be or not? What are the criteria for its authentic performance? And how does it bear witness to the present and future of what God himself, the sole and only authority, daily undertakes for all?

The future of political theology lies with these questions.

## NOTES

1 Immanuel Kant, 'Perpetual Peace', in H. Reiss (ed.), *Kant: Political Writings* (Cambridge, Cambridge University Press, 1970), p. 118.
2 Augustine, *City of God*, bk 4, chs. 3, 4.
3 William Shakespeare, *King Lear*, act 5 scene 3.
4 Augustine, *City of God*, bk 6, ch. 5. Cf. Duncan Forrester, *Theology and Politics* (Oxford, Blackwell, 1988), p. 57.
5 Cf. R. A. Markus, *Saeculum: History and Society in the Theology of St. Augustine* (Cambridge, Cambridge University Press, 1970), pp. 22–44.
6 Gustavo Gutiérrez, *The Truth Shall Make You Free*, tr. Matthew J. O'Connell, (Maryknoll, NY, Orbis, 1990), p. 101.
7 Gustavo Gutiérrez, 'Liberation Praxis and Christian Faith', in *The Power of the Poor in History*, tr. Robert R. Barr (London, SCM Press, 1983), p. 59.
8 Dorothee Soelle, *Political Theology*, tr. John Shelley (Philadelphia, Fortress, 1974), p. 67.

# 14

IVAN PETRELLA

# Globalising liberation theology: the American context, and coda

In August of 1975 the 'Theology in the Americas' conference was held in Detroit. It was an exceptional gathering that brought together major figures of the American theological landscape including, among others, Gustavo Gutiérrez and James Cone, Hugo Assmann and Rosemary Radford Ruether, Juan Luis Segundo and Deotis Roberts, Enrique Dussel and Gregory Baum.[1] To read the proceedings is to be transported to a different time, a time giddy in the hope that the theological transformation brought about by liberation theology would also change society.[2] Passion, urgency, at times anger, emerged from discussions framed around the question – 'What would constitute a "theology in the Americas"?'[3] While this question and the many answers posed obviously mattered deeply to liberation theology's founding figures, whether Latin American, Black, Feminist, Chicano, Native American or White, it is no longer asked. The purpose of this chapter is to ask it again.[4]

Asking this question today, however, requires running against the grain of dominant trends in both scholarship on liberation theology and present-day liberation theologies themselves: the former examines liberation theologies individually while the latter has become a rich and growing forest of theological perspectives that stakes out particular claims for particular communities. The tendency towards particularity emerges, of course, from liberation theology's stress on the contextual nature of the theological enterprise. While unbelievably broad by today's parameters, the Detroit conference itself struggled with how to contextualise the Americas, oscillating between, on the one hand, understanding them as the United States and Canada only, and, on the other hand, understanding them as Latin America, the United States and Canada together. In the former view, the goal was 'to contribute to a new theology that emerges from the historical, social, and religious context of the North American experience'; while, in the latter view, the goal was for the particular contextual liberation theologies to converge, since 'the final Christian vision does not point to a tightly circumscribed context for some only, but to a context that is inclusive of all'.[5]

I will take the latter approach and assume that what unites is more important than what divides different liberation theologies. My approach too will be contextual – no one can escape context – but it will be contextual of liberation theology as a whole; that is, I will think across particular liberation theologies to reveal the overarching context within which a liberation theologian of any stripe must work today. In the process I will surely overlook many important differences, collapse many perspectives, and silence many voices, but I do so to reveal what I see as the central challenge, and equally central failure, that unites all liberation theologies. The argument develops in the following fashion: first, I highlight the social and economic context within which liberation theologians operate. I suggest that this context is best understood as the global expansion of areas of social abandonment.[6] Awareness of this fact should be the starting point of all liberation theology. Second, I present the theological context within which liberation theologians operate. Central to this context is the proliferation of theologies that claim to be 'liberation' theologies but in reality are better labelled as theologies of inclusion. Here I outline what I call the 'debilitating conditions', the different ailments, which keep liberation theologians from properly dealing with the reality of massive poverty. Third, I present a preliminary view of how liberation theology should respond to these contexts. Allow me to add a caveat. While I consider myself a student of all the American liberation theologies, my thinking has been most strongly influenced by the Latin American variant. This emphasis is at this point unavoidable, as Franz Rosenzweig once remarked: 'We all see reality through our own eyes, but it would be foolish to think we can pluck out our eyes to see straight.'[7] I thus ask the reader, where my argument fails, to be guided by its spirit, and revise it, make it better.

## On the social and economic context of the liberation theologian: the poverty of the majority

Hugo Assmann once wrote that:

> any kind of Christian theology today, even in the rich and dominant countries, which does not have as its starting point the historic situation of dependence and domination of $\frac{2}{3}$ of humankind, with its 30 million dead of hunger and malnutrition will not be able to position and concretize historically its fundamental themes. Its questions will not be the real questions.[8]

Assmann was right then, and is still right now. The social and economic context within which liberation theologians must work is only marginally better than it was at the time of liberation theology's inception.[9] As zones of social abandonment spread, more and more people are deprived of the ability to lead a decent and dignified life. There are three main elements to this spread: a ruling and idolatrous logic, the institutions through which the logic is pursued, and its tragic effects.

## The logic that rules

Larry Summers' infamous memo, written while he was the World Bank's chief economist, exemplifies the idolatrous logic that rules the world.[10] Since the memo was written exclusively for internal use, Summers pulls no punches in arguing that it would be more efficient to dump highly polluting industries and waste on the poorest nations: 'Just between you and me, shouldn't the World Bank be encouraging *more* migration of the dirty industries to the LDCs [Less Developed Countries, his emphasis]?... I think the economic logic behind dumping a load of toxic waste in the lowest wage country is impeccable and we should face up to that.'[11] The logic is impeccable because an inhabitant of, say, the United States produces more income and consumes more products than the inhabitant of the 'lowest wage country'. The potential loss of global income and productivity caused by ill health and/or death resulting from pollution is thus far greater in rich than in poor countries. The world is thus run by a simple rule: a person's worth is measured by their capacity to contribute to the global economy. People have value as producers and consumers; since the poor produce little and consume less, they are worthless. What matters is profit, not life.[12] Within a liberationist framework, this is a classic example of idolatry. For liberation theology, God is a God of life – that is, a God that values human life the utmost. Summers, however, places the workings of the global economy above human life. According to him, the global economy works best when the lives of the poor are sacrificed. Within this logic, spreading zones of social abandonment by sacrificing the poor is grounded in sound economics. And, since only idols require human sacrifices – Larry Summers is guilty of idolatry.

## The institutions that rule the world

The spread of zones of social abandonment is not an automatic process or inherent in supposedly natural capitalist dynamics.[13] Instead, it results from the simple fact that Summers' idolatrous logic is incarnated in the institutions that govern the global economy – the International Monetary Fund (IMF), the World Bank and the World Trade Organization (WTO). Not surprisingly, these institutions set rules of interaction between nations that heavily favour the richest countries, and, in particular, the United States. As Henry

Kissinger bluntly stated, 'the basic challenge is that what is called globalization is really another name for the dominant role of the United States'.[14] Liberation theologians have typically focused on the World Bank and the IMF, but it is the WTO that is dictating rules for global economic activity that will ensure that the dynamics of the logic of profit over life operate in the four corners of the globe. In a nutshell, the WTO provides a legal gloss over the global economy that legitimises the interests of the richest countries and their corporations. The stated goal is to 'harmonise' international standards but the end effect is to deprive the national governments of the poor nations of the power to dictate their own economic future. Under the banner of free trade, government subsidies to infant industries, tariffs, quotas, export support, all the mechanisms by which the United States, Europe and, more recently, East Asia became wealthy, are now deemed illegal.[15] In essence, by forbidding any government intervention to favour local industry, the WTO makes a nation's present-day comparative advantage seem given and natural, rather than the long product of partnerships between government and private enterprise. WTO rules, moreover, exclude from the same consideration the developing world's agriculture, textiles and footwear. Europe and the United States are allowed to restrict the entry of products in which poor nations have a comparative advantage, while forcing the latter to open up their economies to products from the former: 'the world trade rules set up by the rich nations freed up global markets for the areas in which they had comparative advantages while protecting their own vulnerable economic sectors, such as agriculture and textiles, from the competition posed by low-wage, poor countries'.[16]

Within the WTO, domestic issues of development for underdeveloped nations are viewed and trumped as issues of trade by North Atlantic corporations; national issues of the Third $\frac{2}{3}$ World are perceived and trumped as issues of a global economic architecture.[17] Take the struggle over global AIDS.[18] Currently, there are 35 million cases of HIV/AIDS in the developing world. While people in wealthy nations have been living longer and healthier lives thanks to antiretroviral therapy, the latter is beyond the reach of the majority of the world's population. The price of drugs in poor countries is dependent on patent rules set by the WTO agreement on Trade Related Aspects of Intellectual Property in 1995 (TRIPS). These rules enforce patent monopolies for products and manufacturing processes and forbid competition from generic producers for at least twenty years from the date of patent filing. Since annual treatment for HIV/AIDS is priced at approximately $15,000 (with an actual cost beneath $10), the new rules practically deny access to drugs for this and other life-threatening illnesses to the poor of the world.[19] Only the intense struggle of developing nations and NGOs allowed for concessions. In 2001 the WTO Declaration on the TRIPS Agreement and

Public Health allowed countries to grant compulsory licences for the production of generic drugs in cases of national emergency, as well as to pursue parallel importing. However, under threat of retaliation from the United States, no nation has yet to grant a compulsory licence.[20] Instead, they produce generic versions of drugs developed before they joined the WTO, and, when trying parallel importing, do so under intense pressure; the United States has even taken Brazil and South Africa to a WTO court to protect the interests of the pharmaceutical industry.[21]

## The world as a zone of social abandonment

Given the idolatry at the very basis of the world's ruling institutions, it is not surprising that fifty years of development have led to a world where more and more people are poor.[22] About one quarter of the world's population lives with less than one US dollar a day, while about half live with less than two dollars a day.[23] Only 20% of the world's population resides in the affluent Northern hemisphere, yet that hemisphere receives 60% of the world's income, engages in 80% of the world's trade, and 80% of the world's health spending.[24] Far from an expansion of economic opportunity, globalisation is marked by 'an accelerated withdrawing, a *shrinking* of the global map, rather than an *expanding* phenomenon, and one which expels ever more people from the interactive circle of global capitalism'.[25] Let me be more specific: the share of developing-country participation in world trade has increased by a mere 3.6% from 1953 to 1996. That increase, however, includes Hong Kong, Korea, Taiwan and Singapore – the Asian Tigers – which account for 33% of the developing world's share of trade while representing only 1.5% of its population. In 1995, once you exclude the Asian Tigers, the developing world's share of global trade was only 18.3%, down from the 1950 share of 25.9%, calculated again excluding the Asian Tigers. Latin America's share of world trade in 1995 was 4.8%, down from 10% in 1950. Recorded growth in world trade, therefore, has bypassed rather than integrated the developing world into the world economy. Similarly, the developing world's share of foreign direct investment (FDI) has dwindled. Up to 1960, the developing nations received half the world's total direct investment flows. By 1988–9 that percentage was down to 16.5%, with over half going to different parts of Asia. The 1990s saw a turnaround with the developing world receiving 38% of FDI by 1997, yet fully one third of this investment is concentrated in China's eight coastal provinces and in Beijing. In fact, in the first half of the 1990s, 86% of all FDI went to 30% of the world's population. All this in a context in which the rich industrial nations consume 70% of the world's energy, 75% of its metals,

85% of its wood and 60% of its food, while becoming proportionally a smaller part of the world's population. So, while the population of the developing world increases, its participation in the global economy and its consumption of the world's resources decreases.

The divide between those included in and those excluded from the global economy, however, is not merely a geographic rich–poor polarisation, it is also a *social* rich–poor divide that 'cuts across territorial boundaries and geographic regions'.[26] Zones of social abandonment are spreading in the First World as well, the United States in particular: 12.1% of the United States population, or 34.6 million United Statesians, fall below the poverty line. At 1.25% of the line, the rate increases to 47.1 million United Statesians; at 1.50 the number increases to 61.1 million. Over 60 million people live below or perilously close to the poverty line in the richest country in the world.[27] This number would increase if the United States focused, like Europe, on relative rather than absolute measures of poverty. While absolute measures define a bottom line standard, relative measures define poverty as a condition of comparative disadvantage. In the former, for example, extreme differences of income are not an issue, as long as the absolute basic standard is met; while in the latter such differences would be taken into account. Still, measured by an absolute standard, the United States falls behind every major industrial nation but the United Kingdom and Australia; while, when measured by a relative standard set at 40% of median income, the United States is the poorest of all – almost twice as poor as the United Kingdom and three times as poor as France.[28] By the absolute measure, child poverty for the United States lies at 18.5%. Measured by a relative standard set at 50% of median income, however, a dramatic 1 in every 4 children is poor. The poverty rate among African Americans is 22.1%, while for Latinos it is 21.2%, almost double the national average.[29] Amazingly, African American men in Harlem have a lower life expectancy than Bangladeshi men.[30] Women, moreover, compose 57% of the poor population.[31] In addition, 40 million working United Statesians have no health care, creating 'a caste of the chronically ill, infirm and marginally employed'.[32]

Of course, poverty in the United States is different from poverty in Latin America and the rest of the Third $\frac{2}{3}$ World. But poverty too is contextual. In *Wealth of Nations*, Adam Smith focused not 'only on the commodities which are indispensably necessary for the support of life, but whatever the custom of the country renders it indecent for creditable people, even of the lowest order, to be without'.[33] That is, social perceptions of poverty are important. So Amartya Sen thinks of poverty as a 'capability failure', the inability to participate fully in society. For him, people with little political voice, little economic and physical security, and little opportunity to improve their lives lack basic capabilities. From this perspective, goods and services are valuable insofar as they help people lead satisfying lives; in highly unequal societies, however, those at the bottom are unable to do so. In the United States, 40% of the country's wealth is owned by the top 1%. In the last forty years, the real value of stock prices has increased by a multiple of more than three and the salaries of company chief executives has grown by a multiple of eleven. Yet the level of a production worker's pay and the minimum wage has barely grown.[34] Indeed, income inequality in the United States – the proportion of the richest tenth to the poorest tenth – is greater than income inequality in India.[35]

## The theological context of the liberation theologian: the poverty of liberation theologies

A liberation theologian today works within a theological context where there is a proliferation of liberation theologies – but not one is prepared to deal with the spread of zones of social abandonment. These liberation theologies are not prepared because the upsurge of race, ethnicity, gender, sexuality and ecology as the organising axis for liberation theology has blurred the fact that material deprivation – that is, the deprivation that comes from one's class standing in society – remains the most important form of oppression. I am not suggesting, however, that oppression based on race or gender or ethnicity or sexuality is unimportant. It is extremely important. But I agree with Leonardo and Clodovis Boff's view that:

> the socioeconomically oppressed (the poor) do not simply exist alongside other oppressed groups, such as blacks, indigenous peoples, women ... It is one thing to be a black taxi-driver, quite another to be a black football idol; it is one thing to be a woman working as a domestic servant, quite another to be the first lady of the land; it is one thing to be an Amerindian thrown off your land, quite another to be an Amerindian owning your own farm.[36]

The most egregious assaults on human dignity most commonly occur not because you are black or because you are female, but because you are poor. To be black and/or female and poor increases a risk that is grounded in class. The economic poor bear the brunt of oppression and yet it is the plight of the economic poor that today is often avoided by liberation theologies in the Americas.[37] To quote Sancho Panza: 'Dos linajes solos hay en el mundo, como decía una abuela mía, que son el tener y el no tener.'[38] Indeed, liberation theologians suffer from 'debilitating conditions' – amnesia, monochromatism and gigantism – ailments that keep them from fully dealing with material deprivation. Often found together, it is useful for analytical purposes to examine them separately.[39]

## Amnesia

Amnesia is the most general of the ailments weakening liberation theologies' critical bite. Theologians with amnesia forget the problems they seek to tackle and the goals they want to pursue. There are three steps: first, the theologian stresses that economic poverty is a key problem to be addressed and that social liberation is a key goal to be realised. Second, the theologian forgets the first step and chooses sources for theological construction that keep the problem from truly being tackled and the goal from really being achieved. Finally, the cultural advancement of a particular ethnic group replaces social liberation as the goal of theology.

Maria Pilar Aquino's programmatic statement 'Latina Feminist Theology: Central Features' provides an example. Aquino writes that 'Latina/Chicana feminism is a critical framework to analyze systematic injustice, both locally and globally, to determine effective strategies for its elimination and the actualization of authentic justice.'[40] Given this liberationist thrust, Aquino provides an analysis of the 'material geopolitical' context which determines the method, the principles for theologising and the tasks for Latina theology.[41] The first level is characterised by global poverty, inequality, social exclusion and social insecurity brought about by 'the current capitalist, neoliberal global economic paradigm'.[42] The second level is characterised by poverty in the United States and the fact that the poverty rates for children, minorities and families headed by women are well above the average of the United States as a whole.[43] The third level is characterised by the exclusion of Latina women from theological activity.[44] Aquino begins, therefore, with an examination of the economic and social context which Latina theology must deal with.

Given the focus on Latina theology's material geopolitical context as the starting point for theology, her description of Latina theology's four main tasks come as a surprise. The first task lies in developing further Latina theology's theological foundations by bringing a feminist critical approach to its sources. The second task lies in Latina women continuing to claim their right to intellectual construction and the development of means and resources for the theological education of Latinas. The third task is drawing a closer connection between theology and spirituality in feminist terms. Finally, the fourth task lies in continuing the theological analysis of the effects of capitalist neoliberal globalisation on the life of grassroots Latinas.[45]

Amnesia has set in. While Aquino begins her essay by highlighting the 'material geopolitical' context which is supposed to determine the method, the principles for theologising and the tasks for Latina theology, as the essay develops, the background of global economic marginalisation as well as the marginalisation of the United States' poor recedes from view, while the theological exclusion of Latinas comes to the forefront. This happens in two main ways: first, Aquino explicitly relegates the critique of economic conditions to the fourth task Latina theology must tackle. Access to theological education and intellectual construction comes first. So does developing further the foundation of Latina theology. Helping people become theologians is given priority to helping people overcome social misery. Second, among the sources she names for Latina theology – *mestizaje*, popular religion, Scripture and Magisterium, interdisciplinary studies and philosophical hermeneutics – disciplines that might help tackle global and local economic marginalisation are nowhere to be found. The upshot of these moves is a theological focus that deals almost exclusively with seeking to address cultural marginalisation through integration at the level of the academy.[46] By the end of the essay, therefore, the 'material geopolitical context' has been forgotten.

### Monochromatism

People with monochromatism suffer from a limited range of vision: they see only black and white. In theology, monochromatism is evident when theologians of a particular ethnic or racial group refuse to look beyond the parameters of that group, as well as the parameters of their discipline, for tools and resources useful to the cause of liberation. Theologians with monochromatism, therefore, stress the goal of liberation, but dramatically limit the pool of resources they can draw upon to actually engage the task. In the end, colour of membership and membership in a professional guild take priority over liberation from material blight.

Take Dwight Hopkins, a prominent Black theologian, as an example.[47] For Hopkins, 'the key to all talk about God from the perspective of the black poor is the spirit of liberation'.[48] By the poor, moreover, he means:

> first the material poor; those who own or control no wealth. For instance, if two people work at a job and they both earn $20,000 a year, it would seem that they are equal. But what if one of those persons owns an oil field in Colorado or Texas? Let's say that both people are fired from their job and lose their income of $20,000. Both people will not suffer equally. Why? Because the one who owns and controls the oil field still has wealth.[49]

Indeed, he stresses that class is the normative thread that runs throughout Black theology.[50] Hopkins thus embraces the preferential option for the poor as a central element of Black theology, an option which involves a 'faith engaged in a radical redistribution of power and wealth on behalf of those whose voices aren't taken seriously in the United States'.[51] He tells us that 'we must avoid an amorphous type of black theology that omits the crucial phrase of *liberation of the poor*. In ambiguity lies the danger.'[52] For this reason, 'one of the key challenges for Black theology is to understand adequately the negative effects of US monopoly capitalism on African American poor and working communities. Faith and practice based on liberation theology must include the need for freedom from the oppressive control of global capital.'[53]

To address this need, Hopkins at times explicitly incorporates political economy into Black theology's sources: 'While interacting with other disciplines, theology seeks to discover how best to get at divine vocation for concrete liberation. For instance, political economy surfaces the issue of power control of politics, culture, and economics ... Furthermore, political economy paints the constructive contours of the new democratic society.'[54] While making political economy constitutive of Black theology is the right move, Hopkins, however, refuses to turn to the best current social, political, legal and economic theory, preferring instead to place his focus on safeguarding the blackness of his sources. So, in *Shoes That Fit Our Feet*, by political economy he means Martin Luther King Jr and Malcolm X. Another more recent essay focuses on Foucault and Cone as sources for a political vision – Foucault for his micro analysis of power relations and Cone for his macro analysis.[55]

Why this insistence on staying within the parameters of blackness when it comes to social analysis and political construction? Why not turn to contemporary social theory of different colours? While Martin Luther King Jr, Malcolm X and James Cone are obvious potential sources for Black theology, they are neither the most current nor the most useful resource if one is interested in developing a political and economic vision of content applicable to the twenty-first century. Hopkins' most recent work fares no better on this front. The 'Communal Political Economy' section of his latest book, *Being Human*, glides through the views of theologians such as Kim Yong-Bock of Korea, Mary Getui of Kenya, Laurenti Magesa of Tanzania, Mario Castillo of Cuba, Ambrose Mayo of Zimbabwe and Kwame Gyekye when it comes to work and the economy. So when dealing with 'political economy' he now restricts his sources to theology *and* blackness (most of them are black). Are there no black African or Third World social scientists and social theorists to whom one can turn? It would seem that turning to the work of social scientists when dealing with political economy is an obvious move. Yet monochromatism keeps Hopkins from looking beyond blackness and theology for tools that might aid the cause of liberation.[56] Seeing only black or not-black, seeing only theological or not-theological, the range of resources available to his theology is severely limited – limiting too his theology's relevance for the liberation of the material poor.

## Gigantism

Theologians suffering from gigantism see giant and monstrous forces oppressing the material poor. Unlike the amnesiac, therefore, the theologian suffering from gigantism does not forget to focus on class. Quite the contrary, economic conditions and social liberation are always the main focus. Unlike the theologian blinded by monochromatism, theologians stricken by gigantism do not limit the range of tools used for liberation. They eagerly embrace recent work from political economy and other social sciences. Their obsession with the gigantic forces oppressing the poor, however, is paralysing. It operates in three steps: first, the theologian asserts the focus on economic oppression and social liberation. Second, the theologian presents a picture of the causes of oppression in which they are of such magnitude that they seem practically insurmountable. Third, given the intractable conditions of oppression, paralysis ensues.

Latin American liberation theology is ripe with examples of gigantism. These can be divided into two related types, gigantism deriving from abstraction and gigantism deriving from demonisation. In the former, the theologian identifies the causes of material poverty with such abstraction that they are impossible to tackle. Thus the poor suffer from evils produced by 'capitalism', 'neoliberalism' or 'globalisation', terms that are used as placemarkers for the cause of oppression but which are rarely carefully examined and concretely defined. The vagueness of the abstraction, moreover, ensures that the placemarkers will be seen as capturing society as a whole. As an example, take Pablo Richard's statement that 'it is not possible to live *outside* the system, since globalization integrates everything, but it is possible to live *against* the spirit of the system'.[57] In this case, the main trait of this opponent is that it remains vaguely defined as a 'system' which it is impossible to escape. Capitalism, moreover, has completely taken over the political sphere as well: 'For *el pueblo* [the people] (the popular sectors, social movements at the base) political power has become impossible (the system does not allow for the orientation of political power in benefit of popular interest), political power has become *irrelevant* (since everything is determined by market logic and it is impossible to govern against that logic).'[58] Given the enemy's awesome scope and power, small wonder the only possible resistance Richard can envision is a vague shift in attitude that leaves the actual structures of oppression untouched.

With demonisation, gigantism is taken to the extreme. Following this line, Leonardo Boff, in a commentary on the Lord's Prayer, declares that the petition to deliver us from evil should be translated as 'deliver us from the evil one … He has a name; he is the capitalism of private property and the capitalism of the state.'[59] Another example is Hinkelammert's claim that 'the world which now appears and announces itself is a world where there is only "one lord" and "master", where there is only one system ... There is no place of asylum ... The empire is everywhere. It has total power and knows it.'[60] Capitalism appears metaphorically as an all-encompassing and absolute empire that cannot be escaped. Take also Hinkelammert's claim that 'today we are before a system of domination which includes even our souls, and which tries to suffocate even the very capacity for critical thinking'.[61] Here capitalism becomes the devil itself; nothing, not even our souls, lies beyond its scope. Capitalism's ability to possess our very being is taken to the limit in the following statement from Boff. For him, 'The capitalist and mercantile systems have succeeded in penetrating into every part of the personal and collective human mind. They have managed to decide the individual's way of life, the development of the emotions, the way in which an individual relates to his or her neighbors or strangers, a particular mode of love or friendship, and, indeed, the whole gamut of life and death.'[62]

Theologians who suffer from gigantism see capitalism everywhere and responsible for everything. Within this conception even envisioning a means of negative resistance is a close-to-impossible task. Where can one anchor change if the enemy is so powerful and all-encompassing? Paralysis ensues.

## A theology for the Americas

These American liberation theologies and the global economy parallel each other. In both, the majority of the world's population is excluded. In some cases, resistance is deemed the only available option, in other cases inclusion is revealed as the goal. The bottom line is that the debilitating conditions ensure that material poverty and social liberation are never successfully placed at the forefront of theology. Properly understanding the theological context within which a liberation theologian currently works means recognising that the material misery of the majority of the Americas is not a central concern to many theologies that dub themselves 'liberation' theologies. Today many 'liberation' theologies do not focus on the poor of the Americas. Today, many liberation theologies are, in intent and/or result, theologies for the middle class. To address properly the material poverty that is the hallmark of liberation theology's social and economic context, therefore, a liberation theology for the Americas must rebel against its theological context; that is, it must refuse to become a theology for the middle class. Only by refusing to trade in liberation for inclusion can a theology be a *liberation* theology. What, then, must we focus on to develop a liberation theology for the Americas? As an initial and preliminary reflection, five points must suffice.

First, the Americas as a whole must be taken as the proper context. This point is especially important for US liberation theologies. If US liberation theologies do not place their claims for justice in the wider American context, then it seems that they are upset only because they have not been given a larger piece of the United States' pie. And if that is what Black, Womanist and Latino/a theologians mean, then from the wider American viewpoint there is little difference between their liberation theologies and non-liberationist US theologies.[63]

Here a theology for the Americas must follow Latin American liberation theology's epistemological break from modern theology; that is, it must move theology away from the perspective of a small and affluent minority towards the perspective of the majority of humankind. The founding figures of Latin American liberation theology saw that, from a global perspective, poverty is not extreme or unusual: poverty represents the way most of the world lives, or, to be more accurate, barely lives. From a global perspective, it is the North Atlantic standard of living that is unusual in that it represents an extreme and unusual case of affluence – an island of prosperity in an ocean of misery. Their critique of modern theology's focus on the sceptic as the object of theology thus sought to highlight the narrowness of that focus; to focus on the sceptic as the object of theology is to organise theology around the material context of a small percentage of humankind.[64]

In breaking from modern theology, therefore, Latin American theologians were engaging in what anthropologist Laura Nader calls 'studying up'. As she puts it:

> Studying 'up' as well as 'down' would lead us to ask many 'common sense' questions in reverse. Instead of asking why some people are poor, we would ask why other people are so affluent. How on earth would a social scientist explain the hoarding patterns of the American rich and middle class? How can we explain the fantastic resistance to change among those whose options 'appear to be many'?[65]

Latin American liberation theologians thus asked questions that unmasked the false normalcy of a dominant theological standpoint that was deemed natural. They were trying to avoid what could be called 'special interest' thinking by reading up the ladder of privilege, 'because privilege blinds us to reality'.[66] While there is no neutral theological ground and thus all theologies are to some degree 'special interest' theologies, some special interest groups (to continue the metaphor) have fewer members and less urgent needs than others. A theology for the Americas, by focusing on the majority, will inherit this radical shift in the perspective from which theology was done.

Second, a theology for the Americas requires that US Black and Hispanic / Latino/a liberation theologies overcome their obsession with legitimising themselves through racial and ethnic categories. This obsession can be traced back to the critical response to Cone's groundbreaking *Black Theology and Black Power*. He tells us that the most powerful critique he received was that his theology was 'black in name only and not in reality. To be black in the latter sense, you must derive the sources and norm from the community in whose name you speak.'[67] In response, Cone and other black theologians sought to ground their theology in products of black culture such as the blues, spirituals and slave narratives.[68] Hopkins' monochromatism is the end result of this move. Instead, a liberation theology for the Americas needs an understanding of blackness that goes beyond skin colour – an understanding that encourages theologians to seek out the best resources for material liberation even if those resources do not come from black hands. Cone himself once wrote that 'being black in America has very little to do with skin color. To be black means that your heart, your soul, your mind and your body are where the dispossessed are ... Therefore, being reconciled to God does not mean that one's skin is physically black.'[69] Such an understanding of Blackness overcomes the monochromatism that plagues Black theology; this is the path to be followed.[70]

The same goes for Hispanic / Latino/a theologies. In his foundational *Galilean Journey*, Virgilio Elizondo tells us that 'the Catholic conquest of the Americas brought with it a new people, a new ethnos – *la raza mestiza*' (mixed clan, family or race).[71] Mexican-Americans are thus neither Mexican nor American, rather they are the product of a 'unique historical process that includes aspects of both but with an originality of its own – the uniqueness of a newborn ethnic strain'.[72] The outsider and marginal position of the *mestizo*, moreover, parallels the marginal position of Jesus. As Jesus breaks the exclusiveness of ancient thought and religion by pointing towards a universal salvation, *mestizo* mixed blood harbours a new humanity where racial and ethnic divides are overcome. While this approach should undermine the focus on limited sources of identity, in Elizondo's hands and that of others, the focus on *mestizaje* has paradoxically led to a theology obsessed with the purity of *mestizo* sources. Indeed, Elizondo's theology ends up providing a divine sanction to race by making *mestizos* the chosen people who will be the carriers of God's promised future: 'God has chosen them [*mestizos*] to be his historical agents of a new unity.'[73] But, if *mestizaje* is really about mixed blood, it should herald the irrelevance of race and ethnicity as a foundation for theology and humanity. *Mestizaje*, therefore, means that the only races that matter are the future races emerging from further mixing – to thus focus on a ghettoed theological/racial project betrays the central insight. In the end, the right question is not 'what makes theology black?' or 'what makes theology Hispanic?' but 'what makes theology liberative to the materially poor?' Yet it is precisely this question that these racial liberation theologies fail to address.[74]

Third, a theology for the Americas must unmask the false neutrality of theological concepts by working out the political, economic and social implications of those concepts. Let me explain: say you and I both agree that a belief in God is central to our thinking and acting. What at the surface seems like a profound agreement may in fact cover deep disagreement. We both believe in God, but what kind of God do we believe in? Say that, in trying to specify what type of God we believe in, we find that we both embrace the liberationist claim that the body is the locus of salvation and that food, water, shelter are part of God's plan for all. This agreement may still hide deep disagreement. To find out whether we really agree requires working out what these ideas mean in practice; we need to develop the implications of that understanding for the way we relate to ourselves, to others and to the way society is organised. For some, it might mean that charity should be an integral part of the Christian lifestyle. For others, it might mean supporting a higher minimum wage and greater welfare benefits, perhaps even socialised health care. For others, it might mean radical structural change such as the replacing of capitalism for socialism or some other system not based on profit and competition. For still others, it might mean that Christians should cease trying to change society and organise their own communities where any of these options may be worked out.[75] Others still would argue that neo-liberal structural adjustment policies are the way to go.[76]

The point, therefore, is that, once one starts to work through concepts, they lose their neutrality. To be stated neutrally, a term must be made too abstract to be interesting or useful. It must be rid of content – if we do not work out our concept of 'God' then we will never know that underneath it lay all these possibilities. As each possibility gets developed further, moreover, different institutional futures emerge.[77] Thus Latin American liberation theology's belief that developing 'historical projects', models of political and economic organisation that might replace an unjust status quo, were necessary to truly work through and understand theological terms. As Bonino once wrote, 'expressions and symbols' such as '"justice", "peace", "redemption", . . . cannot be operative except in terms of historical projects which must incorporate, and indeed, always do incorporate, an analytical and ideological human, secular, verifiable dimension'.[78] By incorporating the development of historical projects as an integral part of theology, liberation theologians were highlighting the emptiness of theological talk that did not work out its implications for society. Theological talk that refuses to do so, moreover, by default falls into the hands of the status quo by leaving things the same. To quote Cone: 'Love's meaning is not found in sermons or theological textbooks but rather in the creation of social structures that are not dehumanizing and oppressive.'[79]

Fourth, a liberation theology for the Americas must incorporate the social sciences and social theory as intrinsic elements of the theological enterprise.[80] Liberation theology needs them to best understand the causes of oppression to give content to its theological terminology, as well as to imagine historical projects. As Cornel West once wrote: 'The possibility of liberation is found only within the depths of the actuality of oppression. Without an adequate social theory, this possibility is precluded.'[81] Indeed, a real liberation theology – one interested in enacting liberation rather than merely talking about liberation – cannot escape an alliance with other disciplines.[82] It is just not enough to rehearse like a mantra concepts like 'liberation' and 'the preferential option for the poor' to place oneself on the side of the continent's poor. Theology and economics, theology and political science, theology and sociology, theology and law are not linked just because the social sciences themselves carry implicit theologies that need to be unmasked. They are linked because, in the final analysis, the social sciences are the realm where God's promise of life succeeds or fails.

Liberation theology, however, must choose among different social science approaches carefully, because the adoption of a social theory – the selection of metaphors one chooses to use as a roadmap to our environment – is inevitably a political act in that social science theories are constitutive of the worlds we inhabit. What really matters, therefore, is how different theories make sense of the world and move people to act in different ways and in different directions. A liberation theology for the Americas must avoid totalising social theories such as dependency theory or world systems theory that present economic and political systems as monolithic wholes. The adoption of these theories is the cause of the paralysing gigantism and demonisation that plagues Latin American liberation theology. Let me stress this point, as it affects every strand of liberation theology as well as much of leftist thought generally.[83] More than a dominant economic model, capitalism should be understood as a dominant discourse that functions to blur the potential for alternatives within itself.[84] Insofar as liberation theologians describe capitalism as all-encompassing and all-powerful, they actually strengthen that which they oppose. Indeed, as William James once suggested, our descriptions add to the world.[85] The task, therefore, is to uncover the alternatives hiding under the discourse of neo-liberal capitalist hegemony. Those alternatives can be found in the wide variety of existing capitalisms – US, German, Asian, Scandinavian, to name just a few – as well as the resistance movements that have emerged in relation to the WTO and other gatherings of world leaders.

From the standpoint of social theory, I believe that the most useful resource for this task is critical legal theory.[86] Critical legal theory allows liberationists to move beyond a blanket condemnation of 'capitalism' and instead examine the way the legal minutiae of the variety of actually existing capitalisms affect the distribution of resources in society. For example, when specifically examined, a market economy is a particular legal regime and so law, in the form of the regime choice, influences the distribution of income achieved.[87] Social interactions – say, for example, the bargaining between labour and capital over wages – can be analogised to a game played under a set of rules.[88] Even if the rules are stated in a way that applies equally to all, they can be examined for their impact on each player's chance for success. The rules of basketball, for example, could be changed to affect the advantage tall players have over short players; lowering the height of the hoop would affect the relative ability of each player. Similarly, the legal rules that set the terms by which capital and labour negotiate are generally deemed as 'background' and thus part of the neutral rules of the game. In this perspective, law only plays a role in distributing power and privilege when it actively intervenes in society to resolve a conflict. Intervention is the exception rather than the rule; the rule being that the law merely sets the apolitical ground rules within which conflict and cooperation can take place. Yet, if one imagines alternative rules, then the background rules are brought forward as far from neutral. Rules are only 'background' rules from the point of view of analyses that operate under the assumption of *ceteris paribus* (other things being equal) – that is, the assumption that those rules remain constant. When the background conditions change, however, they undermine analyses that assume them to be constant.[89] Laws pertaining to collective bargaining, unionisation, duration of strikes, the nature and scope of picketing, and many other details necessarily tilt the scale of power in one direction or another. To change these rules is to change the bargaining power of the groups involved which, in turn, affects the distributional consequences of the capitalism in question. Critical legal theory lets liberation theologians see that the legal ground rules that make particular societies, as well as the global order, can take many different forms – the goal, therefore, is not to replace an abstract 'capitalism' with an equally abstract 'socialism', but instead to examine a social order and find the steps that would democratise access to economic and political opportunity by tilting the rules of the game towards the less fortunate.[90]

Finally, a liberation theology for the Americas will realise that the proliferation of liberation theologies, that nonetheless remain mute to each other, is a sign of health in the academic marketplace, but a sign of disarray in the struggle for liberation. The interests of all the liberation theologies are one. As Leonardo and Clodovis Boff once stated of liberation theology as a whole: 'There is one and only one theology of liberation. There is only one point of departure – a reality of social misery – and one goal – the liberation of the oppressed.'[91] Of course, different liberation theologies are coloured by particular perspectives and localities, yet those perspectives and localities are united by the pangs of hunger that only poverty causes. Among those who are oppressed because of race, gender, sexuality or culture, some die and some do not. Those who do, die because they are poor. A liberation theology for the Americas must remember that life is the foundation for the very possibility of having goals; life is not a goal, it is prior to all goals. In uniting and focusing on material deprivation, a liberation theology for the Americas seeks life – all else can follow. Back in 1977 James Cone wrote that 'we must enlarge our vision by connecting it with that of other oppressed peoples so that together all the victims of the world might take charge of their history for the creation of a new humanity . . . this is the issue black theology needs to address. "Theology in the Americas" provides a framework in which to address it.'[92] The conferences were held, the call was made, but the project was never truly pursued. This time, let us follow it through.

### Coda

Perhaps the future of liberation theology lies beyond theology. At the heart of liberation theology lie two elements: the first is epistemological, the liberationist attempt to do theology from the standpoint of the oppressed. The second is practical/moral, liberation theology's commitment to thinking about ideals by thinking about institutions. Indeed, Latin American liberation theology's attempt to think Christianity in relation to socialism is best understood as a response to a vexing problem in social and political thought – the gap between our ideals and the institutions that are meant to realise them.

Economics, law, medical anthropology, political science, sociology and a host of other disciplines could engage in the same epistemological shift and be fuelled with the same practical/moral drive with revolutionary consequences for each field. These are the disciplines, not theology, which set the intellectual frameworks through which the world is most influentially analysed. The above elements thus need elucidation in disciplines with a wider impact than theology or religious studies.

Perhaps the task is that of disentangling the 'liberation' from the 'theology' in liberation theology. To work in liberation theology today could mean to work outside of it, by finding ways the epistemological and practical/moral elements can infiltrate, undermine and transform other bodies of knowledge. Here the liberation theologian must go undercover and work from within to change a discipline's presuppositions. Here the liberation theologian need not carry the label of 'theologian' and works best under a different disciplinary guise. Could the future of liberation call for the dissolution of liberation theology as an identifiable field of production?

## NOTES

1. Other notable participants included Avery Dulles, Monika Hellwig, José Miranda, Frederick Herzog, José Miguez Bonino, Leonardo Boff, Beatriz Melano Couch, Beverly Harrison, Robert McAfee Brown and Phillip Berryman.
2. For the proceedings see Sergio Torres and John Eagleson (eds.), *Theology in the Americas* (Maryknoll, NY, Orbis, 1976), and Cornel West, Caridad Guidote and Margaret Coakley (eds.), *Theology in the Americas: Detroit II Conference Papers* (Maryknoll, NY, Orbis, 1982).
3. Robert McAfee Brown, 'A Preface and a Conclusion', in Torres and Eagleson (eds.), *Theology in the Americas* p. xviii.
4. I see this question as the natural outgrowth of Ivan Petrella, *The Future of Liberation Theology: An Argument and a Manifesto* (London, SCM Press, 2006; hardback edn by Ashgate in 2004). While that book focused on Latin American liberation theology, I believe the argument has implications for, and can unify, the wide variety of liberation theologies existing today. Indeed, this chapter is a partial bare-bones outline of Petrella, *Beyond Liberation Theology: A Polemic* (London, SCM Press, 2008).
5. McAfee Brown, 'Preface', pp. xviii and xix respectively.
6. I borrow the expression 'zone of social abandonment' from the subtitles of João Biehl, 'Vita: Life in a Zone of Social Abandonment', *Social Text* 1913) (Fall 2001), pp. 131–48, and João Biehl, *Vita: Life in a Zone of Social Abandonment* (Berkeley, University of California Press, 2005).
7. Cited in John Parratt (ed.), *An Introduction to Third World Theologies* (Cambridge, Cambridge University Press, 2004), p. 9. Parratt does not give the original reference.
8. Hugo Assmann, *Teología desde la praxis de la liberación* (Salamanca, Ediciones Sígueme, 1973), p. 40.
9. It all depends: African Americans have civil rights and have made gains in the United States (which does not mean racism is no longer a problem), there is greater gender equality throughout the Americas (which does not mean the struggle for gender equality is over), Latin America is no longer ruled by dictatorships (which does not mean our democracies are exemplary), but poverty is still rampant across the globe, in Latin America, and unacceptable everywhere, and perhaps especially in the wealthiest nation in the world.
10. Summers held the position from 1990 till 1993, when he left to become Clinton's Under-Secretary of the Treasury. He was President of Harvard University until forced out by a series of scandals. This section draws from Susan George and Fabrizio Sabelli, *Faith and Credit: The World Bank's Secular Empire* (Boulder, CO, Westview, 1994). Chapter 5 deals with Summers and the memo.
11. Larry Summers, World Bank Memo, 12 December 1991. Cited in George and Sabelli, *Faith and Credit*, pp. 98–9.
12. Nature too is subject to this logic. The international forestry consultant Bethel refers to tropical forests in the following way: 'The important question is how

much of this biomass represents trees and parts of trees of preferred species that can be profitably marketed ... By today's utilization standards, most of the trees, in these humid tropical forests are, from an industrial materials standpoint, clearly weeds': cited in Vandana Shiva, *Monocultures of the Mind: Perspectives on Biodiversity and Biotechnology* (New York, Zed Books, 1993), p. 24. This logic echoes Summers – if it does not fit in the market, it does not count.

13. This view differs from how liberation theologians typically understand capitalism. For my take, see chapter 4 of *The Future of Liberation Theology*.

14. Henry Kissinger cited in Celia Iriart, Howard Waitzkin and Emerson Merhy, 'HMO's Abroad: Managed Care in Latin America', in Meredith Fort, Mary Anne Mercer and Oscar Gish (eds.), *Sickness and Wealth: The Corporate Assault on Global Health* (Cambridge, MA, South End Press, 2004), p. 69. Not much has changed. According to a 1948 US State Department policy planning study, 'the US has about 50 percent of the world's wealth but only 6.3[%] of its population. This situation cannot fail to be the object of envy and resentment. Our real task ... is to devise a pattern of relationships which will permit us to maintain this position of disparity without positive detriment to our national security': George Kennan, *State Department Policy Planning Study #23* (Washington, DC, US Department of State, 1948); cited in Stephen Bezruchka and Mary Anne Mercer, 'The Lethal Divide: How Economic Inequality Affects Health', in Fort, Mercer and Gish (eds.), *Sickness and Wealth*, p. 12.

15. For a range of studies that document the role of such mechanisms in the wealth of Europe, the United States and East Asia, see Kevin P. Gallagher (ed.), *Putting Development First: The Importance of Policy Space in the WTO and International Financial Institutions* (New York, Zed Books, 2005); Liah Greenfeld, *The Spirit of Capitalism: Nationalism and Economic Growth* (Cambridge, MA, Harvard University Press, 2001); Peter Hall and David Soskice (eds.), *Capitalism: The Institutional Foundations of Comparative Advantage* (Oxford, Oxford University Press, 2001); Alice Amsden, *The Rise of the 'Rest': Challenges to the West from Late-Industrializing Economies* (Oxford, Oxford University Press, 2001); Robert Boyer and Daniel Drache (eds.), *States Against Markets: The Limits of Globalization* (New York, Routledge, 1996); Michael Best, *The New Competition: Institutions of Industrial Restructuring* (Cambridge, Harvard University Press, 1990); and Robert Wade, *Governing the Market: Economic Theory and the Role of Government in East Asian Industrialization* (Princeton, NJ, Princeton University Press, 1990). The WTO freezes a country's endowments and preferences to the present and ignores the fact that in a modern economy comparative advantage is created. In depriving nations of the capacity for creation, these agreements condemn the majority of the globe to poverty. The truth is that every single one of the rich countries grew wealthy through lax intellectual property rights and protected industries. England was protectionist as it tried to catch up with the Netherlands; Germany was protectionist as it tried to catch up with England; the USA was protectionist as it tried to catch up with England and Germany; Japan was protectionist until the 1970s, while Korea and Taiwan were protectionist till the 1990s. Friedrich List once confessed: 'It is a very clever common device that when anyone has attained the summit of greatness, he kicks away the ladder by which he has climbed up, in order to deprive others of the means of climbing up after him ... Any nation which by means of protective duties and restrictions on navigation has

raised her manufacturing power and her navigation to such a degree of development that no other nation can sustain free competition with her, can do nothing wiser than to throw away the ladders of her greatness, to preach to other nations the benefits of free trade, and to declare in pertinent tones that she has hitherto wandered in the paths of error, and has now for the first time succeeded in discovering the truth.' I take the List quotation and this history from Ha-Joon Chang's excellent 'Kicking Away the Ladder: "Good Policies" and "Good Institutions" in Historical Perspective', in Gallagher (ed.), *Putting Development First*, p. 107.

16. Robert Isaak, *The Globalization Gap: How the Rich Get Richer and the Poor Get Left Further Behind* (New York, Prentice Hall, 2005), p. 174.

17. I'm paraphrasing Vandana Shiva, *Protect or Plunder? Understanding Intellectual Property Rights* (New York, Zed Books, 2001), p. 95.

18. What follows draws from Paul Davis and Meredith Fort, 'The Battle Against Global Aids', in Fort, Mercer and Gish (eds.), *Sickness and Wealth*, pp. 145–58; William Tabb, *Unequal Partners: A Primer on Globalization* (New York, The New Press, 2002), pp. 85–120; Shiva, *Protect or Plunder?* pp. 86–93.

19. The hypocrisy: 'In Europe, pharmaceuticals were denied patent protection in some countries until the 1960s and 1970s to promote development of local industry – and control drug prices. By denying such strategies to developing countries, the rich had effectively cut the rungs off the development ladder before the poor were able to climb it': Davis and Fort, 'The Battle Against Global Aids', p. 149.

20. Ibid., p. 149.

21. Another example: 'For some countries, especially developing countries with limited budgets, the possibility of being tried in a WTO tribunal is sufficient to induce them to back down on laws that protect public health and well-being. In 1988, Guatemala adopted the WHO-UNICEF Infant Formula Marketing Code into laws prohibiting infant formula companies from using advertising labels that made their products appear to be healthier than breast milk. For four years US based Gerber Products launched a campaign to eliminate the law and refused to comply. In 1995, Gerber gained US support to challenge the law in a WTO tribunal, and the threat of trade sanctions were enough to have the government exempt imported baby food products from Guatemala's infant health laws': Ellen Shaffer and Joseph Brenner, 'Trade and Health Care: Corporatizing Vital Human Services', in Fort, Mercer and Gish (eds.), *Sickness and Wealth*, p. 82.

22. For an overarching critique of development as a discourse, see Arturo Escobar, *Encountering Development: The Making and Unmaking of the Third World* (Princeton, NJ, Princeton University Press, 1995). For two good overviews of approaches to development, see Richard Peet and Elaine Hartwick, *Theories of Development* (New York, The Guilford Press, 1999), and Ray Kiely, *Sociology and Development: The Impasse and Beyond* (London: UCL Press Limited, 1995).

23. See Bob Sutcliffe, *100 Ways of Seeing an Unequal World* (New York, Zed Books, 2001), Graph #14. This is a fascinating book that provides all sorts of diagrams outlining inequality among and within nations. In this specific case, he gets his data from the World Bank's *Income Poverty – The Latest Global Numbers* (Washington DC, World Bank, 2000) (www.worldbank.org/poverty/data/trends/income.htm). There are two main ways to measure the world's distribution of income, international and global. International distribution takes into account only income differences between countries. It works by assuming that

everyone in the United States, for example, receives the country's average income. In this case, the richest 10% of the world's population are identified as the 600 million people who live in the richest countries. So, essentially, it spreads out wealth and thus lowers the upper bar. According to the international measure of distribution the ratio between the top and bottom 10% of the population in 1997 was 30 to 1. Global measures, on the other hand, incorporate inequality within nations as well. So the richest 10% would not include all of the US population but would include the world's 600 million highest incomes, whether they be from the USA, France or Brazil. Here the ratio is 63 to 1. On these measures, see Sutcliffe, *100 Ways*, p. 8. While the World Bank acknowledges that inequality in the global economy remains severe, it argues that it has diminished in the past two decades. Such a claim, however, remains highly contested. For one counter-argument see Robert Wade, 'The Disturbing Rise in Poverty and Inequality: Is It All a "Big Lie"?', David Held and Mathias Koenig-Archibugi (eds.), *Taming Globalization: Frontiers of Governance* (Cambridge, Polity Press, 2003), pp. 18–46.

24. Sutcliffe, *100 Ways*, Graph #1.
25. See Ankie Hoogvelt, *Globalization and the Postcolonial World: The New Political Economy of Development* (Baltimore, The Johns Hopkins University Press, 1997), p. 70. The following discussion draws from her excellent discussion of global economic trends on pages 67–93.
26. Ibid., p. 64.
27. Mark Robert Rank, *One Nation, Underprivileged* (Oxford, Oxford University Press, 2004), p. 25. I prefer 'United Statesian' to 'North American'. As Justo Gonzalez writes, 'Even the name "America" raises the question: What preposterous conceit allows the inhabitants of a single country to take for themselves the name of an entire hemisphere? What does this say about the country's view of other nations who share the hemisphere with it?': Justo Gonzalez, *Mañana: Christian Theology from a Hispanic Perspective* (Nashville, Abingdon Press, 1990), p. 37. I did not coin the term itself, but have been unable to recover the reference.
28. John Iceland, *Poverty in America: A Handbook* (Berkeley, University of California Press, 2003), p. 62.
29. Ibid., p. 85.
30. Paul Farmer, *Pathologies of Power: Health, Human Rights, and the New War on the Poor* (Berkeley, University of California Press, 2003), p. 46.
31. Iceland, 88.
32. Susan Starr Sered and Rushika Fernandopulle, *Uninsured in America: Life and Death in the Land of Opportunity* (Berkeley, University of California Press, 2005), p. 15.
33. Adam Smith, *An Inquiry Into the Nature and Causes of the Wealth of Nations*, ed. and notes by Edwin Cannan, intro. by Edwin Cannan and Max Lerner (New York, Modern Library, 1937), pp. 351–2; cited in Iceland, *Poverty in America*, p. 11.
34. Sutcliffe, *100 Ways*, Graph #16.
35. Ibid., Graph #41.
36. Clodovis Boff and Leonardo Boff, *Introducing Liberation Theology* (Maryknoll, NY, Orbis Books, 1987), p. 29.
37. Take, for example, the case of disease, an issue not often discussed within liberation theology (Emilie Townes is an exception to this rule). As Paul Farmer has argued, diseases themselves make a preferential option for the

poor. Tuberculosis today has an overall cure rate of over 95%. Yet tuberculosis deaths, which currently number in the millions, are found almost exclusively among the poor, whether in the Third $\frac{2}{3}$ World or the inner cities of the United States. In the year 2000, preventable and treatable communicable diseases – tuberculosis and other respiratory infections, AIDS, diarrheal diseases, perinatal infections – were the cause of 7.7% of deaths among the affluent but the cause of 58.6% of deaths among the world's poor. Crimes such as rape and assault occur among women, but gender alone does not determine who is at risk; it is poor women who are at the greatest risk. Take the case of contemporary slavery. Today slavery is not based on ethnic or racial differences; the key criteria for enslavement today is deprivation – the common denominator is poverty, not colour. The health and poverty data are taken from Farmer, *Pathologies of Power*; on contemporary slavery, see Kevin Bales, *Disposable People: New Slavery in the Global Economy* (Berkeley, University of California Press, 1999).

38. 'There are only two lineages in the world, as my grandmother used to say, the haves and have nots': Miguel de Cervantes Saavedra, *El ingenioso hidalgo Don Quijote de la Mancha* (Madrid, Aguilar S.A., 1993), from memory.

39. In Petrella, *Beyond Liberation Theology*, I discuss a fourth debilitating condition, naiveté, that is often a consequence of the previous three. Space considerations keep me from discussing it here.

40. Maria Pilar Aquino, 'Latina Feminist Theology: Central Features', in Maria Pilar Aquino, Daisy Machado and Jeanette Rodriguez (eds.), *A Reader in Latina Feminist Theology: Religion and Justice* (Austin, University of Texas Press, 2002), p. 136.

41. Ibid., p. 140.

42. Ibid.

43. Ibid., p. 144.

44. Ibid., p. 145.

45. Ibid., see pp. 153–4.

46. Exemplified, for instance, by Aquino's penchant for incorporating words from Nahautl and Spanish into a North Atlantic theological discourse dominated by English, French and German. See ibid., p. 149.

47. Monochromatism, while dominant in Black theology, is not exclusive to it.

48. Dwight Hopkins, *Introducing Black Theology of Liberation* (Maryknoll, NY, Orbis, 1999), p. 46.

49. Dwight Hopkins, *Heart and Head: Black Theology – Past, Present and Future* (New York, Palgrave, 2002), p. 24.

50. Dwight Hopkins and Linda Thomas, 'Womanist Theology and Black Theology: Conversational Envisioning of an Unfinished Dream', in Eleazar Fernandez and Fernando Segovia (eds.), *A Dream Unfinished: Theological Reflections on America from the Margins* (Maryknoll, NY, Orbis, 2001), p. 86.

51. Hopkins, *Heart and Head*, p. 61.

52. Ibid., p. 162.

53. Ibid., p. 49.

54. Dwight Hopkins, 'Black Theology and a Second Generation: New Scholarship and New Challenges', in James Cone and Gayraud Wilmore (eds.), *Black Theology, A Documentary History: Volume II 1980–1992* (Maryknoll, NY, Orbis, 1993), p. 64. See also Dwight Hopkins, *Shoes That Fit Our Feet* (Maryknoll, NY, Orbis, 1993), p. 215, as well as chapters 4–5.

55. See Dwight Hopkins, 'Postmodernity, Black Theology of Liberation and the USA: Michel Foucault and James H. Cone', in David Batstone, Eduardo Mendieta, Lois Ann Lorentzen and Dwight Hopkins (eds.), *Liberation Theologies, Postmodernity, and the Americas* (New York, Routledge, 1997), pp. 205–21.

56. Dwight Hopkins, *Being Human*, pp. 91–98.

57. Pablo Richard, 'Teología de la solidaridad en el contexto actual de economía neoliberal de mercado', in Franz Hinkelammert (ed.), *El huracán de la globalización* (San Jose, Costa Rica, DEI, 1999), p. 228, italics in original.

58. Ibid., p. 233, italics in original.

59. Cited in Iain Maclean, *Opting for Democracy: Liberation Theology and the Struggle for Democracy in Brazil* (New York, Peter Lang, 1999), p. 142.

60. F. J. Hinkelammert, 'Changes in the Relationships Between Third World and First World Countries', in K. C. Abraham and Bernadette Mbuy-Beya (eds.), *Spirituality of the Third World* (Maryknoll, NY, Orbis, 1994), pp. 10–11; cited in Daniel M. Bell Jr, *Liberation Theology After the End of History: The Refusal to Cease Suffering* (London, Routledge, 2001), p. 67.

61. F. J. Hinkelammert, 'Determinación y auto constitución del sujeto: las leyes que se imponen a espaldas de los actores y el orden por el desorden', *Pasos* 64 (marzo–abril 1993), p. 18.

62. Leonardo Boff, *Ecology and Liberation: A New Paradigm* (Maryknoll, NY, Orbis, 1995), pp. 33–4.

63. I am pillaging from James Cone, who saw this: 'If we don't place our claims for justice in a global context, then we will appear to Asians, Africans, and Latin Americans to be black capitalists who are upset only because we have not been given a larger piece of the American pie … If that is what we mean, then there is very little difference between black people and white people in the United States when they are evaluated from the viewpoint of global justice': James Cone, *Speaking the Truth: Ecumenism, Liberation, and Black Theology* (Grand Rapids, MI, William B. Eerdmans, 1986), p. 153.

64. For a classic comparison of modern theology and liberation theology, see Gustavo Gutiérrez, 'Two Theological Perspectives: Liberation Theology and Progressivist Theology', in Sergio Torres and Virginia Fabella (eds.), *The Emergent Gospel: Theology from the Underside of History* (Maryknoll, NY, Orbis, 1978), pp. 227–58.

65. See Laura Nader, 'Up the Anthropologist – Perspectives Gained in Studying Up', in Dell Hymes (ed.), *Reinventing Anthropology* (New York, Pantheon Books, 1972), pp. 284–311; cited in Farmer, *Pathologies of Power*, p. 269.

66. See Chandra Talpade Mohanty, *Feminism Without Borders: Decolonizing Theory, Practicing Solidarity* (Durham, Duke University Press, 2003), p. 4. I take the reference from Nancy Bedford, 'To Speak of God from More Than One Place: Theological Reflections on the Experience of Migration', in Ivan Petrella (ed.), *Latin American Liberation Theology: The Next Generation* (Maryknoll, NY, Orbis, 2005), pp. 95–118.

67. James Cone, *Black Theology and Black Power* (Maryknoll, NY, Orbis, 1997), pp. xi–xii.

68. See, for example, James Cone, *The Spirituals and the Blues: An Interpretation* (New York, The Seabury Press, 1972), and Dwight Hopkins and George Cummings (eds.), *Cut Loose Your Stammering Tongue: Black Theology in the Slave Narratives* (Louisville, KY, Westminster John Knox Press, 2003).

69. James H. Cone, *A Black Theology of Liberation*, C. Eric Lincoln Series in Black Religion (Philadelphia, J. B. Lippincott Company, 1970), p. 151; for this thrust, see also pp. 3 and 17.

70. For an often ignored challenge to monochromatism that comes from Black theology itself, see Victor Anderson's *Beyond Ontological Blackness: An Essay on African American Religious and Cultural Criticism* (New York, Continuum, 1995). Black British social theory has long looked to go beyond monochromatism. See the work of Paul Gilroy and Stuart Hall as examples.

71. Virgilio Elizondo, *Galilean Journey: The Mexican-American Promise* (Maryknoll, NY, Orbis Books, 2003), p. 10.

72. Ibid., p. 19.

73. Ibid., p. 102.

74. Gutiérrez once warned: 'You are Black, you have your point of view; you are Hispanic, you have your point of view; you are Asian, you have your point of view; you are a woman, you have your point of view; you are White, nice White people, you have your point of view. But enough is enough! With this tool, it is impossible to struggle for liberation': West, Guidote and Coakley (eds.), *Theology in the Americas*, p. 83. Similar critiques are emerging from within Latino/a theology itself. Benjamin Valentin has pointed out that Latino/a / Hispanic theologies tend to restrict their discourse to the internal concerns and language of the churches. He also notes that the same theology has limited itself to issues of culture and identity to the exclusion of class and social politics. See Benjamin Valentin, *Mapping Public Theology: Beyond Culture, Identity, and Difference* (Harrisburg, PA, Trinity Press International, 2002), as well as his 'Strangers No More: An Introduction to, and an Interpretation of, U.S. Hispanic / Latino/a Theology', in Anthony Pinn and Benjamin Valentin (eds.), *The Ties That Bind: African American and Hispanic American/Latino/a Theologies in Dialogue* (New York, Continuum, 2001), pp. 51–3. See also Manuel Mejido, 'Beyond the Postmodern Condition, or the Turn Toward Psychoanalysis', in Petrella (ed.), *Latin American Liberation Theology*, pp. 119–46; Mejido, 'Propaedeutic to the Critique of the Study of U.S. Hispanic Religion: A Polemic Against Intellectual Assimilation', *Journal of Hispanic/Latino Theology* 10 (2) (2002), pp. 31–63; and Mejido, 'A Critique of the "Aesthetic Turn" in U.S. Hispanic Theology: A Dialogue with Roberto Goizueta and the Positing of a New Paradigm', *Journal of Hispanic/Latino Theology* 8 (3) (2001), pp. 18–48.

75. This is the 'radical orthodoxy' option. For my views on radical orthodoxy, see chapter 6 of Petrella, *The Future of Liberation Theology*. For an excellent critique of radical orthodoxy from a different angle, see Nelson Maldonado-Torres, 'Liberation Theology and the Search for the Lost Paradigm: From Radical Orthodoxy to Radical Diversality', in Petrella (ed.), *Latin American Liberation Theology*, pp. 39–61.

76. This is the World Bank's position. See F. J. Hinkelammert, 'Liberation Theology in the Economic and Social Context of Latin America: Economy and Theology, or the Irrationality of the Rationalized', in Batstone, Mendieta, Lorenzten and Hopkins (eds.), *Liberation Theologies*, pp. 25–52.

77. John Dewey was also aware of this: 'As for ideals, all agree that we want the good life ... But as long as we limit ourselves to generalities, the phrases that express ideals may be transferred from conservative to radical or vice versa, and nobody

will be the wiser. For, without analysis, they do not descend into the actual scene nor concern themselves with the generative conditions of realization of ideals': John Dewey, *Individualism Old and New* (New York, Milton, Balch & Company, 1930). Also, 'The sense of new values that become ends to be realized arises first in dim and uncertain form. As the values are dwelt upon and carried forward in action they grow in definiteness and coherence. Interactions between aim and existent conditions are at the same time modified. Ideals change as they are applied in existent conditions': John Dewey, *A Common Faith* (New Haven, Yale University Press, 1934), p. 51.

78. José Míguez Bonino, *Doing Theology in a Revolutionary Situation*, ed. William H. Lazareth, Confrontation Books (Philadelphia, Fortress Press, 1975), p. 151.

79. James Cone, 'Black Theology and the Black Church', in James Cone and Gayraud Wilmore (eds.), *Black Theology: A Documentary History, Volume I 1966–1979* (Maryknoll, NY, Orbis, 2003), p. 268.

80. For my views on Latin American liberation theology's faulty understanding of the relationship between theology and the social sciences, see chapter 2 of Petrella, *The Future of Liberation Theology*.

81. Cornel West, 'Black Theology and Marxist Thought', in Cone and Wilmore (eds.), *Black Theology*, pp. 413–14.

82. Another way to put it: liberation theology focuses on making transcendence, rather than explaining transcendence. See Mejido, 'Beyond the Postmodern Condition' in Petrella (ed.), *Latin American Liberation Theology*.

83. See Michael Hardt and Antonio Negri's *Empire* (Cambridge, MA, Harvard University Press, 2000) for a recent influential example.

84. On this point, see J. K. Gibson-Graham, *The End of Capitalism (as we knew it): A Feminist Critique of Political Economy* (Cambridge, MA, Blackwell Publishers, Inc., 1996). I am not suggesting that there is not a push towards the hegemony of one way of institutionalising capitalism. There is. But this push is not the product of essential traits within capitalism, rather it is the product of different power struggles within the global economy and the institutions that are defined by those struggles, such as the IMF and the WTO. There is thus nothing 'necessary' to capitalism. It is the product of history, like everything else.

85. William James, *Pragmatism* (Indianapolis, IN, Hackett Publishing Company, 1981), p. 115.

86. For my take on critical legal theory and liberation theology, see chapter 5 of Petrella, *The Future of Liberation Theology*.

87. Duncan Kennedy, *Sexy Dressing Etc.: Essays on the Power and Politics of Cultural Identity* (Cambridge, MA, Harvard University Press, 1993), p. 97.

88. The basketball example is taken from ibid., pp. 84–5.

89. Fred Block, *Postindustrial Possibilities: A Critique of Economic Discourse* (Berkeley, University of California Press, 1990), p. 30.

90. For an example of what this would look like, see chapter 5 of Petrella, *The Future of Liberation Theology*.

91. Clodovis Boff and Leonardo Boff, *Salvation and Liberation: In Search of a Balance Between Faith and Politics* (Maryknoll, NY, Orbis, 1984), p. 24.

92. Cone, 'Black Theology and the Black Church', pp. 271, 274.

CHRISTOPHER ROWLAND

# Epilogue: the future of liberation theology

Readers of this book may wonder whether its subject-matter is merely a phase of modern political theology at a time when a critical Marxism, unfettered by the rigidities of its Eastern European manifestations, pervaded the social teaching of late twentieth-century Roman Catholicism, only to be snuffed out by a determined reaction from a more traditionalist papacy. That would be a superficial assessment. We are dealing with a movement whose high point as the topic of discussion on the agenda at every theological conference may now have passed, but whose influence, in a multitude of ways, direct and indirect, is as strong as ever. The issues which concern liberation theologians today are more inclusive and extend to questions of race, gender, popular religion, and, more recently, the environment,[1] and have taken root in other situations[2] and religions apart from Christianity.[3] So when the leaders of Roman Catholicism can proclaim that liberation theology is dead, sentiments echoed by some who hitherto have been exponents of liberation theology, they miss the enormous impact that this way of setting about the theological task continues to have in many parts of the world, not least in the citadels of Catholicism itself: 'the fundamental tenets of liberation theology had – almost surreptitiously – been broadly accepted in many parts of the Catholic church'.[4] So, having flourished in the Third World many of the fundamental tenets of liberation theology are firmly established in the First World, sometimes in institutions of higher education, more often in the life of the Church at the grassroots, in popular education and among groups working for justice and peace. In thinking of it as a mere epiphenomenon of the radical social movements of the sixties and seventies, we miss the extent of its impact.

It is true that mainstream theologians in the First World have been slow to accept liberation theology. In fact, there is a growing gap between the use of the Bible in adult theological education departments and many seminaries on the one hand and theology and religious studies departments in universities on the other. Where the ethos of pedagogy is experiential we find educational methods which owe much to the liberationist approach. There may not be many courses on liberation theology in universities, but those basic tenets, the attention to context, and the peculiar perspective of the marginalised (though with an impact on economically comfortable sectors of the Church[5]), are a feature, for those with eyes to see, of much modern theology, both inside and outside the academy. One senses that there *is* a risk of a polarisation, in which the two streams of theology, that in the traditional academy and that in the Church in adult education, go their own ways, but the Latin American experience of theology suggests that it need not be so and that there is a way that they can be held together and, indeed, benefit one another. Modern biblical and theological study is in a hermeneutical maelstrom, and it would be a pity if European and North American academic theology and exegesis did not allow itself to be influenced by currents of interpretation which are fructifying both Church and academy in the Third World.

Two conversations I had on my first visit to Latin America illustrate the contrasting fortunes and future of liberation theology. In the first an exponent of the theology of liberation, based in Mexico, whose writing had secured him a wide audience in Europe and North America when liberation theology first came into vogue, treated me to a very gloomy set of predictions about the future of the theology of liberation: 'All that will be left of it in a few years' time will be our books', he said. In some respects, even that now looks optimistic. If book sales offered an accurate guide to its continuing influence, the situation would seem to be rather hopeless. Whereas books on the subject might have been expected to sell a decade ago, there is little market for them now.

The tone of the second conversation was in marked contrast, however. A Brazilian theologian spoke of the Basic Christian Communities (the CEBs) as a potent force in Brazilian life which could not be stopped. He said that, whatever the attempts by forces of reaction to put a stop to the process of change and renewal in the Church leading to involvement in action for social change, there could be no putting the clock back. Or, as he more graphically put it, once the toothpaste has been squeezed from the tube there can be no putting it back in again!

There are elements of truth in both comments. Over recent years in many countries of Latin America, particularly Brazil, there has been a spate of appointments at episcopal level which has seen the progressive bishops replaced with conservatives or moved to peripheral dioceses. This has meant a clear shift in the balance of power away from the progressive, and often politically controversial, style of recent years, suggesting that the Church is everywhere on the retreat back to altar and presbytery. There is a crisis for the Church at the grassroots, both in terms of its role, so obvious in a period of oppression, and from the challenge of an all-pervasive Pentecostalism.[6] Yet despite all that, at the grassroots the Church as the people of God is as involved as ever. Thousands of ordinary men and women, whose names will never make the theological libraries of Europe and North America, are struggling in the midst of hardship and injustice, convinced that their faith emboldens and enables them to engage in activity which confronts the powerful and provokes them to struggle for better conditions for themselves and the poor here and now. One hears in the language used by them echoes of the voices of Scripture: the experience of being an alien; and the unexpected insight into Scriptures hidden from those in more comfortable circumstances, which comes neither from learning or status, and thereby opens doors of the reign of God.

'A new genre of theology is waiting to be born,' writes Charles Villa-Vicencio. 'It will need to look to the spoken and unspoken word, often so deep within the human psyche that it cannot be adequately articulated.' What has been set in train in South Africa is a tender shoot, 'a spirituality which creates and sustains people . . . a struggle for symbols that unite and stories that bind'. The experience of celebration, worship, varied stories and recollections, in drama and festival, characterises the kind of theology worked out in the Basic Christian Communities. It is an oral theology in which story, experience and biblical reflection are intertwined with the community's life of sorrow and joy, reflecting the Scriptures themselves, which are the written deposit of a people bearing witness to their story of oppression, bewildered and longing for deliverance. The Bible has become a lens through which one might read the story of today and thereby lend it a new perspective. For all its apparent novelty what is happening is a rediscovery of older methods of scriptural interpretation which stress the priority of the spirit of the word rather than its letter.

So the seeds of hope have been sown. Yet everywhere the situation which prompted liberation theologians to write and explore a different way of engaging in theological reflection from what had become the norm, has not improved. In many parts of the world it has become worse, and it is this continuing context which prompts a continuing need for the kind of theological engagement we find in liberation theology.

As Jon Sobrino has put it:

> . . . what takes my breath away is when people keep saying that liberation theology has gone out of fashion. Poverty is increasing in the Third World, the gap between the rich and the poor countries is widening, there are wars – more than a hundred since the last world war and all of them in the 'Third World'. Cultures are being lost through the imposition of foreign commercial

cultures ... Oppression is not a fashion. The cries of the oppressed keep rising to heaven ... more and more loudly. God today goes on hearing these cries, condemning oppression and strengthening liberation. Anyone who does not grasp this has not understood a word of liberation theology. What I ask myself is what theology is going to do if it ignores this fundamental fact of God's creation as it is. How can a theology call itself 'Christian' if it bypasses the crucifixion of whole people and their need for resurrection, even though its books have been talking about crucifixion and resurrection for twenty centuries? Therefore if those doing liberation theology are not doing it well, let others do it and do it better, but someone must keep on doing it. And for the love of God let's not call it a fashion.[7]

## NOTES

1 See, e.g., L. Boff, *Cry of the Earth, Cry of the Poor* (Maryknoll, NY, Orbis, 1997).

2 N. Ateek, *Justice and Only Justice: Towards a Palestinian Theology of Liberation* (Maryknoll, NY, Orbis, 1989).

3 E.g., M. H. Ellis, *Towards a Jewish Theology of Liberation* (Maryknoll, NY, Orbis, 1987), and F. Esack, *Quran, Liberation and Pluralism: an Islamic Perspective of Interreligious Solidarity against Oppression* (Oxford, Oneworld, 1997).

4 I. Linden, *Liberation Theology Coming of Age?* (London, CIIR, 1997), p. 50.

5 A. F. Evans, R. A. Evans, W. B. Kennedy, *Pedagogies for the Non-Poor* (Maryknoll, NY, Orbis, 1987).

6 See M. A. Vásquez, *The Brazilian Popular Church and the Crisis of Modernity* (Cambridge, Cambridge University Press, 1997); R. Shaull, 'El quehacer teológico en el contexto de sobrevivencia en Abya-Yala', in J. Duque, *Por una sociedad donde quepam todos* (San José, DEI, 1996); and M. H. Ellis, *The Future of Liberation Theology: Essays in Honour of Gustavo Gutiérrez* (Maryknoll, NY, Orbis, 1989).

7 J. Sobrino, *Companions of Jesus. The Murder and Martyrdom of the Salvadorean Jesuits* (London, CIIR/CAFOD, 1990), pp. 50–1. See also Jon Sobrino, *Compassion: The Shaping Principle of the Human and the Christian* (Regina, University of Regina, 1992), p. 15.

# SELECT BIBLIOGRAPHY

## SOURCES

Cone, J. H. and G. S. Wilmore, ed., *Black Theology: A Documentary History*, Maryknoll, NY, Orbis, 1979; 1993.

Hennelly, A. T. ed., *Liberation Theology. A Documentary History*, Maryknoll, NY, Orbis, 1990.

*The Kairos Document: A Theological Comment on the Political Crisis in South Africa*, London, CIIR, 1985.

King, U., *Feminist Theology from the Third World, A Reader*, London, SPCK, 1994.

*Medellín Conclusions* (Second General Conference of Latin American Bishops), New York, US Catholic Conference, 1973.

*Puebla Conclusions* (Third General Conference of Latin American Bishops), London, CIIR, 1973.

Radford Ruether, R., *Woman Guides: Readings toward a Feminist Theology*, Boston, Beacon, 1985.

*Santo Domingo Conclusions* (Fourth General Conference of Latin American Bishops), London, CIIR, 1993.

Sugirtharajah, R. ed., *Voices from the Margins*, London, SPCK, 1992.

Walsh, M. and B. Davies, eds., *Proclaiming Justice and Peace*, London, CIIR/CAFOD, 1984.

## PROCEEDINGS OF THE ECUMENICAL ASSOCIATION OF THIRD WORLD THEOLOGIANS (EATWOT)

Torres, S. and V. Fabella, eds., *The Emergent Gospel: Theology from the Underside of History*, Maryknoll, NY, Orbis, 1978.

Torres, S. and K. Appiah-Kubi, eds., *African Theology en Route*, Maryknoll, NY, Orbis, 1979.

Fabella, V. ed., *Asia's Struggle for Full Humanity*, Maryknoll, NY, Orbis, 1980.

Eagleson, J. and S. Torres, eds., *The Challenge of Basic Christian Communities*, Maryknoll, NY, Orbis, 1981.

Fabella, V. and S. Torres, eds., *The Irruption of the Third World: Challenge to Theology*, Maryknoll, NY, Orbis, 1983.

*Doing Theology in a Divided World*, Maryknoll, NY, Orbis, 1985.

Abrahams, K. C., ed., *Third World Theologies: Commonalities and Divergences*, Maryknoll, NY, Orbis, 1990.

Abrahams, K. C., and B. Mbuy-Beya, eds., *The Spirituality of the Third World: A Cry for Life*, Maryknoll, NY, Orbis, 1994.

## GENERAL

Batstone, David, Eduardo Mendieta, Lois Ann Lorentzen and Dwight N. Hopkins, *Liberation Theologies, Postmodernity and the Americas*, London, Routledge, 1997.

Berryman, P., *Liberation Theology: the Essential Facts about the Revolutionary Movement in Latin America and Beyond*, London, Tauris, 1987.

Boff, L., *Cry of the Earth, Cry of the* Poor, Maryknoll, NY, Orbis, 1997.

Boff, C. and L. Boff, *Introducing Liberation Theology*, London, Burns and Oates, 1987.

Cooper, T., *Controversies in Political Theology: Development or Liberation*, London, SCM Press, 2007.

Croatto, J. Severino, *Mito y hermenéutica*, Buenos Aires, El Escudo, 1973, pp. 7–11.

Ellis, M. H., *The Future of Liberation Theology: Essays in Honour of Gustavo Gutiérrez*, Maryknoll, NY, Orbis, 1989.

Evans, A. F., R. A. Evans and W. B. Kennedy, *Pedagogies for the Non-Poor*, Maryknoll, NY, Orbis, 1987.

Freire, P., *Pedagogy of the Oppressed*, London, Penguin, 1972.

de Gruchy, J., *Christianity and Democracy*, Cambridge, Cambridge University Press, 1995.

Houlden, J. L. (ed.), *The Interpretation of the Bible in the Church*, London, SPCK, 1995.

Kee, A., *Marx and the Failure of Liberation Theology*, London, SCM, 1990.

Linden, I., *Liberation Theology Coming of Age*, London, CIIR, 1997.

McGovern, A. F., *Liberation Theology and its Critics*, Maryknoll, NY, Orbis, 1989.

New Blackfriars, *A Theology of Liberation Twenty Years On*, Oxford, Blackfriars, 1991.

Nolan, A., *God in South Africa*, London, CIIR, 1988.

O'Donovan, O., *The Desire of Nations*, Cambridge, 1996.

Petrella, Iván, *The Future of Liberation Theology. An Argument and a Manifesto*, London, Ashgate, 2004.

*Beyond Liberation Theology: A Polemic*, London, SCM Press, 2008.

Rowland, C., *Radical Christianity*, Oxford, Polity Press, 1988.

Rowland, C. and M. Corner, *Liberating Exegesis*, London, SPCK, 1990.

Scott, J. C., *Domination and the Arts of Resistance: Hidden Transcripts*, New Haven, Yale University Press, 1990.

Smith, C., *The Emergence of Liberation Theology*, Chicago, University of Chicago Press, 1991.

Soelle, D., *Political Theology*, Philadelphia, Fortress, 1974.

Turner, D., *Marxism and Christianity*, Oxford, Blackwell, 1983.

## LATIN AMERICA

Aguilar, M., *The History and Politics of Latin American Theology*, vol. I, London, SCM Press, 2007.

*The History and Politics of Latin American Theology*, vol. II, London, SCM Press, 2008.

Assmann, H., *A Practical Theology of Liberation*, London, SPCK, 1975.

Azevedo, M. de C., *Basic Ecclesial Communities in Brazil*, Washington, Georgetown University Press, 1987.

Berryman, P., *The Religious Roots of Rebellion*, London, SCM, 1984.

Boff, C., *Theology and Praxis*, Maryknoll, NY, Orbis, 1987.

Boff, L., *Church, Charism and Power*, London, SCM, 1985.

Bonino, J. M., *Doing Theology in a Revolutionary Age*, London, SPCK, 1975.

Bruneau, T. C., *The Catholic Church in Brazil. The Politics of Religion*, Austin, University of Texas Press, 1982.

Burdick, J., *Blessed Anastacia: Women, Race, and Popular Christianity in Brazil*, London, Routledge, 1998.

*Legacies of Liberation: The Progressive Catholic Church in Brazil at the Start of a New Millennium*, Aldershot, Ashgate, 2004.

Burdick, J. and W. E. Hewitt, *The Church at the Grassroots in Latin America: Perspectives on Thirty Years of Activism*, Westport, CT and London, Praeger, 2000.

Burdick, M., *Looking for God in Brazil: the Progressive Catholic Church in Urban Brazil's Religious Arena*, Berkeley, University of California Press, 1993.

Chopp, R. S., 'Latin American Liberation Theology', in D. Ford, ed., *The Modern Theologians*, Oxford, Blackwell, 1997, pp. 409–25.

Cook, G., *The Expectation of the Poor*, New York, Orbis, 1985.

Dussel, E., *Ethics and Community*, London, Burns and Oates, 1988.

*A History of Liberation Theology*, Grand Rapids, Eerdmans, 1981.

Ellacurìa, I. and J. Sobrino, eds., *Mysterium Liberationis*, Maryknoll, NY, Orbis, 1993.

Ferm, D. W., *Latin American Liberation Theology. An Introductory Survey*, Maryknoll, NY, Orbis, 1985.

Gutiérrez, G., *A Theology of Liberation* (rev. edn.), London, SCM, 1988.

*The Power of the Poor in History*, London, SCM, 1983.

*The Truth Shall Make You Free*, Maryknoll, NY, Orbis, 1990.

*We Drink from Our Own Wells*, Maryknoll, NY, Orbis, 1984.

*Essential Writings*, ed. J. Nickloff, London, SCM, 1996.

Hinkelammert, F. J., *The Ideological Weapons of Death*, Maryknoll, NY, Orbis, 1986.

Kay, C., *Latin American Theories of Development and Underdevelopment*, London, Routledge, 1989.

Mainwaring, S. and A. Wilde, eds., *The Progressive Church in Latin America*, Notre Dame, University of Notre Dame Press, 1989.

Mesters, C., *Defenseless Flower*, London, CIIR, 1989.

Petrella, I., *Latin American Liberation Theology: the Next Generation*, Maryknoll, NY, Orbis, 2005.

*The Future of Liberation Theology: An Argument and a Manifesto*, Aldershot, Ashgate, 2004, and London, SCM Press, 2006.

Regan, D., *Church for Liberation. A Pastoral Portrait of the Church in Brazil*, Dublin, Dominican Publications, 1987.

Segundo, J. L., *The Liberation of Theology*, Maryknoll, NY, Orbis, 1976.

Sen, Amartya, *Development as Freedom*, Oxford, Anchor Books, 2000.

Sobrino, J., *Christology at the Crossroads*, London, SCM, 1978.

*The True Church and the Church of the Poor*, London, SCM, 1985.

*Jesus in Latin America*, Maryknoll, NY, Orbis, 1989.

*Companions of Jesus. The Murder and Martyrdom of the Salvadorean Jesuits*, London, CIIR/CAFOD, 1990.

*Compassion: The Shaping Principle of the Human and Christian*, Regina, Saskatchewan, University of Regina, 1992.

*Christ the Liberator: A View from the Victims*, Maryknoll, NY, Orbis, 2001.

Tombs, D., *Latin American Liberation Theology*, Boston, Brill Academic Publishers, 2002.

Torres, S. and J. Eagleson, eds., *Theology in the Americas*, Maryknoll, NY, Orbis, 1976.

Vásquez, M. A., *The Brazilian Popular Church and the Crisis of Modernity*, Cambridge, Cambridge University Press, 1997.

## FEMINIST THEOLOGY

Althaus-Reid, Marcella, *Indecent Theology. Theological Perversions in Sex, Gender and Politics*, London, Routledge, 2000. Also translated into Spanish as *La Teología Indecente*, Barcelona, Bellaterra, 2005.

*From Feminist Theology to Indecent Theology*, London, SCM, 2004.

*Liberation Theology and Sexuality*, London, Ashgate, 2006.

Butler, Judith, *Gender Trouble. Feminism and the Subversion of Identity*, London, Routledge, 1990.

Chamorro, Graciela, *Teología Guaraní*, Quito, Abya Yala, 2004.

Chopp, R. S., 'Feminist and Womanist Theologies', in D. Ford, ed., *The Modern Theologians*, Oxford, Blackwell, 1997, pp. 389–404.

Daly, M., *The Church and the Second Sex*, Boston, Beacon, 1968.

*Beyond God the Father*, Boston, Beacon, 1973.

Fabella, V., *Beyond Bonding: a Third World Women's Journey*, Manila, EATWOT, 1993.

Gilligan, C., *In a Different Voice? Psychological Theory and Women's Development*, Cambridge, MA, Harvard University Press, 1982.

González, Roberto and Norberto D'Amico, 'Love in Times of Dictatorships: Memoirs of a Gay Minister from Buenos Aires', in Marcella Althaus-Reid, ed., *Liberation Theology and Sexuality*, London, Ashgate, 2006, pp. 179–89.

Grant, J., *White Women's Christ and Black Women's Jesus: Feminist Christology and Womanist Response*, Atlanta, Scholars Press, 1989.

Hampson, D., *Theology and Feminism*, Oxford, Blackwell, 1990.

Newsom, C. A., and S. Ringe, eds., *The Women's Bible Commentary*, London, SPCK, 1992.

Radford Ruether, R., *Sexism and God-Talk*, London, SCM, 1983.

*Women-Church: Theology and Practice*, San Francisco, Harper and Row, 1985.

Riley, M., *Transforming Feminism*, London, Sheed and Ward, 1989.

Rostagnol, Susana, 'Posibilidades y limitaciones del activismo sexual en el contexto uruguayo', in Josefina Fernández, Mónica D'Uva and Paula Viturro, eds., *Cuerpos ineludibles. Un diálogo a partir de las sexualidades en América Latina*, Buenos Aires, Ají de Pollo, 2004, pp. 27–38.

Schüssler Fiorenza, E., *Discipleship of Equals*, New York, Crossroads, 1993.

*Searching the Scriptures. A Feminist Introduction*, London, SCM, 1993.

*In Memory of Her: a Feminist Reconstruction of Christian Origins*, London, SCM, 1983.

Tamez, E., *Against Machismo*, Yorktown Heights, Meyer-Stone, 1987.

Trible, P., *God and the Rhetoric of Sexuality*, Philadelphia, Fortress, 1978.

Williams, D. S., *Sisters in the Wilderness: the Challenge of Womanist Theology*, Maryknoll, NY, Orbis, 1993.


## ASIA

Amaladoss, M., *Life in Freedom: Liberation Theologies from Asia*, Maryknoll, NY, Orbis, 1997.

Balasuriya, T., *Planetary Theology*, Maryknoll, NY, Orbis, 1984.

Bock, K. Y. ed., *Minjung Theology: People as the Subjects of History* (rev. edn.), Maryknoll, NY, Orbis, 1983.

Crusz, R., M. Fernando and A. Tilakaratne eds., *Encounters with the Word: Essays to Honour Aloysius Pieris SJ on his 70th Birthday*, Colombo, Ecumenical Institute for Study and Dialogue, 2004.

Fabella, V. ed., *Asia's Struggle for Full Humanity: Towards a Relevant Theology*, Maryknoll, NY, Orbis, 1980.

*Asian Christian Spirituality. Reclaiming Traditions*, Maryknoll, NY, Orbis, 1992.

Kyung, C. H., *Struggle to the Sun Again: Introducing Asian Women's Theology*, London, SCM, 1991.

Pieris, A., *An Asian Theology of Liberation*, Maryknoll, NY, Orbis, 1988.

Song, C. S., *Theology from the Womb of Asia*, Maryknoll, NY, Orbis, 1986.

Thomas, M. M., *The Christian Response to the Asian Revolution*, London, SCM, 1966.


## BLACK THEOLOGY AND THEOLOGY IN SOUTHERN AFRICA

Cone, J. H., *A Black Theology of Liberation* (rev. edn.), Maryknoll, NY, Orbis, 1986.

de Gruchy, J. W., 'African Theology: South Africa', in D. Ford, ed., *The Modern Theologians*, Oxford, Blackwell, 1997, pp. 445–54.

Frostin, P., *Liberation Theology in Tanzania and South Africa: A First World Interpretation*, Lund, Lund University Press, 1988.

Hopkins, D. N., *Down, Up, and Over: Slave Religion and Black Theology*, Minneapolis, Fortress Press, 2000.

Mosala, I. J., *Biblical Hermeneutics and Black Theology in South Africa*, Exeter, Paternoster, 1989.

Setiloane, G., *African Theology: an Introduction*, Johannesburg, 1986.

Thomas, L. E., ed., *Livingstones in the Household of God: The Legacy and Future of Black Theology*, Minneapolis, Fortress Press, 2004.

Villa-Vicenzio, C., *Theology of Reconstruction*, Cambridge, Cambridge University Press, 1992.

West, G., *Biblical Hermeneutics of Liberation: Modes of Reading the Bible in the South African Context*, 2nd edn., Maryknoll, NY, Orbis, 1995.

## ECONOMICS AND LIBERATION THEOLOGY

Duchrow, U., *Alternatives to Global Capitalism*, Utrecht, International Books, 1993.

Gorringe, T., *Capital and the Kingdom*, London, SPCK, 1994.

Hay, D. A., *Economics Today: a Christian Critique*, Leicester Apollos, 1989.

Hinkelammert, F. J., 'Liberation Theology in the Economic and Social Context of Latin America: Economy and Theology, or the Irrationality of the Rationalized', in David Batstone, Edwardo Mendieta, Lois Ann Lorenzten and Dwight N. Hopkins, eds., *Liberation Theologies, Postmodernity, and the Americas*, New York, Routledge, 1997, pp. 25–32.

Hobgood, M. E., *Catholic Social Teaching and Economic Theory: Paradigms in Conflict*, Philadelphia, Temple University Press, 1991.

Kay, C., *Latin American Theories of Development and Underdevelopment*, London, Routledge, 1989.

Meeks, D., *God the Economist: the Doctrine of God and Political Economy*, Minneapolis, Fortress, 1973.

Schubeck, T. L., 'Liberation Theology and Economics: God's Reign and a New Society', in J. M. Dean and A. M. C. Waterman, eds., *Religion and Economics: Normative Social Theory*, Boston, Kluwer Academic Publishers, 1999, pp. 69–84.

Sen, A., *Inequality Re-examined*, Cambridge, MA, Harvard University Press, 1992.

United Nations Development Programme, *Human Development Report*, NY, 1996.

United Nations Research Institute for Social Development, *States of Disarray: The Social Effects of Globalization*, Geneva, URISD, 1995.

Viner, J., *Religious Thought and Economic Society*, Durham, Duke University Press, 1978.

www.cafod.org.uk/policy_and_analysis

Zweig, M., 'Economics and Liberation Theology', in M. Zweig, ed., *Religion and Economic Justice*. Philadelphia, PA, Temple University, 1991, pp. 3–49.


## 'THE MIDDLE EAST'

Ateek, N., *Justice and Only Justice: Towards a Palestinian Theology of Liberation*, Maryknoll, NY, Orbis, 1989.

Ellis, M. H., *Towards a Jewish Theology of Liberation*, Maryknoll, NY, Orbis, 1987.

Esack, F., *Quran, Liberation and Pluralism: An Islamic Perspective of Interreligious Solidarity against Oppression*, Oxford, Oneworld, 1997.


## USEFUL ADDRESSES

Catholic Fund for Overseas Development (CAFOD), 2 Romero Close, Stockwell Road, London SW9 9TY. web page: http://www.cafod.org.uk/

Catholic Institute for International Relations (now Progressio), Unit 3, Canonbury Yard, 190a North Road, London N1 7BJ.

Christian Aid, 35 Lower Marsh St, London, SE1 7RL. web page: http://www.christianaid.org.uk/

Church World Service, 28606 Phillips St, PO Box 968, Elkhart IN 46515

DEI, Apartado 389–2070, Sabanilla, Montes de Oca, San José Costa Rica.

EATWOT, www.eatwot.org/mainfile.php/about.
ISEDET, Camacuá 282, DOF 1406c Buenos Aires.
Kairos Europa, Hegenichstr. 22, 69124 Heidelberg.
Orbis Books, Price Building, Box 308, Maryknoll NY 10545-0302, USA.
Orbis Books web page: http://www.orbisbooks.com/contact.htm
The Urban Theology Unit, 210 Abbeyfield Road, Sheffield S4 7AZ (www.
    utusheffield.fsnet.co.uk).